Thinking in Dark Times

THINKING IN
DARK TIMES

HANNAH ARENDT ON ETHICS AND POLITICS

Edited by Roger Berkowitz, Jeffrey Katz, and Thomas Keenan

FORDHAM UNIVERSITY PRESS   New York 2010

Frontispiece: Shy Abady, *Dark Times*, 2004, mixed media on paper.

Library of Congress Cataloging-in-Publication Data

Thinking in dark times : Hannah Arendt on ethics and politics / edited by Roger Berkowitz, Jeffrey
    Katz, and Thomas Keenan. — 1st ed.
        p. cm.
    Includes bibliographical references and index.
    ISBN 978-0-8232-3075-4 (cloth : alk. paper) — ISBN 978-0-8232-3076-1 (pbk. : alk. paper)
1. Arendt, Hannah, 1906–1975—Political and social views. 2. Political ethics. 3. Political science—
Philosophy. I. Berkowitz, Roger, 1968– II. Katz, Jeff (Jeffrey) III. Keenan, Thomas, 1959–
    JC251.A74B47 2010
    172—dc22
                                                                                2009027934

Printed in the United States of America

12 11 10   5 4 3 2

First edition

Contents

Figures

Preface

This book originates in an unusual conference that was held at Bard College to celebrate Hannah Arendt's one-hundredth birthday. For the conference, "Thinking in Dark Times: The Legacy of Hannah Arendt," we invited a wide range of public intellectuals, artists, journalists, and academics from across the disciplines to address the relevance of Arendt's thinking. The speakers were given particular questions to respond to, questions such as, "Is totalitarianism a present danger?" "What is the activity of democratic citizenship?" "What does it mean to think about politics?" In addition, we asked the participants to limit their remarks to ten minutes. The effort was to encourage talks that avoid the regalia of disciplinary posturing and specialized jargons and move straight to the provocative questions at the very heart of Arendt's project.

Looking over the transcripts after the conference, we quickly recognized that the talks not only spoke in a provocative and incisive way, but they also revealed the passionate and engaged embrace of political and ethical thinking that is too frequently lost among the layers of interpretation and scholarship that deadens much writing about Arendt. We therefore asked the participants to expand and polish their essays for publication. At the same time, we asked that they make an effort to preserve the style and form of the original oral presentations. The essays that follow are the result. They are as a whole shorter than typical academic essays, and they have fewer footnotes and scholarly trappings. Instead, they present efforts to think with and, at times, against Arendt in her call for thinking.

The book, like the conference that inspired it, is very much rooted in Bard College. Bard has a long and meaningful association with Hannah Arendt. Her husband, Heinrich Blücher, taught at Bard for seventeen years and was instrumental in designing Bard's common-course core curriculum. Arendt herself was a professor and friend of Bard's current president, Leon Botstein. Blücher and Arendt both are buried on the Bard campus, a short walk from Arendt's personal library, which is currently housed at Bard's Stevenson Library. In addition, Bard hosts the Hannah Arendt Center for Ethical and Political Thinking. To give a feel for Arendt's intellectual life and to offer to others a glimpse into world of her personal library, we include in this volume a wide range of images taken from the books and manuscripts of the Hannah Arendt Library.

RB, JK, TK

Acknowledgments

This volume is a work of twenty-five contributors and three editors and would never have been finished without the assistance of many others. From the beginning, Bard's President Leon Botstein encouraged and supported our efforts. Funding for the conference, which also supported publication of this book, was generous and came from Michael Steinhardt, Richard Gilder, Wendy and Alex Bazelow, Barbara Dobkin, and the Center for Constitutional Rights.

In planning the original conference, we were assisted greatly by Debra Pemstein and Mary Strieder. In addition, a number of Bard students—Alice Baker, Cassandra Cornell, Anthony Daniel, Noah Levine, and Elizabeth Snowden—assisted in preparing the manuscript for publication. Serena Randolph donated time and talents to photograph material from the Arendt Library. Cassandra Cornell took on the responsibility of organizing the index. Finally, we are deeply indebted to Helen Tartar, Thomas C. Lay, and Eric Newman at Fordham University Press.

This book is dedicated to Jenny Lyn Bader and Mary Katz.

Editors' Note

Hannah Arendt intentionally wrote *antisemitism*, *antisemitic*, and *antisemite* instead of *anti-Semitism*, *anti-Semitic*, and *anti-Semite* throughout her work. She did so for the simple reason that, as she wrote in *The Origins of Totalitarianism*, there is a difference between "Jew-hatred" on the one hand and "antisemitism" on the other. There is no such thing as a pro-Semitic "Semitism" that an "anti-Semitism" opposes, but only an ideological "antisemitism." Following Arendt's reasoning and her practice, the essays in this volume will speak of antisemitism, antisemitic persons and ideas, and antisemites.

HERMANN BROCH
DIE SCHULDLOSEN

1951—, warum mußt du's dichten?
Wen willst du damit verpflichten?
Ach, in diesem Tal von Wichten,
die ich lieber möcht' vernichten
als im Bilde zu belichten,
gibt es Menschen äußerst schlichten
Kindessinnes, die mitnichten
je geneigt sind auf Geschichten,
wie sich's ghörte, zu verzichten.
Freunde sind es, zwar perverse,
aber sie sind voll Verzeihn:
ihnen sollen die paar Verse
und dies Buch gewidmet sein.

    Für Hannah und Monsieur

Neujahr 1951   Hermann

Thinking in Dark Times

∷

ROGER BERKOWITZ

In Bertold Brecht's poem "To Posterity," the poet laments:

> Truly, I live in dark times!
> An artless word is foolish. A smooth forehead
> Points to insensitivity. He who laughs
> Has not yet received
> The terrible news.
>
> What times are these, in which
> A conversation about trees is almost a crime
> For in doing so we maintain our silence about so much wrongdoing!
> And he who walks quietly across the street,
> Passes out of the reach of his friends
> Who are in danger?[1]

Brecht's poem inspires the title of one of Hannah Arendt's less celebrated books, *Men in Dark Times.* For Arendt, dark times are not limited to the tragedies of the twentieth century; they are not even a rarity in the history of the world. Darkness, as she would have us understand it, does not name the genocides, purges, and hunger of a specific era. Instead, darkness refers to the way these horrors appear in public discourse and yet remain hidden. As Arendt observes, the tragedies to which Brecht's poem refers were not shrouded in secrecy and mystery, yet they were darkened by the "highly efficient talk and double-talk of nearly all official representatives who, without interruption and in many ingenious variations, explained away unpleasant facts and justified concerns."[2] Similarly today, the various outrages—environmental, economic, and governmental—that confront us daily are hidden in plain sight. Dark-

Facing: Inscription from Hermann Broch to Hannah Arendt on the half-title page of Broch's novel *Die Schuldlosen.* The inscription is a poem written to Arendt and Blücher dedicating the book to them. The poem reads: "1951—, Why must you write it?/Whom do you wish thus to bind?/Ah, in this valley of dwarfs,/Whom I would rather paint a clear picture of/Than destroy./There are men of an extremely simple/Childlike cast of mind, who are not at all/Inclined to do without stories,/as would be fitting./They are friends, though admittedly perverse,/But they are full of forgiveness:/These few verses/And this book are dedicated to them./For Hannah and Monsieur/New Years, 1951/Hermann." Courtesy of the Hannah Arendt Collection, Stevenson Library, Bard College.

ness, for Arendt, names the all-too-public invisibility of inconvenient facts, and not simply the horror of the facts themselves.

In *Men in Dark Times*, Arendt responds to what she, borrowing from Martin Heidegger, calls the light of the public that obscures everything. The black light of the public realm is, of course, the chatter and talk that drown the reality of life in "incomprehensible triviality." It is the vapid clichés that mar speech on TV news channels and by the water cooler. For Arendt, as for Heidegger, "everything that is real or authentic is assaulted by the overwhelming power of 'mere talk' that irresistibly arises out of the public realm."[3] And yet, Arendt, unlike Heidegger, resists the philosophical withdrawal from the public world into a realm of philosophical contemplation.

Instead of world-weary withdrawal, Arendt writes with the conviction that "we have the right to expect some illumination." The darkness of the public spotlight is, she insists, not inevitable. On the contrary, it is possible and even necessary that darkness cede to light.

In seeking light in the public realm, Arendt shuns the embrace of rationality, democracy, and universal values that are the source of the optimism driving much of political thinking in modern times. Al Gore, for example, has recently argued that the crisis facing the nation and the world has been allowed to flourish because reason is under attack. In his book *The Assault on Reason*, Gore argues that a "faith in the power of reason—the belief that free citizens can govern themselves wisely and fairly by resorting to logical debate on the basis of the best evidence available, instead of raw power—was and remains the central premise of American democracy." That faith, he writes, is under assault. He blames TV, advertising, and the corporatization of press—all of which have undermined what Gore, citing Jürgen Habermas, calls "the structure of the public forum."[4] In the face of the dangers posed by dictators and environmental disaster, Gore embraces Habermas's claim that reasoned deliberation can yield rational and thus decent decisions.[5] For Gore, as for Habermas, dark times demand the light of reason.

The faith in reason that animates both Gore and Habermas is seductive. It speaks to the pride of man: that we, as rational beings, can come together and dispassionately and rationally move ourselves—fitfully at times—toward a better world. Our faith speaks to our scientific age, in which we believe that we can understand and improve both the natural and the political worlds. And our conviction reflects the fundamental claim of enlightenment: that our reason will set us free.

For Arendt, however, to reassert our rationalist tradition in the face of its rampant violation is to ignore the facts of our times. If the last hundred years have taught us anything, it is that "the subterranean stream of Western history has finally come to the surface and usurped the dignity of our tradition."[6] It is questionable whether any universal affirmation of the values of human reason and human dignity can offer a meaningful bulwark against the temptations of evildoing. The pressing need for rationally decipherable human values—let no one deny the need is pressing—does not, alas, render those values actual. Mature thought requires, Arendt implores us repeatedly, that we trade the fantasies of wish fulfillment for the honest work of thoughtful comprehension.

To comprehend the failure of rationality as the guarantor of a peaceful and prosperous life is not merely to recognize the limits of reason's universal knowability. Beyond the charge of relativism, Arendt insists that we face squarely the possibility that the claims of rationality itself offer no protection against the very horrors that Gore and Habermas enlist it to oppose. On the contrary, all too often the arguments in favor of genocide, torture, and terror are made in the voice of reason. Arendt reveals how the totalitarian and dictatorial regimes of the twentieth century counted upon and received popular support. Today, suicide bombers rationalize their use of terror as the most efficient way to address their political claims even as democratic governments rationalize their use of torture in their elusive pursuit of security. Indeed, the normalization of terror and torture shows how ordinary men can reason themselves into justifying what ought to be unthinkable. Reason, Arendt warns, risks fitting "man into the iron band of terror."[7] Reason, she insists, reasons, it does not think.

If reason risks descending into the justifications and rationalizations that spread darkness in our times, Arendt argues that the only reliable source of light in dark times is found in the activity of thinking. From the beginning to the end of her writing life, Arendt situates herself as a thinker even as she warns against the dangers of reason. In *The Origins of Totalitarianism*, her grand inquiry into the roots of totalitarianism in rootlessness, loneliness, and thoughtlessness, Arendt frames her inquiry as an effort of comprehension, by which she means "the unpremeditated, attentive facing up to, and resisting of, reality—whatever it may be." In *The Human Condition*, she explains her project as a "matter of thought" that opposes the thoughtlessness that "seems to me among the outstanding characteristics of our time." And in her engagement with what she saw as the thoughtlessness behind Adolf Eichmann's evil deeds, she asks: "Could the activity of thinking as such be among the conditions that make men abstain from evil-doing or even actually 'condition' them against it?"[8] Thinking, Arendt suggests, is the only reliable safety net against the increasingly totalitarian or even bureaucratic temptations to evil that threaten the modern world.

By thinking Arendt means something quite specific, namely the silent dialogue with oneself that Socrates describes in Plato's *Theaetetus*. Only one who speaks with oneself will worry that in acting unethically he or she will have to live with a criminal. It is Socrates' habit of thinking with his other self, his *daimon*, that Arendt argues stands behind Socrates' moral claim that "it would be better for me that my lyre or a chorus I direct were out of tune and loud with discord, and that most men should not agree with me and contradict me, rather than that I, being one, should be out of tune with *myself* and contradict *myself*."[9] Arendt repeatedly returns to this line of Socrates' and highlights his claim that an individual person, though one, can be out of tune with himself or herself. "If I disagree with other people," Arendt writes, "I can walk away." I cannot, however, walk away from myself unless I cease the internal dialogue of myself with myself. Because the activity of thinking means that I must live with myself—with my other self—thinking is the one activity that can stop men and women from doing great wrongs. For who, she asks, is willing to live their lives in such close confines with a criminal?

The political implications of thinking are brought front and center in Arendt's discussion of the argument from the lesser evil as it arose in response to the actions of German citizens and even Jews during the Nazi era. In her coverage of the trial of Adolf Eichmann for *The New Yorker*, and later in her book *Eichmann in Jerusalem*, Arendt reported on a disturbing fact that struck her, and many others, at the trial. Eichmann, she noted, was decidedly average. The evil of his deeds was indisputable; yet, notwithstanding what he had done, Eichmann's motivations seemed grounded in typical bourgeois drives. Eichmann was ambitious. He sought the recognition that came from success. And he wanted to excel at his profession. These banal motivations could, under the Nazi system of rule, lead him to participate in some of the most wrongful deeds in the history of man. How could such a simple man do such extraordinary evil?

Confronted with the normalcy of one responsible for such evil, Arendt drew parallels with others who participated in the Nazi government but escaped judgment for their complicity with the Nazi regime. While not at all equating members of the *Judenräte* (the Jewish Councils that worked with the Nazis to administer life in and deportation from the Jewish ghettoes) with Eichmann's orchestration of the machinery of death, she nevertheless condemned those Jewish leaders for participating in the selection of who should die and who should live. And while not in the least obscuring the difference between Eichmann's role in genocide and the everyday role of those German bureaucrats who accommodated without supporting the Nazis—many of whom easily made the transition from Hitler's to Adenauer's civil service—Arendt also condemned normal, average, everyday Germans who chose to work within the Nazi government. What unites the German civil servants and the Jewish leaders in Arendt's telling is their willingness to justify morally suspect actions in the name of doing an unethical job as ethically as possible. They claimed, in other words, that their cooperation was a lesser evil that helped to prevent an even greater evil. This, she argued, was the very same argument Eichmann employed.

The argument of the lesser evil is endemic to our society. It is typically the case that both sides in a given political or ethical argument invoke reasoning of the lesser evil to buttress their position. In Israel today, for example, supporters of humanitarian aid for the Palestinians argue that giving food and medicine to the Palestinians and thereby normalizing and even supporting the blockade of Gaza is the lesser evil when compared to the starvation and deaths that would otherwise occur. Opponents of the humanitarian mission argue, with the same logic, that allowing some to die is a lesser evil than supporting and thus legitimating an inhumane blockade.[10] Similarly, arguments in the United States over the Iraq war and the war on terrorism most often revolve around the question of the lesser evil, torture in the name of safety or potential deaths in the name of freedom and civil liberties.

In pointing out the pervasiveness of the argument of the lesser evil, Arendt argues that it is itself rooted in a deeper phenomenon, namely the "widespread fear of judging" that has nothing to do with the biblical "Judge not, that ye be not judged."[11] She connects the increasingly common recourse to the argument of the lesser evil with the even more pervasive unwillingness to judge in general.

This fear of judging is wide-ranging in society. We see it in social issues like euthanasia, where what was once considered deeply wrong is now often justified as a lesser evil to the pain of a slow death.[12] We see the fear of judging in the law where the embrace of mandatory sentences reflect the view that the loss of individualized judgment and individualized punishment are lesser evils than the risk of shorter sentences by lenient judges. And those of us in the academic world are witness to the fear of judging in the rampant inflation of grades, a reflection of the increasing unwillingness of professors to evaluate student work honestly.

To Arendt, both the fear of judging and the embrace of the argument of the lesser evil that accompanies it stem from the same two causes. First, the fear of judging is rooted in the rise of social science and determinism, practices that reduce human freedom to the conformity of norms, statistics, and probabilities. The more that social events and even personal actions are seen to be calculable, predictable, and manipulable through sociological norms and rules that are discoverable by sociologists, economists, and political scientists, the less responsible people are for their actions. If what we do, what we read, and what we buy can be plotted on a bell curve, we trade the rarity of action for the normalcy of behavior. And the diminished responsibility of persons leads to an unwillingness to judge those who are not responsible for what they do.[13]

The second, and less often acknowledged, ground of the fear of judgment is the modern belief in equality. Judgment, Arendt writes, presupposes self-confidence and pride: "what former times called the dignity or the honor of man."[14] Only one who believes oneself right can judge another; thus, judgment presupposes a certain authority and superiority. The judge must have a feeling of distinction, what Nietzsche calls a "pathos of difference," in order to arrogate to himself or herself the right to judge. There is, Arendt recognizes, a necessary arrogance to judging that is increasingly absent in our age in which pride is either absent or at least tempered by a mock modesty that denies oneself the right to judge.

The problem of judgment is widespread. Take, for example, the outcry over President George W. Bush's description of Saddam Hussein as a bad man. Immediately the intelligentsia condemned the simplicity of Bush's worldview that would dare to divide the world into good and evil. Such a black-and-white approach, critics held, misses the nuances and shades of gray in moral judgment. While Saddam killed many people, he also held Iraq together and raised the standard of living. To judge him a mass murderer is thought to be a vulgar judgment lacking in sophistication. There is, of course, much to criticize in President Bush's decision to label Saddam evil. One could wonder at his selective vision. And one can certainly reject his conclusion that the United States is justified in invading any country led by an evil leader. To judge the war morally wrong, or to judge it as an unnecessary risk, reflects a sound mind. To condemn the characterization of an autocratic and cynical despot who gasses his own citizens as evil is something else. The unwillingness to make such stark judgments of guilt is indicative of a "deep-seated fear . . . of passing judgment, of naming names, and of fixing blame."[15]

In raising the question of personal responsibility under a dictatorship, Arendt suggests that first and foremost, one must be able and willing to judge. When asked or ordered to participate in an evil government, the citizen must make a judgment, one that does not depend on a rational or intellectual calculation of the lesser or greater evil. Those who judged the Nazi regime wrong belonged to no particular class and shared no common educational background. The nonparticipants were not the intellectuals or the most respected members of the community. Those who resisted and those who simply withdrew into private life did not rationally consider the question of whether it was good to murder Jews. Instead, those who judged that to coordinate their actions with the regime was not a lesser evil but evil plain and simple were the ones who "never doubted that crimes remained crimes even if legalized by the government." Faced with laws and commands that rationalized actions they held to be wrong, these individuals said no; their no was based neither on a universal rationality nor social norms. They simply said "This I can't do."[16]

What is needed in dark times, Arendt shows us, are people who think and who, in thinking, make for themselves the space to judge. Instead of reason, Arendt teaches the supreme importance of thinking—the habit of erecting obstacles to oversimplifications, compromises, and conventions. "When everybody is swept away unthinkingly by what everybody else does and believes in," Arendt wrote, "those who think are drawn out of hiding because their refusal to join in is conspicuous and thereby becomes a kind of action."[17] The thinker is the one who stands as a beacon not to some particular ideology or policy, but to following one's conscience.

The essays that follow are explorations of the power and impact of Arendt's thinking. Thinking, as George Kateb writes, has multiple meanings in Arendt's writing, many of which are intimately woven into her equally political idea of judging. As important as judging is for Arendt, thinking remains, Kateb argues, the core activity that makes possible any resistance to political atrocities. Thinking, as these essays make clear, is at the very core of Arendt's understanding of politics.

Some of these authors address the place of thinking in Arendt's work head on. Mark Antaki explores the connection between thinking and politics and argues that thinking, as the thinking about nothing—the freeing oneself from any and all positive ideologies—is a kind of political judgment that makes room for spontaneity and freedom. Thinking is political, he argues, because it is thinking that clears a space for action and politics.

The path through judgment to thinking begins, Shai Lavi argues, with Arendt's lifelong attempts to respond to evil, first in her confrontation with totalitarianism and later with Adolf Eichmann. Tracing the development of Arendt's approach to reconciliation, forgiveness, and revenge as responses to human failings, Lavi argues that Arendt's turn to judgment does not offer a solution to her questions but returns her more powerfully to the Heideggerian approach to thinking that she had earlier sought to escape.

Kateb, too, brings thinking together with judgment to argue that one capacity of thinking—to imagine that the people we are harming are people like ourselves—is our only meaningful defense against the poisonous fictions that reduce a world of plurality into a single and consonant ideology. Since the most dangerous ideologies depend upon the construction of stable enemies, the thoughtful imagining of others to be like ourselves is, Kateb argues, the most important defense against the unyielding human drive to do evil.

While Arendt understands that evil arises in many forms, she argues that perhaps the great danger of evil in modern times rests upon the drive for social equality. Uday Mehta goes to the heart of Arendt's critique of modern politics: its concern with remedying social inequality, a concern that for Arendt threatens to replace the injustices of inequality with the bonds of terror. In opposing the social and the danger of tyranny, Arendt pursues a vision of politics that, as Mehta sees, has instructive similarities with Mahatma Gandhi's. For Arendt, as for Gandhi, the love of difference commits them to a politics that resists the effort to erase prejudices, a politics that rejects a naturalist yet unthinking brotherhood for the thoughtful work of friendship.

Christopher Hitchens shares Arendt's skepticism regarding naturalist ideals of brotherhood. He begins by asking whether Arendt too, at least once, was too caught up in a hopeful fantasy of brotherly unity. Of concern is the postscript celebrating the 1956 Hungarian Revolution that Arendt added to the second edition of *The Origins of Totalitarianism*. Arendt then removed the postscript from future editions, an act that Hitchens reads as an admission of a certain naïvete. The removal, Hitchens argues, comes about because Arendt came to recognize that the revolution was planted in the fertile soil of antisemitism. Her oversight, Hitchens suggests, comes from a misplaced faith that the dangers of antisemitism are different from hatred of Jews.

Antisemitism is one of the political lies that, as Arendt expresses it, attack the very fabric of reality. The political lie, as Peg Birmingham and Cathy

Caruth remind us, is at the center of Arendt's reflections on politics from *The Origins of Totalitarianism* through to her later engagement with American politics. Arendtian politics calls for thinking most explicitly at moments when fictional constructions of reality—the very stories and legends that give our world meaning—harden into ideologies and certainties that obscure reality.

Birmingham points to the particular problem that the political lie raises in an age in which the loss of a clear boundary between fact and lie elevates the problem of political deception to the highest of political and philosophical importance. The total lie opens the door to the totalitarian lie and transforms the political lie from an act of politics in the name of particular interests to an attack on the framework of reality itself. Politics now is marshaled to defend and preserve the lying reality asserted by the modern political lie. Since lying is central to the political project of unifying a plurality, lying and politics become an essential support for totalitarian government.

For Caruth, the importance of Arendt's engagement with the political lies exposed in the Pentagon Papers is that the papers have the force of a revelation even though all the information they contained was already known. Much like the publication of the Red Cross Report on the torturing of prisoners in Guantánamo, the release of the Pentagon Papers explodes the frame of the media's complicity in the political lie through the media itself. The Red Cross's decision to leak its report, like Ellsberg's own leak, has the form of a decision to break one's promise to remain complicit in the lying political order. Precisely such an explicit decision to break up the reality of the lie is what Caruth sees as the thoughtful essence of witnessing as a response to a lying world order.

Many of the authors explore Arendt's politics through her own political commitments. Seyla Benhabib looks to three particular political periods of Arendt's life to suggest that against a realm of pure or theoretical politics that Arendt is often thought to embrace, Arendt's politics is one of active engagement. Arendt helped Jewish children escape to Palestine during World War II; after the war she was active in debates about the state of Israel. Later, Arendt's political involvements shift from Jewish to American questions. For Benhabib, as for Leon Botstein, the original influence of Judaism on Arendt's politics is replaced by the increasing importance she sets on being an American. Through political engagement, Arendt develops, according to Benhabib, a unique understanding of politics founded upon the demand for judgment grounded in the practice of thinking.

The need for thinking in politics underlies Arendt's lifelong reflections on the proper activity of democratic citizenship. For Patchen Markell, the chief characteristic of democratic citizenship is the experience of freedom. Reading Arendt's *On Revolution*, Markell argues that the experience of "inadvertence" lies at the center of meaningful political action. Against a politics governed by conceptual aims, Arendt's politics is rooted in the unruly experience of the new. Focusing on experience as the core of politics, Markell warns that democratic freedom is threatened not only by the restriction of liberties but also by withdrawal from the activity of politics in a society where the primary political activity is voting for others who will actually govern.

For Verity Smith, Arendt's essay *Civil Disobedience* is central to her political thinking. Tracing Arendt's constitutional thinking back to Montesquieu, Smith argues that Arendt's constitutionalism opposes the rule of a unitary sovereign. Civil disobedience pluralizes the sources of power, advancing the great virtue of constitutional government. Because the civil disobedient contests the status quo even as she accepts the general legitimacy of the laws and the government, civil disobedience can thus promote both change and stability. In this way, the civil disobedient is, Smith argues, deeply engaged in the citizenly activity of reconstituting a government.

In a similar vein, Jay Bernstein argues that because civil disobedients act and speak with others, they help form a political community bound together by common opinion. Every act of founding a political community must begin, Bernstein argues, as an act of dissent that has made itself the ground of a new voluntary consensus. Legitimate power can emerge only when there is a meaningful possibility for dissent, which is why civil disobedience is the source of modern constitutional power.

Arendt's insights into the power of thought come to the fore nowhere more than in her attempts to makes sense of her experience of Adolf Eichmann. Eichmann appeared less an evil man than a thoughtless man, and Arendt, struck by Eichmann's thoughtlessness, asked herself whether thinking itself might in some way inoculate those who think from participation in systematic programs of evildoing. It might, she suggests, to the extent that evil is something banal. As a thoughtless evasion of responsibility, the banality of evil might, she speculated, be vulnerable to the activity of thinking.

Arendt's discovery of the banality of evil has been, writes Richard Bernstein, widely and badly misunderstood. The phrase "banality of evil" appears, as Bernstein reminds us, only once in Arendt's account of the Eichmann trial. The banality of evil is in no way a simplification or washing away of the evil in Eichmann's acts. It is, he argues, an attempt to recognize that evil might arise in many ways, from fanatical sociopaths and, more likely in our times, from the thoughtless compliance of normal people with systematic evil.

Peter Baehr takes issue with Arendt's banality of evil thesis. The banality of evil, he argues, is an example of silly cleverness, a resonant but ultimately hollow turn of phrase. While Arendt's account of Eichmann makes visible the strange and important interdependence of evil and thoughtlessness, her claim that evil is banal ignores the reality of evil that seeks the destruction and injury of others. Baehr argues that Arendt overreached in arguing that evil is banal.

For Yaron Ezrahi, the dispute over the banality of evil has been superseded by the success of Arendt's thesis itself. Having worked its way into the popular consciousness, the banality of evil now exists independently of Arendt.

And this, for Ezrahi, is a good thing. What he calls the second career of the banality of evil has the potential to reframe endemic disputes like the Israeli-Palestinian conflict. Where opposing parties view each other as evil, the banality of evil idea offers an opportunity to depersonalize the crimes committed by the opposing sides. The banality of evil opens the door to a less essentialist view of criminal conduct that can, Ezrahi argues, change the conditions and forms of consciousness that contribute to the production of evil itself.

Jennifer Culbert argues that we must turn our attention from debates over the essence of evil to questions about the way evil appears. To see evil as it appears in the world is to learn to judge, to see what is. She finds an example of such seeing in Arendt's judgment of Eichmann; Arendt's judgment that Eichmann must be hanged even though he was not guilty of a legally recognized crime is based not on an evil will or on a demand for revenge grounded on the pain of his victims. Instead, Arendt judges that the deeds he participated in were evil and that he, by participating in them, does evil. What is needed is to learn to see an evil that demands to be punished.

Eichmann in Jerusalem was controversial not only for its claims about the nature of evil as banal. The book was condemned by Jewish leaders for whom Arendt's comparison of Eichmann with Jewish leaders who cooperated with the Nazis was unforgiveable. One effect of the controversies that isolated Arendt from the Jewish community has been to deemphasize Arendt's Jewishness and to ignore the roots of her thought in both her Judaism and her experience of antisemitism during the war. However, as the essays by Benhabib, Botstein, Jerome Kohn, Ron Feldman, Elisabeth Young-Bruehl, and Suzanne Vromen make clear, Arendt's engagement with Judaism was at the core of her political thinking.

Little was known of Arendt's involvement in Jewish questions before the publications of *The Jew as Pariah: Jewish Identity and Politics in the Modern Age* (1978), edited by Ron Feldman, and, more recently, *Arendt's Jewish Writings* (2007), edited by Jerome Kohn and Ron Feldman. The essays in these volumes, as Feldman argues below, reflect a deep engagement with Jewish politics, antisemitism, and Zionism, even as Arendt stands opposed to what Kohn sees as her more general suspicion of identity politics.

Suzanne Vromen writes against the description of Arendt as a "non-Jewish Jew" by Richard Wolin. Vromen argues that in spite of the uproar over *Eichmann in Jerusalem*, Arendt's experience as a Jew was "the foundation of all her thinking." Specifically, her political embrace of her Judaism led to her choice to become a pariah. As Feldman puts it, the experience of being a Jew taught Arendt the value of standing apart from society, offering her the opportunity to embrace her role as a conscious pariah, someone who was able to transcend the duality of nationality and particularity and stand apart while still influencing the wider world of European and American life. Arendt's Judaism is essential to her desire to remain rebelliously outside a realm of homogenized social equality while at the same time demanding full political equality.

Elisabeth Young-Bruehl also explores Arendt as a cosmopolitan thinker. She approaches Arendt through Karl Jaspers' understanding of the Jews as one of the "Axial Age" peoples. She argues that Arendt, in conversation with Jaspers, develops a cosmopolitan thinking based on a sense of the plurality of the new as a basic experience of the human condition. Her cosmopolitanism, rooted consciously and unconsciously in her Jewish identity, is for Young-Bruehl one deep source of Arendt's approach to politics.

While denying the importance of Arendt's Jewish identity, Jerome Kohn finds in Arendt's experience of being a Jew one of the important foundations for her political thought. Her experience of antisemitism, Kohn argues, underlies her valuation of plurality and her experience of being excluded from the public world that leads to her valuation of action over thinking. Moreover, her experience of horror at what man is capable of leads Arendt back to the value of thinking—the activity of thinking—as that activity which can resist evil in the modern world.

Leon Botstein argues that Arendt's distinctive understanding of the separation of the political and the social spheres is rooted in her engagement with the Jewish question, first in modern Europe up to 1941 and later in the United States. Behind Arendt's political thinking, he writes, was the effort to allow Jewish culture and identity to continue to exist in the private and social spheres while at the same time enjoying full equality in the public sphere of politics. Botstein traces how Arendt's vision of politics found its expression in her study of America, where neither assimilation nor subordination was required in order to live a vibrant and free public life.

A free and equal political sphere where the many can speak and act in public is the sine qua non of Arendt's politics. And yet the essays in this volume seek to shift the singular focus away from Arendt's discussion of the public sphere and to explore the ways that thinking itself is at the root of Arendt's vision of political action. The shift from public to private passes through solitude. Since politics depends upon thoughtfulness that is nourished in solitude, I argue, in my essay, that political thinkers need to attend to Arendt's defense of the private realm.

If many of the contributors to this volume embrace Arendt's thinking as a cautionary impediment to getting carried away in fictional ideals, Drucilla Cornell argues that we need to risk recommitting ourselves to ideals. Against Arendt's worry that the dignity of the European moral tradition has crumbled, Cornell calls for the reimagining of new ideals of dignity that could uplift the human spirit. Turning to the development of a dignity jurisprudence in South Africa, Cornell suggests that the South African ideal of legal dignity offers the promise of a political ideal that might restore the lost dignity of the human condition that Arendt so carefully explores.

This collection ends with an artists' statement, an interview, and an exploration of the Arendt Library at Bard. Shy Abady's short statement provides the background for his two portraits of Arendt reproduced in this volume. As efforts by an Israeli artist to enter into her world, Abady's portraits set Arendt in and against the events and symbols of the twentieth century. An interview with Arendt's friend Jack Blum allows a window into a more personal Arendt, and yet one that shines light on Arendt's thinking. Discussing Arendt's intimate and creative relationship with her husband, Heinrich Blücher, Blum offers insight into the way she herself imagined the boundaries between the private and the political.

Since this volume began as a celebration of Arendt's one hundredth birthday sponsored by the Hannah Arendt Center and the Hannah Arendt Library at Bard College, it appropriately includes Reinhard Laube's characterization of Arendt's personal library. The library, he writes, was both a working library and a reference collection; as a whole, it offers a unified glimpse into Arendt's approach to writing and also into the professional and personal circles in which Arendt traveled.

PART I

Politics

Reflections on Antisemitism

C H R I S T O P H E R   H I T C H E N S

In October 1956, exactly fifty years ago to the month that we celebrate Hannah Arendt's one-hundredth birthday, the two Cold War colossi were being simultaneously convulsed by the uprising in Budapest and its repression by Soviet tanks. At the same time, the final act of Anglo-French imperialism in the Near East—you might prefer to say Middle East, or Western Asia—was taking place, in collusion with the state of Israel, with the invasion of Suez.

We know that the events in Hungary had an enormous emotional and intellectual impact on Hannah Arendt. The nature of this effect is somewhat enigmatic, which is why I want to begin with it. We know that she wrote a separate epilogue on these events for the second edition of *The Origins of Totalitarianism*, an epilogue she later removed. She didn't airbrush it. She was candid about having removed it, as having, as she put it, "become obsolete in many details."[1] But she never actually said why it was that she had decided that her tribute to the Hungarian rebels wouldn't stand the test of republication.

I want to begin by asking, "Why was that?" And that involves revisiting the events of 1956. Not alone were the Soviet tanks involved in the repression of the Hungarian revolution. There must also be dealt with, as was discussed by Hannah Arendt and many others, the betrayal of the Hungarian revolution by the statecraft of the United States—particularly by its Central Intelligence Agency, which, not unlike its performance in the year 1991 in Iraq, was content to issue incendiary broadcasts to the insurgents in Budapest, promising them help as long as they would continue to die. The poet e. e. cummings, I remember, wrote a song at that time called "Thanksgiving 1956," which ends by saying: "so rah-rah-rah democracy / let's all be thankful as hell / and bury the statue of liberty / (because it begins to smell)."

If one takes the trouble to find her missing epilogue, one finds it's full of surprisingly naive optimism—and surprisingly naive optimism is not a qual-

Facing: Hannah Arendt's notes from the front endpaper of Gershom Scholem's *Major Trends in Jewish Mysticism*. Arendt selects 11 topics that form an outline of the main topics of Scholem's text. The topics include the Kabbalah, esoterica, mysticism, and the problem of superstition. Her notes focus on two core questions: first, how to maintain the mysterious without going to superstition; and second, the relation of legalism and formalism in the rabbinic texts. Courtesy of the Hannah Arendt Collection, Stevenson Library, Bard College.

ity most saliently associated with the name of Hannah Arendt. I say it was naive because it stressed the spontaneous democracy of the worker's councils that were set up in Budapest. I think perhaps here she was expressing a nostalgia—even a little romance—for the German revolutions of 1919 in Munich and elsewhere, in which her future husband Heinrich Blücher had played such an honorable part.

Arendt's epilogue was naive also because it laid great stress on what she called the peaceful and orderly and good-humored crowds of Budapest. She rather romanticized the good-naturedness of the Hungarian revolution. Now, this optimism may possibly be justified in the long term, which is why it's worth looking up that epilogue again. After all, in 1989, not more than three decades later, there was a peaceful, bloodless, and orderly velvet revolution; it had its beginning in Budapest when the Hungarians allowed their East German brethren to resist by transiting Hungarian soil without hindrance. It led, in the end, to the fall of the Berlin Wall. And that was a classic case of the recovery of what Arendt so beautifully called, I think, the lost treasure of revolution.

The lost treasure of revolution is the common property to which Hannah Arendt alludes, very lyrically, in the opening passages of her collection *Between Past and Future*. She describes this ability to recover freedom: the spirit of an unforced liberty that is latent, she thought, in all people and which she claimed to detect in "the summer in 1776 in Philadelphia, the summer of 1789 in Paris, and the autumn of 1956 in Budapest."[2] Which, as you can see, is putting 1956 in Budapest on quite a high pedestal and threshold. Now this concept of the hidden treasure, the treasure that's always hidden but that can be reclaimed, is remarkable for its lack of what a Marxist would call concreteness. Here's how it appears according to Hannah Arendt, this treasure: It appears only "under the most varied circumstances, appears abruptly, unexpectedly, and disappears again under different mysterious conditions, as though it were a *fata morgana*,"[3] or, so to say, as a will of the wisp or *ignis fatuus*. The lost treasure of the revolution is a very, very elusive, almost ethereal concept for Hannah Arendt to be dealing with. And let me say, one of the nice things about reading and rereading Hannah Arendt is to discover how nice it is when she is fanciful every now and then.

But is the fantastical element of the lost treasure the reason why she so sternly decided to remove that epilogue? I think I know why she did it. Further research and disclosure of what happened that time in Budapest had brought it to her attention that those events in 1956 hadn't been as beautifully spontaneous as she had supposed. Mixed into the grandeur of the Hungarian rebellion was quite a heavy element of ultra-Magyar, ultra-Hungarian nationalism. The revolution also included quite a lot of antisemitism, directed at the strongly Jewish membership and character of Hungary's Communist elite. Many of the Jewish communist leaders had been denationalized from Hungary, having spent the war in the Soviet Union, in Moscow, some of them becoming Russian citizens. They came back to take over Hungary, which was still largely a Catholic, rural, and conservative country, and they did so only with the support of Red Army bayonets. The resentment aroused by the returning Jewish Communist leaders was considerable. The revolution did not lead to pogroms in the true, ghastly, meaning of the word, but there were some ugly lynchings of Jewish communists and some nasty rhetoric. And I think this must have weighed very much with her.

Arendt once noted approvingly, echoing a judgment made by Peter Nettl, in his marvelous biography of Rosa Luxemburg: "she [Rosa Luxemburg] was more afraid of a deformed revolution than she was of an unsuccessful one."[4] Nettl says this of Luxemburg, and Arendt underlined it. In a small way, Arendt too was a bit of a perfectionist in the moral and ethical, political world; she would have been happier with defeat than with a shameful victory. I, by the way, think that that's a huge clue to her character and identity. In any case, antisemitism, for her, was the most toxic possible sign of deformity, and for good reason.

It's remarkable, when one goes over it, how deeply the Hungarian revolution of fifty years ago was influenced by different strains of anti-Jewish feeling, both from above and from below. There's a wonderful recent study of the Hungarian revolution called *Twelve Days*, by a young Hungarian Jewish exile called Victor Sebestyen, who has had access to the Soviet archives. We now know that the Soviet Union was not fooling itself as much as we thought it was, about the popularity of communist rule in Hungary. Indeed, it knew that its Hungarian proxies had so alienated themselves from the population as to pose a very serious danger of counterrevolution. And, after Stalin's death, the leader of the Hungarian communist party, a man named Mátyás Rákosi, was summoned to Moscow to a meeting, which was organized by: Georgy Malenkov, Stalin's successor; Nikita Khrushchev, who was to be Malenkov's successor; and Lavrentiy Beria, the most famous secret policeman, probably, in history. Beria is a man whose command of Stalin's secret police was the most feared element of the great purges of the gulag right through the 1930s and '40s. At this meeting the party comrades left the talking to Beria, and Beria addresses Rákosi in these terms: "Listen, comrade Rákosi, we know that Hungary has had Hapsburg emperors, Tartar Khans, Polish Princes, Turkish Sultans and Austrian Emperors, but as far as we know, she has never yet had a Jewish king. And that is what you are trying to become. You can be sure we will never allow it."[5]

What had happened in the previous Hungarian revolution of 1919, also led by a Jewish communist, Béla Kun—with Georg Lukács, the great Hungarian philosopher, as Minister of Education—was a short-lived Hungarian commune. Actually, Lukács also came out of retirement to be Minister of Education in the 1956 revolution, and, I will allow myself a digression. After its crushing he was taken to a castle in Transylvania, and interned there for some considerable time, and never told when he was going to be let out or when he was going to be brought to trial, at which he is said to have commented, "So," after a pause, "Kafka was a realist after all."[6]

These memories of what had happened in 1919—the deformed revolution, the revolution that had betrayed itself and disgraced itself—and the relevance of such a revolution to her beloved Heinrich Blücher, would, I think, have weighed with Arendt. And remember, this is happening—this Soviet démarche to the Jewish deputy Rákosi in Budapest—only a few months after the doctor's plot, the terrible scare that Joseph Stalin threw into Russian society by his mad conviction that his Jewish doctors had formed a cabal to try and slowly poison him. Had he not died—not, I'm sorry, of poison, but of natural causes—the orders had been given already for what looked like a general roundup and internment of the Jews of Russia, which we were only just to be spared.

So all this was in the air at the time of the '56 events. And note the contempt with which Beria and his cohorts speak to Rákosi, their Jewish underling. Antisemitism comes in more than one guise. This is a man they're half ashamed even to be using. Bear that in mind while I just allude to what's happening at the same time in Egypt.

The British and French armies, navies, and air forces were bombing the airports of Egypt. Making use of a secret agreement they had made with the government of Israel, they were seeking to recover the Suez Canal zone for Britain and to try to eliminate Nasser's support—the support of Egypt's new dictator—for the Front de Libération Nationale (FLN) in Algeria. It was believed that if they could get rid of Nasser, they could dry up the sources of rebellion in Algeria. Which, of course, was an illusion.

But had the Arab world ever come to know of the secret meeting, of the secret collusion between France, Britain, and Israel that fall, I think there would have been even more anti-Jewish paranoia on Arab radios and in Arab propaganda than there was already. A meeting took place on October 22, 1956, at the Villa Bonnier de la Chapelle in Sèvres, just outside Paris and the site of many previous failed treaties. Present were Ben Gurion, General Moshe Dayan, and Shimon Peres (the only person from that meeting who is still alive). Israel's demands were: to be given the West Bank; for the rest of Jordan to be given to—guess which country?—Iraq; for control of Lebanon up to the Litani River; and for the Gaza Strip. All in return for their acting as proxy to stage an attack on Egypt, which the British and French could then claim to be intervening in order to prevent or forestall—or, as they put it, "separating the combatants."

There sometimes are conspiracies in history, there's no way 'round it, this was one; and if it wasn't a Jewish conspiracy, it was a conspiracy that involved Israel, and also Israel acting as proxy. Proxy for whom? Well, again, Sir Anthony Eden, the British Prime Minister, was one of the most notorious antisemites ever to be produced by the British foreign office, which is saying quite a lot. While he was Churchill's foreign secretary during the Second World War, he discounted all the wartime news of the Final Solution—the *Endlösung*, the

Holocaust, the Shoah, whichever you agree to call it—as mere Jewish propaganda. He strove to keep those leaky boats full of Jewish refugees—the boats like the *Struma*—away from the coast of Palestine where they could sink. His private secretary, Oliver Harvey, made a wartime entry in his diary saying that Sir Anthony Eden is "immovable on the subject of Palestine—he loves Arabs and hates Jews." He told Harvey in 1941, "If we must have preference let me murmur in your ear that I prefer Arabs to Jews."[7] This is the man who, in 1956, wants to use Israel as his proxy, just as the Jew-baiting Stalinists of Moscow knew that they had to rely on Rákosi, and his group in Budapest. The mutual contempt is alarming to reflect upon.

The British radio in the Middle East, while the invasion of Egypt was being readied, denounced Nasser for being a tool of the USSR and denounced the USSR for being too pro-Israeli and too friendly to Judaism. "It's high time," said the British radio, "that the Arab leaders who believe that Russia would support them against Israel, should know the truth about Russia. It is Moscow who has advised the Arabs to accept Israel's existence; it's the British Prime Minister who has given expression to Arab demands."[8] In other words, the British were attacking the Russians as being "soft on Jewry." And Nasser was denounced on British radio as being a "secret Zionist . . . also a secret freemason"—rather overegging the pudding. Meanwhile, the French Prime Minister, Guy Mollet, as he was arriving, made a point of coming up to Shimon Peres and assuring him that he had no anti-Jewish feelings of any kind. He had indeed, he said, himself suffered in the war and possessed very many Jewish labor friends.

So if I've drawn this picture successfully, and if you are taking my drift, we have the government of Israel going to war on behalf of one British antisemite and one Frenchman who hysterically claims that his best friends are Jews— not a very pretty picture. But the scene is of interest because it shows the mutations that antisemites can undergo. I might add in this context that some of Hannah Arendt's worst enemies were Jews. Some of you, I'm sure, have read the letter published by the *New York Times* in December 1948, protesting the visit to New York of Menachem Begin, the leader of Israel's Herut Party and later an Israeli prime minister. In it, Arendt denounced Begin's party as a fascist party based on racist and nationalist phenomena, on a leader cult, and on the preaching of violence. The letter was signed by her, Albert Einstein, Sidney Hook, and Seymour Melman.

To return to what I said about mutations of antisemitism, the antisemite is convinced, in spite of his prejudice, that the natural talent of the Jew for secret world domination might turn out to be quite useful. Thus, people who did, in a sense, hold that prejudice, were capable of exploiting their Jewish connections, and that, I think was of consuming interest to Arendt. She had always been fascinated by the way in which Jews could be not just persecuted and maltreated by those who did not like them, but also exploited and made use of, even by those who sought their destruction. Her attention, very famously, in the controversy over Eichmann, was much more on the Kapo, the collaborator, the *Judenrat*, and the mentality of those who make use of what they fear and make use of those whom they despise.

Now, her multiple reflections on antisemitism or Judeophobia, which are expressed best in the *Origins of Totalitarianism* are, in a way, to be regarded as an Enlightenment project. They are an attempt, if you read them closely, to reduce this fugitive mysterious prejudice to rational and explicable dimensions. It is an attempt to try to anatomize and diagnose it, to see how it can be understood with a view to its cure or banishment. She was always hoping to be able to consign atavism and medievalism and bigotry to some remote era of the past. This can be seen also in her attitude toward developments in the Soviet Union. Responding to the Soviet trial of Yuri Daniel and Andrei Sinyavsky in 1966, which was a frame-up with anti-Jewish and anti-intellectual overtones of its own, Arendt called it an "ugly reminder of something one had hoped had passed into history."[9] Two months before she died, she told Radio Liberty that she thought Andrei Sakharov was now the greatest of the intellectual dissidents in Russia. She added, "Which doesn't mean I have anything against Solzhenitsyn, except that I'm not sure pan-Slavism will work." I can just hear her saying that in her husky way.

When one has analyzed all the different strains and the contradictions that materialize or that constitute antisemitism, whether it's the Jewish middlemen in the French scandal over the Panama Canal shares, or whether it's the role of the Rothschilds in financing this or that bourgeois revolution, or whether it's the extraordinary preeminence of Arendt's hero and antihero Benjamin Disraeli in forwarding the cause of British imperialism in India, one is still increasingly impelled to doubt that the thing will yield to an analysis, even one that's as deft and thorough as hers is. Kurt Blumenfeld once quoted an observation, with which Arendt greatly agreed, that was made by his friend and publisher Salmon Schocken as early as 1914. Schocken had said, "In the emancipation period for Jews, one asked: 'What do you believe?' Today one only asks: 'Who are you?'"[10] And the answer was always, to that question, as Arendt had to concede, that whatever you believe, you still have to answer that you are a Jew.

Now, this is a depressing conclusion, because it suggests that the analysis and combating of antisemitism lies somewhere outside the rationalist and Enlightenment universe. The contradictory nature of antisemitism has a strong connection, I think, to Arendt's work on the totalitarian principle. She might have saved herself a little trouble and achieved a slightly greater concision in her study of this if she pointed out the real sense in which all forms of racism are totalitarian by definition. The indictment of the victim of racism is an absolute one. The victim of racism is unable to alter himself or herself. That is what makes racism totalitarian and also absolutist. And the means required to enforce a racist policy are also absolutist and totalitarian in that they have to obliterate completely the distinction between the public and the private spheres—they abolish private life. One of the foundations of the totalitarian system is that the racist who wants to cleanse the body politic of the "wrong race" must mount an inquisition into heredity, kinship, and marriage. To do so, he must scrutinize birth records and, in all other ways, be a slave to the constant, impossible quest for more and more purity: that's totalitarianism by definition. How odd it is—I sometimes think, and when I get the chance to, also write—how odd it is that racists are ever accused of discrimination. The ability to discriminate is the one faculty that the racist does not possess. They can't tell one from another of the target group. It's a very conspicuous failing on their part.

This very month of October 2006—fifty years later—comes the news that crowds shouting anti-Jewish slogans are marching on the parliament in Budapest. Again, the protests followed the admission of some rather gross economic policy deceptions on the part of the ruling Hungarian Socialist Party. Meanwhile, all across Europe, its almost commonplace, including among conservatives, in fact more and more often among conservatives, to hear that Israel has outlived its usefulness to the empire, and is, in effect, to be dumped over the side. Now, by no means is all of this resentment attributable to sympathy for the plight of the Palestinians—I think that's the way I'll choose to understate that.

At the same time, on the website of the party that currently holds the majority of the seats in the Palestinian parliament, you may easily find that otherwise quite hard to get publication, *The Protocols of the Elders of Zion*. It's on the Hamas website, you can download it anytime. In fact, adhesion to the doctrine of the *Protocols of the Elders of Zion* is in the founding charter of the Hamas organization, which is, as you probably know, the bastard child of the Muslim brotherhood under another name among the Palestinians. Also in Hamas proclamations are other very gross emanations of antisemitic paranoia, such as the apparently ineradicable belief that the Matzoh for a Jewish Passover must be sweetened with the blood of a non-Jewish child. Now, I disagree with Hannah Arendt's formulation, which has been generally accepted, of the Protocols, which she called a forgery. I think there's a danger lurking in that definition of the Protocols. After all, a forgery is an attempt to replicate a true bill; it's an attempt to make a copy of something genuine. There is no genuine basis of which the Protocols could be said to be a forgery—it would be better to say that they're a whole cloth concoction, or fabrication, actually undertaken by the Russian secret police under the Czar, and brought to Europe by the White Russian emigration, and adopted by the National Socialist movement, but it's not a forgery, it's a flat-out fraud. And it might be encouraging to consider that Muslims have no such tradition of their own. They don't have the Protocols, they don't have the "blood libel" about the Christian babies butchered at Passover, they have to borrow—when they want to be anti-Jewish—the rubbish of medieval Roman Catholic and Eastern Orthodox antisemitism. Isn't that a heartening thought? Sad to say, though, there are references to Jews being the descendants of coupling with pigs and monkeys, which are, as some of you will recognize, taken directly from the Koran. These are not a plagiarism of Christian antisemitic propaganda.

The Grand Imam of al-Azhar University—the nearest institution the Sunni Muslim world has to the Vatican—the Grand Imam Muhammad Sayed Tantawi has produced a long Koranic script using only Muslim sources for his polemic called "Jews and the Koran and the Tradition," which is an explicit incitement of violence against Jews based only on Muslim material.

While I'm doing this *tour d'horizon* of the recrudescence of antisemitic prejudice, it is worth recalling Mel Gibson, whose film *The Passion of the Christ* is an attempt to revive what the Vatican disowned only in 1966. This is the charge of "deicide" made against not just the Jewish Sanhedrin, but the Jewish people themselves and their "uttermost generations"—as is said in one verse of one gospel of the New Testament, the one that Gibson sought to revive cinematically. His film is an open incitement to antisemitic hatred. It would normally have been forbidden screening in the Middle East. You can't show films like *Ben-Hur* or *King of Kings* in the Muslim world because they physically represent one of the prophets who is mentioned in the Koran, namely Jesus of Nazareth. But an exception was made in the case of Mel Gibson's *The Passion of the Christ*, and I have a feeling I understand why that was. In case you're resting your view of Mr. Gibson and his agenda purely on his alcoholic tussles on the Malibu Highway, I call your attention to the Catholic splinter sect of which he's a member, which is founded by his father, Hutton Gibson, a man who Mel Gibson says has never told him a lie, and who is his moral and intellectual hero. Mr. Hutton Gibson commented on Joseph Ratzinger's statement, when he was a cardinal, that though the Jews did not, alas, recognize the Christian revelation, they were, at least it could be said, earlier in adopting monotheism and thus might be regarded in the light of an elder brother to Christianity. It's not great, the Ratzinger formulation—it's a bit condescending—but it's better than some Catholic statements on the Jewish question. Hutton Gibson's comment on this: "Abel had an elder brother." I think we know what we're talking about here.

This is the situation. Antisemitism is back, and it's back in quite a big way. It's being preached with impunity and shown on screens in the United States. In Europe the situation is getting steadily worse. It's eight hundred percent more likely, according to studies of public opinion, that if you are a Muslim you will report negatively on Jews than if you are a Christian.

Another way in which racism is totalitarian by nature is the extent to which it claims to explain absolutely everything. Once one knows the key bit of information, as Hofstadter says about the paranoid—the paranoid already has all the information he needs—once one is in possession of the key thing, the secret, in other words, of Jewish world government, then everything is suddenly explicable: how simple it all now seems.

I humiliated myself a few years ago looking at the list of names of people killed in—I should say murdered in, obliterated in—the World Trade Center. I'd read so many reports, not just from the Middle East, but from Europe too, saying that all the Jews had left the building just before the planes hit. And I thought to myself, "Why am I doing this? This is disgusting to be looking to see if there are Jewish names there." Something in me made me do it: this is what I've been reduced to. And this is what I mean by the toxic nature of prejudice and the way it spreads like a weed. If I had been told that none of the Jews turned up to work that day, I suppose I might possibly have thought, well—it could bear checking. In fact it would be checkable. But millions of people around the world believe something that is literally and figuratively unbelievable—that all the Jews managed to leave just before the planes hit. They believed that the first time they heard it, and still do.

Hannah Arendt is a great prop and stay and comfort in dark times like these, because she was always very acute on the morbidly stupid element of totalitarianism. The morbidly stupid element is totalitarian's saving grace. It is a mentality that is so dumb as to say that extreme and fanatical means and measures must be used with complete mobilization to achieve an end that is, in any case, historically inevitable. What could be more absurd than that?

The absurdity of totalitarian thinking is related to its attack on the life of the mind. Arendt was quite right to insist on confronting this anti-intellectual element of totalitarianism and the racist element in it; and she was right, I think, to insist on the centrality of the Dreyfus case to a meaningful understanding of antisemitism. She saw that antisemitism bears an odd relationship to the life of the mind. It is at once anti-intellectual—highly anti-intellectual—and also pseudo-intellectual. The very word *intellectual* originates, in fact, as a term of abuse, from the time of the Dreyfus case. It was the charge thrown by the anti-Dreyfusards at the partisans of Dreyfus and his friends Émile Zola and Georges Clemenceau. The intellectual was the rootless person with no real connection to the land or the *patrie*, to the tribe or the country, or to the tradition. He is someone who simply lived with his mind and had no loyalties beyond this; he didn't have an organic relationship—if you like—to the rest of society. I personally think that the word *intellectual* should never quite lose this taint of insult, as it does when fatuous formations like "public intellectual," for example, are used among us.

However, antisemitism, although it has this anti-intellectual origin, also has a pseudo-intellectual character. Someone who dislikes West Indians, shall we say, or Mexicans, or Haitians, as it might be, is usually expressing a straight-out feeling of superiority over them, and of contempt for their inferiority as a race or an ethnicity. It is the contempt for a lesser breed, usually mingled with disgust over their birth rate, if you listen clearly, and, whether you listen or not, obviously fear of their sexuality. Racism takes grossly physical forms. It talks about the nastiness of their cooking, the way they breed like rabbits, their bathroom habits, the possibility of sleeping with them—this kind of thing. That's common racial bigotry.

Antisemitism is not like that. After all, nobody says that people from Chiapas province or from Haiti have a secret plan to take over the stock exchange or Wall Street. Antisemitism is more like a theory, and when you read its productions, you'll see that certain continuing tropes will occur: gold, the role of gold in history, and the hoarding of it; banking, with the secrecy that banking implies; blood and soil; and the possibility of a Jew being able to conceal himself, to avoid detection. Also, of course, mythology, deicide, and the fact that the Jews were the first to encounter both Jesus of Nazareth and the prophet Muhammad, and to conclude that neither of them was authentic (something for which it is unlikely that they'll be forgiven by their successor monotheists). To discuss with an antisemite is a quite different proposition from discussing with an ordinary, vulgar, racist demagogue. We are talking about either conspiracy theories, or—as I wouldn't dignify the World Trade Center innuendo even with that sobriquet—fantasy theories, based on the apprehension of something very dark and hidden.

There was another woman of very considerable mind and courage and intellect who, like Arendt, thought deeply about antisemitism in modern Europe—Rebecca West. I chanced to have been writing the introduction to the Penguin Classic version of her *Black Lamb and Grey Falcon* this summer. And when she was traveling through the Balkans in the 1930s—with extremely acute antennae—she saw the way that antisemitism was going in that part of Europe and elsewhere, and how unappeasable it probably was going to be. And at one point she has the following insight regarding the relationship between antisemitism and anti-intellectualism. She writes, "Now I understand another cause for antisemitism. Many primitive peoples must receive their first intimations of the toxic quality of thought from Jews. They know only the fortifying idea of religion. They see in Jews the effect of the tormenting and disintegrating ideas of skepticism."[11] I think that's extremely well put.

The extent to which the anti-intellectual aspect of antisemitism is joining with—or is it perhaps becoming?—anti-Americanism, is I think worth our attention. In many of the great tirades we hear today, against the massive temple of modernity, commerce, and globalization, it's perhaps not wrong to detect the undertones of a much older complaint against the cosmopolitans, the merchants, and the rootless: it is the complaint against those who disturb the order and the calm of the settled, organic, and pious societies. I have a feeling that there's a transference—it's an echo I keep picking up in Europe and in the Middle East—of old antisemitic caricatures into a general characterization of these United States. There's actually one very bizarre, anecdotal piece of evidence for this: namely, the slang word, the punk word, the street word used by the insurgents in Iraq—I mean the people who do the kidnappings, the video beheadings, the destruction of each other's mosques, the throwing of acid in the faces of unveiled women. I mean that lot who are politely called by the *New York Times* the "insurgents." Their slang word for the soldiers of the United States Army is *"yehud"*—the Jews. "Here come the Jews, take cover, scatter, the Jews are coming." This is anecdotal evidence for my view that there's a convergence between those whose ideology is suicide and Islam, and those who've had a more traditional attitude towards the mongrel, denatured melting pot commerce of the United States. And some of the prejudice takes a secular form.

It was Arendt who was one of the first to notice the drift away, by the campus left, from anything resembling classic Marxism. As she was writing her essay "On Violence" in the 1960s, she noted how the left abandoned Marxism for flirtations with the Maoism that taught of political power flowing from a gun barrel, or with the fantasies of Sartre and Fanon on the cleansing qualities of violence, or the heroic qualities of provocations that were designed to elicit backlashes, and, above all, the cult of youth. If you separated them out from their political context and you knew no more about them, they would, taken together, remind you, as they did her, of some of the building blocks and emotions of fascism.

Let me conclude by saying that I think it may be time to take the temperature of antisemitism again, and to take it seriously. This may involve admitting what we might rather not think: that there is something protean and ineradicable about the prejudice. It's always able to take different forms, and to recur at different times, and in different places, and different idioms and different vernaculars. The most obvious literary analogy for this would be, I propose, the rats in *La Peste*, Albert Camus's classic about the plague in Oran, where the plague bacilli, and their carriers, hide themselves and bide their time, always waiting, as Camus says, for another chance to send their rats up to die again in a free city. But wouldn't it be horrible if that image was not the worst one? The depressing, further thought occurs to me: What if this is also like Arendt's buried and hidden treasure—the protean treasure that she discusses in *Between Past and Present*? What if it's a will of the wisp and *fata morgana*—an impalpable thing that can never be netted, identified, pinned down, or diagnosed, let alone cured? What if antisemitism is something that has the power to manifest itself in unpredictable seasons and unexpected places, and is always to elude the work of the mind of the analyst? If that comparison were valid, which I have to say I rather hope it isn't, we would be looking right down the corridors of our past and uncovering the original scenes of tragedy.

Power process –

CHAPTER X

OF POWER, WORTH, DIGNITY, HONOUR, AND
WORTHINESS

Power.   THE POWER *of a man*, to take it universally, is his present means, to obtain some future apparent good; and is either *original*
or *instrumental*.   *= original*

Natural power, is the eminence of the faculties of body, or mind: as extraordinary strength, form, prudence, arts, eloquence, liberality, nobility. *Instrumental* are those powers, which acquired by these, or by fortune, are means and instruments to acquire more: as riches, reputation, friends, and the secret working of God, which men call good luck. For the nature of power, is in this point, like to fame, increasing as it proceeds; or like the motion of heavy bodies, which the further they go, make still the more haste.

The greatest of human powers, is that which is compounded of the powers of most men, united by consent, in one person, natural, or civil, that has the use of all their powers depending on his will; such as is the power of a commonwealth: or depending on the wills of each particular; such as is the power of a faction or of divers factions leagued. Therefore to have servants, is power; to have friends, is power: for they are strengths united.

Also riches joined with liberality, is power; because it procureth friends, and servants: without liberality, not so; because in this case they defend not; but expose men to envy, as a prey.

Reputation of power, is power; because it draweth with it the adherence of those that need protection.

So is reputation of love of a man's country, called popularity, for the same reason.

Also, what quality soever maketh a man beloved, or feared of many; or the reputation of such quality, is power; because it is a means to have the assistance, and service of many.

Good success is power; because it maketh reputation of wisdom, or good fortune; which makes men either fear him, or rely on him.

Affability of men already in power, is increase of power; because it gaineth love.

Reputation of prudence in the conduct of peace or war, is power;

Fiction as Poison

:: G E O R G E K A T E B

I translate the question, "What does it mean to think about politics?" into "What does it mean to think about politics today in the spirit of Hannah Arendt?" Thinking in the spirit of Arendt signifies among other things that we should summon up attentive worry about the fate of constitutional government in times of both real and artificial crisis; at the same time, we should expect developments that demonstrate the fragility of constitutional government and that simultaneously increase that fragility because of the establishment of precedents that will further erode constitutional democracy in the future.

For Arendt, constitutional government is a high practicable ideal that unlike other high ideals may be regularly institutionalized. In particular, the U.S. Constitution is, in her judgment, perhaps the greatest achievement of constitutionalism in human history. But she was extremely sensitive in her lifetime to the ubiquitous assaults all over the Western world on the structures of, and aspirations to, constitutional democracy—free, popular, limited, lawful, and moderate government. In the United States, she was particularly worried by the assaults of McCarthyism and related Cold War tendencies in the 1950s. But the encroachment on constitutionalism, owing in large part to an adventurist foreign policy, did not monopolize Arendt's attention. She was attentive to foreign policy for its own sake and found in it much cause for worry. The Vietnam War called forth acute analysis and eloquent worry in her essay on the Pentagon Papers, "Lying in Politics." We can say that there is an affinity, not only a causal link, between an unnecessary and hence aggressive war abroad and encroachments on constitutionalism at home: both phenomena display an urge to violate, to destroy prescriptive barriers and cross lawful boundaries. War provides a cover for anticonstitutionalism, which in turn intensifies the illusion that war is necessary and urgent. Each is thus a contrived means for the other, and each is an end that leads beyond itself into a

Facing: Chapter 10 of Hannah Arendt's heavily annotated copy of Thomas Hobbes's *Leviathan*. This page shows Arendt's note-taking, which fills many of her books with selective underlinings and marginalia. The heading "Power process" is written at the top of the page, emphasizing her reading of Hobbes's "nature of power" as a process. Courtesy of the Hannah Arendt Collection, Stevenson Library, Bard College.

thrilling sense of indefinite potentiality for transgression. Besides the urge to violate and its two modes of fulfillment, there are other unscrupulous urges bred from too much wealth and power.

Arendt's attentive worry was, of course, born in her experience of the Nazi movement and was then intensified by its years of rule. This worry fed her studies in the extremist nature of European imperialism in the nineteenth century and of long-standing European racism, including antisemitism. These studies help us to understand the cultural conditions that made up a large part of the background that favored the triumph of Nazism. It should be noticed, however, that she insists that Nazism was neither their inevitable outcome nor a merely incremental advance in the same direction. Nazism in its fully developed policies was an unpredictable phenomenon, and it could not be grasped by inherited modes of understanding political life.

Running through Arendt's work, even aside from her studies of totalitarianism, is the conviction that attentive observers of political life will always have cause to worry. That is so for many reasons, but in her analyses, one reason stands out, and that is the ferocious human proclivity to become enclosed in ideologies or fictions; this proclivity is frequently combined with another, which is to become obsessed with images—that is, with appearances, with notions and symbols of prestige and reputation. When I speak of appearances, I do not refer to her celebration of shining appearances, the beauty that memorable deeds and creations bestow on observers, but rather appearances closer to Machiavelli's sense: deceptive or illusionary manipulations carried out in speech or actions. Yet, just as those who disseminate ideologies to the mass are those who are most prone to believe them, those who manipulate appearances are themselves taken in and come to believe—perhaps always believed—what they want others to believe. Both the ideological enslavement and the self-deception of warmakers figure in "Lying in Politics."

In her analysis of totalitarianism, Arendt gives special explanatory emphasis to the attractiveness of mental constructions—especially ideologies—that reduce reality to an all-encompassing story or picture, that are revered or idolized as the truth about reality or some higher reality, and that are cartoon-like and ruinously untrue to reality. Ideologies, which are action-doctrines, are the most poisonous fictions. The passion is to coerce the world into total consonance with the pattern fantasized in an ideology. People may find these constructions initially attractive because they promise harm to designated enemies, or, on the other hand, prove so attractive that eventually they enable followers to disregard or overcome all restraint in dealing out harm to these enemies. The most perverse ideologies are built on the *manufacture* of enemies. But if totalitarianism originally made the study of ideology crucial for Arendt, and if totalitarian ideologies are the cruelest and the most distant from truth, the fact remains that ideologies are everywhere and help to define and energize political life, often with destructive results. This is not to deny that fictions of other kinds can incite wickedness.

Thus, if her work leaves the reader with a net impression of pessimism about politics—actual politics all through time and in the present—and succeeds in inducing pessimism in her readers, the cause is not that Arendt has a theoretical pessimism concerning human nature. She does not lament allegedly innate and transgressive human instincts, appetites, and drives. For short, let us say that she does not harbor an Augustinian or a Hobbesian pessimism. We cannot pin her down in this way. She is unorthodox in her pessimism. She also refuses to have a fallback cynicism that locates in sharp-eyed and tireless self-interest the key to unlock all political mysteries. In fact, she is intent on showing how for both good and bad, political actors can unexpectedly disregard self-interest. Even more, she discourages the tendency to make wrongdoing glamorous or psychologically deep by attributing to political actors a steady disposition to be villainous or sadistic, or to do harm out of spite or gratuitous malice. I believe nonetheless that she does in fact give serious cause to be pessimistic about politics. Her attention is constantly addressed to the reality that injustice, oppression, and evil are constantly streaming forth from the decisions and actions of political agents, whether leaders or officials or activists, whether in democracies or dictatorships. Human susceptibility to fictions that give political life vivid meaning and false transparence lies at the foundation of political wrongdoing.

An important formulation occurs in Arendt's letter to Gershom Scholem (1963), replying to his criticism of the notion of the banality of evil in *Eichmann in Jerusalem*. She says, "Evil is never 'radical,' that it is only extreme, and that it possesses neither depth nor any demonic dimension. . . . Only the good has depth and can be radical." Human evil can "lay waste the whole world precisely because it spreads like a fungus on the surface" (*The Jewish Writings*, 471), while moral goodness, which she begins to explore at length a year later in "Some Questions of Moral Philosophy" and then elsewhere, is a rare gesture that emanates from the depths of the constantly self-questioning and hence equally rare soul.

Arendt's hard truth, perhaps her hardest truth, is that when many if not most of the awful events in political life happen, not only the evil of totalitarianism, the leading perpetrators do not feel, as, say, Macbeth does, that they are doing or even intending wrong; rather, they usually think sincerely that they are serving a mission of some kind. They are not haunted by guilt. Hitler and Stalin would be prime instances because they carried this tendency as far as it has been carried in human history up to now. There is an ineffaceable human tendency to feel guiltless while doing great wrong; this is the substance of her pessimism. Typically, wrongdoers do not assume that their actions are lamentable but necessary. Instead, they think that they are doing the positively and purely right thing. Beyond questions of moral good and evil, extremist political actors believe that they are doing what is historically or metaphysically or aesthetically right. In what they do, if they notice at all the costs in human life and in the ability of people to live decently, they regard these costs as far less important than the achievements they plan to attain or have already attained. In the propaganda they use to rebut criticism, achievements are made to justify the costs, whenever they sense the need to justify these costs. Indeed, the costs are not costs, except to one's side; and even then they are made little of. The costs paid by the other side are merely the exactions of destiny or history's vengeance.

Arendt's lesson is that we should always expect the worst in political life because human beings live by simplified ideas and distorted reductions, by ideologies, fictions, stories, patterns, and images that enchant them. Enchanted, they will do great wrongs while convinced that they are conceiving or doing great deeds. By her emphasis on ideology and other fictions, I think that Arendt's work makes the opaque subject of political motivation, of the energies behind politics, somewhat less opaque. It is an enormous contribution that her analyses have made to understanding not just the evil of totalitarianism, but also all systematic uses of violence and coercion.

Her writing confronts the fact that there has always been much scholarly and popular incuriosity about what moves political actors, as if actions spoke for themselves, presented no puzzle, and required little interpretation; or as if the motives of the living, not only the dead, are always too opaque for sustained analysis. The usual advice is to stay content with a few easy rules like these: assume the basest motive, follow the money, be assured that all politics is local politics, realize that politics is always the same old story, and therefore never be surprised, much less shocked, and so on; or go in the other direction and imitate the establishment by attributing to all actors the honorable will to do their best; or throw up your hands and say that officials are dazed by their power and don't quite know what they're doing but like doing it anyway, or don't fully mean what they do, but are trying to respond to events as if they didn't cause them, so that they can just get through the day. These are the counsels of happy resignation and blank complacency.

In any case, Arendt drives home the idea that it is rare to do wrong when you bring yourself to acknowledge the fact that it is or would be wrong, especially in the essentially abstract realm of political policy and action. In face-to-face life, it may require an irresistible impulse to block perception, but politics is not marked by the irresistible impulses of officials. Politics is the home of those who are often innocent—premoral, postmoral, supermoral, or amoral—to themselves; their minds do not move outside their framework; they are mesmerized inside it. They have little inclination to see themselves as tragic figures who must practice the doctrine of the necessary and lesser evil or the method of dirty hands. (Perhaps political actors who spurn the tragic pose as pretentious are sometimes commendable. Ideas of the dignity or moral heroism of using violence are likelier to fill the heads of theorists than actors.) Although those who do wrong on a large scale may be innocent to themselves, they need not, however, be innocent to the observer; and if not innocent, not possessed of tragic dignity, either.

Thinking and Judging

There are instructive complexities in Arendt's approach to understanding the drives behind the ravages of political life. The first is that she provides two apparently divergent methods: understanding political actors from within (for example, her empathic discussion in *The Origins of Totalitarianism* of the Boers in their encounter with African natives), and yet imposing on them from the outside an interpretation that they would not accept and in which, some of the time, they would not even recognize themselves (for example, her defamiliarizing conceptualization in *Origins* of totalitarian leaders as prisoners of their ideological fictions who succeed in likewise imprisoning their followers). Arendt engages in empathy with brilliant if disturbing results, but she also finds meanings that hide from those who do the deeds and from many observers as well. The impressive fact is that she bestows empathy not only on actors she admires or has sympathy for, but also on actors that fill her with disapproval or even horror; and she imposes interpretive meaning similarly.

The second instructive complexity is that Arendt undertakes a remedial enterprise: she explores mental processes that conduce to keeping before us the idea that those with whom we deal are as valuable to themselves as we are to ourselves; and if they are our adversaries, they are as human as we are and are not to be oppressed or degraded or treated as nonhuman or subhuman. She tries, that is, to undermine those ideological attitudes that work to make it easy to kill and waste people and destroy the conditions of their lives. These sentiments of equality are meant, however, to accompany the realization that human beings are not equally capable of the most remarkable feats of both inhuman policy and extraordinary and praiseworthy creation.

In the course of trying to suggest the motives behind totalitarianism, Arendt opens up the general question of political motivation, especially the motivation behind systematic uses of violence and coercion. At the same time, she contributes to those human capacities that can retard or resist all kinds of political excess and atrocity. I would therefore like to turn now to the second complexity, Arendt's remedial enterprise, which consists of her methods of undermining those beliefs (including ideologies) that make it easy to kill and waste people and destroy their conditions of life. She applies her methods to opposing such harms as war and other violence, not just resisting totalitarianism or tyranny. The principal methods are *thinking* and *judging*, especially thinking. What helps to reduce susceptibility to murderous ideologies and fictions? It is cultivating the readiness to think for oneself and to form one's judgment in the actual or invisible company of those who think for themselves. In what follows shortly, I will mention some of the leading kinds of thinking and judging that Arendt singles out as especially useful in diminishing susceptibility. The absence or feeble existence of these mental processes is what enables ideologies and other fictions to take hold and govern leaders and followers in their pursuit of excesses and atrocious policies.

The first two volumes of her projected three-volume work *The Life of the Mind* explore thinking and willing. Both volumes are full of suggestions concerning various relationships between action (not only political action) and mental processes. She did not live to write the third volume, on judging, which was for her the most politically relevant sector of the life of the mind. In the writings we have, what she makes clear is that thinking rather than judging is more relevant in resistance to political atrocities. After the fact, judging is essential to comprehending political events when they are novel, whether atrocious or creative, and in need of unfamiliar conceptualization.

An irony should be noticed: thinking is not just a main source of resistance to policies of atrocity, but it is also an unwitting source of those theoretical systems that in simplified or caricatured form help to engender the ideologies and other fictions that inspire, facilitate, or rationalize atrocities. Thinking must sometimes remedy itself.

At the risk of simplifying Arendt's reasoning and depriving it of its inimitable texture, I propose to bring together some of her key ideas on thinking and judging. She offers at least a sketch, if not always a worked-out view, of all the kinds of judging and thinking that I am about to list; and her work exemplifies all of them as well. With the exception of system building, they all play a part in constituting the attention that grows out of and focuses political worry; and some play a part in perfecting the will to resist. I suppose it would be fair to say that her implication is that political theorists and historians as well as poets, novelists, and moral essayists should and often do aim to perfect these operations of remedial intellect. But it is precisely the scarcity of these mental traits in the population at large that produces the bulk of events in life; and these events are the stuff that necessitates and often joyously entangles thinkers and scholars in the project of understanding. I mean that her work is directed at making sense of those who, because they act, are too busy to think (as she recurrently says), or who are enslaved to fictions and cannot think and judge, or who in the mass are prone to incuriosity. Those who try to understand want to understand those who do not want to understand—either themselves or others. That is one very important division of labor in life. The political urgency comes from the effort to understand the emergence of great wrongs, past and present, some of them unprecedented, and to awaken us, her readers, whether we are near or distant in time or place in relation to what has happened or is happening; especially to awaken us to terrible effects.

The mental processes, then, are judging and thinking. It must be said that the distinction between them is not always sharp, and that they tend to blend into each other. Certain instances of each could be taken for the other. Obviously, not all thinking or judging is politically relevant. In what follows, my emphasis is on the political relevance of these mental processes.

1. *Judging* for the purpose of ascertaining whether a given political phenomenon is a novel occurrence, rather than being in most respects familiar and

amenable to being subsumed under prevailing categories or patterns. Her effort in *Origins* to demonstrate the unprecedented qualities of totalitarianism in its militant extremism and its extermination of races or classes or other groups, and its absolute distinction from historical tyrannies and despotisms, is her most famous act of judgment in this sense. Then, too, "Lying in Politics" tries to isolate the novel feature of the Vietnam War—novel at least in American history—and finds it in two main motives: leaders were obsessed by the aim of protecting the image of American power and determination, and bureaucrats were gripped by the project of solving problems, no matter how artificially created a particular problem was and no matter what the so-called solution might cost human beings. The war was the pure politics of appearances: the struggle was to keep up the reputation of strength and resolve, when it was never in doubt; and superimposed on it was the game in which technocrats unleashed their passion for abstract victory. Her implication is that there was no danger that losing the war would have any negative effect on American reputation, and that persisting in the attempt to win the war was a rationalist simulacrum of madness.

She also denies, though unpersuasively, that the United States is and has been an imperialist society, and for her that makes the remote war against a distant and unthreatening country even more unusual. Yet we can say instead that U.S. imperialism is probably a new kind of imperialism on the world stage, an imperialism that is not comprehensible by reference to Athens, Rome, or Britain, despite flashes of similarity to all three. It needs an act of judgment—inspired by Arendt but in disagreement with her conclusion—to delineate its at least partial novelty. I am sure she would have found novelty in the war against Iraq, but it would be a mistake to try to guess how she would have identified it.

2. *Judging* as the effort to bring home the reality of various phenomena. (Thinking as reflection—the ordinary sense of the word that appears in the question "What does it mean to think about politics?"—is indistinguishable from judging in the second sense.) In some cases, this effort supplements the delineation of the novelty of phenomena. To bring home the reality of a given phenomenon is especially necessitated by the resistance one feels in oneself to making such an effort, mostly because of horror or aversion, but it can also be necessitated by intoxicated pride or by shame; and when the phenomenon itself, in its deliberate or unavoidable opacity, seems to resist the effort to be understood. Arendt had to overcome what she called her "speechless horror" at the death camps in order to begin writing about Nazism and disclose the obsessive and invincible attachment to racial ideology in its most terrible and grandiose form. Beyond the resistance in oneself, one must face the resistance of others who are averse to perceiving reality because it depresses them or burdens them or importunes them to respond; or, in contrast, fills them with unexamined satisfaction. It is also true that Arendt sets about unearthing

admirable phenomena. She strives to retrieve the "buried treasure" of authentic politics in such works as *The Human Condition*, *Between Past and Future*, and *On Revolution*. She gives an unusual importance to the role played by the exhilaration of political participation in attracting people to politics and keeping them in it, apart from goals and ends, even though many observers and even many participants who, in their self-important solemnity, do not perceive or wish to acknowledge such exhilaration.

3. *Judging* as impartiality, whether in the form of appreciating the skills of one's adversaries and the pathos of their struggle, or in the form of one's ascent above the fray in order to look at both sides fairly. Arendt praises Homer, Herodotus, and Thucydides in *Between Past and Future* and *Lectures on Kant's Political Philosophy* for these kinds of judgment. She could not extend this receptive generosity to those who have ever done absolute evil, but when such evil is not involved, she is rarely eager to pass moral judgment on historical events. She loves Athens but does not hate Sparta.

4. *Judging* as the effort to form one's taste in general, and to form one's opinion about a given artwork or human phenomenon by means of an enlarged mentality that takes into account the opinions of others when they are known, or imagined as what they would be, given the different positions in life that others hold. The essays on particular thinkers in *Men in Dark Times* are a major expression of this kind of judgment, because Arendt seeks to show the grounds of her admiration for diverse writers and their achievements.

5. *Thinking* as the effort to retain the conviction that human beings actually exist and therefore to weaken the tendency to substitute for their reality figments of one's egocentric fantasy or the monsters of one's ideologically debauched imagination. Her discussions of Socrates always return to this theme of the human reality of the Other.

6. *Thinking* as empathy, as the effort to understand even the most abhorrent or outlandish human beings as they understand themselves. Actually, Arendt denounces empathy by name as an impossible attempt to know what she believes cannot be known: what it is like to be another person. Each of us can know from the inside, or seek to know, only what it is to be oneself. One cannot be two people at the same time: one cannot experience being another person while simultaneously remaining oneself. (The "two-in-one" of the self conversing with itself is not a process in which one practices empathy on oneself.) Yet this manifestly correct view coexists with a contention in *The Human Condition* that seems to go in an opposite direction: only others can know me; I cannot know myself. It is possible that this apparent inconsistency is resolved by saying that no one can know their identity (*who* they are) because identity is a mystery, but that others can describe our traits and qualities (*what we*

are) far better than we can. In any case, Arendt does indeed perform acts of empathy, more properly understood. She tries to imagine what other people feel and think when they are substantially different from herself, by filling out the significance of their deeds or of their actual recorded expression. She proceeds by enhancement or elaboration in a manner not exactly like that of a novelist but not entirely dissimilar. Empathy matters especially for any political analyst, including Arendt, when morally terrible or questionable deeds demand explanation. Is this act only imagining how one would feel and think if one found oneself in the condition or circumstances of other agents? She sometimes sounds as if this is what she means. But if it is, that indicates that all people in the same condition or circumstances would think and feel in the same way. That couldn't be true. People are different in temperament and disposition; they are not all the same person with one identity who happens to find himself in an indefinite variety of circumstances. She celebrates the power of imagination as indispensable to the moral life, but she simply will not say a good word for empathy, which is simply another name for that sort of imagination. She could have said, but did not say, that one basis of imagination lies in the incipient presence in all human beings of potentialities that go unrealized, but that if inwardly detected in oneself through an act of attentive courage, permit a person to recognize that what is apparently alien and remote or repellent in others is truly a part of anyone's possible but unrealized self.

7. *Thinking* as the attempt to invest the world with meaningfulness by constructing systems of thought in metaphysics or theology. *Thinking*, the first volume of *The Life of the Mind,* is Arendt's extended discussion of the relation between systems of meaning and the activity of thinking. These systems are without warrant, yet they must be created because thinkers often cannot live without some higher comprehensive meaning that they claim to detect in the nature of things. In reduced ideological form, these systems turn into fictions that seduce followers into trying to remake the world to conform to the fiction. The fictions turn murderous because the products of thinking are consumed unthinkingly or thoughtlessly. Arendt is fascinated by systems in part because she herself espouses the cause of meaningfulness, at least in local and particular contexts, because it allows people to be at home in their world or in the world altogether. Less alienated, perhaps, they would be less inclined to destruction and cruelty. But her great worry is the conversion or mutation of theoretical systems into ideologies that cast a spell over masses of people and lead them to do or cooperate with atrocities. This ironic turn in the fate of thinking instigates another kind of thinking.

8. *Thinking* as the effort to undo systems by continuous questioning. This is Socratic thinking. It is a potent weapon against systems that try to impose a higher and comprehensive meaning on the world. By relentless but incon-

clusive eristical inquiry, or by self-doubting dialectical inquiry in cooperation with others, any given system is exposed as harboring errors and unexamined assumptions that vitiate its conclusions. Thus, one kind of thinking
must struggle against the corrupted versions of another kind. Thinking in the
form of continuous questioning achieves on the purely intellectual level what
thinking as the strain to acknowledge the reality of the Other, and the further
strain of practicing empathy, achieve in a more personal way.

Let us notice that thinking in two forms—the effort to acknowledge the
reality of the Other, and the effort to practice empathy—is essentially aimed
at understanding those who, above all in political life, have no interest in understanding the motives or culture of their adversaries, and hence regard
them as nonpersons, as having no inwardness and no humanly recognizable
attachments. Political actors also have little interest in understanding themselves; they are allergic to self-examination. All unthinking people—all of us
most of the time—in politics or out, say: I alone am real, I alone am real to
myself, I alone deserve to be understood as I understand myself; or they substitute "we" for "I" in these attitudes. But if most people on all sides are unthinking, the better side, if there is one, is not necessarily made up of people
who think or judge better.

Understanding and Forgiving

Arendt's views raise the general question as to whether she excuses political
wrongdoing by representing it as often unaccompanied by little, if any, sense
in the wrongdoers that they in fact do wrong. As I have said, she often represents them empathically, as they understood themselves, which often means
that they saw themselves as doing right in some sense that makes moral right
irrelevant or minor. She certainly makes it clear that the Nazi death camps
were unforgivable evil, whatever the mentality that created and administered
them. However, her capacity to make political phenomena understandable as
the action of those who have no interest in understanding, no interest in judging and thinking, does not issue in even the slightest inclination to forgive
the Nazis. Was she unforgiving about the evils of most wars? If she wasn't, we
should be. But what about lesser wrongdoing—say, the brutalities and restric-
tions of police states, or gross violations by the U.S. government of the Constitution at home and abroad? We know where her sentiments lie or would lie.
But does her capacity to make political phenomena understandable teach us,
when confronted with our troubles, to try to understand their motivational
source, and though we remain worried, to permit our wisdom to increase our
disinclination to act? To be attentively worried, but also, in a countermove-
ment, less disposed to condemn policies that are enacted by perpetrators who
have little or no idea that they deserve condemnation, so insulated are they
by their fictions or ideologies or concern for image? In teaching us how to
understand political actors who are thus rendered morally incapacitated, no

matter what side they are on, does Arendt's work reconcile us to wrongdoing, provided it doesn't reach the depths of Nazi evil? There may be such a temptation. But there are resources in Arendt's work that enable resistance to that temptation.

Thinking and Individualized Imagination

I suggest that what Arendt wants to condemn—perhaps as much as anything else—is the absence of the simple ability to think (item 5 in our list), to imagine that the people we are harming are people like ourselves but in different circumstances, that they are real, that they matter to themselves as much as we matter to ourselves, and that they are noumena (imperfect as they are), not phenomena. This ability is normally not within the reach of almost all of us, which means that the ability to think is rare in all sides to a struggle. As I suggested, there is no difference in inwardness between those who fight on a good side and those who fight on a bad one. Her most famous and controversial example of this inability is Eichmann. The banality of evil is simple-mindedness to the point of moral imbecility in those administrators of evil who are zealously dutiful, but not zealously ideological; they cooperate with what they would never have had the ideological passion to originate. An inability to think makes all action potentially immoral. In Eichmann's case, the inability to think existed in one of its most acute forms; he administered policies that were absolute evil, not simply oppressive or unjust. For Arendt his unthinking is unforgivable, whereas lesser wrongdoings can sometimes be forgiven by those on whom they are inflicted. Eichmann represents many hundreds of thousands of bureaucratic types who have ever served to implement policies of atrocity.

The inability to think is what William James calls moral blindness in his great essay, "On a Certain Blindness in Human Beings" (1899). Following Arendt, we can say that the aim of fighting off moral blindness is served by the exercise of what she sometimes calls imagination and sometimes Socratic thinking, and what I could call individualized imagination. Only by such thinking can we come to believe that others are as real to themselves as we are to ourselves. But since this kind of imagination always exists in short supply, the undeveloped imagination of otherness facilitates the explosion of the politics of inflamed imagination, which is always morally blind, always invincibly thoughtless. Anyone who wields discretionary power or serves it is necessarily alienated from the effects his decisions cause, especially if these effects are invisible and at a distance. A candid administrator would say, in a sudden flash of evanescent insight, I could not do my job, or could barely do it, if I knew what I was doing, if I knew what effects I was causing. Remoteness from effects, owing to a failure of imagination, indicates remoteness from the meaning of what one does and hence from the very meaning of the words one uses in speaking about what one is doing. One doesn't know what one is saying: the abstractions cut the speaker off from reality. As for those who can literally see what they are doing, such as soldiers on the battlefield, self-preservation and camaraderie blunt the impact of too much reality.

Of course the danger in dividing up the world into those who can think and those who cannot or do not think is to become presumptuous. One presumes that one is able to think when it matters most because those around one are acting thoughtlessly. One may be badly mistaken in both attributions. Socrates believed that most people do not care about themselves or others in the right way, while he cared about them all. What is acceptable in Socrates is not for the rest of us. Still, we should try to understand where we can, whatever the risk of presumptuousness. It is also right that we should not allow the occurrence of totalitarianism to distort moral reasoning by an exclusive preoccupation with the horrors of extermination. Although totalitarianism is the worst evil, perhaps because its millions of designated enemies are innocent, it is not the only evil. Evil is abundant because war is always taking place. In its mastery over people and the absoluteness of its destructive effects, war is not completely dissimilar from totalitarianism. There are other serious wrongs, which are endemic conditions or daily events all over the world. And when we try to understand, we encounter the strong possibility, thanks to Arendt, that an inability or (a refusal) to think helps to explain the prevalence of ideologies and fictions, which in turn helps to explain the prevalence of wrongdoing, without supplying a complete account of it.

Guilt and Innocence

We are left with a tangle. People who initiate or facilitate evil (and I would add the smaller wrongs of oppression and systematic injustice) often think they are exempt from moral scrutiny because the mission they serve is in the eyes of history or philosophy higher than any morality. How can we hold those who are thus deluded or spiritually intoxicated morally responsible? In addition, if wanting to think for oneself and judge in the company of those who think for themselves, is a rare passion, how can we hold the overwhelming majority of people responsible for not arming themselves against the seductive splendor of ideological stories and pictures of the world? Yet we want to condemn.

If most of us are led to fortify and cooperate with political wrongdoing because we are drawn to ideologies and stories that invest the world with vivid meaning and spurious coherence, and are usually disposed not to think for ourselves or to judge in the company of those who also think for themselves, are we better or worse than those who act out of viciousness because of their urge to inflict suffering on others? Are we better persons when we are duped or seduced and uninterested in finding out our true state than if we are calculatingly but not ideologically villainous out of self-aggrandizement and envy? Is an all-to-human "innocent" agent of wrongdoing better than the person who knows from the start that he is guilty and persists in his crime? My answer—based on Arendt's "Some Questions of Moral Philosophy"—is that although the innocent have much better character in everyday life as long as they are not too sorely tempted or tested, and in fact make the continuance of decent everyday life possible, they make grave political wrongdoing inevitable and hence are responsible for far more harm in the world than the guilty. Such innocence cannot possibly be innocent. But with exceptional luck, the innocent will not, for a stretch of time, be presented with ideologies and stories that catch them up into systems or projects of evil, oppression, or injustice.

What is the point of condemnation when there are no long-lasting lessons that will inoculate us against the enchantment of ideologies and stories and therefore prevent terrible policies and events? To preserve a record of opposition? Why do that? It has no pragmatic value because people can never learn to live in a world made bare and barren by the absence of ideological constructions and comprehensive fictions. As Arendt teaches, contemplative wonder at the mere fact that there is a world can be sufficient to sustain a life only for a comparative few. There is some worth, however, when teachers discourage as many as possible from succumbing to ideological temptation and withhold their intellectual support from constructing delusions and spreading their influence.

Let me highlight a consideration to which Arendt does not pay much attention. The human imagination is addicted to group identity, and therefore to *group-religious* or *group-historical* or *group-political* fictions, stories, ideologies, fantasies, and images, which create much of the harm in political life. They do so in what Nietzsche, in his brilliant analysis in *The Genealogy of Morals*, calls "good conscience." The group as such is always prepared for wrongdoing. (Arendt would never say such a thing, even though it is perfectly Augustinian.) In opposition to the terrible power of this hallucinatory imagination is individualized imagination, which grows when a person, retreating to moments of solitude, tries to withdraw from the delusional constructions intrinsic to political and social life and tries to "see," to imagine human beings in their plurality, to conceive of each of them as an individual human being, and even if deficient in thinking and judging, a member of the only infinite species, and therefore except in the most dire circumstances, not to be harmed, despite his or her readiness to harm others.

Arendt advises us to expect the worst of politics because of the terrifying strength of the idolatrous human imagination. The scarcity of judging and thinking in the general population, but especially thinking, provides room for idolatry and for the crimes of idolatry. But she also insinuates the hope that some of us can individualize our imaginations, and then, whether concerted or not, we will offer glimpses and episodes of creative resistance. If resistance is still too much to hope for at any given time, then she teaches her readers by the example of her impassioned and honest thinking and judging, at least. The times are always dark, but not always pitch black—and then, too, there are moments of brightness.

SAN REMO

VISITATE IL CASINO MUNICIPALE

POSTE ITALIANE 75

Mme

Hannah Stern

Paris

60 rue de Seine

A Discriminating Politics

:: UDAY MEHTA

Every attempt to solve the social question by political means leads to terror.
HANNAH ARENDT, *On Revolution*

Terror and its cognates have come to signify the darkest excesses of contemporary and twentieth-century political life. They include in their fold aggressive claims to purity; murderous manifestations of programmatic and religious self-certainty; paranoid and devastating responses to threats to national security; and more generally, an intensity of instrumental forms of thinking and acting that give to individuals, groups, and states a broad warrant for deploying violence as a means to their purposefulness. Hannah Arendt reflected deeply on the implications of such high-minded and bellicose purposefulness. Understanding terror was a sustaining motif of her political thought from the time she left Germany in 1933. Yet, precisely because she reflected with such moral seriousness about terror and politics, it is important, as the epigram suggests, to recognize that Arendt also associated terror with something utterly commonplace, whose reach and provenance extended well beyond the twentieth century—namely, in the political attempt to address ubiquitous social questions.

In Arendt's view, the propensity to terror stemmed from a simple hubris in which politics, as a kind of activity, did not abide by its own appropriate limits and instead was seduced by the prospect of offering what it could not deliver. Terror was an implication of this hubris, which also endangered politics itself. It is striking that Arendt saw in this transgressing of politics—beyond its own legitimate bounds—not merely a failure but also the immanence of terror. After all, such terror is not, at least obviously, sanctioned by the monstrous, the banal, the incomprehensibly strange or the recklessness

Facing: Postcard from Walter Benjamin to Hannah Arendt. It reads: "Dear Hannah [Arendt] Stern, Both of us have been, each on our own initiative, seeking French discoveries this summer. This mountainous region [on the postcard], with the fort by Vauban in the background, has won me for the Dauphiné for a long time. *Perhaps there will be a chance one day to display our finds.* In the meantime, I had hoped to see you and H[einrich] B[lücher] on my last evening in Paris. I am very sorry that nothing came of this. I hope to find H. once again proof against all weathers on the command bridge when I return. This will have to happen quite soon. My "horses" (i.e., knights in chess) are already neighing impatiently to exchange bites with yours. With all my compliments, Benjamin." Courtesy of the Hannah Arendt Collection, Stevenson Library, Bard College.

with which it is today typically associated. Instead, it stems from something Arendt understood to be constitutive of modern politics: the social question, namely the impulse to redress the needs of the body and to make good on the promise of equality. Since by the social question Arendt meant issues of material destitution, suffering, and inequality—the very features with which politics is now so closely, indeed inextricably, linked—her view is an especially trenchant perspective on the implications of the general contours of politics and its purposefulness. As such, it widens the possible causes and ambit of terror well beyond the familiar horrors with which it is associated in the twentieth century and in the contemporary era. It is a view that highlights the contrast between her conception of politics and that which has undergirded the predominant tilt of modern, and especially twentieth-century, constitutionalism. Could something as ubiquitous and mundane as social issues implicate politics with an inevitable complicity with terror and violence? Arendt thought it could, and her deep-seated skepticism regarding modern politics is substantially anchored in this thought.

The claim about the relation between the social question and terror was one of the central planks by which Arendt distinguished the American and the French revolutions and the constitutional settlements that followed them. For her, the singular calamity of the French Revolution, on account of which it led to terror and constitutional instability, was that the revolution did not constitute itself as a moment for securing public freedom, but rather by the redress it prospectively offered on issues of destitution and social inequality. It offered this redress via the political framework it brought into being, namely a capacious form of constitutional government. In contrast, in the American case, by substantially ignoring the social questions of the day, the Constitution was able to limit the ambit of political power and hence, according to Arendt, secure the domain of public freedom. Arendt was well aware that questions of slavery, the material plight of slaves, and the treatment of Native Americans were also largely ignored at that founding moment. Moreover, it was the singular good fortune of the Americans that mass poverty among the citizenry was also substantially absent in late-eighteenth-century America. That propitious predicament alleviated the social pressures on the American Revolution and further encouraged the founders to be substantially indifferent to such social urgencies. In contrast, the French faced a much more dire social landscape.

For Arendt, the decision made by the Americans to ignore social inequality as a political issue was far-reaching in its consequences and judicious in its implications. It comports with a central feature of her political vision: that for power to be chastened and public freedom secured, political institutions must be exempt from—and must exempt themselves from—shouldering the burden of redressing the material and social inequalities of the day. It was the intermingling of political power with social questions that led the former to become absolute and to exact a heavy price on freedom. Indeed, Arendt even saw the reference to the pursuit of happiness in the Declaration of Independence as an embryonic form of this intermingling, harboring the potential compromising of an autonomous and circumscribed political domain. Nevertheless, in her view, the American Constitution served as an ideal in which public freedom was secured and national unity anchored in the chastened structures of political institutions. All this was possible only because the social questions were kept at bay and the demanding exigencies of the body limited.

Whatever one might say about Arendt's neo-Aristotelian conception of politics—as an agonistic public domain for the expression of ideas and ideals, bounded by an imaginary agora and substantially relieved of quotidian social pressures—her conception stands out as an alluring and enduring ideal. It is a powerful reminder that politics, even when it is not in obvious and familiar ways absolutist, can be drawn into an orbit without limits precisely because it is implicated with concerns that tend to be without limits. But, and as an aside, clearly a lot more can be said about her conception of politics, including the critical claim, recently and most forcefully associated with the work of Amartya Sen.[1] In the social democratic tradition whose basic insights Sen sharpens and extends, freedom, far from being secured through a disassociation with issues of development, is in fact conditional on the success of such a linkage. The enlargement of the domain of freedom relies on enlarging and securing the social capabilities on which, in that view, the exercise of freedom rests.

While one may question Arendt's conception of politics, what cannot be disputed is her claim that it has been the French revolutionary legacy that has been overwhelmingly influential in the subsequent history of revolutions and constitutionalism. Thus, in Russia, Latin America, and Asia, it is the French approach to the articulation of the powers of the state, as something constitutionally alloyed with a commitment to social uplift and redressing entrenched inequality, that has been front and center in revolutionary and constitutional practice. In the twentieth century, in line with the French revolutionary model, political power has been braided with issues of social uplift. It is from within this tradition that terror and absolutism found their strongest votaries.

For Arendt the process, which drew politics into this absolutism and terror, had to do with the realm of necessity. Issues such as mass poverty, illiteracy, and ubiquitous destitution, which characteristically inform twentieth-century constitutionalism, belong to the realm of necessity. To a great extent they are the instigators of modern politics and the imperatives through which mass politics has extended its reach. This is true even when political activity is authorized under the emancipatory banners of nationalism or anti-imperialism or anticommunist hegemony. Social questions put human beings under the pressing dictates of their bodies and their relative standing with others to whom they are linked. Politics, when it concerns itself with these questions, draws on the existential urgencies of suffering, injustice, historical inequality, and discrimination. To the extent that political power concerns itself with these dimensions of life—and under modern conditions it has to—politics, too, is subject to a corresponding necessity. Thus, during the last two hundred years, political citizenship has almost always expressed itself as a response to a social predicament. The power of the state, including that of constitutional and democratic states, has become similarly a promissory rejoinder to redress that predicament.

Arendt may have been wrong, or at any rate overreaching, to identify a politics that concerns itself with social questions as inevitably leading to terror. But it is an error of overstatement and exaggeration, which does not evacuate the force of the basic insight. For what she captures is a tendency and a pressure that politics is under once it is conjoined with the necessities of the body. There is an absolutism implicit in this necessity—an absolutism that at its limit can take the form of terror. Here absolutism refers not to the capriciousness of the prince or the Leviathan who can make his will synonymous with right and power. Constitutionalism, especially democratic constitutionalism, clearly checks that aspect of absolutism. But what Arendt's insight identifies is a tendency of power, once it is committed to alleviating the pressing exigencies of life, to lose the ability to be discriminating. Its choices are always braced by necessity. Hence, there can be few absolute or even fundamental limits on power. In this ambit there can be no prior or fundamental constraint placed on the political and the power that it wields. This simple logic transforms power from its concern with freedom to a concern with life and its necessities. Freedom exists as something prospective, as something that must be deferred because it is just one term in a complex calculus of national social utility. This is perhaps most vivid in poor and newly independent countries, where social issues—including, of course, issues of identity, which in these contexts are almost always conjoined with social grievances—have led to an abridgement of public freedom, and a corresponding amplification of the power of the state. Hence the familiar fact that in such countries constitutions become amenable and amendable on account of the constantly shifting sands of popular social necessity. But even in wealthy countries the intensity of mere life, including the security of the body politic, can, as we know, be a warrant for torture and much else that recalls and even condones terror. Not unlike the Jacobins who viewed the suffering French people as the ground of French unity, contemporary politicians and political thinkers see poverty, illiteracy, and destitution as constitutional warrants for much of the progressive social agenda of modern constitutionalism. There is hence clearly an awkward tension between Arendt's constitutionalism and modern constitutionalism, a tension decided in favor of the latter; for constitutional thinkers and actors today have largely ignored Arendt and understood their mandate as giving primacy to social questions.

Arendt's abiding concern with public freedom is part of a piece with a conception of politics that must be discriminating and deliberative. In this she is plainly an heir to Aristotle's emphasis on politics being anchored in the human ability to speak and to reason under conditions of human diversity. She is resolute in her opposition to politics' being subsumed by any one of many likely surrogates that threaten to dissolve its distinctive concern with freedom, diversity, and the making of choices.

One familiar way in which modern politics has asserted this distinctiveness is by a critique of kinship and a reassessment of the role of blood. It is an account in which the lineaments of the flesh are superseded by those of the word and where the word itself points to the gathering importance of contract, textuality with its link to constitutional politics, and individual rationality as the anchor to choice and individual rights. It is a familiar story that modernity writes about itself. The flesh and the body are mortified, the word and the text triumph, the rule of men is displaced by the rule of law, authority is chastened by words rather than by the lineal associations of blood, writing replaces violence, and most importantly, politics no longer reflects and relies on the passive commonality of familial and lineal bonds. Instead, modern politics is meant to exemplify the potential for associations that are the product of active and discriminating individual choice. In brief, as Weber noted, in the critique of the familial, just as in the trials and executions of Charles I and Louis XVI, there is a prefiguring of the conditions that make possible modern citizenship with its reliance on a depersonalized legal order and a rationality that is evinced in individual choice.

Much of this is concisely evident in John Locke. In articulating the broad and enduring terms of liberal and democratic politics, Locke begins, both philosophically and textually, by uncoupling, and thus invalidating, Robert Filmer's braiding of fatherhood, property, and political authority. Locke is of course undermining the claims of absolute monarchy, which Filmer had defended. But he does this by first limiting and displacing the very role of blood and of the familial, because on his reckoning political authority and citizenship would henceforth have an altogether different basis, one that would feature consent and not the gendered and hierarchical ascriptions associated with blood, family, and lineage.

All this Arendt would have emphatically concurred with. It is suggested in the following sentence, "He wanted to be the friend of many men, but no man's brother."[2] The sentence comes from an essay on the political language of Lessing, where Arendt opposes the virtue of friendship to the political vice of brotherhood. The bond of friendship, Arendt claims, entails by its differentiation and discrimination the activity of choice, while that of brotherhood implies a passive commonality that enters politics spurred by a familial ideal only to destroy such choice. Friendship, one might say, and this was Arendt's point, must think of itself in terms of differentiation *as such*, not merely the differentiation between friend and enemy. In friendship, there is no antecedent to choice; choice, as it were, goes all the way down, never mysteriously blending into some shared corporeal lineage. In contrast, the presumption of brotherhood in politics assumes a false unity—which, once it encounters the diversity that is essential to *polis* life, can only seek to destroy a politics of choice.

This emphasis on choice and against attempts to vitiate its constantly demanding implications, such as kinship, leads Arendt to a dispassionate acceptance of prejudices as something constitutive of politics. Prejudices are the reservoir of convictions that make choices politically meaningful—"Any response that places man at the center of our current worries and suggests he must be changed before relief is to be found is profoundly unpolitical."[3] The idea of absolving politics from prejudices is itself a prejudice against politics and an attempt at depoliticizing everyday relations.

Here notwithstanding their many deep differences, Arendt echoes Gandhi, who was insistent in his objection to a politics anchored in kinship and the evacuation of both prejudice and choice. What Gandhi feared in the context of modern India, and more generally in the context of modern civilization, was that political relations increasingly occurred only through the mediation of the state, which served as the arbiter of individual and group interests. For Gandhi, such arbitration of interests effectively depoliticized the everyday relations between Indians. A politics of pure interests was one in which politics had become sovereign, and thus wholly sequestered from ethics. In this form politics could have only an instrumental relationship to the ethical—that is, a relationship that effectively destroyed the ethical. As Gandhi so often put it, political relations were reduced to a commercial logic, namely the trading and negotiating of interests.[4] In such negotiations the threat of violence was always the ultimate backstop and the state with its power the inescapable third party to all human relations.

This was especially the case in the febrile context of sectarian relations between Hindus and Muslims. Gandhi approached this sublimation of everyday politics by making the very prejudices that linked and separated Indians into the ground for the differentiation and discrimination of friendship. The importance of prejudices, such as those that were evinced among different religions, castes, and very occasionally ethnic groups, was that they could become the subjective and normative ground for resisting the state's impulse to reduce politics to a negotiation of interests, and hence to an instrumental relationship with no ethical content beyond the shifting vagaries of political expedience. Moreover, for Gandhi it was the absence of prejudices, or rather their displacement, that made for the severest hatred and violence, particularly hatred that deployed the false language of brotherhood. After all, it is not the citizen as stranger, but rather the citizen as brother, who was hated for betraying his fraternity to a contract of interests mediated by the state. Arendt hinted at a similar thought when she said, "The freer a person is of prejudices of any kind, the less suitable he will be for the purely social realm."[5]

In his writings on Hindu/Muslim relations, especially in the 1920s during the aftermath of the British abolition of the Khilafat in Istanbul, Gandhi articulated an argument and a movement in which the bonds of brotherhood, common ethnicity, and shared origins between Muslims in India and Turkey and between Hindus and Muslims in India played no role. Instead Gandhi forged the movement opposing the abolition—a movement that in India was constituted, largely through Gandhi's efforts, by Hindus—by first identifying the distinct prejudices within different religious groups, and then making these very prejudices the ground for a unconditional, or at any rate nonnegotiable, politics of friendship. It was in such friendship that choice and discrimination were essential and appropriately political. Religious sentiments, for Gandhi, were at their core prejudices. They could not and should not be reduced or translated into interests, and hence could not serve as the ground for a false kindred or even national unity. They stood beyond the reach of a contractual economy, and also beyond the reach of the state, which attempted to project itself as arbiter of such interests. Gandhi insisted on resisting the mediation of religious prejudices precisely because they constituted an absolute, a kind of kernel of selfhood, that should not be divided. In the context of the Khilafat movement, as in the later context of the partition of India and Pakistan, Gandhi wanted to forge ethical and political relations between Hindus and Muslims that would be grounded in their differences, and not in a imperial and nationalist logic that would view these differences as fungible assets that could be traded in the face of extant pressures and available expedience. A politics that recognized prejudices was not necessarily divisive or partitioning. Instead, it had the potential of expressing a unity that was willed and chosen and as such was both political and ethical.

On Gandhi's reckoning, Indian Muslims were engaged in a world historical struggle that had to remain at the level of a religious ideal: "The Khilafat," he wrote, "is an ideal and when a man works for an ideal, he becomes irresistible. The Muslims, who represent the ideal, have behind them the opinion of the whole mass of the Indian people."[6] And because the issue turned solely on the matter of religion, Gandhi, with complete seriousness, invited Christians into the movement: "What I venture to commend to . . . Christians . . . is to join the defense of the Khilafat as an ideal, and thus recognize that the struggle of Non-cooperation is one of religion against irreligious."[7]

The idealism of the Khilafat cause, which was at once also the prejudice of religious conviction, provided Gandhi with a position from which to focus on the generality of Indian relations and to develop them politically. He did this by insisting on the irreducibility of prejudices; real prejudices could not be negotiated into interests and thus rendered amenable to a reason—which, in the context of the empire, was always a reason of state. For Gandhi, religious sentiments had the dual feature of being an ideal and a rigid constraint. They constituted, as he says, a "bind" on the believer and were hence an essential aspect of his or her self. To view them as negotiable or divisible, and available to mediation, was to distort the self who was bound by them. Consider the blunt facticity with which Gandhi characterized Muslim sentiments: "I cannot regulate the Mohammedan feeling. I must accept his statement that the

Khilafat is with him a religious question in the sense that it binds him to reach the goal even at the cost of his own life."[8]

The most spectacular avowal of Gandhi's understanding of prejudice was evident in his denial of the very mutuality of compromise so characteristic of liberal contractual politics. It came with his refusal to make Hindu participation in the Khilafat movement conditional, whether upon Muslim support for Indian political reforms which at that time were being agitated for, or upon Muslim abstention from cow slaughter. The specific issue could not have been more serious in its tactical and strategic importance. Yet Gandhi refused to countenance either consideration: "I trust that the Hindus will realize that the Khilafat question overshadows the Reforms and everything else."[9] And then, he went on:

> The test of friendship is assistance in adversity and, that too, unconditional assistance. Cooperation that needs consideration is a commercial contract and not friendship. Conditional cooperation is like adulterated cement which does not bind. It is the duty of the Hindus, if they see the justice of the Mohammedan cause, to render cooperation. If the Muhammadans feel themselves bound in honor to spare the Hindus' feelings and to stop cow killing, they may do so, no matter whether the Hindus cooperate with them or not. Though, therefore, I yield to no Hindu in my worship of the cow, I do not want to make the stopping of cow-killing a condition precedent to cooperation. Unconditional cooperation means the protection of the cow.[10]

The last sentence made the protection of the cow audaciously depend upon the very lack of agreement between Hindus and Muslims. If the slaughter of cows by Muslims was to be proscribed, it had to depend entirely on an unconditional act of friendship and choice and not on political barter, which in effect vitiated the discriminating aspect of politics. Neither Hindu support for the Khilafat nor Muslim refusal to slaughter cows could be part of a mutual and balancing equation.

For Gandhi, the individual Muslim's loyalty to a Muslim state, however far removed from his or her everyday context, stemmed from the tenacity of a religious prejudice. The fact that Hindus did not participate in this prejudice, perhaps did not even understand it, was not reason for inviting mediation or of conceiving of the situation as representing an interest via which Hindus and Muslims could forge a contractual connection. Gandhi was loath to posit some third entity as a mediating ground for relating or linking Hindus and Muslims.[11] A politics that relied on power, or the state, in being able to connect everything and everyone was really commercial, and not political, in the sense that it could put a price on anything and hence establish a unified field of equivalences. For Gandhi, such political unity and the corresponding claim to political sovereignty rested on an implicit desire to divest individuals from acting on their deepest convictions.

This is what he and Arendt feared about modern politics, notwithstanding their attitudinal differences and profoundly different sensibilities. As she put it, "That prejudices play such a large role in daily life and therefore in politics is not something we should bemoan as such, or for that matter attempt to change. Man cannot live without prejudices."[12] For Arendt and Gandhi, prejudices referred to those values and practices whose denial would constitute a profound and anti-political dispossession of the self. This is admittedly an imprecise idea, but it is meant simply to suggest that not all preferences, not even all attachments, qualify as prejudices. The edge that marks out a prejudice from a mere preference or attachment is some notion of constitutive selfhood as distinct from merely an accident of the self. Gandhi, though he never fully articulated it, implicitly had something of an Aristotelian distinction between essence and accident in mind. With regard to prejudices, the idea of error is not relevant; in contrast, regarding preferences and attachments, errors and hence the possibility of correcting errors were eminently possible. Thus, for example, Gandhi's response to those upper-caste Hindus who claimed that the belief and practice of untouchability was constitutive of their Hindu identity, was to retort that such an identification was in fact an error, and thus not constitutive. And because it was an error, it could and should be reformed by an alternative set of practices.

The new practices, in this instance of cleaning toilets by upper-caste Hindus, would, in Gandhi's view, correct their false beliefs. What Gandhi did not demand of such Hindus is that they deny their Hinduism. It is striking that Gandhi, to the best of my knowledge, despite his deep familiarity with Islam and Christianity, never calls for the reform of these other religions. His restraint on these matters should be seen as another way in which Gandhi himself was bound by his own prejudices. The reformer, Gandhi appeared to be saying, must speak from within the horizons of a prejudice. Only then does one's view become properly epistemic, and only then can the possibility of change and correction be led by conversation and nonviolence and not via the mediation of power. Like Burke, who spoke of the "eternal separation of India and Britain" if they could not first converse with each other, Gandhi was deeply suspicious of associations and forms of linkage that required the emollient of power. He was a reformer, but one who saw the limitations of what he could change. Many putative prejudices, for instance racial prejudices, would for Gandhi not qualify as real prejudices but rather simply errors of fact and judgment. They would not meet the standard of a genuine prejudice, namely as something whose denial would lead to a profound dispossession of the self.

By way of conclusion, let me refer to an American example that, even though it pertains to a horribly destructive war, would, I suspect, have found favor from both Gandhi and Arendt. At the end of his first Inaugural Address, just before the oft-quoted sentence about the "mystic chords of memory," Lincoln says: "We are not enemies, we are friends. We must not become enemies."

In characterizing the relations between the North and South in these terms, Lincoln was eschewing what was to become the dominant metaphor for the Civil War as a fraternal conflict. It was a metaphor in which, once the hostilities had ceased, one could, in the imagination at least, return to a condition of natural familial unity. There was in this view no fundamental difference in prejudice between the North and the South because their unity had already been spoken for in the language of blood and fraternity. Slavery and the issue of the relations among whites and African Americans, on this view, were not matters of fundamental political choices and actions. They did not draw on two sets of distinct prejudices, and, for that reason, they did not require a distinctly political and ethical volition and discrimination to redress. Lincoln, on my reading, by invoking the language of friendship, perhaps anticipated the amnesia that would set in if the war were seen such fraternal terms. By that view, that second great American political experiment, which Arendt admired not less than the first, would have been reduced to a political nullity by being incorporated into a given family unity.

Instikt 683   Sammler 675

Verlorene Inf. 722

Geschwister — 764 (Kafka) 532, 556, 614

Jerusalem — Hebr. 488, 493,-4, 497, 505, 531, 535,
579, 655,

Brecht 474, 514, 518, 594, 596, 599, 602, 628, 631, 658,

Hofmannsthal 498, 502, |669/70, 712, 716, 764, 727,

Kommunismus 506, 521, 523f., 537, 553, 604, 646,
640, 662,

Scholem 510-12, 513, 525, 533, 740, 764, 767,

Klages 515!

Familie, Finanzen 520, 542, 547, 563, 566 (1933), 600

Akademie — George Kreis 523 |624, 636, 651, 655, 636,
810, 814

Produktion höh. g. Lesen 539

Bibliothek 544

Wissenschaft 557, 561, 568, 572, 624, 652, 662, 665,

Emigration — 595, 660, 703, 717, |474-683, 683, 737,
740, 781,   810, 825
Kafka 617, 629,   814, 827, 824,

Kraus 623

Buchlese Sammler 653,

Autobiogr. — 662-3,

Bretzischa in Abfällen 685

Baudelaire — erste Version — 778, 782-786; 795,
800, 811 (Ms. in Scholems Archiv), 823,

S. 841

Nr. 299 Kafka Brief

Scholem g Urverwangand
vor allem gegen
Brecht
Urverwangand 676
Scholem

Planet — 618

f

Gas in Wien 820

Flaneur 784!

Frankreich 600

Grotto — 698

Tradition — 760 ff

Hannah Arendt's Political Engagements

:: SEYLA BENHABIB

There was a special poignancy to our celebrations of Arendt's centenary in 2006 through many conferences, since so many of us were and are still gripped by concern with the "crises of our republic," as one of those conferences was called. Many fear that what Jonathan Schell has aptly named the age of "Arendtian revolutions,"[1] of nonviolent peoples' movements that brought democracy to power in countless countries, from the Philippines to the Czech Republic, from South Africa to the Ukraine throughout the 1980s and 1990s, is over. In their place have emerged amorphous global jihadist movements, exploiting weak and failed states in Asia, Africa, and the Middle East. These movements are fractured, incoherent, and violently at odds with one another. Juxtaposed to them is a big-power rhetoric of a war without end, without democratic authority or legitimization—President Bush's war of shadows. Against this background, Arendt's concepts of totalitarianism, radical evil, and even the "banality of evil," roll easily off the lips of journalists as well as academics. Speculation is rife about what she would have said, could have, or should have said about Islamic totalitarianism, contemporary antisemitism, and new forms of political evil.[2]

In this essay, I will not engage in speculative counterfactuals. Instead, I would like to examine three episodes in Arendt's political life and consider Arendt's own political engagements as they illuminate her conception of political agency. I am hereby continuing a challenge, which I have posed elsewhere, to an influential view of Arendt's understanding of the political which argues that for her, the political is the sphere of authentic action that redeems us and permits us to escape immersion in everyday routines and to approach a more transcendent ideal. Building on Heidegger's critique of modern society as the realm of "das Mann," or everyman, these commentators claim that the political is about self-disclosure and forms of self-revelation lying beyond ordinary moral or normative constraints.[3] But Hannah Arendt's own involvements as a

Facing: Hannah Arendt's notes on the endpaper of her copy of Walter Benjamin's *Briefe*. The notes take the form of a personal index in pencil, including references to pages she has underlined and marked. The main headings are: Jerusalem, B[erthold] Brecht, [Hugo von] Hoffmannstahl, Communism, [Gershom] Scholem, [Ludwig] Klages, Family and Finances, The Stefan George Circle, [Theodor Adorno] Wiesengrund, [Franz] Kafka, and [Charles] Baudelaire. At one point she writes: "Scholem and Wiesengrund, however, above all Brecht." Indeed, Brecht is cited the most often. Courtesy of the Hannah Arendt Collection, Stevenson Library, Bard College.

political agent flatly contradict this view of the political, which was always motivated by justice, was egalitarian as well as sagacious, and sought to balance an ethics of conviction with an ethics of conscience, in the Weberian sense of these terms.[4] There are at least inconsistencies, if not contradictions, between this metatheory of the political and her own political engagements, and it is to the latter that I wish to turn. I want to do so by singling out several important episodes in Arendt's own political activism.

Let me follow her understanding of political agency across the following moments: First is her Jewish politics in the interwar years, from 1926 to 1941; second is the phase from 1941 to 1948, which I will name the "heartbreak over the Jewish state"; and third is her engagement with the American republic from the early 1960s onward, which may be named "citizenship in a new republic."

Jewish Politics in the Interwar Years

Arendt met Kurt Blumenfeld, the German Zionist leader, in 1926, when she was a student at the University of Heidelberg.[5] Deeply impressed by him, she started to collect materials for the upcoming World Jewish Congress, documenting antisemitism and the exclusion of Jews from German professional associations. In 1933 the Gestapo arrested her. She somehow managed to escape with her mother from Germany across Czechoslovakia to Paris, where she settled as a refugee. Arendt became a stateless émigré and was deeply involved in Jewish politics and in settling Jewish children in Palestine. She was part of a wide circle of European antifascist and anti-Stalinist resistance. She was well familiar with these circles through her husband, Heinrich Blücher, who had been a member of the left-wing social democratic German Spartacist party until the murder of Rosa Luxemburg. In this period, communist militants were eliminated by Stalin for not toeing the party line; those who managed to escape came back to Europe with reports about the collapse of the "worker's paradise" and the emergence of Stalinist totalitarianism. Militants who fought in the Spanish Civil War, socialists of all stripes, and Bundists—who were Jewish nationalists who thought there could be room for a Jewish republic within the newly declared Soviet Socialist Republics—met and fought and argued with each other, and tried to survive as émigrés and stateless peoples in European capitals such as Paris.

This group of militants constitutes Arendt's and Blücher's circle of friends in emigration; they are members of "the other Europe" of antifascist resistance,[6] which is brilliantly documented in works such as Manes Sperber's *Like a Tear in the Ocean* and Arthur Koestler's *Darkness at Noon*.[7] Through this circle Arendt becomes deeply familiar with the critique of Soviet totalitarianism, and thus her inclusion of the Soviet regime, alongside with Nazi Germany, as a "totalitarian" form of government in *The Origins of Totalitarianism*[8] is less a consequence of Cold War anti-Marxism than the deep influence left upon her by the knowledge and experience of these disappointed anti-Stalinist, communist militants about the Soviet experiment.

This period ends when, in 1941, Hannah Arendt and Heinrich Blücher manage to board a ship from Lisbon to the United States and arrive in New York.

The Heartbreak Over the Jewish State

In the years from 1941 to 1948, we witness the most explicit manifestation of Arendt's thinking about politics. Following the principle that in politics one defends oneself under the identity that is under attack, Arendt on the one hand is concerned to alert her American readers to what is really being done to Jews on the continent; on the other hand, she is busy militating among American Jewish circles for resistance to the Nazis, and she is following developments in British-occupied Palestine with growing anxiety and concern. She writes articles for *Der Aufbau*, the German-language daily published in New York, with titles such as "The Jewish Army: The Beginning of a Jewish Politics" and "The So-called Jewish Army."[9]

Also composed in this period are the brilliant essays "Zionism Reconsidered" (1945) and "To Save the Jewish Homeland: There is Still Time" (1948). Until recently these essays were available to us only in a collection edited by Ron Feldman, *The Jew as Pariah: Jewish Identity and Politics in the Modern Age* (1978); fortunately, they have now been republished in a more comprehensive version as *Hannah Arendt's Jewish Writings*,[10] edited sensitively by Jerome Kohn and Ron Feldman.

Arendt is anguished about the fate of the Jewish populations still remaining in Europe. She is also in despair about the blindness of the Zionist establishment toward the plight of Palestinian Arabs. She fears that Zionists are repeating the worst mistakes of European nationalism in a new continent and in an environment largely alien to the idea of the European-style nation-state. Repeatedly, she returns to the question: How can we establish a Jewish homeland—not a nation-state—that will be fair and egalitarian to the Arab population? Yet the logic of the Zionism of that period is leading either to the mass emigration, whether forced or voluntary, of Palestinian Arabs or to their becoming second-class citizens in a new Jewish entity—or to both. Arendt was right: After the partition of Palestine and the Israeli War of Independence in 1948, this is precisely what took place. She warns that Israel will remain a pariah among her neighbors, and she predicts that there will be continuing war.

Was there really any alternative for the Jews of Palestine and the Zionist leadership? Caught between the Holocaust proceeding apace in Europe, the needs of desperate refugees trying to reach Palestine, and surrounded by hostile Arab populations, what were the Jews to do but defend themselves? This is the Zionist reply to Arendt's criticisms in this period, and it is not easy to dismiss.

Nevertheless, it is important to understand that Arendt's critique of Zionism was never a critique of aspirations for Jewish self-determination. Hers is a utopian vision, which distinguished sharply between the idea of a Jewish state and a Jewish homeland, but it may be a vision from which one can still learn. Arendt is sympathetic to the Brit Shalom movement, founded mainly by German Jewish intellectuals, which included among its supporters the first president of the Hebrew University, Judah Magnes, and the philosopher Martin Buber. The goal of this movement was to establish Jewish-Arab councils of cooperation and governance.[11] Arendt envisaged such an entity, which she referred to as "the Jewish homeland," as being integrated into a Mediterranean federation of peoples.[12] Just as she thought that there would be room for a Jewish republic in postwar Europe, in Palestine as well, she imagined a Jewish political entity, integrated within a Mediterranean comity of peoples. Revealed here is Arendt's enduring passion for institutions of local self-governance and for federal systems of cooperation and organization at the international level.

For her to think politically means looking at the hard facts without being blinkered by ideological commitments or bureaucratic constraints. Although she supported efforts to build a "Jewish homeland," she was deeply aware of the plight of Palestinian Arabs and the emerging Arab hostility to a Jewish entity in the Middle East. Also paramount in her considerations was always the interdependence between Europe and other parts of the world. Just as European totalitarianism had developed as the practices of European imperialism from the colonies in "the heart of Africa" were brought to the heart of Europe, so too, Zionism exported the failed ideology of the nation-state to the Middle East.[13] It is her portrayal of the complex interdependencies of peoples' fates across continents and the sad ironies of politics that make for such fascinating reading of her contributions from this period.

A Citizen in a New Republic: The 1960s

Arendt quit active engagement in Jewish politics after being booed by a Jewish audience in Massachusetts during a speech she gave upon the death of Judah Magnes on the idea of Arab-Jewish coexistence.[14] During the controversy over *Eichmann in Jerusalem* that erupted in 1962–63, few were aware of Arendt's lifelong and active involvement in Jewish politics since her student days in the 1920s. Arendt did not only focus on the Eichmann controversy but instead began grappling with the political legacy of the American Republic and engaging the soon-to-erupt turmoil of the 1960s. In works such as *On Revolution, On Violence,* and *Crises of the Republic,*[15] Arendt engaged the social and political upheavals of her new home: the civil rights and the anti–Vietnam War movements, the Black Power movement, violence in American cities, and the Watergate hearings.

One of Arendt's most controversial essays, and oddly one of the few that serve as a link between her understanding of Jewish politics in Europe and the new realities of racial divide in the United States, is "Reflections on Little Rock." After significant controversy, the editors of *Dissent* magazine published the essay with a disclaimer, distancing themselves from the views expressed therein about the desegregation of schools through the intervention of federal marshals. The essay is highly critical of attempts to force school integration through the use of force by the federal government and is particularly critical of black parents who send their children to school when violent confrontation is so imminent. Arendt writes, "The most startling part of the whole business was the Federal decision to start integration in, of all places, public schools. It certainly did not require too much imagination to see that this was to burden children, black and white, with the working out of a problem which adults for generations have confessed themselves unable to solve."[16] Arendt's concern for the politicization of the life of children had its roots in her memories of totalitarian politics, be it in their National Socialist or Communist variants, when political movements and party organizations would intrude into familial life and turn children against their parents. How could she be so sure, however, that this is what took place during struggles in the American South as well? In this one case, was she not using lenses that actually blinkered rather than aided her vision of what was at stake?

In an interview with Robert Penn Warren, Ralph Ellison commented that "Hannah Arendt's failure to grasp the importance of this idea [the ideal of sacrifice] among Southern Negroes caused her to fly way off into the left field in her 'Reflections on Little Rock,' in which she charged Negro parents with exploiting their children during the struggle to integrate the schools."[17] After this intervention, Arendt wrote a letter to Ellison, admitting that African American parents' sending their children to schools under conditions of civil violence, accompanied by policemen, was an act of public courage and not simply the instrumentalization of those children for political purposes. This letter was not made public during Arendt's lifetime, to my knowledge, but it is now available through the Library of Congress and can be accessed online.

In general Arendt is deeply unsettled by the spiraling of the civil rights movement into violence through the rise of the Black Power movement. For her, violence in politics is almost always an abdication of the real telos of the political, which is the creation of power through action-in-concert of the many, united-in-diversity, through the plurality of their views. In remarks surprising for their candor and judgmentalism, she takes on the leaders of the Black Power movement at a time when many American intellectuals either fell silent in view of the excesses of this movement or idealized its violence.[18]

There were many moments of joy and excitement, as well as concern, for Arendt when the student movement erupted in Europe and the United States after May 1968. When the son of her émigré friends from her period in Paris, Daniel Cohn-Bendit (also known as "Danny the Red," less on account of his politics but more on account of his unwieldy red hair) emerged as one of the student leaders in France and Germany, it was as if a circle of life had been completed. For Arendt, the student movement was proof that every generation could bring something new into the public-political world, that the capacity for "natality," for initiating something new and unprecedented and the capacity for "plurality," for discovering and enjoying the world through action-in-concert, were not exhausted. Cohn-Bendit embodied both.

In 1975, after the extent of the Watergate scandal and Richard Nixon's knowledge of and involvement with the tapping of the Democratic headquarters in Washington by members of his circle had become clear, Arendt published "Home to Roost" in the *New York Review of Books*,[19] linking the illegality of the Vietnam War and the illegality of actions at home. She recalled once more a lesson she had already articulated in *The Origins of Totalitarianism*, namely "the boomerang effect": Wars in the periphery, in faraway lands, come "home to roost"; the mentalities cultivated in such wars, the personnel engaged in them, the practices hammered out in the absence of vigilant oversight by representative institutions, sooner or later, come home to haunt and undermine the republic in whose name they were undertaken. If those lessons seemed so pertinent then, how much more so are they for us today after the experiences of Abu Ghraib, Guantánamo, and the activities of private contractors such as Blackwater in Iraq? The torture memo issued by Attorney General Alberto Gonzales, the violation of habeas corpus for Guantánamo detainees until restored by the U.S. Supreme Court, and the "renditions" of American prisoners to undisclosed locations where they could be interrogated and tortured without the oversight of U.S. law—these and many other practices and doctrines are instances when the chickens come home to roost in our times. They sap at the roots of the republic's freedoms and laws.

In conclusion, I would like to briefly discuss Hannah Arendt and Carl Schmitt. A number of contemporary authors, most notably Giorgio Agamben, today revive Hannah Arendt's work in the context of a "politics of the exception." In this explosive amalgamation of Arendt, Foucault, and Schmitt, many of Arendt's own distinctive contributions are distorted.[20] I want to distinguish among her understandings of the *unprecedented*, *the new*, and *the exceptional*. For Arendt, the unprecedented almost always represents the moment of the destruction of tradition. The "new," by contrast, signifies an original configuration. Politics at its best opens the possibility of reconfiguring elements of traditions that have been destroyed by creating new and unexpected modalities of action, new modalities of perception and thinking. This is the task not only of politics but also certainly of art and philosophy, which aid in the reconfiguration of the commonplace. For Arendt, the French anti-Nazi resistance, an all-Jewish army to fight the Nazis that fought in Europe during the Second World War, and the Arab-Israeli local self-governance councils, as well as the kibbutzim, student, and civil rights movements—all represented the new in politics.

By contrast, and it is amazing that this contrast has not been noted by commentators, "the exception" (usually referred to as *die Ausnahmezustand*) in Carl Schmitt's work[21] is always about the latent moment of violence. The exception signals that moment when the illusions of liberalism and the consensus that marks liberal politics breaks down. It is when the sovereign emerges as the one who decides on the exception, and the latent violence and arbitrariness on which all liberal-democratic politics rests, in Schmitt's view, is revealed. This is not Hannah Arendt's conception of the "new" in politics at all; she has a radically different view of violence. Violence is coercive and hides the need for the legitimation of decisions rather than revealing and disclosing political options. Arendt sees no redemptive value in violence.

The most important point of contact between Arendt and Schmitt is their understanding of the "autonomy of the political." Arendt distinguishes the political from economics on one hand and from psychoanalysis and psychology on the other. In this respect, she is close to Schmitt who also argues that the political needs to be viewed as its own autonomous sphere. Whereas Schmitt, however, sees the political as being marked by the "existential conflict between friend and foe," Arendt emphatically rejects this notion. We have to understand her concept of "judgment" to see why this is so.

Arendt's concept of judgment is about transcending the "friend/foe" distinction, via cultivating "the enlarged mentality" and by learning in politics and morals to take the "standpoint of the other." Be it when thinking about the predicament of the Arabs in Palestine, the psychology of the white colonizers in South Africa, or the fear of black children in the segregated South, Arendt tries to exercise reasoning from the standpoint of the "other." The political world has an inevitable perspectival quality, and the political actor as well as thinker, have to make present again all these perspectives to themselves. Arendt names this the capacity to exercise "the enlarged mentality" (*die erweiterte Denkungsart*), and it is her reading of Kant's *Critique of Judgment* that is crucial to developing this concept.[22]

Let me finally mention Arendt's passion for the republic. Arendt has often been charged with elitism, and some have accused her of "polis envy."[23] This is a silly phrase because it fails to appreciate Arendt's profound political egalitarianism and moral universalism, her distaste of any kind of groupthink, her deep dislike of nationalism, and her insistence on the disjunction between nationalism and the rule of law in the modern state. Jeremy Waldron has named this Arendt's "democratic republicanism,"[24] a felicitous term in the sense that, for Arendt, there is not an elite of class, an elite of income, an elite of talent that has the privilege to engage in politics; rather, political life brings forth a self-appointed elite, a self-chosen elite, and these are the people who care for "the public thing," for the *res publica*. In every generation there will be people who care for the *res publica*, and it is the legacy of revolutions that, like a Fata Morgana, they appear and disappear, bearing witness to the human capacity for natality—for letting the new shine forth in politics.[25]

PROF. DR. CARL SCHMITT

Der Begriff des Politischen

HANSEATISCHE VERLAGSANSTALT HAMBURG

What Does It Mean to Think About Politics?

:: MARK ANTAKI

Hannah Arendt was a thinker who concerned herself with, more than any-thing else, politics. But what does it mean to think about politics? There is a difference in Hannah Arendt's thought (and on this point she presents her-self as a follower of Kant) between, on one hand, thinking, which aims af-ter meaning or sense, and, on the other hand, understanding, which aims after truth or knowledge.[1] Indeed, Arendt insists that knowledge is, in some of its forms, antithetical to thinking. Knowledge—the knowing of things—does not belong integrally to thinking as Arendt grasps it. Accordingly, this essay concerns itself with the sense, the significance, the meaning of a certain kind of thinking—namely, thinking about politics.

The question of the meaning of thinking about politics is not reducible to, though perhaps it encompasses, the question, "What is politics?" Nor is the question reducible to, though perhaps it encompasses, "What is thinking about politics?" or, perhaps, "What is political theory?" This essay is not an at-tempt to proffer a definition of thinking or of politics. Rather, I seek to reflect on the existential import of thinking about politics. The aim is not to learn something about thinking that can be positively expressed as a conclusion or proposition and fixed as known. In fact, as we will see, for Arendt, thinking is essentially negative.

I propose the following: the existential import of thinking about politics is a double confrontation with the nothing. In short: for Arendt, politics is the relating of human beings to one another around the space of the world—the empty center of the polis—and hence a confrontation with the nothing. Thinking itself is engaging in the activity of dissolving, and—particularly in modern times—a dwelling in the gap between past and future, and hence itself a confrontation with the nothing. Thinking about politics carries with it this double negative, which gives it its meaning, or existential import.

Thus, I am going to address two negatives: first the negative involved in thinking, and second the negative involved in politics. In my discussion of thinking, I will emphasize, as Arendt sometimes does, the relation of thinking

Facing: Cover of Hannah Arendt's heavily annotated copy of Carl Schmitt's *Der Begriff des Politischen*. There are a total of nine books by Schmitt in Arendt's collection. Courtesy of the Hannah Arendt Collection, Stevenson Library, Bard College.

to politics.[2] I will end with the suggestion that the beginnings of an answer to the question of the meaning of thinking about politics lead back to Kant and to the negativity that belongs to his thought: the refusal of absolutes tied to the embrace of the absolute.

The First Negative: What Does It Mean to Think About Politics?

Thinking, according to Arendt, is essentially negative. Arendt describes thinking as "the quest for meaning which relentlessly dissolves and examines anew all accepted doctrines and rules."[3] In "Thinking and Moral Considerations," she revisits the idea of the banality of evil introduced in *Eichmann in Jerusalem*,[4] that is, the question of the relation between wrongdoing and thoughtlessness (or the inability to think). In so doing, Arendt turns to the example of Socrates to emphasize the capacity of thinking to free human beings from the tyranny of established creeds and "prescribed rules of conduct."[5] She turns to Socrates as well to show the manner in which the thinking of a human being, the "soundless dialogue . . . between me and myself,"[6] necessarily involves acceptance of, and even delight in, the fact of plurality, the defining feature of human being-in-the-world.[7] The promise of thinking, then, lies both in its capacity to free the thinking human being from received, unexamined beliefs, but also in its capacity to free the thinking human being to the actuality of others and otherness, and even to friendship.[8]

According to Arendt, nihilism is a possibility inherent in the activity of thinking. Thinking is essentially negative: it is a turn away from what we usually take for granted. The possibility of nihilism inherent in thinking, however, is not simply tied to thinking's negativity but, rather, is tied to thinking turning against itself and forgetting its own negativity. Thinking turns against itself when it erects the opposite of what it negates as positive, thereby forgetting that its own fruits are negative: "The quest for meaning . . . can at every moment turn against itself, as it were, produce a reversal of the old values, and declares these as 'new values.'"[9] Whereas, in relation to action, thinking produces a kind of paralysis,[10] thinking itself is characterized by an utter restlessness, a constant movement—even a constant turning-away-from. The coming of thinking to rest—rooted in the desire that thinking bear positive fruit—makes possible its transformation into nihilism. Nihilism, then, appears as an incomplete confrontation with the nothing.

The coming to rest of thinking makes possible not only nihilism but also wrongdoing—and even acts of great evil. Thus, though thinking is usually "a marginal affair in political matters,"[11] in "emergencies," that is "when everybody is swept away unthinkingly by what everybody else does and believes in, those who think are drawn out of hiding because their refusal to join is conspicuous and thereby becomes a kind of action."[12] Indeed, thinking's negativity, "its purging element . . . is political by implication."[13] Thinking is political by implication because it makes possible the judgment and discernment so crucial in times of emergency, in dark times. In dark times, thinking brings much needed light and clarity.

It is striking that, in several places in her work, Arendt transforms thinking—sometimes quietly, sometimes less quietly—into judging. In "Thinking and Moral Considerations," Arendt refers to the ways in which the wind of thought manifests itself, that is, the way thinking is concretized. She asserts that thinking is concretized in judging; in other words, thinking is made manifest in the "ability to tell right from wrong, beautiful from ugly."[14] In both *Between Past and Future* and *The Life of the Mind*, thinking is also transformed into judgment. Thus it is no accident that Arendt conceives of thinking as critical thinking. If we listen to "critique," we hear *krinein*, which is Greek for discrimination, for judgment. *Krinein* is also tied to crisis.[15] There is a fascinating, and intentional, slide or transformation in Arendt's work from thinking to judging, and this slide or transformation brings to the fore the relation between dark times and the necessity of proper judgment.

As Roger Berkowitz writes in his contribution to this volume, in times of crisis, in times of mass conformity, thinking becomes perhaps the most elevated form of action. This elevation of thought to action brings to mind Karl Jaspers, one of Arendt's exemplary "Men in Dark Times." Jaspers remained "firm in the midst of catastrophe"[16] because of his attachment to the public realm, its plurality, its demands for clarity and for human responsibility for the world. This elevation of thought to action also brings to mind (how Arendt grasped) Adolf Eichmann's thoughtlessness: his willingness to go along with whatever rules and standards were current at the time. Eichmann's attachment to clichés and catchphrases points us in the direction of "Politics and the English Language," a text in which Orwell asserts the belonging together of, in my words, proper speech and proper sight.[17] In my words again: the abuse of language leads to dissimulation and to the dimming, shrouding, even shrinking of the world. World and word are co-primordial. Human responsibility for one is human responsibility for the other.

In addition to the extremes of Jaspers and Eichmann in dark times, we should also think of thinking becoming crucial in moments of opportunity, moments where an existential possibility opens up, moments in which radically new beginnings are possible. These moments are also moments of crisis, moments where discernment is sorely needed. Thus, one of Arendt's aims in *On Revolution* is to free revolutionaries from the scripts inherited about revolution from the past, scripts that tied foundation to violence and to the appeal to a transcendent source of authority.[18] Thinking becomes crucial in freeing ourselves from the scripts or standards that we take for granted not only in moments of crisis—the way we tend to understand them, the darkest times—but also in moments when we have the brightest possibilities before us. Thinking, I suggest, is not only a way of safeguarding a future or preserving a world in dark times but also a way of opening up a future where we can found or find a world.

So: thinking is essentially negative, and thinking is often transformed into judgment, discernment, and discrimination. And judgment is crucial in times of crisis. Thus, aside from, or perhaps as a result of, its being a good-in-itself, thinking manifests itself, concretizes itself, in politics. Thinking's essential negativity does not mean that thinking is not "positive" in some way. Thinking is positive insofar as it reclaims the clearing, the space in which human beings see, speak, and act. Because thinking is essentially negative, it makes room for spontaneity and freedom: thinking makes room for action and politics. The "positivity" of thinking lies in its "negativity."

We moderns are, according to Arendt, particularly called to thinking, to "settling down in the gap between past and future."[19] The metaphor of the gap signifies that thinking is "settling down"—making oneself at home—with the nothing. This settling down with the nothing is a particularly modern challenge because we no longer have the Roman trilogy of tradition, authority, and religion.[20] The loss of tradition, authority, and religion means that we no longer have at our disposal those institutions that have historically covered up the gap between past and future. We are now left or abandoned in the gap, the abyss of the present. In this gap, Arendt calls for thinking. Thinking is a settling down in the gap: making oneself at home with the nothing makes possible human freedom and politics.

The Second Negative: What Does It Mean to Think About Politics?

Thinking is not only necessary for politics, but thinking is also like politics insofar as politics, too, is to be understood as a human comportment in the face of the nothing. To think about politics is to think about nothing. One can hear or see this intimate relation between politics and nothing in the word "politics" itself. One hears the Greek *polis* in politics, and in *polis* one hears the Greek verb *pellein*, which means "to rise in a circular motion."[21] The circular nature of the polis is telling: the pole is nothing but an emptiness around which the lives of human beings revolve. The polis is a space in between us, an existential center, but in itself, it is nothing. The polity to which we belong is nothing positive. Thus, Arendt refers to action, "the political activity par excellence," as "the only activity that goes on directly between men without the intermediary of things or matter."[22] Politics, which "deals with the coexistence and association of different men,"[23] unites a plurality of human beings around nothing.

This tendency to withhold a substantive content from politics is a noteworthy strand in modern political thought. Weber famously defines the state (our word for the modern political entity) in relation to its means rather than in relation to its activities or ends. According to Weber, "a state is that human community which (successfully) lays claim to the monopoly of legitimate physical violence within a certain territory."[24] In the work of Carl Schmitt, and to a lesser extent in the work of Schmitt's follower Julien Freund, no unchanging, determinate, substantive content is ascribed to politics. Thus, Schmitt famously asserts that "the specifically political distinction to which political actions and motives can be reduced is that between friend and enemy" while reminding his reader that "this provides a definition in the sense of a criterion and not as an exhaustive definition or one indicative of substantial content."[25] To the friend-enemy distinction or relation, Freund adds "the relation of command and obedience" on one hand and "the relation of public and private" on the other hand.[26] He sees command and obedience as "the basic presupposition of politics in general" while, according to him, the public-private relation characterizes domestic politics, and the friend-enemy relation characterizes foreign relations.[27] Freund's three relations summarize rather well key elements in the history of Western thinking about politics.

Without necessarily attacking the relevance of these accounts or criteria, Hannah Arendt's thought begins to pick away at them, sometimes casting them in a different light—often disputing the claim that they characterize what is most important about or constitutive of politics. First, Arendt challenges the idea that relations of command and obedience are primordially political by appealing to a Greek conception of politics in which, she argues, relations of subordination, of command and obedience, of ruler and ruled, were understood to be pre-political.[28] Indeed, the Greeks bequeathed to us the possibility of grasping politics as the practice of freedom rather than as simply a means to freedom.[29] Second, Arendt's work appears to challenge the centrality to politics of the relation of friend and enemy. To be sure, politics is about being together in a way that is not merely "social," but politics is not necessarily about being for or against one another as allies and enemies. For example, Schmitt imagines a united world, a world without the possibility of war and enmity, as one in which the political has disappeared, has been reduced to mere administration. Arendt, as much as Schmitt, fears the reduction of politics to mere administration, but she is willing to countenance, even yearn for, the possibility of a world at once political and united along federal lines.[30] Although the friend-enemy relation can be helpful in identifying an aspect of the political, the relation does not go to what is essential about politics.

We are left with the public-private relation. This relation is much more difficult to relativize in Arendt's work on politics. Though politics may not have a determinate content, politics requires a public space, "a space of appearance between acting and speaking men."[31] Arendt's emphasis on appearance also makes it difficult to translate completely the public-private distinction into a mere opposition between freedom and necessity—though Arendt strongly tends to associate the public with freedom and the private with necessity.[32] Nevertheless, there have been fruitful criticisms of or engagements with Arendt's reliance on or conception of the public-private distinction.[33] Without resolving the question, it is possible that we might have to let go of (at least some of) the public-private distinction as well—though without letting go of the need for a space or clearing in which human beings can appear to one another. And so we might be left with an even greater emptiness with respect to what is politics. We might be left with nothing. We might be left with nothing in order to decide what is political and what is not. Nothing to tell us *when* we are engaging in political action, nothing to tell us *that* we are engaging in political action. Nothing but Arendt's insistence that the "the meaning of politics is freedom."[34]

From Politics to Ethics

I wish to conclude by suggesting that grasping the full extent of the meaning of Arendt's thinking about politics requires, perhaps surprisingly, an engagement with the absolute. I invoke the absolute knowing full well that Arendt explicitly excludes the absolute from politics. Arendt shares with Schmitt and other thinkers the refusal to reduce politics to something else. More specifically, Arendt refuses to reduce politics to morality—or, to be more precise, moralism. This refusal is a great and difficult one. For Arendt, the moralization of politics is suspect because it abstracts and detaches from context, from concreteness. Moralization, in its modern guise as humanitarianism, also reduces politics to the status of a mere means to be used to "solve" the human condition (read: the social question). Moralization absolutizes, doing away with the plurality of persons, perspectives, and possibilities that, for Arendt, is characteristic of politics. It is partially along all of these lines that Arendt, in *On Revolution*, asserts that "the absolute . . . spells doom to everyone when it is introduced into the political realm."[35]

For Arendt, the Rights of Man led to the Terror because the project they captured aimed for an immediate (that is, absolute) solution to the social question. As articulations of absolute goodness, the rights of man spelled doom to the political realm. For Arendt, the realm of politics is one of contingency, persuasion, appearance—the "relations" of human beings to one another. The absolute and, in particular, absolute moral claims have no place in this realm because they introduce (mechanical) necessity into a realm of human freedom. Absolute claims leave no room for speech or persuasion, that is, for humans as humans.

Indeed, one of the defining parts of Arendt's account of politics is her refusal of absolutes: absolutes shall not enter the realm of politics, for this realm is a realm of human freedom. This refusal of absolutes appears to belong to her great secularism and to her great modernism. This refusal of absolutes also underlies her turn to Kant's *Critique of Judgment* rather than to his practical philosophy to ground her political philosophy. In his critique of the faculty of judgment, Kant is most concerned with human beings in the plural whereas, Arendt argues, in his moral philosophy, Kant reduces men to man.[36]

Nevertheless, Kant's moral philosophy is also marked by the great refusal of absolutes that characterizes Arendt's thought. Put negatively rather than positively, the transformation of any determinate end or good into an abso-

lute good is "prohibited" by the very structure of human freedom.[37] This "pro-
hibition" is the same injunction, it seems to me, that Arendt wishes to use to
shed light on politics and to preserve the human freedom that is politics.

Of course, Kant's refusal of absolutes was also an embrace of the absolute.
Claims made in the name of some "specific" absolute can never be absolute
because the absolute, as such, always already has claimed us. Kant's moral philosophy may even require that we keep empty the space we traditionally fill
with the absolute. Like thinking, ethics may consist much less in affirmations
than in negations, negations that keep reclaiming the space in which humans
beings see, speak, and act. And these negations are crucial if human beings
are to free themselves to the actuality of others and otherness, to friendship,
but also to politics.

It is quite possible that, for Arendt, "politics" is one name for this prior
claim of the absolute. Arendt's account of politics can be criticized, and has
been criticized, for its emptiness or nothingness—that is, because it points
to that with which politics should not directly or predominantly be concerned
but does not point to that with which politics should be concerned. In this
respect, Arendt's account of politics is materially empty in the same way as
Kant's categorical imperative. And yet, for Arendt, politics is where human
freedom resides, the freedom of human beings whose condition is characterized by the most radical—that is, original—plurality. The challenge for contemporary thinking about politics, then, may not be to think through politics
free from the absolute but to think through the absolute politically (and for
Arendt this means non-metaphysically). To think through the absolute, politically, is to return to ethics.

PART II

Lying and Politics

Don't you know that there is a state of mind half-way between wisdom and ignorance?" "What do you mean?" "Having true convictions without being able to give reasons for them," she replied. "Surely you see that such a state of mind cannot be called understanding, because nothing irrational deserves the name; but it would be equally wrong to call it ignorance; how can one call a state of mind ignorance which hits upon the truth? The fact is that having true convictions is what I called it just now, a condition half-way between knowledge and ignorance." "I grant you that," said I. "Then do not maintain that what is not beautiful is ugly, and what is not good is bad. Do not suppose that because, on your own admission, Love is not good or beautiful, he must on that account be ugly and bad, but rather that he is something between the two." "And yet," I said, "everybody admits that he is a great god." "When you say everybody, do you mean those who don't know him, or do you include those who do?" "I mean absolutely everybody." She burst out laughing, and said: "Well, Socrates, I don't see how he can be admitted to be a great god by those who say that he isn't even a god at all." "Who are they?" I asked. "You are one of them and I'm another." "What can you mean?" "It's perfectly easy; you'd say, wouldn't you, that all gods are happy and beautiful? You wouldn't dare to suggest that any of the gods is not?" "Good heavens, no." "And by happy you mean in secure enjoyment of what is good and beautiful?" "Certainly." "But you have agreed that it is because he lacks what is good and beautiful that Love desires these very things." "Yes, I have." "But a

80

being who has no share of the good and beautiful cannot be a god?" "Obviously not." "Very well then, you see that you are one of the people who believe that Love is not a god."

'"What can Love be then?" I said. "A mortal?" "Far from it." "Well, what?" "As in my previous examples, he is half-way between mortal and immortal." "What sort of being is he then, Diotima?" "He is a great spirit, Socrates; everything that is of the nature of a spirit is half-god and half-man." "And what is the function of such a being?" "To interpret and convey messages to the gods from men and to men from the gods, prayers and sacrifices from the one, and commands and rewards from the other. Being of an intermediate nature, a spirit bridges the gap between them, and prevents the universe from falling into two separate halves. Through this class of being come all divination and the supernatural skill of priests in sacrifices and rites and spells and every kind of magic and wizardry. God does not deal directly with man; it is by means of spirits that all the intercourse and communication of gods with men, both in waking life and in sleep, is carried on. A man who possesses skill in such matters is a spiritual man, whereas a man whose skill is confined to some trade or handicraft is an earthly creature. Spirits are many in number and of many kinds, and one of them is Love."

'"Who are his parents?" I asked. "That is rather a long story," she answered, "but I will tell you. On the day that Aphrodite was born the gods were feasting, among them Contrivance the son of Invention; and after dinner, seeing that a party was in progress, Poverty

81

A Lying World Order

POLITICAL DECEPTION AND THE
THREAT OF TOTALITARIANISM

:: PEG BIRMINGHAM

I want to address the question whether totalitarianism is a threat today. I think a caveat is in order as I make some remarks about this question; and that is that for Hannah Arendt totalitarianism was the crystallization of several elements that together constituted this event. I say this because I think, first of all, that for Hannah Arendt there is no form of totalitarianism in the way that Montesquieu, for instance, might outline a form of government such as the republic or the monarchy. Second, we should keep in mind that these elements of totalitarianism might themselves change. There may be unpredicted and unprecedented elements of totalitarianism facing us today that would constitute or reconstitute the event of totalitarianism again, but in ways that might look very different from the analysis that Arendt gives in the *Origins of Totalitarianism*.

That said, I do think that there is one element of totalitarianism that Hannah Arendt was herself very concerned about, and one that we are facing today. And that is what Arendt calls a "lying world order."[1] It is not often enough noted that the problem of political deception occupies a central, indeed inaugural place, in Hannah Arendt's analysis of totalitarianism. At the outset of *Origins of Totalitarianism*, prior to her analysis of antisemitism, imperialism, and radical evil, Arendt raises the issue of political deception, considering the difference between the ancient and modern sophists and their relation to truth and reality. She argues that while the ancient sophists were satisfied with "a passing victory of the argument at the expense of truth," modern sophists want a great deal more, namely, and again citing Arendt, modern sophists want "a lasting victory at the expense of reality itself."[2] In these early pages of *Origins of Totalitarianism*, Arendt claims that the characteristic that

Facing: Pages 80–81 of Hannah Arendt's heavily annotated copy of Plato's *Symposium*, translated by W. Hamilton. Arendt's copies of Plato's *Symposium* and *The Republic* are two of the most heavily annotated texts in the library. Her annotations frequently correct the translation and also reflect her thematic interests. At the bottom of p. 80, she writes, "The 'right opinions.'" At the top of the page she provides the Greek original of the sentence indicated, highlighting that "true convictions" translates To orta doxadzein. On p. 81, she crosses out the English "deal" and replaces it with "mix" to render the sentence: "God does not mix directly with man." She also corrects the translation of spirit as daimonon and writes at the top of page 81: "daimonon is between a god and a mortal." Courtesy of the Hannah Arendt Collection, Stevenson Library, Bard College.

sets totalitarianism apart from tyrannical and dictatorial regimes is precisely the modern sophistic victory at the expense of reality, a victory that, she argues, institutes a lying world order. Indeed, her discussion of radical evil in the *Origins of Totalitarianism* cannot be understood apart from her continuing preoccupation with the problem of this particular kind of political deception.

When she writes, in 1945, that the problem of evil will be the fundamental question of postwar intellectual life in Europe, Arendt is indicating that the problem of radical evil is not by any means eradicated with the defeat of totalitarianism. To my mind, this is in large part because of totalitarianism's inseparable link with the political lie. The political lie, for Arendt, has nothing to do with what we understand by falsehood, error, or even the deliberate lie, which are the ways in which deception, in all its guises, is traditionally distinguished from truth. Falsehood and error are the opposites of truth, while a deliberate lie is the intentional dissimulation of the truth. The political lie is something else altogether, insofar as it introduces, and these are Hannah Arendt's words, "a mutation into the history of the lie."[3] The mutation, for Arendt, is the deliberate attempt to transform a lie into reality.

In her 1945 essay "The Seeds of a Fascist International," Arendt writes,

> It was always a too little noted hallmark of fascist propaganda that it was not satisfied with lying, but deliberately proposed to transform its lies into reality. For such a fabrication of lying reality, no one was prepared. The essential characteristic of fascist propaganda was never its lies, for this is something more or less common to propaganda everywhere, and of every time. The essential thing was that they exploited the age-old occidental prejudice which confuses reality with truth, and made that true, which until then, could only be stated as a lie.[4]

Arendt gives the example of this mutation by pointing to the statement, "my wealthy aunt is dead." If someone should say, "But I saw your aunt just a moment ago at the market," all I have to do to make my statement true is to go home and murder my aunt. For Arendt the transformation of a lie into a truth introduces a mutation into the history of the lie: "One can say that to some extent fascism has added a new variation to the old art of lying—the most devilish version—that of lying the truth."

For Arendt, our only defense against a lying world order is our establishing of factual truth, and nothing could be more difficult. For unlike rational truths such as 2 + 2 = 4, factual truths are characterized by their contingency. They are the result of action, and there is no necessity to action; this is what makes factual truths unexpected and unpredictable. Arendt's example, for instance, was that there was no necessity to France's not being a victorious superpower at the end of World War II, nor was there any necessity for Germany to invade Belgium in 1914. The problem we run into with factual truths is that we usually view action from the point of view of its completion, rather than its inaugural moment. So the paradox of factual truth is that it possesses both, for Arendt, a stubborn thereness and an absolute contingency, and it is the contingency of factual truth that makes it the kind of truth most like doxa. Yet, for all of Arendt's insistence on the public space as a space of doxa, she is not one who celebrates doxa over factual truth. Indeed, she insists on the distinction between the two. Doxa is always open to persuasion, and there is always a plurality of doxa that together make up the public space as a space of opinion. Factual truths, on the other hand, while "political in nature," are not strictly speaking part of the public space, if by that is meant a space of persuasion, contest, and debate. In other words, while factual truth and opinions occupy the same realm, namely, the public space, they are in different locations. Factual truths, Arendt argues, provide the limits of the public space as a space of action and of contested and debatable opinions. In this way, they function more like laws that provide the walls of the public space. Unlike the law, she argues, which provides the boundary and border of the public space, factual truth provides the ground of the public space itself. Without this factual ground, there simply is no public space whatsoever.

Moreover, factual truths are not open to persuasion. I can try to persuade you for the next many months that Belgium invaded Germany, or that France was a great superpower after the war, but even if I succeed in changing your mind, I have not thereby altered the reality of what occurred. The best way to destroy factual truths, however, is to reduce them to so many opinions that can then be easily dismissed as "just another opinion," open to dispute, contest, and interpretation. Arendt argues, "facts and opinions, though they must be kept apart, are not antagonistic to each other, they belong to the same realm. Facts inform opinions, and opinions, inspired by different interests and passions can differ widely and still be legitimate as long as they respect factual truths. Indeed, the best way to destroy factual truth is simply to reduce them to so many opinions which can thus be easily dismissed as, just simply, your opinion."[5]

To establish the validity of factual truths requires witnesses and testimony: factual truth "is always related to other people; it concerns events and circumstances in which many are involved; it is established by witnesses and depends upon testimony."[6] Arendt suggests that without the testimony of the witness, there is no public space whatsoever; the witness establishes the very ground of reality, factual truths, the very condition of the public space, without which the perseverance of this reality is threatened. Asking the Kantian question of whether truth should be sacrificed for the survival of the world, Arendt answers, and I quote, "What is at stake is survival, the perseverance of existence (*in suo esse persevare*), and no human world, destined to outlive the short life span of mortals within it, will ever be able survive without being willing to do what Herodotus was the first to undertake consciously, namely *legein ta eonta*, to say what is. No permanence, no perseverance and existence can even be conceived without those willing to testify to what is, and appears to them because it is."[7] If totalitarianism is characterized as the complete eradication of the public space, then the loss of factual truth, and those who are willing to say it, is one of totalitarian's necessary conditions.

Certainly Arendt's insights, to my mind, on the pervasiveness and threat of political deception have lost none of their urgency. Indeed, it is my claim that the issue of political deception has today become an even greater political and philosophical problem.

Politically, there is no lack of examples for the decline and fall of factual truth in the public space, as suggested by the subtitle of Frank Rich's book *The Greatest Story Ever Sold: The Decline and Fall of Truth from 9/11 to Katrina*. Rich quotes a White House aide in his introduction as saying, "A judicious study of discernable reality is not the way the world works anymore; we create our own reality."[8] Rich gives an account of the deceptions of the George W. Bush administration, an account that reveals the accuracy of Arendt's claim that political deception would be one of the most difficult problems of the contemporary world.

The decline of factual truth and creation of lying realities is unfortunately not an anomaly. For Arendt, philosophy itself opens the door to the possibility of what she calls "a lying world order." In her essay "On the Nature of Totalitarianism," she claims, "If Western mentality has maintained that reality is truth, for this is of course the ontological basis of the *adaequatio rei et intellectus*, then totalitarianism has concluded from this, that we can fabricate truth in so far as we can fabricate reality, that we do not have to wait until reality unveils itself and shows us its true face, but we can bring into being a reality whose structure will be known to us from the beginning, because the whole thing is our product."[9] And I think, for those of us here, in a conference titled "Thinking in Dark Times," this implication of philosophy in the problem of deception may be the most difficult for us. Philosophically, I submit, deception is an even greater problem today, precisely because postmodern philosophy has rejected the notion of *adaequatio rei et intellectus* in favor of a notion of reality as performative and truth as a performative fiction. I say "postmodern" in a very broad and general sense, by the way, and I agree with many of postmodern philosophy's claims regarding the performative nature of reality.

The question, for us, is how we grasp the phenomenon of the lie, if reality is constituted through a performativity that seemingly renders the very notion of factual truth invalid. If there is no objective reality or objective truth—and I think Arendt herself subscribes to that view—and further, if facts are dependent upon their modes of representation, then what happens to the very notion of factual truth, which, Arendt argues, seems to be one of the most imposing bulwarks against totalitarianism and radical evil? If we think of this in terms of narration and interpretation, then it would seem, out of this framework, that for any particular narrative or representation, there could always be a counter narrative, even contradictory facts. If reality is performative, given only its reality in its various representations, then what would prevent us from performing or representing reality in a way that better corresponds to how we wish it to be? In other words, taking the postmodern critique of objectivity seriously, is there any philosophical basis by which to make a distinction between on the one hand a true performance or a true representation, and on the other hand lying the truth?

I will conclude by suggesting that perhaps the answers to at least some of these questions can be found by paying close attention to the final chapter of *Origins of Totalitarianism*, "Ideology and Terror." It may be that this ending returns *Origins of Totalitarianism* to its beginnings, for the problem of ideology is, for Hannah Arendt, the problem of political deception. Ideology, for Arendt, is the mutation that establishes the lying world order, by replacing reality with an ironclad fiction. In other words, ideology is the "most devilish version of the lie"; these are Hannah Arendt's words, and we should hear her claim that the "banality of evil" is, at its very heart, ideology. With both its hellish fantasies and its clichés, the "banality of evil" is characterized by a strident logicality—a logic through which the whole of reality is thoroughly and systematically organized, according to a fiction with a view to total domination.

tate those who are most excellent, so that if he does not attain to their greatness, at any rate he will get some tinge of it. He will do as prudent archers, who when the place they wish to hit is too far off, knowing how far their bow will carry, aim at a spot much higher than the one they wish to hit, not in order to reach this height with their arrow, but by help of this high aim to hit the spot they wish to.

I say then that in new dominions, where there is a new prince, it is more or less easy to hold them according to the greater or lesser ability of him who acquires them. And as the fact of a private individual becoming a prince presupposes either great ability or good fortune, it would appear that either of these things would in part mitigate many difficulties. Nevertheless those who have been less beholden to good fortune have maintained themselves best. The matter is also facilitated by the prince being obliged to reside personally in his territory, having no others. But to come to those who have become princes through their own merits and not by fortune, I regard as the greatest, Moses, Cyrus, Romulus, Theseus, and their like. And although one should not speak of Moses, he having merely carried out what was ordered him by God, still he deserves admiration, if only for that grace which made him worthy to speak with God. But regarding Cyrus and others who have acquired or founded kingdoms, they will all be found worthy of admiration; and if their particular actions and methods are examined they will not appear very different from those of Moses, although he had so great a Master. And in examining their life and deeds it will be seen that they owed nothing to fortune but the opportunity which gave them matter to be shaped into what form they thought fit; and without that opportunity their powers would have been wasted,

and without their powers the opportunity would have come in vain.

It was thus necessary that Moses should find the people of Israel slaves in Egypt and oppressed by the Egyptians, so that they were disposed to follow him in order to escape from their servitude. It was necessary that Romulus should be unable to remain in Alba, and should have been exposed at his birth, in order that he might become King of Rome and founder of that nation. It was necessary that Cyrus should find the Persians discontented with the empire of the Medes, and the Medes weak and effeminate through long peace. Theseus could not have shown his abilities if he had not found the Athenians dispersed. These opportunities, therefore, gave these men their chance, and their own great qualities enabled them to profit by them, so as to ennoble their country and augment its fortunes.

Those who by the exercise of abilities such as these become princes, obtain their dominions with difficulty but retain them easily, and the difficulties which they have in acquiring their dominions arise in part from the new rules and regulations that they have to introduce in order to establish their position securely. It must be considered that there is nothing more difficult to carry out, nor more doubtful of success, nor more dangerous to handle, than to initiate a new order of things. For the reformer has enemies in all those who profit by the old order, and only lukewarm defenders in all those who would profit by the new order, this lukewarmness arising partly from fear of their adversaries, who have the laws in their favour; and partly from the incredulity of mankind, who do not truly believe in anything new until they have had actual experience of it. Thus it arises that on every opportunity for attacking the reformer, his opponents do so with the zeal of partisans, the others

Lying and History

:: CATHY CARUTH

I would like to address the problem of violence in the political realm by focusing on a question that, I believe, emerges out of several late works by the twentieth-century political thinker Hannah Arendt: What is history in the time of what Arendt calls "the modern lie"? In "Truth and Politics" (1967) and "Lying in Politics" (1971), Arendt reflects on what she considers a profound philosophical conundrum at the heart of politics and the political: an intimate and foundational relation between politics and the lie that has momentous implications for the way we think about political history (and, more widely, about history as such). Beginning from a reflection on the nature of political action in the context of lying, Arendt ultimately enables a rethinking of the very nature of history around the possibility of its political denial. What does it mean, she asks, for political history to be fundamentally linked, at certain points in modern times, to its erasure or lack of witness? And how might it be possible to witness from within this history?

Politics and the Lie

The question of history arises, in "Truth and Politics," in the context of Arendt's concern with the pervasive role of lying within the political sphere in the modern world. As Arendt had suggested in her earlier work, *The Human Condition*, the sphere of politics is important because it is the exemplary place in which man displays his essential capacity, as man, to act and thus to bring into the world "something new . . . which cannot be expected from whatever may have happened before."[1] This concept of political action arose specifically in the Greek *polis*, she says, when words and deeds replaced the mute force of violence and created a public sphere in which men appeared before each other and created the world anew in unpredictable and unexpected ways. But the political sphere maintains itself, Arendt adds, not only as the site of action but also as the site of its remembrance, for "speech and action . . . possess an enduring quality of their own because they create their own remembrance."[2]

Facing: Pages 20 and 21 of Hannah Arendt's heavily annotated copy of Max Lerner's edition of Machiavelli's *The Prince and the Discourses*. Written at top of the page is: "*Fortuna* & *virtu*: Constitute an *active* Harmony." Courtesy of the Hannah Arendt Collection, Stevenson Library, Bard College.

More specifically, they create political bodies that establish the conditions for remembrance, "that is, for history."[3] History thus seems central to the functioning of the political world, both as its memory and as the ground upon which the political world builds a future.

In the modern world, however, Arendt will point out in "Truth and Politics," the public realm has become a realm of deception, a place dramatizing, in effect, the "clash of factual truth and politics, which we witness today on such a large scale."[4] Arendt draws on a number of examples, remarking, for instance, on the disappearance of Trotsky from the history books of the Soviet Union, and on the German and French representations of their actions during World War II. Unlike the ancient world, in which the notion of politics first appeared, she suggests, the public realm in the modern world is not only the place of political action that creates history but also, and centrally, the place of the political lie that denies it. Focusing on the ubiquity of the lie in the modern world, then, Arendt ultimately asks the following question: What kind of politics is possible in a world in which history is regularly and systematically denied?

The topic of the denial of history emerges, for Arendt, after the great wars. The phenomena had been analyzed in the work of another great writer, Sigmund Freud, in terms of the psychological forms of denial in the face of catastrophic events, and especially those of World War I.[5] But Arendt's explicit concern in her essay is of another nature, a form of deliberate political deception that also emerges after that war but, in a surprisingly brazen way, arises directly and consciously in the political sphere and attacks the fundamental facts of history that had previously been considered indestructible:

> During the twenties, so a story goes, Clemenceau, shortly before his death, found himself engaged in a friendly talk with a representative of the Weimar Republic on the question of guilt for the outbreak of the First World War. "What, in your opinion," Clemenceau was asked, "will future historians think of this troublesome and controversial issue?" He replied, "This I don't know. But I know for certain that they will not say Belgium invaded Germany." We are concerned here with brutally elementary data of this kind, whose indestructibility has been taken for granted even by the most extreme and most sophisticated believers in historicism.[6]

The responsibility for the outbreak of World War I—a matter of profound political significance between the wars—is a factual truth that, in an earlier period, might have seemed unassailable even in the contested world of politics. But in the political world that emerged in the ensuing period, even this crucial and well-known fact had come under debate:

> It is true, considerably more than the whims of historians would be needed to eliminate from the record the fact that on the night of August 4, 1914, Ger-

man troops crossed the frontier of Belgium; it would require no less than a power monopoly over the entire civilized world. But such a power monopoly is far from being inconceivable, and it is not difficult to imagine what the fate of factual truth would be if power interests, national or social, had the last say in these matters.[7]

In her allusion to the totalitarian states that arose after World War I, Arendt suggests that the world in which facts could be agreed upon is in danger of changing forever and that not only individual facts, but the fate of "factual truth" as such is in danger in this new and emergent reality. The danger to the political world in modern times is the loss of the factual world that emerges, paradoxically, at the heart of the political realm that ordinarily creates, and depends upon, historical remembrance.

What is of interest to Arendt is that the lie comes not from without, but precisely from within the realm of political action and is in fact tied to it by a fundamental similarity between action and lying. Facts are fragile in the political sphere, she says, because truth-telling is actually much less political in its nature than the lie:

> The hallmark of factual truth is that its opposite is neither error nor illusion . . . but the deliberate falsehood or lie. Error of course is possible. . . . But the point is that with respect to facts there exists another alternative, and this alternative, the deliberate falsehood, does not belong to the same species as propositions that, whether right or mistaken, intend no more than to say what is or how something that is appears to me. A factual statement—Germany invaded Belgium in August 1914—acquires political implications only by being put in an interpretative context. But the opposite proposition, which Clemenceau, still unacquainted with the art of rewriting history, thought absurd, needs no context to be of political significance. It is clearly an attempt to change the record, and as such it is a form of *action*.[8]

If the lie "changes the record" of history, it does so, Arendt suggests, not as a falsehood that negates a truth (a falsehood that could be a mere error without being a lie), but as an act of speech intended, like political action, to make a change in the world. The liar thus prevails in the political world because, like the actor, he is exercising freedom:

> While the liar is a man of action, the truth teller . . . most emphatically is not. . . . The liar needs no accommodation to appear on the political scene; he has the great advantage that he always is, so to speak, already in the midst of it. He is an actor by nature; he says what is not so because he wants things to be different from what they are—that is, he wants to change the world. He takes advantage of the undeniable affinity of our capacity for action, for changing reality, with this mysterious faculty of ours that enables us to *say*,

"The sun is shining," when it is raining cats and dogs. . . . In other words, our ability to lie—but not necessarily our ability to tell the truth—belongs among the few obvious, demonstrable data that confirm human freedom. That we can change the circumstances under which we live at all is because we are relatively free from them, and it is this freedom that is abused and perverted through mendacity.[9]

Like the political actor, the political liar wishes to change the world, to be free from things as they are given. Since his denial of the world is also a form of action, the act of lying is, in itself, a demonstration of freedom. The lie does not appear in the political realm only as the denial of the historical acts of the past, then, but also as a kind of *action of beginning* that, potentially, has its own political and historical unfolding.[10]

It is this independent historical unfolding that, in fact, Arendt describes as the site of the danger of the lie when she narrates the passage of the lie from its traditional role, within politics, as another means of effecting true political action, to a wholly independent and all consuming activity that replaces action (and its history) altogether. Thus at first, Arendt argues, lying serves the interest of politics: it is used by and aimed at individuals. Traditionally, the lie concerns particular facts and serves specific political ends. In this sense the lie works within political history and is subordinated to particular political purposes. But over time a fundamental change takes place. The lie is now aimed at facts everyone knows; it deceives not only particular individuals but also everyone in society (including the liars themselves); and it is aimed not at particular facts but at the entire framework of factuality as such. The lie moves out of its subordinate position, in other words, to become an absolute framework in which nothing but the creation of the lie acts in the world.[11] In this sense, Arendt appears to suggest, there is a certain reversal in the course of political history, in the relation between the lie and politics: if the traditional lie worked within the realm of action defined by politics—and thus served to confirm and further its history as freedom—politics now works within (and serves) the modern lie. At this point the lie is no longer limited to traditional acts of lying by individuals, but rather takes over and exceeds individual intention, driving forward a political process no longer serving purely political ends.

The danger of the lie is thus not a covering over of history but a substitution of its own action (and history) for that of true political beginnings. In totalitarianism, as Arendt suggests in her book *The Origins of Totalitarianism*, the "mass rewriting of history" not only denies the history of the past but also moves forward as the creation of an "entirely fictitious world."[12] This world is made to be fictitious both in the sense that its fictions are enforced upon reality and in the sense that through "organized" propaganda and terror it eliminates the capacity for human beings to act and makes a world of marionettes acting in entirely predictable and mechanical ways. The action of lying is thus not simply a covering over of reality (as in traditional deception) but a replacement of reality altogether with the fiction of an overarching lie:

> All these lies, whether their authors know it or not, harbor an element of violence: organized lying always tends to destroy whatever it has decided to negate, although only totalitarian governments have consciously adopted lying as the first step to murder. . . . In other words, the difference between the traditional lie and the modern lie will more often than not amount to the difference between hiding and destroying.[13]

The violence of the modern lie consists in the absolute loss of the reality that it denies. But we could also say that the violence of the lie, in this process, consists in substituting the action of destroying the facts of reality for the action of beginning, replacing a history of beginnings with a history of their total erasure.

The historical newness of the lie, as Arendt describes it—its unfolding as a true history—thus consists in the conversion of the process of political action into the action of this substitution. But how do we understand the historical moment that leads to this kind of usurpation? In Arendt's repeated reference to the outbreak of World War I, she hints at the possibility that this shift takes place when the massive destructiveness of this war—a kind of destruction that, she will say elsewhere, inaugurated a new world of technological violence—is itself denied. The denial of the responsibility for the beginning of the war, which she refers to repeatedly in her examples, may be the first lie, in fact, that leads to this modern world. To understand the nature of the historical progress of the lie we must understand, then, the way in which the violence of war becomes entangled with the violence of its denial. The question of history in the world of the lie thus ultimately becomes, as I interpret Arendt, the question: What does it mean for the historical violence of war to become the history of the violence of the lie?

Lying and War

It is this question that, I will suggest, lies at the heart of Arendt's analysis of the Vietnam War. "Lying in Politics" is a response to Daniel Ellsberg's release of the so-called Pentagon Papers, the "top-secret" history of the decision-making processes in the war that was leaked to *The New York Times* in 1971 at the height of the conflict, which created shock waves throughout the public sphere because of their revelation of the systematic and pervasive use of lies on all levels in the war. As Arendt notes, this lying involved, among other things, "the phony body counts of the 'search and destroy' missions, the doctored after-damage reports of the air force, and the 'progress' reports to Washington from the field written by subordinates who knew that their performance would be evaluated by their own reports,"[14] among other kinds of deception. For Arendt, it is the centrality of deception (as opposed to error or illusion) that constitutes the major lesson of the Papers: the centrality of deception as not only a secondary but also a fundamental factor in the decision-making process shaping the development of the war:

> The Pentagon Papers . . . tell different stories, teach different lessons to different readers. . . . But most readers have now agreed that the basic issue raised by the Papers is deception. . . . The famous credibility gap . . . has suddenly opened up into an abyss. The quicksand of lying statements of all sorts, deceptions as well as self-deceptions, is apt to engulf any reader who wishes to probe this material, which, unhappily, he must recognize as the infrastructure of nearly a decade of United States foreign and domestic policy.[15]

To the extent that deception appears in the war, it appears not only as a secondary matter in a larger political and military process—a "gap" between the public version of the war and its political realities—but as an "abyss" that opens up within the infrastructure of the policymaking process itself. Drawing on the currently popular description of the war as a quagmire in her own figure of the "quicksand" of lying statements, Arendt shifts the center of action from the actual process of military engagement—presented, in the quagmire model, as a well-intentioned but misguided step-by-step entrance into the conflict—to the process of lying itself, which thus usurps the place of politics as the fundamental action driving the decision-making process of the war.

The process of deception in the war, as Arendt analyses it, can thus be understood as a new, non-totalitarian version of the *modern* lie. This "more recent variety" of lying she refers to specifically as "image-making,"[16] which involves two different, but apparently related, kinds of images: those that change or distort the facts (the images disseminated by the mass media describing the war) and those that guide the war-making decisions themselves. Both kinds of image making are part of a new phenomenon, and Arendt seems to be touching, quite farsightedly here, on the specificity of a world that is dominated by the mass media. I will suggest, however, that while both kinds of image making are new, the essential feature that appears to constitute the image as a form of the modern lie is the way in which the image making involved with the selling of the war is transformed into the image making that guides the decision-making process itself. It is in the transformative process that takes place *between* the two kinds of image making, in other words, that the war is not only *hidden as a fact* but also *created as a history*.

We can discern this dynamic relation between the images in Arendt's first description of the two kinds of image making, that of the "public relations managers" and that of the "problem-solvers." On one hand, Arendt tells us, are the "public relations managers" who "learned their trade from the inventiveness of Madison Avenue," and believe that half of politics is "image-making" and the other half the art of making people believe in the images.[17] These image-makers thus *make images*, in effect, *to sell the war.* The problem solvers, on the other hand, are intellectuals and game theorists who were brought to Washington to calculate scenarios with "game theories and systems analyses" in order to solve the "problems" of foreign policy.[18] The problem solvers, who are "different from ordinary image-makers," are striking because they lie, "not so much for their country—certainly not for their country's survival, which was never at stake—as for its image."[19] The problem solvers thus lie, in other words, *in the service of* an image. Arendt's description of the structure of image making at the heart of the war, as I interpret her argument, thus seems to operate around a reversal that repeats, somewhat differently, the one that governed the transformation from the traditional to the modern lie: if the public relations managers *make images to sell the war*, the problem solvers *make war to sustain an image.* The war is thus created and sustained, Arendt seems to suggest, for the production of its own image.

Arendt's analysis of the progress of the war in terms of its shifting goals can indeed be understood as a reflection on the way in which the images that sell the war come to take over the decision-making process that guides it. Since "nearly all decisions in this disastrous enterprise were made in full cognizance of the fact that they probably could not be carried out,"[20] Arendt notes, the goals had constantly to be altered. At first these shifts involve the way in which the war is presented to the public. For example, the goal of the war is described originally as "seeing that the people of South Vietnam are permitted to determine their future" but also "assisting the country to win their contest against the . . . Communist conspiracy."[21] As the war worsens, however, the image making is not only aimed at convincing the public to support the war but is also incorporated into the conception of the war itself as a kind of image-making process:

> From 1965 on, the notion of a clear-cut victory receded into the background and the objective became "to convince the enemy that *he* could not win" . . . Since the enemy remained unconvinced, the next goal appeared: "to avoid a humiliating defeat"—as though the hallmark of a defeat in war were mere humiliation. What the Pentagon papers report is the haunting fear of the impact of defeat, not on the welfare of the nation, but on the *reputation* of the United States and its President.[22]

What emerges as the war grows more difficult—and the goals themselves become less reality-oriented—is not a decision-making process concerning the winning of an actual war but the creation of an "image of omnipotence" that ultimately appears to drive the entire process:

> To "convince the world"; to "demonstrate that U.S. was a 'good doctor' willing to keep promises, be tough, take risks, get bloodied and hurt the enemy

badly" . . . to keep intact an image of omnipotence, "our worldwide position of leadership" . . . in short to "*behave* like" the "greatest power in the world" for no other reason than to convince the world of this "simple fact" . . . this was the only permanent goal that, with the beginning of the Johnson administration, pushed into the background all other goals and theories.[23]

What lies behind the decision-making process is not, as one might expect, an adjustment to events but rather the production of, and adherence to, an "image of omnipotence" that increases in dominance, paradoxically, as true power is lost.

It might seem that the image of omnipotence could itself operate as another traditional form of the lie created in the service of wielding additional power. From this point of view it would remain part of what is ultimately a military and political process in which the image would serve as a traditional political tool. But Arendt argues that the creation of the image of omnipotence actually *undermines* power and puts itself in its place:

> The ultimate goal was neither power nor profit. Nor was it even influence in the world in order to serve particular, tangible interests for the sake of which prestige, an image of the "greatest power in the world," was needed and purposefully used. The goal was now the image itself, as is manifest in the very language of the problem-solvers, with their "scenarios" and "audiences," borrowed from the theater. . . . Image-making as global policy—not world conquest, but victory in the battle "to win the people's minds"—is indeed something new in the huge arsenal of human follies recorded in history.[24]

The "image of omnipotence" has, in fact, no relation to actual power or any other interest to which it might be subordinated, but rather becomes the principle *in itself* that subordinates all other realities to it. And this is what then constitutes it, paradoxically, as "new" (the hallmark of all true political action): that political decision making would not serve as a true action but as the action of creating an image that empties this process of any power except that of the image itself.

The "image of omnipotence," then, is not created in this war in order to wield more power—as it might be, says Arendt, in "a third-rate nation always apt to boast in order to compensate for the real thing"—but operates in spite of its actual effect of undermining effectiveness in the real world. Wishing to show "how considerable were the chances for a global policy that was then gambled away in the cause of image-making and winning people's minds,"[25] Arendt notes two incidents revealed in the Pentagon Papers, the first involving Ho Chi Minh, who had written President Truman in 1945 and 1946 to request support from the United States, and the second involving Chou En Lai, who in 1945 had approached President Roosevelt to establish relations with China so that China could "avoid total dependence on the Soviet Union." Both overtures were ignored because, as Arendt cites one scholar on the China incident, they "contradicted the image of monolithic Communism directed from Moscow,"[26] an image that would, presumably, be necessary to sustain the converse image of an omnipotent United States winning over a monolithic antithetical power. The creation of the image of omnipotence thus involves the undoing of actual power.

The sustaining of the image is, in this manner, tied to what Arendt calls the process of "defactualization" at the heart of the war by which the decision-making process simultaneously loses its grounding in reality and becomes unable to observe the loss of its own ground. The Vietnam War is, she argues, a war whose very genesis and history serve the establishment of what Arendt calls an entirely "defactualized world."[27]

History of the Image

What kind of history (and what kind of witness) is possible in the movement toward an entirely defactualized world? Arendt's description of the transformation of the image from the tool to the framework of the decision-making process seems to involve a machinelike mechanism that makes reflection (and truly historical action) increasingly unlikely. Arendt indeed describes a process in which both aspects of the image-making activity have already been essentially cut off from reality. Thus, she explains, the attempt to sell the war becomes, for the image-makers, a battle in which the war is displaced onto the selling process: in thinking of the image-making process as "the battle for people's minds"[28] the public relations managers essentially allow the image making itself to take on the properties of the war. The war, for the public relations managers, thus disappears into the image as advertising the war becomes the primary site of the action.

On the other hand, in the case of the problem-solvers (those who lie for the image), the image making has left the realm of deception and self-deception entirely, since "disregard of reality was inherent in the policies and goals themselves."[29] *The war itself*, for these policymakers, *has taken on the properties of image making*. In this quasi-mechanical manner the world and the war thus come to sustain the image that empties this world of any true political significance and ultimately serves only the image's own ongoing and ruthless perpetuation. "One sometimes has the impression," Arendt says, "that a computer, rather than 'decision-makers,' had been let loose in Southeast Asia."[30] The violent history of the war becomes, in this process, subordinated to the violent historical unfolding of the image.[31]

It is the unfolding movement of this self-erasing image that seems to mark the war *as* an event—a new event—within the larger context of the modern lie. The new aspect of the lie as image making can itself be traced back, in fact, to an earlier event in history that Arendt will go on to describe. Thus the problem-solvers, Arendt says, were preceded by the Cold War ideologists who had once been communists and needed a "new ideology to explain and reliably foretell the course of history."[32] The "sheer ignorance of facts" in this process produced the "theories" of the younger generation (the problem-solvers) that "shielded men from the impact of reality."[33] And this history—a history not of *facts* but of *defactualization*— has a beginning in the occurrence of a specific event that is a crucial event in history but also an event in the history of the modern lie:

> There are historians today who maintain that Truman dropped the bomb on Hiroshima in order to scare the Russians out of Eastern Europe (with the result we know). If this is true, as it might well be, then we may trace back the earliest beginnings of the disregard for the actual consequences of action in favor of some ulterior calculated aim to the fateful war crime that ended the last world war.[34]

At the "earliest beginnings" of defactualization—at the beginning, Arendt implies, of the kind of image making that usurps the decision-making process in the Vietnam War—is a single and inaugurating act, the decision to drop the atomic bomb. If this decision is the beginning of a new mode of the modern lie, however, of image making of the kind she has analyzed in the war, then the "action" of this decision (and its violent consequences) as a "beginning" is subordinated to the image it creates. Rather than taking place as a historical event that provides a framework in which the modern lie will develop, the dropping of the bomb (within the logic of Arendt's analysis) converts the frame of political and historical events into the framework of the lie's own self-generation.

The dropping of the bomb, as I would expand on what I discern in Arendt's argument, would not be meant to wield real power but rather to create the image of power, an event that replaces itself with its own image. The bomb is not only a "beginning" of the nuclear age, but also the beginning of a certain mode of image making, a beginning that erases itself as such in this very process. This is particularly striking in the case of the bomb, since as actual, technological power the bomb would seem to embody precisely the omnipotence it would represent as image. Yet this technologically destructive power (and its political potential) is instantly transferred into the image making that subordinates its present, factual reality (including the reality of its destruction) to the image of a future omnipotence ultimately related only to its power to destroy itself as a fact. The bomb is not dropped in order to wield power that would allow for victory, but rather for the "pursuit of a mere image of omnipotence" that lies in the future.[35]

And yet, it would seem, "image" of itself is also an actual image, insofar as the bomb, in its technological function, is associated with the production of a blinding light (it is often compared to a sun) as well as an image that represents its power, the "image of omnipotence" in the shape of the "mushroom cloud" in which the explosive power of the bomb appears. The bomb thus posits its own image as something that—like the modern lie—is seen and not seen at the same time. The decision to drop the bomb, we could say—which is, or starts as, a true form of action—is covered over, or erased, by the power of the image produced in the actual falling of the bomb, the "mushroom cloud" that gives the falling of the bomb a kind of inevitability (and becomes the term used to make future wars seem inevitable rather than acts of decision making). The erasure of the act of decision making (the process by which a true decision took place) in the dropping of the bomb—the way in which the decision is erased by the image—could be considered the creation of a new kind of fact, one that erases itself in its own production, and in so doing moves forward toward a blinding future. The beginning—and hence futurity—constituted by the "decision" to drop the bomb thus becomes the future "of the image," a history determined by a technological image-making power that determines the future as an explosion annihilating both past and future history.[36]

The end of World War II is ultimately the beginning of the image, a dark (or blindingly light) doubling, perhaps, of the historical process encapsulated at the end of *The Origins of Totalitarianism* in Arendt's claim that "every end in history necessarily contains a new beginning."[37] The history of the lie, in its new form as the history of the image, would be a history constituted by its own erasure. And this is also how we would have to understand its violence: not only as the actual destruction made possible by the bomb, but also as the means by which destruction and violence are made, in their very appearance, inaccessible as knowledge. This is indeed the absolute destruction of fact that Arendt names in the very first section of "Lying in Politics" as another mode of omnipotence: "Total lying can be done only through radical destruction . . . the power to achieve it would have to amount to omnipotence . . . to kill all contemporaries and to wield power over the libraries and archives of all countries of the earth."[38]

Explosive Histories

If the dropping of the bomb is the advent of the image, however, Arendt's own writing also bears witness to the trace of another explosion, an explosion, moreover, associated with an exemplary fact. This fact—mentioned in the quotation from "Truth and Politics" with which we began—also marks the beginning of a war and is repeated four times in the essay as representative of both the coerciveness of facts and of their fragility: "the fact that on the night of August 4, 1914, German troops crossed the frontier of Belgium." In *The Origins of Totalitarianism*, however, this fact has a complicated structure, since it marks, as it turns out, the transition from the pretotalitarian to the totalitarian world and opens the famous chapter ("The Decline of the Nation State and the End of the Rights of Man") that pivots between them:

It is almost impossible even now to describe what actually happened in Europe on August 4, 1914. The days before and the days after the first World War are separated not like the end of an old and the beginning of a new period, but like the day before and after an explosion. Yet this figure of speech is as inaccurate as are all others, because the quiet of sorrow which settles down after a catastrophe has never come to pass. The first explosion seems to have touched off a chain reaction in which we have been caught ever since and which nobody seems able to stop. . . . Every event had the finality of a last judgment, a judgment that was passed neither by God nor by the devil, but looked rather like the expression of some unredeemably stupid fatality.[39]

The "fact" (which is also a date) of August 4, 1914, derives from an event of a special kind, a transitional event between two worlds that constitutes a radical change in political history, from the post-revolutionary world to the world in which much of European politics was ultimately subordinated to the totalitarian movements. As such it heralds something new in history, although, Arendt notes, it is not the newness of a beginning but rather of an "explosion," a gap in time that does not produce a future but rather appears to annihilate it. Indeed, the atomic nature of the explosion (related to a chain reaction) suggests, on a figural level, a link between this historical event marking the beginning of World War I and the literal event of explosion that marks the end of World War II, a chain of explosions in which the beginnings and the ends are equally destructive and seem to produce a history constituted only as the repeated erasure of the histories that precede them.

The explosion of August 4, 1914, indeed marks a transition, specifically, between the world of the traditional lie and the world of the modern lie. As such, the explosion is precisely the advent of the modern lie as an historical event, but an event of a new kind: an event heralding the possibility of its total erasure. The history of explosions would thus constitute the historical unfolding of the modern lie as a repetition of erasures, each both eliminated and passed on by the one that follows.

The figure of explosion that Arendt uses here, however, also delineates this repetitive history in its *difference from* the pure mechanicity and determination of the bomb, insofar as it *reverses* the order of explosion and chain reaction: "Yet this figure of speech is as inaccurate as are all others, because the quiet of sorrow which settles down after a catastrophe has never come to pass. The first explosion seems to have touched off a chain reaction in which we have been caught ever since and which nobody seems able to stop." Whereas in an ordinary, single event of atomic explosion the chain reaction would precede the explosion, here the explosion precedes the chain reaction, which then causes another explosion and another into the future. The explosion, that is, does not take place except insofar as it creates another one, a figure not so much of purely mechanical processes as of a repetition of explosions whose impact always lies in the future of explosions to come. If the advent of the modern lie, in history, is also the advent of history's erasure (as event), this reversal suggests that this erasure never quite occurs, that it is only half-erased and transmitted to the future where it leaves its traces in the violent imprint (and in the technology associated with it) that accompanies the bomb. In Arendt's text, then, the violent and blinding light of the bomb, *as an image*, bears with it the *trace of a figure* that is passed on through the very process of its (partial) erasure.[40] The distinction between the image and its figure would permit, here, a nonmechanistic, nondeterministic historicity of the modern lie—and the possibility of its witness—to begin to emerge.

The Possibility of Witness

It is the trace of this self-erasure of the historical fact that Daniel Ellsberg might indeed be understood as describing when he says, in *Papers on the War*, that he leaked the Pentagon Papers in order to reveal an "invisible war"[41]—not only a war that was invisible to the public but also, perhaps, a war constituted by its self-elimination as a traditional fact. Ellsberg's revelation of the Pentagon Papers is indeed not the revelation of a simple secret, as Arendt notes at the end of her essay:

> What calls for further close and detailed study is the fact, much commented on, that the Pentagon papers revealed little significant news that was not available to the average reader of dailies and weeklies; nor are there any arguments, pro or con, in the "History of the U.S Decision-Making Process on Vietnam Policy" that have not been debated publicly for years in magazines, television shows, and radio broadcasts.[42]

While Arendt emphasizes the availability of the facts because she wishes to insist on the importance of a free press, I believe that her recognition that the Pentagon Papers do not reveal new facts points to a reinterpretation of the way in which the media could be understood as working in their disclosure. If the Pentagon Papers have the force of a revelation, it cannot be because they reveal any facts that are not known (including the facts of the lies themselves) but rather because they produce, from within the very medium of the image (the public press), the force of an explosion that transmits and makes legible the explosion of the fact in the modern world. It is, perhaps, the performance of a kind of *explosion of the frame* of the media through the very media that create this frame.[43]

Ellsberg himself, in fact, describes his decision to leak the Pentagon Papers not in terms of revelation or truth but in terms of the breaking of a promise—the breaking of the secrecy oath that, in an essay on the subject, he identifies as a promise to lie.[44] Ellsberg's decision is a peculiar kind of speech act: not a promise—a central kind of political action in Arendt's work—but the *breaking of a promise to lie*. This new kind of action would have to be understood as an action that forgoes the possibility of straightforward truth-telling yet serves, nonetheless, as a form of political witness. What occurs here is not the telling of truth, that is, but the testimony to erasure: the exposure, in Ellsberg's words, of an "enigma,"[45] the enigma of an "invisible war"—that is, a *witness to invisibility*.

In Arendt's response to this witness, I would propose, we may also discern, not so much the truth of the lie's history, but the possible outlines, and performance, of a certain historicity—passing through the beginning of World War I, the end of World War II, the endless war in Vietnam, and a future of wars (and of lies) that Arendt could not know would arise out of the post-Vietnam era but about which she seemed to write so presciently—a historicity that does not submit itself entirely to the absolute violence of the lie. Only by thinking through the possibility of total erasure, Arendt shows us, can we also conceive of the possibility of a decision to witness that itself, *as* an action, has political and historical consequences—the possibility for a witness from *within* the world of the lie. In Arendt's own writing, it is at the point at which we discern the radically self-annihilating historicity of the bomb that we may also trace the figure of an explosion not entirely determined by its self-erasure. The trace of this figure would not necessarily be a promise, but might serve, instead, as testimony to the possibility of another history.

PART III

Citizens

three CITIES or republics, the largest were entitled to *three* votes in the COMMON COUNCIL, those of the middle class to *two,* and the smallest to *one.* The COMMON COUNCIL had the appointment of all the judges and magistrates of the respective CITIES. This was certainly the most delicate species of interference in their internal administration; for if there be any thing that seems exclusively appropriated to the local jurisdictions, it is the appointment of their own officers. Yet Montesquieu, speaking of this association, says: "Were I to give a model of an excellent Confederate Republic, it would be that of Lycia." Thus we perceive that the distinctions insisted upon were not within the contemplation of this enlightened civilian; and we shall be led to conclude, that they are the novel refinements of an erroneous theory. PUBLIUS

From the New York Packet, Friday, November 23, 1787

THE FEDERALIST NO. 10

(MADISON)

To the People of the State of New York:

AMONG the numerous advantages promised by a well-constructed Union, none deserves to be more accurately developed than its tendency to break and control the violence of faction. The friend of popular governments never finds himself so much alarmed for their character and fate, as when he contemplates their propensity to this dangerous vice. He will not fail, therefore, to set a due value on any plan which, without violating the principles to which he is attached, provides a proper cure for it. The instability, injustice, and confusion introduced into the public councils, have, in truth, been the mortal diseases under which popular governments have everywhere

The Experience of Action

:: PATCHEN MARKELL

"What is the activity of democratic citizenship?" That is a provocatively odd question with which to frame a discussion of the legacy of Hannah Arendt's thought, and particularly a discussion of her thought about *thinking* and its political significance. From one angle, the question seems straightforward enough: it asks us to identify the activities appropriate to the citizens of democracies as citizens, the practices through which they can most effectively steer their community safely past the hazards endemic to democratic politics. Reasoned deliberation, regular participation in the associational life of civil society, the vigorous questioning of entrenched assumptions and settled institutions: these are just a few of the more familiar possible conceptual specifications of "democratic citizenship" that circulate in the field of political theory today, sometimes with an Arendtian imprimatur. Still, understood in these terms, the question ascribes to the theorist who answers it, no matter how egalitarian his or her commitments, a certain kind of supervisory expertise over the manifold of human activities—an expertise that might remind us of the theoretical knowledge claimed by that perpetual Arendtian nemesis, the Platonic "statesman," the one who does not himself "perform practical tasks" but knows what is to be done and when, and assigns those tasks to those who do perform them, thereby "weaving everything [in the city] together in the most correct way."[1] This has not been an unfamiliar rhetorical stance in postwar academic political theory, but it was not Arendt's. Is there a way to engage the question of democratic citizenship while refusing the invitation to subordinate political activity to the disposing power of expert thought?

We might start by hearing the question differently: not as a call for conceptual specification—which subset of the multitudinous human activities *counts* as the activity of democratic citizenship?—but rather as a call for an enriched description; and in particular (since the object of the description is an activity, undertaken by an agent) for a phenomenological description: what is it

Facing: Page 53 of Hannah Arendt's heavily annotated copy of *The Federalist Papers*. She notes that Federalist no. 10 is to be read in conjunction with no. 39. She writes on the left margin, "Two kinds of popular gov: republic & Democracy." At the bottom of the page, she writes, "Faction based on interest, i.e. of Will, can't be argued with!" Courtesy of the Hannah Arendt Collection, Stevenson Library, Bard College.

like to engage in this activity? In what follows I explore this possibility with the help of Arendt's *On Revolution*, and in particular by attending to some of her characterizations of the American revolutionaries' experiences of, and in, political action. These characterizations throw a distinctive light both on the question of what threatens, and what might help sustain, the activity of democratic citizenship, and on the question of the relations among political activity, thinking, and theory. They do so not only in virtue of what they say about the American revolutionaries, but also by exemplifying the generatively idiosyncratic way Arendt uses the fraught idea of "experience." To bring that idiosyncrasy into the foreground, it will be helpful to start with a few more general words about *On Revolution* and its context.[2]

On Revolution[3] is a curious book. Conceived and written between 1959 and 1962, and first published in 1963—the same year as *Eichmann in Jerusalem*—it was, as Elisabeth Young-Bruehl has put it, an "overshadowed sibling," at least at first; though as the decade proceeded it became increasingly widely read, with a mixture of admiration and skepticism, on the democratic left.[4] Still, there may be more to the dull thud with which the book initially landed than its rivalry with *Eichmann*, or Arendt's penchant for irritating professional historians. It is worth recalling the historiographic moment at which *On Revolution* appeared. In 1963, none of the landmark texts of what would be known as the "republican revival" in early American history had yet been published—Bernard Bailyn's *Pamphlets of the American Revolution* was still two years away—nor had the techniques and concerns of the new social history yet coalesced into the transformative movement they would become.[5] Instead, the most recently ascendant approach was what its critics had begun to call "consensus" or "conservative" history.[6] Reacting against the prominence of the themes of economic and sectional conflict in the work of Beard, Turner, and their followers, such scholars as Louis Hartz, Daniel Boorstin, and Clinton Rossiter had emphasized the fundamental continuity of an American history unscarred by deep-seated social divisions and resentments.[7] The Revolution itself, from this perspective, was to be understood as a uniquely American effort to conserve the colonial tradition of political liberty—"hardly a revolution at all," as Boorstin put it, "in the modern European sense of the word."[8] While their critics charged them with "carrying out a massive grading operation to smooth over America's social convulsions,"[9] these historians' portraits of the American political tradition as detached from Europe's fierce ideological strife, and of the American Revolution as utterly different in kind from its terrible kin in France and Russia, resonated with readers eager to affirm American liberalism while avoiding the doctrinal rigidity that had fed "the characteristic tyrannies of our age."[10]

Arriving onto this scene, *On Revolution* must have cut a puzzling figure. Some of its most prominent themes would have seemed to place Arendt squarely in the camp of the consensus historians—several of whom she read as part of her self-education in American history, and whom she cites, mostly approvingly, in the book—including her focus on the fateful differences between the French and American Revolutions and her celebration of the American Revolution's "success"; her insistence on the fortunate impotence of the "social question" in an America that knew little in the way of abject poverty; her harsh jab at Charles Beard, comparing his search for economic motives behind the making of the Constitution with Robespierre's terroristic "passion for [the] unmasking" of hypocrisy; and her presentation of the American revolutionaries as having set out merely to recover "the rights and liberties of limited government" that were their birthright as British subjects, and which had been a vital part of colonial practice.[11]

Still, much of *On Revolution* would also have confounded such efforts to place her on a familiar historiographic map. For all Arendt's insistence on the differences between the French and American cases, her trains of association often carry her writing across national boundaries—particularly in the exposition of the idea of the council system in the book's final chapter, in which Arendt bounces among Monticello, Paris, St. Petersburg, Budapest, and Berlin with impunity. Her celebration of the American Revolution's success is likewise muted by her extended elegy for the lost "revolutionary spirit," and her suggestion of an antagonism between that revolutionary spirit and the Constitution—which she says eventually "cheated [the American people] of their proudest possession"—shares the *pathos*, if not the economism, of the old Progressive interpretations of the Constitution as an effort not to realize but to constrain revolutionary democracy.[12] And despite her evident debt to the consensus historians' accounts of the conservatism of the revolutionaries and of the continuities between colonial and revolutionary practice, Arendt also insists, as they did not, that the American Revolution was genuinely *revolutionary*, an expression of the human capacity to initiate something unprecedented and new.[13]

What could Arendt have meant in characterizing the Revolution in such apparently contradictory terms? The route to an answer lies through one final comparison between *On Revolution* and its historiographic surroundings. As Arendt was working on *On Revolution*, the term "experience" was enjoying a certain currency in American historical writing thanks to the work of Daniel Boorstin, who had just published the first volume of a history of America subtitled *The Colonial Experience*, to be followed by *The National Experience* and *The Democratic Experience*.[14] Several years earlier, in his Walgreen Lectures, Boorstin had proposed that the "genius" of American politics, and its most powerful insulation against European-style ideological warfare, lay in its allergy to the abstract speculations of political theory. That allergy had first been contracted by the Puritans, who arrived in America as dogmatists but slowly learned to "seek their standards in their own experience"; and it was inherited by the revolutionaries, whose writings were always practical, experimental responses to concrete legal and institutional challenges, not dogmatic treatises in political philosophy, and whose ingrained faith in the sufficiency of past and present experience lent the Revolution its conservative character.[15] Later, Boorstin filled in this sketch of early America with rich detail, recounting with didactic sarcasm an early and ill-fated project, planned with "fantastic neatness," for the colonization of Georgia—"the only flaw in this scheme was that it had to be carried out by real people at some real place on earth"—and waxing eloquent about colonial pragmatism wherever he found it.[16] Boorstin's America is well emblematized by his characterization of the spirit of eighteenth-century American medicine: "By allowing crude, fluid experience to overflow the ancient walls between departments of medical knowledge, men might see relations in nature which had been obscured by guild monopolies and by the conceit of learned specialists."[17]

"Experience" is a key term in *On Revolution*, too. Throughout the book, Arendt's concern is with the "experience of a new beginning"—which is to say, for her, with the "experience of being free"—that the French and American Revolutions "brought to the fore," and which they subsequently, each in its own way, helped to obscure.[18] Sometimes her use of the term "experience" echoes Boorstin's, as when she contrasts the Americans, with their extensive experience of colonial self-government, with the French revolutionaries, who were "theoretical in the extreme" because they "had no experience to fall back on, only ideas and principles untested by reality to guide and inspire them."[19] Yet Arendt's use of "experience" also departs from Boorstin's in crucial ways. For Boorstin, "experience" was first and foremost a source—he called it a "fund"—of insight and practical guidance, built up gradually through deliberate experiment and direct observation, which represented a wholesale alternative to "theory": the American experience made theory "superfluous."[20] In *On Revolution*, by contrast, experience is not primarily important as a source of reliable knowledge or good judgment—much less as a satisfaction of the craving for the immediacy of "life," unfettered by concepts.[21] The paths of revolutionary experience Arendt traces are too crooked, too shot through with both surprise and opacity, to serve those familiar purposes.[22]

In Arendt's telling, for instance, the experience of the eighteenth-century revolutions was an experience of "inadvertence."[23] Her revolutionaries did not set out to begin something new; instead, quite in accord with conservative historiography, they had a "disinclination for novelty" and were "firmly convinced that they would do no more than restore an old order of things that had been violated."[24] Once their undertaking was underway, however—"in the course of the event itself," as she repeatedly puts it—"what they had thought was a restoration, the retrieving of their ancient liberties, *turned into* a revolution."[25] This transformation was not simply a function of the accelerating accumulation of unintended consequences, though that phenomenon had played a significant role in Arendt's account of "action" in *The Human Condi-*

tion.[26] It was "in the very nature of their enterprise," she says, that the revolutionaries

> discovered their own capacity and desire for the "charms of liberty," as John Jay once called them, only in the very act of liberation. For the acts and deeds which liberation demanded from them threw them into public business, where, intentionally or more often unexpectedly, they began to constitute that space of appearances where freedom can unfold its charms and become a visible, tangible reality. Since they were not in the least prepared for these charms, they could hardly be expected to be aware of the new phenomenon. It was nothing less than the weight of the entire Christian tradition which prevented them from owning up to the fact that they were enjoying what they were doing far beyond the call of duty.[27]

Likewise, as the last sentence of this passage already intimates, the "experience" Arendt ascribes to the revolutionaries was hardly something to which its subjects had privileged, unobstructed access: indeed, on Arendt's account, the shape of revolutionary experience was peculiarly obscure to those who lived it.[28] This was not simply because their supposedly pure experience had been corrupted by concepts.

Arendt makes this obscurity within revolutionary experience clear later in *On Revolution* in her one explicit engagement with Boorstin's writing, where she firmly rejects his sharp contrast between European philosophizing and American pragmatism. "Experiences and even the stories which grow out of what men do and endure, of happenings and events," she insists, "sink back into the futility inherent in the living word and the living deed unless they are talked about over and over again. What saves the affairs of mortal men from their inherent futility is nothing but this incessant talk about them, which in its turn remains futile unless certain concepts, certain guideposts for future remembrance, and even sheer reference, arise out of it." Thus, *contra* Boorstin, to the extent that Americans *have* displayed an "aversion to conceptual thought," the result has been not the salutary insulation of experience against ideological perversion, but the creation of a dangerous vacuum: "The reason America has shown such ready receptivity to far-fetched ideas and grotesque notions may simply be that the human mind stands in need of concepts if it is to function at all; hence it will accept almost anything whenever its foremost task, the comprehensive understanding of reality and the coming to terms with it, is in danger of being compromised."[29]

These features of revolutionary experience, which on more conventional uses of the term might seem to drain "experience" of its power, or to undermine its claim to authority, are, for Arendt, central to the phenomenon. First, they help to explain how the same revolution can rightly be characterized as both "conservative" and "revolutionary." The element of surprise present in the course of revolutionary experience works like a joint: on the one hand, it allows for the bends, the transformations in direction and significance, that arise during the course of the event itself and that do not conform to the aims and expectations of its agents. On the other hand, it also keeps the conservative and revolutionary trajectories of the event intimately connected to each other: the surprise that strikes the revolutionaries does not result from the shattering of their routines by an external force; instead, it is, precisely, surprise at the nature and intensity of their enjoyment of what they are already doing. Just as in *The Human Condition* the work-world in which human beings relate instrumentally to durable objects is not altogether separate from the world of action, in which things and people appear and take on significance through their involvement in the stories of unique human beings—the way Arendt put it there was that the "physical, worldly in-between" is "overlaid and, as it were, overgrown with another, altogether different in-between which consists of deeds and words"[30]—in *On Revolution* the revolutionary character of the American Revolution arises not out of a sudden break in the orientation of the revolutionaries' activities, but out of the fact that *in* doing one thing, the work of liberation, they *also* turned out to be doing something else: appearing in public.[31]

Second, these features of revolutionary experience also help Arendt make sense of what she calls the "failure of thought and remembrance" that has contributed to the loss of the "revolutionary spirit" in America.[32] It is tempting to think that this lost "revolutionary spirit" is something like a spirit of persistent rebelliousness, an antipathy to the constraint involved in every settled political form, and that an Arendtian politics would therefore involve an unending alternation between the stable forms and settled procedures that democratic politics inevitably requires if it is not to deteriorate into anarchy, and the unruliness and perpetual self-questioning that democratic politics also requires if it is not to solidify into a new despotism.[33] Yet Arendt says that the idea of an opposition between "the concern with stability" and the "spirit of the new" is in fact the "*symptom* of our loss"— that is, it is a manifestation of the revolutionaries' failure, not its cause;[34] and she sees the first signs of that misleading sense of an opposition—she calls it a "fallacy"—in Jefferson's own swing from the endorsement of periodic anticonstitutional rebellions to the endorsement of periodic constitutional refoundings.[35] The real source of this loss, Arendt suggests, lies in the fact that the revolutionaries, in need of concepts with which to make sense of their impermanent and elusive experience, turned reflexively to traditional frameworks of political thought, rather than inventing "another comprehensive way of communicating and stating their own experiences."[36] Jefferson's succession of schemes for "tearing down and building up," for instance, represented a series of efforts to "provide for . . . an *exact repetition* of the whole process of action which had accompanied the course of the revolution," conceived at different stages in the movement of the event.[37] What such schemes could not provide for, however, was precisely the *course* of the event, simultaneously continuous and innovative, and characterized by an element of surprise. In this, Jefferson's schemes shared something with the attitudes of those twentieth-century revolutionaries who were convinced that they "knew beforehand the course a revolution must take,"[38] and they demonstrated the continuing influence of certain "Platonic notions" in Jefferson's political thought—including especially the idea that "action is fundamentally no more than the execution of knowledge."[39] For political thought to do justice to revolutionary experience, it would need not to use different concepts, but to use concepts differently.

The significance of Arendt's account of the American Revolution for larger questions about the activity of democratic citizenship—and about thinking and politics—should now be coming into view. Most obviously, Arendt's observations about the inadvertence and surprise that are characteristic of revolutionary experience indicate the difficulty of invigorating democratic citizenship as part of a theoretical design. If the experience of political freedom is something that actors do not typically pursue deliberately or as a discrete project, but that arises instead out of a surprising encounter with what they are *already* doing, then experience of that kind will resist the best efforts of the theoretically informed statesman to schedule, prescribe, or command it—though not, again, because the experience is intrinsically an experience of unruliness. Indeed, Arendt's insistence that the revolutionary experience of novelty retains a kind of attachment to the given, as that out of which it emerges and to which it responds, also helps identify a serious and peculiarly insidious threat to the activity of democratic citizenship. Such activity can, of course, be stifled through the explicit restriction of civil and political liberties; but it can also be suffocated indirectly, through the narrowing of the range of things and events that show up *to* citizens as occasions for their active response, as things that are their business to attend to or worry about. (This is the gentle side of the paternalism of today's security state, which does not so much deny our capacity to think and act for ourselves as try to relieve us of the time-consuming responsibility of actually doing so.[40]) It is also the sort of danger to political activity to which, on Arendt's reading, Jefferson did eventually respond in his late letters, in which he articulated what Arendt called his "most cherished political idea," the subdivision of the country into the little "elementary republics" that he called "wards"—an institutional arrangement whose aim was not to produce a precise repetition of a particular course of action or to ensure the performance of a specific kind of activity, but to establish the background conditions against which the experience of action *might* emerge, if at all, as it must: on its own time.[41]

None of this, finally, should be taken to suggest that thinking and theory have nothing to offer politics, or that their contributions to politics can only be negative in character. It does not mean that, while the restless activity of thinking can helpfully dissolve prejudice and loosen sedimented assumptions in a way that prepares citizens to exercise political judgment, it necessarily becomes pernicious when it begins to congeal into fixed conceptual forms.[42] To be sure, Arendt was sensitive to the tension between the "relentless and repetitive" activity of thinking, which on its own produces no results, and the "reification" performed by the writer, which makes thought fit to appear in the world only at the cost of interrupting and stilling its lively activity.[43] But Arendt was a writer no less than a thinker, and as we have seen, when she discusses the failure of "thought" in *On Revolution* she is referring to thinking in its reified state, in which it belongs to the world of durable artifacts from which the ongoing processes of action and thinking take their orientation.[44] What matters to Arendt is not that thinking remain immaterial, but that, in its reified form, it "remain bound to incident as the circle remains bound to its focus."[45] Such thinking produces concepts that are also figures, as irregular as the courses of events to which they are tethered. Their function is neither to dissolve rigid ideologies nor to prescribe courses of action, but to accustom readers to certain shapes of event, and perhaps thereby to let them see and understand features of their own experience that might otherwise have eluded them.

Chapter VIII

HOW EQUALITY SUGGESTS TO THE AMERI–
CANS THE IDEA OF THE INDEFINITE
PERFECTIBILITY OF MAN

EQUALITY suggests to the human mind several ideas that would not have originated from any other source, and it modifies almost all those previously entertained. I take as an example the idea of human perfectibility, because it is one of the principal notions that the intellect can conceive and because it constitutes of itself a great philosophical theory, which is everywhere to be traced by its consequences in the conduct of human affairs.

Although man has many points of resemblance with the brutes, one trait is peculiar to himself: he improves; they are incapable of improvement. Mankind could not fail to discover this difference from the beginning. The idea of perfectibility is therefore as old as the world; equality did not give birth to it, but has imparted to it a new character.

When the citizens of a community are classed according to rank, profession, or birth and when all men are forced to follow the career which chance has opened before them, everyone thinks that the utmost limits of human power are to be discerned in proximity to himself, and no one seeks any longer to resist the inevitable law of his destiny. Not, indeed, that an aristocratic people absolutely deny man's faculty of self-improvement, but they do not hold it to be indefinite; they can conceive amelioration, but not change: they imagine that the future condition of society may be better, but not essentially different; and, while they admit that humanity has made progress and may still have some to make, they assign to it beforehand certain impassable limits.

Thus they do not presume that they have arrived at the supreme good or at absolute truth (what people or what man was ever wild enough to imagine it?), but they cherish an opinion that they have pretty nearly reached that degree of greatness and knowledge which our imperfect nature admits of; and as nothing moves

33

Dissent in Dark Times

HANNAH ARENDT ON CIVIL DISOBEDIENCE AND CONSTITUTIONAL PATRIOTISM

... there can be no patriotism without permanent opposition and criticism.
HANNAH ARENDT, Letter to Gershom Scholem (1963)

:: VERITY SMITH

There has been much talk of late regarding the so-called paradox of democratic constitutionalism in debates surrounding constitutional design, amendment, and interpretation.[1] As Frank Michelman puts it, "constitutional theory is eternally hounded, if not totally consumed, by a search for harmony between what are usually heard as two clashing commitments: one to the ideal of government constrained by law ('constitutionalism'), the other to the ideal of the search for government by act of the people ('democracy')."[2]

In this essay, I explore the place of civil disobedience in Hannah Arendt's work to generate an account of constitutionalism in which the rule of law and democracy are mutually constitutive rather than opposed principles. The first section argues that Arendt is what I call an "agonistic constitutionalist." The second section delineates her debts to Montesquieu in this regard. The third section takes up civil disobedience as a constitutionally regenerative practice of reverent disobedience.

Hannah Arendt: Agonist or Constitutionalist?

Hannah Arendt may not immediately spring to mind as a constitutional thinker.[3] It is understandable that this is so, for she does not articulate an easily identifiable doctrine, theory, or model of constitutionalism, or, for that matter, of democracy, emphasizing instead the language of freedom, plurality, and action-in-concert. Moreover, complexities abound, as she is critical of theories of law and contract based on natural rights, as well as theories of rule based on will or sovereignty, *including* theories in which the rule of law is legitimated by popular sovereignty (and vice versa). In *On Revolution*, the work in which she most directly addresses processes of revolution, foundation, and constitution, she is critical of the centralizing tendencies and

Facing: Page 33 of Hannah Arendt's heavily annotated copy of Alexis de Tocqueville's *Democracy in America*. At the top of vol. 2, part I, chapter 8, Arendt writes: "man: animal perfectible: = change of human nature? = no human nature." Courtesy of the Hannah Arendt Collection, Stevenson Library, Bard College.

"vertical" or hierarchical nature of representative institutions. She seems here and elsewhere to call for acts of political insurgency in ways that seem anti-constitutional.[4] She is also explicitly critical of liberalism's emphasis on "negative liberty." Her emphasis on action-in-concert, free communication, and the public sphere has facilitated collectivist, communitarian, and deliberative democratic readings. And her account of the heroically performative politics of the Greek polis has led many to read her as agonistic in either a Nietzschean or classical mode.[5] Aspects of her work make all of these readings available, and even persuasive.

And yet, Arendt also stresses the importance of the institutional *structure* that makes political life possible. In particular, she invokes the language of laws as boundaries, hedges, or walls within which men can act. Law she says, is literally the "framework of stability" required for public life.[6] At times, Arendt is almost maddeningly contrarian, sounding as if she is writing in riddles: What kind of walls are without foundation? How can activity provide stability? The paradox, it seems, is that Arendt is at once an institutionalist proponent of the rule of law, *and* an anti-institutionalist agonist or radical democrat.

Accordingly, it may seem that the participatory elements of her idea of democracy are in tension with the constitutional, limiting, and constraining elements. But Arendt's essay "Civil Disobedience" illuminates a way in which we can see those two sides together. That is, the activity that best embodies the way we can hold together these two elements—the desire for limited constitutional government and the need for vital, active, and participatory contestation—is civil disobedience.

At the heart of her insight into the constitutionality of civil disobedience is Arendt's attempt to frame civil disobedience as an activity that mediates between a need for change and a need for stability. Civil disobedience is not a fully revolutionary activity—in that such disobedient dissonance accepts the general legitimacy of the system of laws. But neither is it fully counter-revolutionary—in that the civil disobedient does want to contest the way the frame of authority is interpreted and applied. In some sense, the civil disobedient engages in the essential activity of *reconstitution*.

Indeed, Arendt contends, "It would be an event of great significance to find a constitutional niche for civil disobedience—of no less significance, perhaps, than the event of the founding of the *constitutio libertatis*, nearly 200 years ago."[7] Arendt's point is that constitutional continuity is preserved only through contestation. Constitutionalism thus has a democratic, agonistic aspect as well as a stabilizing one. Moreover, civil disobedience and dissent by diverse sets of actors is understood as a critical means of constitutional maintenance and preservation. We might even say that Arendt thinks about civil disobedience and dissent as forms of *constitutional patriotism*—thus presaging both Habermas's advocacy of "constitutional patriotism" (*Verfassungspatriotismus*)[8] and the so-called republican revival in constitutional theory.[9]

Understanding the ways in which Arendt is adapting aspects of Montesquieu's constitutionalism is essential to understanding how this works in her thought. Not only are Arendt's debts and affinities to Montesquieu far more significant than previous scholarship has recognized, but many of the apparent paradoxes in Arendt's constitutional politics also dissolve, or are at least relaxed, when viewed in his light.[10] Her vision of constitutionalism is in several respects a return to a seventeenth- and eighteenth-century worry that sovereignty needs mediation or pluralization, and that constitutional contestation is the way to do this. On this model, the very stability of a constitutional framework depends, paradoxically, on its contestation and continuous revitalization.

Arendt and Montesquieu may at first seem more dissimilar than not. Montesquieu is most often characterized as a liberal constitutionalist, advocating a form of limited monarchy. He is perhaps best known as the author of *The Spirit of the Laws*, and he is frequently called the "father of constitutionalism" insofar as his work was of critical importance to both Blackstone and the American founders. His best-known legacy is that of the separation of powers and the independent judiciary, and he is known for moderation, not the sort of agonistic action with which Arendt is typically associated. But Arendt was profoundly influenced by Montesquieu's theorization of the dangers of absolute sovereignty—whether monarchical or popular—as well as by his activity-centered understanding of constitutionalism. As Arendt began to associate the origins of twentieth-century totalitarianism with sovereign theories of will and national identity, she increasingly skipped back over the intervening centuries to recover aspects of Montesquieu's constitutional alternative.

Indeed, Arendt adapted numerous aspects of Montesquieu's work to her own. She appropriated his notion that only power arrests power, the federal principle, the importance of intermediary institutions, the concept of "animating" or "inspiring" principles, and the concept of the "spirit of the laws." She found his view of man as "a flexible being" chilling and prescient, and she worked through his thinking about despotism and the loss of traditional bases of authority at great length in attempting to find a new framework for understanding and judgment in the wake of totalitarianism. Arendt refers to Montesquieu hundreds of times in her published work, often singling him out for praise as the exceptional prerevolutionary thinker to forgo absolute foundations, or natural law, or sovereignty, or will, and so on. And there are many more instances in which she uses Montesquieu's language or concepts without naming him outright. Moreover, her unpublished lectures, correspondence, and notes treat Montesquieu in an extended way, demonstrating the tremendous depth and breadth of his importance for her thought.[11]

In particular, Montesquieu influenced Arendt's account of the "inspiring principles"—or motive force—of political action.[12] The book Arendt originally planned to write after *Origins of Totalitarianism*, on totalitarian elements in

Marx's thought, was meant to include a lengthy section on Montesquieu.[13] Thus, in the early 1950s, while Arendt was revising the first edition of *Origins of Totalitarianism*, she produced a number of essays and lecture notes in which she appropriated Montesquieu's concept of the animating or motivating "principles" that set each form of government in motion, extending this notion to all human freedom and action. What most struck Arendt was Montesquieu's account of the difference between the nature or structure of government and its principle—or what makes it act.[14] The latter he calls "human passions" in motion. For democracy, the principle is virtue; for aristocracy, moderation; for monarchy, honor; and for despotism, fear.

In 1955, Arendt began work on a book called *Introduction Into Politics* that would have examined "the various modi of human plurality and the institutions which correspond to them." This project would, she says in her Rockefeller Foundation grant proposal, "undertake a re-examination of the old question of forms of government, their principles and their modes of action."[15] Importantly, she conceived of this book as a companion to *The Human Condition*, insofar as she thought she had discovered in Montesquieu's notion of *animating principles* the idea that humans have a basic capacity for free action—one they may be able to recover through concerted and continuous political action even when the traditional bases of authority are gone. While Arendt never wrote either of the planned books, many of her key ideas surfaced in other writings, including the essays in *Between Past and Future* and *On Revolution*.[16]

Arendt celebrates Montesquieu's question, "What makes a government act as it acts?" as an entirely original one.[17] She thought his discovery that each government had not only a particular "structure" but also a "principle" that sets it in motion of great relevance insofar as it introduced "history and historical process" into structures of government, contrary to the "unmoved and unmovable" formulations of the Greeks.[18] Arendt thus credits Montesquieu with providing *the principles of motion* that modify Aristotelian categories regarding forms of governance.

Arendt further praises Montesquieu's understanding of law as *rapports* or relations that connect people as a salutary revival of the Roman *lex*—law as a formal or lasting tie between people. This she contrasts to the Greek *nomos*, which is more of a wall. The former requires action; and the Romans accordingly understand legislation and foundation as political acts. The Greek conception, by comparison, cordons off the founding or legislative act as a pre-political act of fabrication—treating acting as if it were making; thus introducing a dimension of instrumentality or violence. Here, she alternatively blames Greek philosophers and the members of the polis themselves. She credits Montesquieu as having sidestepped this problem by not worrying about absolute foundations or absolute validity; instead, drawing on a "Roman" view of law as "rapports" and preferring processes of *amendment* to revolution.[19] On this conception, law is not the expression of the sovereign's will (whether that sovereign is one or many). Roman law, Arendt maintains, is itself political and non-absolutist.

But perhaps most importantly, Montesquieu and Arendt shared a *summmum malum*, though Arendt approaches it from distinctly her own angle. That is, a *fear of undivided sovereignty* runs through all of her work, which parallels Montesquieu's fear and condemnation of despotism or lawlessness as well as his worry regarding the unity and homogeneity of ancient republics. It is undivided sovereignty that she sees at work and condemns in her writing on nationalism, cosmopolitanism, the sovereign state, absolutism, tyranny, philosophical theories of will, identity, democratic popular sovereignty, and especially totalitarianism. It is the threat of undivided sovereignty, I contend, that links her fear and animus of all of these ills. This is also what leads her to such a committed constitutionalism, as well as to the *particular form* of her constitutionalism. For Arendt, undivided sovereignty brings about the erasure or collapse of the public space necessary for plurality and human diversity. This fear commits her to a constitutional framework for politics as well as to a constant contestation of the framework—not as a form of *disruption*, but, rather, as a kind of *conservation* of the framework.

Civil Disobedience and the Politics of Reverent Disobedience

Arendt is thus committed to the rule of law, as well as to the ongoing agonistic contestation of the law. And the startling notion that contestation is actually a form of reverence, and even preservation, is Montesquieuian to the core. This may seem an odd claim, in that Montesquieu is famous for his praise of moderation. But what Montesquieu calls "moderation" may also be read as indicating a healthy non-unity—an anti-absolutism or, in Tzvetan Todorov's phrase, "a marker of complexity."[20] Montesquieu's insistence on legality as a complex weave of forces maintains a complicated equilibrium, issuing in plurality. For Montesquieu, a well-conceived constitution not only balances power so that power can check (*arrête*) power, but this very activity of contestation and mediation generates more power, ultimately ensuring the polity's stability. Thus, a good constitution will permit social heterogeneity and a plurality of moral standards, which are, Montesquieu argues, moderating and stabilizing.[21]

Moreover, Montesquieu contends that legality requires active maintenance—sometimes quite spirited maintenance to the point of loyal disobedience on the part of intermediary bodies and honorable aristocrats, including the "illegal means of maintaining the law" that was built into the very structure of the limited monarchical constitutional regime.[22] Ultimately, that is, the monarchy would not be possible without the cooperation of the intermediary orders of nobility. And this means devolving power to those bodies so that, as Montesquieu famously put it, "No monarchy, no nobility; no nobility, no monarchy."[23]

From Montesquieu, Arendt inherits the notion that it is unity or singularity that leads to excess, and thus to tyranny. Unity has a static quality that leads not just to tyranny, but also ultimately to instability—whether internal implosion or external overthrow. This supports Arendt's paradoxical notion that civil disobedience is actually preserving a constitutional framework by disrupting it, dissenting from it, and contesting it. Constitutional continuity is preserved only through constitutional contestation by diverse sets of actors, thus ensuring the dynamic appropriation and revision of constitutional norms, principles, and practices. Arendt thus makes the Montesquieuian claim that "political institutions, no matter how well or how badly designed, depend for continued existence upon acting men; their conservation is achieved by the same means that brought them into being. Independent existence marks the work of art as a product of making; utter dependence upon further acts to keep it in existence marks the state as a product of action."[24]

It is this priority of action that leads Arendt to express the wish in *On Revolution* that Jefferson's proposal for council politics had been incorporated into the structure of representative government, as a way of keeping constituent power alive in constituted government. It is also the source of her more Madisonian celebration of intermediary groups and institutions, and of federation. For Arendt, the great risk of losing intermediary institutions is that there is then no space built in for plurality or action.[25] Intermediary institutions, bodies, or powers, following Montesquieu, are sites of political action, and mediation is not simply a matter of constitutional engineering, but an activity both facilitated by and enacted through the constitutional framework.

Arendt thus draws on Montesquieu in developing a contestatory constitutionalism of reverent disobedience, and nowhere is this more evident than in her reflections in the essay "Civil Disobedience." There, in a series of appropriating moves, Arendt argues that "consent and the right to dissent" are the "inspiring and organizing principles of action" that guide citizens living in the American constitutional order.[26] Here, Arendt is once again deploying Montesquieu's conception of "inspiring principles" that move and guide a regime. Civil disobedience, she argues, is thus part and parcel of the "spirit of the laws" in the United States, insofar as that spirit entails "active support and continuing participation in all matters of public interest."[27]

Montesquieu's device of "the spirit of the laws" is meant to point to norms, practices, and traditions, which we can mobilize to critique the positive law in the name of a larger constitutional order. Contesting the constitutional order in the name of its principles thus becomes a way of demonstrating our more ongoing support and allegiance to that order insofar as "dissent implies consent, and is the hallmark of free government; one who knows that he may dissent knows also that he somehow consents when he does not dissent."[28] Exercising our right to dissent transforms our otherwise tacit consent into a more active and even "voluntary" consent to the general framework of governance (though not, of course, to "specific laws or specific policies," since we may think these imperfect or wrongheaded applications of constitutional ideals).

Arendt's civil disobedients, then, perform the mediating function that Montesquieu attributed to the nobility. They are perhaps best understood as a kind of intermediary order or voluntary association—an idea Arendt adapts from Tocqueville's reading of Montesquieu.[29] But Arendt's creative appropriation considers the importance of intermediary institutions in terms of practices and relations of mediation. And rather than be tied to fixed social stations, as were the nobles of Montesquieu's day, Arendt's elites are self-selecting, public-spirited citizens who rule no one but work in organized minorities and voluntary associations of all sorts to further democratic ideals by mediating the forces of centralization and hierarchy. These elites act to invigorate but not replace mass democratic politics and representative institutions, acting as a kind of supplement to constituted government so that democratic ideals do not ossify. They also break up the oligarchic tendencies of mass society by acting in "elementary republics" or partial publics. In effect, Arendt suggests that we ought to view these organized minorities as supplemental sovereigns perpetually enacting something like the Lockean "horizontal version of the social contract"—in which the people are bound to one another with one another by their promises to constitutional fidelity—prior to the vertical contract they then make with a sovereign (popular or otherwise).[30]

Importantly, Arendt takes care to distinguish civil disobedience from conscientious objection, stressing both the explicitly countermajoritarian and group-oriented nature of this kind of action-in-concert: "The civil disobedient, though he is usually dissenting from a majority, acts in the name and for the sake of a group; he defies the law and the established authorities on the ground of basic dissent, and not because he as an individual wishes to make an exception for himself and get away with it."[31] In fact, Arendt goes further, and claims "that civil disobedients are nothing but the latest form of voluntary association" which means that "they are thus quite in tune with the oldest traditions of the country"[32]—that is, they are a part of the spirit of the law:

> Ever since the Mayflower Compact was drafted and signed under a different kind of emergency, voluntary associations have been the specifically American remedy for the failure of institutions, the unreliability of men, and the uncertain nature of the future . . . . [T]his republic, despite the great turmoil of change and of failure through which it is going at present, may still be in possession of its traditional instruments for facing the future with some measure of confidence.[33]

By linking civil disobedience to voluntary associations, and associational life to the spirit of the law, Arendt renders dissent essential to the very preservation of our constitutional framework. Such unruly reverence prevents the ossification of the law, heading off stasis by adapting the letter of the law to the needs of the day, thus protecting its spirit.

It is this notion that leads Arendt to celebrate civil disobedience not only as a remedy to potential failures of judicial review, but also as a politically enacted mechanism of amendment, and an ongoing process of constitutional interpretation. Civil disobedience, on her account, allows us to augment and restore our constitutional tradition at the same time. Here and elsewhere, Arendt thus invokes the Roman term *augere*, which is a form of constitutional maintenance—even restoration—*and* of change. In some sense we inherit, but in another we invent. Most importantly, it is this ongoing process of amendment or augmentation that ensures the very stability of the structure of the constitution and wards off the excesses of revolution. Thus, the very limits of the constitutional framework *must* be continuously contested through intermediary institutions, voluntary associations, civil disobedience, and other partial publics: not in order to *disrupt* the framework, but paradoxically, to preserve the space in which plurality might thrive. As Arendt was fond of saying (quoting René Char): "*Notre heritage n'est precédé d'aucun testament.*"

Finally, for Arendt, as for Montesquieu, the concept of the "spirit of the laws" provides a way to critique the letter of the positive law, without recurring to natural legal foundations. It also moves us away from originalist accounts in which the ultimate grounds of legitimacy are sought in a founding act that reflects the unified, sovereign will of a homogeneous people. In effect, Arendt does a kind of end-run around Rousseau, recovering from Montesquieu a model of citizenship that abjures sovereign *grounds* for legitimacy in favor of ongoing, open-ended processes of democratic legitimation. This also gives us another way to think about the aforementioned "paradox of constitutional democracy." For Arendt, the rule of law and democracy are not conflicting but rather mutually constitutive principles (put another way, constituent power and constituted governance happen together). Constitutionalism is thus not a static set of institutional constraints, but, rather, a dynamic set of contestable practices.

Facing: The Hannah Arendt Library at Bard College. Photo, Serena Randolph. Courtesy of the Hannah Arendt Collection, Stevenson Library, Bard College.

TRANSCENDENTAL DOCTRINE OF ELEMENTS

FIRST PART

TRANSCENDENTAL AESTHETIC

§ I[1]

IN whatever manner and by whatever means a mode of knowledge[2] may relate to objects, *intuition* is that through which it is in immediate relation to them, and to which all thought as a means is directed. But intuition takes place only in so far as the object is given to us. This again is only possible, to man at least,[3] in so far as the mind is affected in a certain way. The capacity (receptivity) for receiving representations through the mode in which we are affected by objects, is entitled *sensibility*. Objects are *given* to us by means of sensibility, and it alone yields us *intuitions*; they are *thought* through the understanding, and from the understanding arise *concepts*. But all thought must, directly or indirectly, by way of certain characters,[4] relate ultimately to intuitions, and therefore, with us, to sensibility, because in no other way can an object be given to us.

The effect of an object upon the faculty of representation, so far as we are affected by it, is *sensation*. That intuition which is in relation to the object through sensation, is entitled *empirical*. The undetermined object of an empirical intuition is entitled *appearance*.

That in the appearance which corresponds to sensation

---

[1] [In A the sub-sections are not numbered.]   [2] [*eine Erkenntnis.*]
[3] [*uns Menschen wenigstens* added in B.]
[4] [*vermittelst gewisser Merkmale* added in B. Cf. Kant's *Nachträge zur Kritik* (edited by B. Erdmann, 1881), xi: " if the representation is not in itself the cause of the object."]

Promising and Civil Disobedience

ARENDT'S POLITICAL MODERNISM

:: J. M. BERNSTEIN

Since this essay offers a dense sliver of a much longer exposition, let me begin by simply stating my conclusion. Premise: when she wrote *The Human Condition*, Hannah Arendt did not and could not have truly grasped the meaning of her own basic concepts: beginning, action, founding, principle, promise. Only when, in *On Revolution*, Arendt relocates her political theory from Greek antiquity into modernity can these emphatically modernist concepts and their corollaries take on their appropriate shapes: principles and promises are articulated through the idea of a founding constitution, and the notion of action as beginning, as bearer of novelty, becomes exemplified in revolution, and hence in acts that found a state. State-founding, however, is rare. And that rarity is the point. As Sheldon Wolin eloquently states the thesis:

> The loss of the political [which is the orienting experience governing Arendt's entire project] is a clue to its nature: it is a mode of experience rather than a comprehensive institution such as the state. The thing about experience is that we can lose it, and the thing about political experience is that we are always losing it, and having to recover it. The nature of the political is that it requires renewal. It is renewed not by unique deeds whose excellence sets some beings apart from others [Arendt's baroque fantasy synthesizing Homeric heroes with Greek democracy], but by rediscovering the common being of human beings.[1]

Wolin means these words to be a criticism of Arendt, but in fact they state precisely the content of her doctrine of civil disobedience.

Civil disobedience, I want to argue, reveals that the truth of revolutionary founding is always a re-founding. If action is essentially beginning, and

Facing: Page 65 of Hannah Arendt's heavily annotated copy of Immanuel Kant's *Critique of Pure Reason*. Above the section heading for the Transcendental Doctrine of Elements, Arendt lists four notes that are definitions or summaries of primary Kantian terms: "*Representation*: intuition a form of representation not vice versa!/*The affection itself is not yet representation./**Sensation = affection capable of representation/+Intuition instead of traditional terms (*Empfindung*) sensation." She also offers a number of cross references to other pages in the *Critique of Pure Reason* and to a quote from the *Prolegomena*: "An intuition is such a representation as immediately depends upon the presence of the object." Courtesy of the Hannah Arendt Collection, Stevenson Library, Bard College.

beginning is best exemplified by revolutionary founding, and founding finally is completed in the re-founding that is civil disobedience, then civil disobedience is the fulfillment of Arendt's political doctrine.[2] Civil disobedience as re-founding is renewing; it is the return of the new in its double conditionality: always dependent on the radical past it exceeds and the repressive present it repudiates; because so conditioned, it reveals the political as always failing (ready to be lost, again).

The idea that civil disobedience is a re-founding and renewal depends upon three distinct ideas. First, the form of sociality proper to us as beings who speak and act is promising. Promising, in all its Nietzschean hyperbole— "To breed an animal that is *permitted to promise*—isn't this the paradoxical task nature has for itself with regard to man? Isn't this the true problem *of man?*"[3]—forms the absolute center of Arendt's late political ontology, her account of how it is and what it means for us to be bound together in the mode of speaking and acting. Second, it is the kind of bonding that occurs through collective mutual promising—above all in the constitutional contract—that constitutes what Arendt means by power. Power is the proper name for the kind of social bond realized by a community of promisors. And third, the rational force of the principles, in Arendt's technical sense of that concept, under which those who commit civil disobedience act is analogous to the kind of force possessed by a modernist work of art. Kant calls it "exemplary validity"; in it the rational force and normative authority of an idea (concept, value, universal) is *revealed* through a particular act or work. This is what revolutionary action and constitution making share with modernist artworks; it is equally how founding and creating become capable of achieving authority and validity. On this account, the Constitution of the United States possesses exemplary validity, a validity dependent on its revolutionary emergence, that is reauthorized —and so our political being together is re-founded—in exemplary acts of civil disobedience. Since promising and exemplary validity are political morality and rationality as always conditioned, always contingent, always failing or falling or dissolving, hence always in need of renewal, then Arendt's political doctrine is unequivocally modernist. Political modernism arguably achieves a defining statement in Arendt's thought.[4]

The Power of Promising

What distinguishes Arendt's version of radical democracy from other, analogous accounts is the centrality she gives to the notion of founding, and in her account of founding the place she accords the American Constitution and constitution making generally. Founding is the most direct transcription of Arendt's conception of natality and beginning into a political, collective register. For Arendt we take responsibility for our presence in the world by acting; we take responsibility for the world itself, for all that is sedimented in the institutions and practices we inhabit, when we act to found a state. While we cannot literally make the world, we can fashion the boundaries of our being together and the terms of our encounter with one another in the world. Politics in part involves the collective taking responsibility for our being together in the world by fashioning the categorical forms of mutual belonging. Political founding is, at this level of analysis, the collective corollary of the existential fact of natality and the character of action to begin something: we say who *we* are in the institution of the principles joining us.

Surprisingly, perhaps, Arendt exemplifies the revolutionary act of founding with the American Constitution, and thereby in constitution making generally. For her a constitution is the act through which people constitute a government,[5] which is to say, it is the act through which they constitute themselves as *a* people with binding institutional rules regulating their life together. Hence constitution always possesses a double register for Arendt: it is the *act* through which a people constitutes itself as a people, and hence a performance of some kind; and it is the *object* of that act, what is constituted, hence the legal document, the laws, and institutions that are set in place in the light of that acting. It is the two-sidedness of constitution, political and legal, act and object, that is at the center of Arendt's version of constitutional democracy. Getting right how, even in principle, the existential urgency of founding can be carried through into everyday practice in all its legal and institutional trappings is the pressing issue bequeathed by constitution's essentially two-sided character. One can hear something of the existential pathos Arendt attributes to constitution in her approving quote of John Adams: "A constitution is a standard, a pillar, and a bond when it is understood, approved and beloved. But without this intelligence and attachment, it might as well be a kite or balloon, flying in the air."[6] We might say that the plausibility of Arendt's constitutional theory turns on her capacity to demonstrate exactly how we can and why we should understand, approve, and love the constitution in order that it can be a standard, pillar, and bond, so that its standing can be internally related to the regard it is accorded by citizens in a manner that adequately reflects the impetus of the founding act. Constitutions without constitutional patriotism, and the activities necessary to make such patriotism actual, are empty. They are kites or balloons. Constitutional patriotism, were it ever to exist, would be the political presence of the founding act, the existential gravity of founding, relayed into (quotidian) present practice.

Arendt begins to secure her idea of constitutional founding through a distinctive development of social contract theory. Arendt's route into contract theory emerges out of her understanding of promising, which, in the first instance, she considers from the perspective of neither politics nor morality, but, rather, as a component of her phenomenology of action as praxis. In *The Human Condition*, promising is posited as the remedy for the "chaotic uncertainty of the future"[7] since it speaks to our capacity to legislate our future actions in a way our fellows can count on; "I promise to be there every morning at six" suddenly gives our life together a predictability, a solidity, and a human form it could not otherwise have. Brute regularity can give the future a predictable visage, but with only the past as its support. Promising reaches out toward the future through the very gesture in which one individual reaches out toward her other; in the act of promising the *I* binds herself to her other to form a *we* whose future together the act of promising legislates. In promising, a we and an orderly future arise together.

For Arendt, promising along with forgiving are distinguished by being the only moral precepts that "arise . . . directly out of the will to live together with others in the mode of acting and speaking."[8] Promising is a potentiality of action in that promising is itself nothing other than an action. Promising is a disposing of one's future in the present in relation to one or more others; it occurs through the medium of a written or verbal act—for example, stating the words, "I promise." To promise is a performative utterance: the making of the utterance "I promise" is binding me to others by binding the future course of my will, undertaking now to do or forgo particular future actions.

Echoing the Nietzschean remarking of promising as what distinguishes humans from other animals, Arendt, in a rather remarkable passage, avers that without being bound to the fulfillment of promises, we would never be able to keep our identities: "We would be condemned to wander helplessly and without direction in the darkness of each man's lonely heart, caught in its contradictions and equivocalities—a darkness which only the light shed over the public realm through the presence of others, who confirm the identity between the one who promises and the one who fulfils, can dispel."[9] The negatives in this statement are significant for Arendt's account of promising. Arendt conceives of promising as about more than the problem of the unpredictability of human action and the consequent need to develop modes of mutual reliability and action coordination. Issues of reliability and action coordination ride on the back of the problem of human inwardness, the darkness of human motives and desires even or especially for agents themselves, and the corresponding fundamental indeterminacy of individual identity. If our deepest desires and motives are complex, equivocal, opaque and variable, then unless there were some other register for the determination of identity, the answer to the questions, "Who are you?" and "What did you mean in acting so?" addressed to each would have to be just as equivocal and contradictory as the torsions of psychic life itself. If psychic life is conceived this way—and even Kant assumed the fundamental opacity of the human heart—then promising does not and cannot be conceived of as a fundamental inflection of spontaneous human inwardness, a complex self-relation projected outward. Promising works from the outside in rather than from the inside out; promising is a mechanism for the *social* fashioning of the self, for public soul making, for a normative social construction of the self. In saying that promising is a form of action that depends on others, that its force arises directly out of the will to live together with others in the mode of speech and action, and that it confers identity upon the speaker, Arendt is ascribing to promising the status of being the paradigmatic form a social bond takes that resides firmly within the domain of sociality. For Arendt, promising is sociality itself; it is the exemplary revelation of the normative authority of speaking and acting as essentially social events, as events that acknowledge plurality and natality.

Promising for Arendt is thus not a mere intention, undertaking, commitment, or self-binding—all of which presume the logical priority of inwardness and psychological identity over social connection. On the contrary, and here is the crux of the matter, it is the opposite that is the case: the very ideas of intending, undertaking, committing, and binding oneself, as well as, following Nietzsche, all the collateral normative concepts—responsibility, obligation, duty, guilt, and conscience—are all either constituted through or structurally bound to the intrinsically linguistic institution of promising. Nietzsche's hard but simple thought is that we *learn* to keep promises by having the requirement to pay off our debts to others burned into our memory through cruel and painful regimes of training and punishment.[10] The point of Nietzsche's account is not to deny that there is a psychology of promising; it is to claim that this psychology is the shadow of being held to account by others, and that such being held to account has it locus in behaviors that only afterward secrete the appropriate dispositions and moral psychology. Only by being made accountable—only by being made time and again to behave outwardly as we promised to behave, and when failing to do so to be punished—do we learn to hold ourselves accountable; our self-relation thus, in fact, finally only an inflection of our irreducible relation to our others. In the case of promising, not only is its psychology a consequence of social training, but the moral psychology it generates also remains a shadow of social practice.

So much is evident in the physiognomy of the concept. The force of promising does not depend on any "inner" psychological state, say, promising in my heart, but on my word being my bond irrespective of my heart. This is why excuses, which routinely apply to actions, do not apply to promises: we cannot have promised accidentally or inadvertently or unknowingly or by mistake, our words belying or falsely transcribing an opposing inner state. Crossing my fingers behind my back as I say "I promise" does not nullify or empty or prohibit the promise from meaning just what its wording says; at most, my inner duplicity simply sets my inner self against my public self, where that inner self is just what the public act of promising has evacuated of authority—that evacuation is in part the point of the public act. *Saying* the words "I promise" abruptly places me in an emphatic spiritual relation to my speaking partner: I am bound to her by my future being bound to her. Promising words, by so binding and bonding, stake the self, hence lend that self an imposing moral stature and standing. Promising lifts me out of the equivocalities of my heart into a space I share with others. Hence, if my word is my bond, and it is that which gives to promising its terrifying character, its character of locating me, presenting me in a social relation to others over which I am no longer free to dispose of as I please, that is, my words place me socially with respect to others in a manner necessarily exceeding my accompanying desires or willings (since their spiritual urgency is formed by the normative import of the words), then if I forfeit my bond, I forfeit myself, become hollow, unworthy, lose face and standing.

Of course, not all promises are momentous ("I promise to take out the garbage"), or difficult to keep, or of a kind where failing them is failing one's place in the world. But promises can be all that, and when they are, this is because "since no word is really mine to dispose of as I wish . . . what I forfeit is language itself. . . . Forfeiting my word when my word is my bond would be like forfeiting my body."[11] This, from Stanley Cavell, sounds exorbitant, but is plainly entailed: If promising bestows upon me a public identity in relation to others, then forfeiting a promise is forfeiting that identity (myself for others). If I have that identity in the light of the words I speak, then as promisor I am bound to the life of those words; when I forfeit my bond, I forfeit not my word here, but my standing as a speaker: having failed that promise, my words no longer have the power of binding. Since my words are my spiritual presence for others, when my words no longer bind and bond, then I no longer possess a spiritual presence for others. Hence, forfeiting my word when my word is my bond is like forfeiting my body—it is forfeiting my linguistic-spiritual body, which is my public spiritual presence for others.

The spiritual content of promising depends on the kind of institution it is, its way of binding us to others and a future which thereby, if the institution is to flourish and mean in the ways its lineaments project, solicits subjects for whom saying, "My word is my bond," becomes something fateful for them and all those they address. In *The Human Condition*, promising appears as, for the most part, simply the moral precept intrinsic to the life of action, saving us from the predicament of unpredictability. Yet, the implicit subtext of her brief remarks gives to Arendt's account the wider compass I am suggesting, one that becomes thematic in *On Revolution*. What is at stake in promising, what makes it an exemplary institution, especially for us moderns, is its revelation of the power, authority, stakes, and potentialities embedded in the mere fact of our speaking and acting together. Promising exemplifies the spiritual density of speaking and acting together. Cavell (whose Austin-inspired account I have been drawing on) eloquently states the thesis: "The price of having spoken, or remarked, taken something as remarkable . . . is to have spoken forever, to have entered into the arena of the inexcusable, to have taken on the responsibility for speaking further, the unending responsibility of responsiveness, of answerability, to make yourself intelligible."[12] In Arendt this thought comes with a Nietzschean pedigree, but its salience is the same: *speaking with others is to promise*. There is, she maintains, a stratum or dimension of all speaking that contains a promissory, non-instrumental aspect. If each saying comes with, at least, a small bundle of presuppositions and entailments, then in speaking with others we become responsible for those presuppositions and entailments. It is no accident that we spontaneously apologize for misinformation, for being misleading about plans and intentions, for speaking without sufficient evidence, for lack of clarity or precision, for rambling or for mumbling. We apologize because we hold ourselves accountable to others for these things as what speaking with them involves. While it might be tempting to suppose that there are independent norms here, as Jürgen Habermas does,[13] the Arendt/Nietzsche claim is that such norms would be utterly idle unless we were essentially implicated in their having force; the beauty of the promissory interpretation of these moral ideas is that being bound to others is not the happy upshot of possessing moral ideas but their practical, social origin. The binding power of promising is hence the power invested in the space of appearances, our appearing to one another in the modes of speaking and acting.

For Arendt, it is mutual promising, not justice, which is to be the bond of political community. Promising is "higher than justice" because it is the condition for it. The force of the claims of social justice is, at least in part, parasitic upon mutual promising because, in a secular world, no idea or norm can be politically authoritative unless it derives from our collective deliberation. But the authority of our collectively deliberating derives from how we are bound together as a deliberating body. The substance of that body is formed by our speaking and acting having a promissory status: we are bound together as a community of promisors, and hence *our* word is *our* bond. This is the fundamental source of Arendt's anti-moralism; morality is too individualistic, too private, too bound to the whims of conscience, to be an adequate basis for collective living.[14]

Power is the bond formed through speaking and acting together. Arendt was continually struck by instances in which the difference between power and violence became manifest, when power overpowers or at least challenges those in possession of the means of violence: the colonists against the English, Gandhi's campaign against the British, the Hungarian revolution, the Vietnamese against the Americans, the civil rights movement, and so on. Where traditional theory is premised on the difference between might and right, Arendt focuses on the less common but phenomenologically equally evident difference between power and violence. A good deal of the import of Arendt's distinction depends on the fact that unlike the idealist fact/value duality, power and violence have been conflated with one another, and, at least on the surface, appear to belong to the same semantic family. Power, which is the ability to act in concert, has five distinguishing aspects: (1) power possesses normative legitimacy in opposition to the sheer capacity for destruction in the means of violence (the single area of direct overlap with the tradition); (2) power is the possession of a collective, it is what *emerges* in acting and speaking together; power is an emergent property that comes into being through speaking and acting together; which is why, (3), in cases of power, unlike the means of violence where one with sufficient means can overcome the many no matter how powerful, numbers matter; (4) power is the source

of authority, it is what gives authority—the capacity to be obeyed unreflec-
tively—to governments and leaders; (5) power is a kind of strength, the kind
that emerges from the first three items, the kind that becomes manifest in
the bonding of promising.

Arendt's resistance to considering politics as for the sake of social justice
is routinely misunderstood. Her fundamental objection to the moralizing of
the political is that it instrumentalizes our very being together as an irreduc-
ibly political community, a community formed through speaking and acting.
Making social justice the constitutive end of political community makes political community for the sake of something that exists independently of it,
hence operates a vicious act of self-instrumentalization. It is this viciousness
that Arendt detects in the Terror. For Arendt, the power created through mutual promising is thus best construed as the replacement for the Aristotelian
doctrine of friendship as the antecedent to and surplus beyond justice that is
the fundament of political community. Arendt says this explicitly. Power like
peace is an end in itself. To say this is not to deny

> that governments pursue policies and employ their power to achieve pre-
> scribed goals. But the power structure itself precedes and outlasts all aims,
> so that power, far from being the means to an end, is actually the very condi-
> tion enabling a group of people to think and act in terms of the means-ends
> category. . . . And since government is essentially organized and institution-
> alized power, the current question What is the end of government? does not
> make much sense.[15]

Arendt's first stretch of argument against means-ends rationality and the te-
leological, work model of action reaches its conclusion in her conception of
power as the end in itself specific to human sociality. Government is not for
the sake of anything because it has power as its fundamental condition of possibility. Since power is the emergent property of speaking and acting in their
promissory modes, then power and the experience of power are the existential
excess accompanying all merely non-instrumental collective action.

Because power is the necessary condition for the possibility of government, it most emphatically displays itself when the very possibility of government is at issue: in revolution and in founding. Here is the sentence that
has been orienting my discussion up until now: "The grammar of action: that
action is the only human faculty that demands a plurality of men; and the syn-
tax of power: that power is the only human attribute which applies solely to
the worldly in-between space by which men are mutually related, combine in
the act of foundation by virtue of the making and keeping of promises, which,
in the realm of politics, may well be the highest human faculty."[16] The act of
foundation is the institution of power, the creation of a particular social bond
that occurs through an explicit effort of mutual promising.

There is one further aspect to founding: the *content* of the mutual promise. Arendt contends that "the absolute from which the beginning is to derive its own validity . . . is the principle which, together with it, makes its appearance in the world . . . . [T]he principle inspires the deeds that are to follow and remains apparent as long as the action lasts."[17] Principle, in modernity, becomes equivalent to the content of the mutual promise of founding, that is, principle is no longer some antique idea (honor or excellence or love of equality), but the constitution itself. The founding promise has as its content the terms that are to regulate and govern the community formed through it.

The constitution is awesome because it is itself both a promise and the demanding terms of living a life based on nothing but mutual promising with others; the constitution is the promise to live a life with others in accordance with the norms implied by the very idea that community is fundamentally the life of a being that makes promises. Hence, on Arendt's reading, the constitution is the final making explicit of the whole series of implicit promissory relations upon which normatively governed sociality is premised: if promising is the making explicit the implicit promissory character of all speaking and acting together, then the constitution is itself the social mechanism through which that making explicit of promising becomes explicitly the terms of our life together. In brief, a constitution is the institutional elaboration and reflective enunciation of what it is to be a being who can keep promises and hence can organize a form of life normatively grounded in our capacity to speak and act together. And, again, since it is through promising that we attain a social and normative identity in our being with others, then the constitution, its creation/consolidation/acknowledgment/making explicit of our standing as a community of promisors, is the mechanism through which we attain an ongoing normative identity with respect to one another. We call this identity being a citizen. While citizenship is, formally, the bestowal on an individual of the battery of rights and duties that make her one of us, *being a citizen* is the social identity in which possessing those rights and duties is taken as becoming responsible for the form of living together projected by them. Being a citizen is the promise to all other citizens to uphold the founding promise through which we all have become politically united. This is the fundamental reason for Arendt's fierce opposition to liberalism, and her equally fierce fidelity to civic republicanism: constitution making as a form of promising necessarily leaves the private individual behind. To make a constitutional promise is to become a citizen for oneself and for others; one's political responsibilities and entitlements flow from one's identity as a citizen—one's identity as, essentially, a promisor.

This still leaves unanswered the question of what, apart from being the content of a mutual promise, is the status of the principles and practices announced in the constitution? If political community is not reducible to moral community, is not grounded in a priori moral norms, then what validity can its founding principles possess? Of course, there is a deep constraint on these principles: they must be compatible with the very idea of regulating our life together based on an act of mutual promising; hence, again, in part, the constitution has for its contents the formal specification of what it means, what is to be involved in living a life together premised only on the promise to live a life according to mutual promising. But such specifications, for instance, that there shall be three branches of government, cannot be deduced from the idea of mutual promising itself as the ground of our life together. To draw on the conceptuality Arendt will later find in Kant's aesthetics, principles in *On Revolution* possess an *exemplary validity*. In modernity, art is the domain in which there occurs a thematizing of the new, of the human power for fashioning authoritative, novel unique particulars, items whose worth is not dependent on falling under an antecedent concept or norm. Kant develops the idea of exemplary validity in order to explain how this is possible. How is it possible for an item that is not the product of an antecedent concept or idea to make original sense, create a new universal? Artworks are items for which no rule can be found but that nonetheless themselves serve "as a standard or rule for estimating."[18] Artworks are hence paradigmatically what principles are for Arendt: a rule or standard or norm or value that becomes manifest in a concrete empirical item, and through that manifestation legislative for both itself and what might follow. The litmus test for exemplarity, what demonstrates that an item has that authority, is succession, that is, the production of further instances that do not imitate (as constitutional originalism would have it) but rather "create from the same sources out of which the former himself created, and to learn from one's predecessor only the way to proceed in such creation oneself."[19]

The burden of modernity, and hence the continuing insistence of Arendt's modernism, turns on the discovery that in the realm of human affairs the only kind of authority that principles (norms, standards, values) may have is exemplary validity. To say that the kind of authority the constitution is to possess is that commensurate with the Preamble to the Declaration of Independence in which the contents are bracketed within the mutual promise that forms it—"We *hold* these truths"—is to make the authority of the principles that follow exemplary. This is to say two things. First, the manner in which the U.S. Constitution itself appears, its contents, needs to be seen as analogous to the way in which a work of art appears. The Constitution is a particular; its contents need to be understood as both rules and a blueprint for government, and as the disclosure of the world in which such a notion of government can be received and have an impact. Like artworks, constitutions create their audience by creating the terms for their own reception; they create the terms for the latter by projecting a world in which those terms form the categorial conditions of possibility of both that world and its ideal inhabitants: state and citizen. Beginnings are the beginning of a world, are world making. But the authority of that world making is the reconfiguring of the known world in the light of its projected shape. Hence, the constitution is an item in the world that means to re-describe the world, give it a new look and appearance.

Second, what Kant calls "succession," Arendt thinks in terms of amendment and augmentation: "the very authority of the American Constitution resides in its inherent capacity to be amended and augmented."[20] What Arendt is crediting to the American Constitution, albeit with a retrospective glance, is the recognition that its validity rests on the only kind of authority available under conditions of modernity. Call it revolutionary authority. Revolutions typically fail, Arendt avers, because they seek to make absolute their founding moment. The genius of the American Revolution was the recognition that it formed *a* beginning, not the beginning, and that any beginning is only *a* beginning, hence contingent, hence in continual need of preservation, augmentation, and amendment.

Now, if legitimate authority is essentially revolutionary authority because only it sufficiently acknowledges the absence of absolute foundations, the insufficiency of traditional authority, the contingency of the social bonds binding us one to another, and the necessity of a moment of self-binding in any social bonding, if founding is thus the paradigmatic political moment, then what happens *after*? In *On Revolution*, what gives Arendt's account a suspect utopian cast is her supposition that the current state of affairs is deficient for lack of an appropriate commitment to a pyramidal ward or council system. But what such a system amounts to in Arendt's thought is the continual dissolution of the *poesis* of democratic *praxis* back into itself, as if each moment of democratic politics could draw the contents created, with their inevitable *durée*, back into the act of their creation, and hence become the simultaneous realization of its three temporally dispersed aspects (founding, empirically continuing, re-founding). So in dissolving the gap between founding and continuing, every moment of American democratic life would have the solidity, urgency, and authority of the original founding. For whatever the reason, in *On Revolution* Arendt still had the idea of an ideal polity—as represented by an idealized construction of the American Revolution—against which contemporary reality might be measured. In so doing, she in fact robs her theory of its modernism, and hence of its intrinsic radicalism.

It is just this theft that she comes to recognize in "Civil Disobedience." The fact of the fabrication of government and state in all their institutional and bureaucratic complexity and density, which (ideally) is the product of every founding, entails that the everyday life of a modern representative democracy will inevitably over time detach power from the people and rigidify exemplary validity into habit, command, and coercion. Call this the tendency toward totalitarian tyranny—the rule of no one—built into every modern, large-scale bureaucratic institution. Bureaucratic rationalization is the "natural" way modern democratic institutions fail and political experience is lost.

In a quiet piece of self-criticism, Arendt agrees that while the Lockean conception of the social contract, in which people contract with one another, is a legal and historical fiction, she is now minded to argue that it is not an existential or theoretical fiction. Further, for the first time, Arendt acknowledges that social contract theory *implies* a notion of consent. Hence, her question becomes: how can we align the role of consent with the promissory understanding of contract? She begins with the obvious assumption of social contract theory, namely, that tacit consent is given by birth since we are necessarily dependent on society for having a life at all. But tacit consent is hardly voluntary since, again, it derives from a situation of dependency. In acknowledging unsurpassable social dependency, Arendt is for the first time acknowledging the empirical reality internally conditioning, everywhere and always, political life itself. There is no absolute "outside" to the necessities of the body, to economic necessities, to the thick institutional and personal dependencies constituting nonpolitical social life. Political life does not emerge after our life of mutual dependency is settled, which is the fantasy of *The Human Condition*, nor when the life of mutual dependency is not urgent or pressing, the fantasy of *On Revolution*, but rather from *within* a world always already constituted by dependencies—natural, social, historical, and political. What this means is that the tacit consent we must give to the laws and norms governing our everyday lives, the consent entailed by our participation in and benefiting from life in a representative democracy, while truly a form of consent, does not on its own match the terms for legitimacy represented by the existential and theoretical truth of contract theory. In this situation, consent can become truly voluntary if and only if we have the power of dissent (the power of voice and exit). Dissent implies consent. So dissent keeps consent alive, giving it back its actuality.[21] However, our consent is not to statutory laws but to the constitutional settlement (and only thereby to routine laws). In binding ourselves to the Constitution, we leave ourselves free to dissent from particular laws.

In making dissent the cornerstone of her theory for consent, Arendt is doing nothing more than making explicit what is already implicit in her revolutionary theory. Because she was absorbed by the ideas of actions as beginnings, with founding as the primary political moment, and with mutual promising as the formative act in that founding, Arendt had previously downplayed the significance of the fact that revolutions are, in the first instance, acts of dissent and rebellion, acts of negation and transgression, acts of saying "No!" If consent is bound to the moment of founding, then *every act of consent presupposes a dissent made good*. Actual consenting includes the potential for dissent, and actual dissent becomes the central mechanism through which tacit consent can become actual, appear, and become explicit. Said differently, if all founding is only a beginning and not the beginning, then authentic founding entails re-founding. Re-founding is the *truth* of founding; it is, to use Kant's language, to create anew out of the same sources from which the original emerged; in

augmenting the original founding, it reveals that founding as authoritative—
as if for the first time.

Because "active support" for the constitutional settlement cannot be fully
or adequately provided by the ordinary mechanisms of a representative democracy, and because the everyday world of such a democracy involves the
congealing of power in government in opposition to the people whose power
it is, then the paradigmatic mechanism for re-founding, for the dissent proper
to democratic consent, becomes civil disobedience. As she describes it, civil
disobedience is the central mechanism for re-founding, for augmentation and
amendment in the ordinary world of constitutional democracies. Civil disobedience always concerns the constitutional order itself, referring to either its
augmentation or its restoration. Although dissenting from the majority, the
disobedient one "defies the law and established authorities on the ground of
basic dissent,"[22] that is, as a citizen; because civil disobedience is the work of
citizen dissent, then it is the work of a minority standing in for a presently
absent constitutional majority.

If this is correct, then civil disobedience involves, precisely, the two defining features of revolutionary authority: first, those who commit civil disobedience are a community bound together by "common opinion"[23] rather than
common interest; they are an essentially political community bound together
in the mode of speech and action in opposition to government. This is why,
when effective or nearly so, such groups appear powerful. But, second, their
power cannot derive solely from the form of their communal binding. It is in
acts of civil disobedience that the characterization offered earlier concerning the disclosure of principles becomes most evident. Acts of civil disobedience are efforts of both political argument and world-disclosure, that is, again,
the revelation of the world in which the argument is to have its place. Civil
disobedience is theatrical in that it always involves the revelation of a scene
where the absent majority becomes visible in or through the dissenting minority voicing the polemical principle unheeded by the actual majority. Civil
disobedience is the materialization of the power of the people under the sign
of the (constitutional) principle currently flouted by government, the principle (of equality, of justice, of law) necessary for governmental legitimacy.[24] For
Arendt, civil disobedience and revolution are structurally the same; civil disobedience is thus the analogue of revolutionary founding that occurs within
the ordinary world of representative, constitutional democracies.

PART IV

Evil and *Eichmann in Jerusalem*

(handwritten notes — partly legible)

Left page

Industrial canon in 1930 followed by ulterior aid;
the first was things in reason by and the others allies,
the latter by slaughter — notably China where the
alliance with Chiang Kai-shek was followed by Canton
rising — explained in relation from ?: the Westerners
because he did not believe in "neutralist"; he
served because he had to "conform". — 401 ff.

(Stalin's fear of a successful revolution)
                                                S. 414
405/06: he saw no explicit left for doubters,
who thereupon assumes simple neglect.

The rising in March 523

The value of the book predicated until the trials —
consequently taking up to them of imponderable use —
if Stalin should have falled the arguments. The
others still alive in their understanding made
even to fake historically real.

Doubters' fear to be like those who reacted to the
Terror — and overestimated it — of the French
Revolution.
The prediction or the framework of the past.

Doubters' "sense": "to drive barbarism out of
Russia by barbarous means" — that the concept of
justified opposition. 568
Characteristically: denounces ... 's cunning and de-
plores spiritual degeneration and economic non-
sense — Does not mention the persecutions.
                        567/565
Murder and inadequate field of mind experience —

Right page

The Rostovsky - big bolyy -
Stalin's "sadism": is lack of guilt, inferiority feeling
and resentment.

"The Domination of the World ..."
Hazard of promotion: 112
Stalin's last steps to rule: 214
Early "sentimentalism" 178 ff

faith of Johns Wallace 189

Stalin's "realism" — approval of doubter's
past. Dominion of occupying etc.

The persecution of everything: origin of the
law cases — 137. origin of the purges —
Everything becomes an instrument of police.
                Exp.
The Rostollincton all the Russia Rev. preceded by
the Russia distillation about a Cr. Revolt.
Real trying: career of Stalin — 215

Why should the table on p. 203 be authentic ? ?

Turn to Totalitarianism: 10 "conquer of thee
the Kronstadt rising —
This is one of the most peculiar settings in the book:
for us Stalin !

Stalin's implicit guide: is it possible that different parties typed
                        393
him peculiar with all Trotsky in the early struggle ?
                        395
"honour or gold" — legend of the Revolution 387

Is Evil Banal?
A Misleading Question

RICHARD J. BERNSTEIN

I have been asked to address the question "Is evil banal?" I am going to be confrontational because I think that this question is badly formulated. This is the type of question that invites serious misinterpretations of Arendt. I find the question objectionable for three reasons. First, the question suggests that Arendt has a general *theory* or thesis about the nature of evil. This is absolutely false. Over and over again she insisted that she was not proposing a general *theory* when she spoke about the banality of evil. She was calling attention to a factual phenomenon that she observed at the trial of Adolf Eichmann in Jerusalem. Second, the question obscures the most important aspect of Arendt's thinking about evil. From the time that she discovered what was happening in the Nazi death camps—especially Auschwitz—until her death, she sought on a number of occasions to comprehend what was distinctive about Nazi evil. One needs to follow the twists and turns of her thinking to appreciate fully her subtle and complex reflections on evil. Third, the question obscures a distinction that is crucial for Arendt—the distinction between the doer and the deeds. "The banality of evil" describes the character and motivations of the doer (Eichmann), not his deeds—the monstrous actions that he committed, and for which he was fully responsible. She categorically rejected the "cog" theory—that Eichmann was simply a cog in a complex machine. Remember, she supported the court's decision to hang Eichmann. The suggestion—still quite common—that Arendt was trivializing the evil of the Shoah by speaking about Eichmann's banality is a slander.

To justify my critical remarks, one has to say a few words about Arendt as a thinker. The metaphor that best characterizes Arendt's style of thinking is "thought trains."[1] She was not a theoretician who proposed general and comprehensive theories. She pursued different thought trains; sometimes these intertwine and reinforce each other, and sometimes they conflict and even contradict each other. She was an independent thinker (*Selbstdenker*); she did

Facing: Hannah Arendt's notes on the front endpaper of her heavily annotated copy of Isaac Deutscher's *Stalin: A Political Biography.* These notes highlight Arendt's practice of intense engagement with a text by outlining and indexing the major themes on the front or back endpapers. The notes are in pencil and difficult to decipher, but they highlight sections in which Deutscher discusses his own Bolshevik past and suggest that Arendt thinks he excuses the Communists unduly for the turn to totalitarianism. Courtesy of the Hannah Arendt Collection, Stevenson Library, Bard College.

not follow fashions or schools of thought. This is why she is still so thought-provoking—she makes us think. On any topic that she discusses—whether it is action, politics, freedom, or evil—there are various *strands* in her thinking that need to be carefully discriminated. This is emphatically true of her reflections on evil.

If we turn to *The Origins of Totalitarianism*, we discover that she initially characterized Nazi evil as *absolute* or *radical* evil. And by radical evil, she means the evil of making human beings superfluous as human beings:

> Difficult as it is to conceive of an absolute evil even in the face of its factual existence, it seems to be closely connected with the intention of a system in which all men are equally superfluous. The manipulators of this system believe in their own superfluousness as much as that of all others, and the totalitarian murderers are all the more dangerous because they do not care if they themselves are alive or dead, if they ever lived or never were born. The danger of the corpse factories and holes of oblivion is that today, with populations and homelessness everywhere on the increase, masses of people are continuously rendered superfluous if we continue to think of our world in utilitarian terms.[2]

Arendt claimed that the concentration and death camps served as "laboratories" for the Nazis: "The camps are meant not only to exterminate people and degrade human beings, but also to serve the ghastly experiment of eliminating, under scientifically controlled conditions, spontaneity itself as an expression of human behavior and transforming the human personality into a mere thing, into something that even animals are not."[3] Arendt subsequently questioned whether what she was describing should be called "radical evil," because "radical" (referring to the root) suggests that there is something deep about evil. She came to think that evil is always on the surface. "It can overgrow and lay waste the whole world precisely because it spreads like a fungus on the surface."[4] But she never rejected her claim that making human beings superfluous as human beings is evil—transforming them into something that is less than human.[5]

I want to focus on the phrase the "banality of evil" because it is still badly misinterpreted. The expression "the banality of evil" appears only once—in the final sentence of her report (just before her epilogue). Arendt comments on "the grotesque silliness" of Eichmann's final words before being hanged. Eichmann is reported to have said: "After a short while, gentlemen, *we shall all meet again*. Such is the fate of all men. Long live Germany, long live Argentina, long live Austria. *I shall not forget them*." This is Arendt's comment:

> In the face of death, he had found the cliché used in funeral oratory. Under the gallows, his memory played him the last trick; he was "elated" and he forgot that this was his own funeral.

It was as though in those last minutes he was summing up the lesson that this long course in human wickedness had taught us—the lesson of the fearsome, word-and-thought-defying *banality of evil*.[6]

That's it! There is no further commentary or explanation of what she means by the phrase "the banality of evil." When her critics attacked her, she declared, "When I speak of the banality of evil, I do so only on the strictly factual level, pointing to a phenomenon which stared one in the face at the trial."[7]

One of the clearest statements of what she means by the banality of evil appears in a lecture that she gave in 1971, "Thinking and Moral Considerations":

> Some years ago, reporting the trial of Eichmann in Jerusalem, I spoke of the "banality of evil" and meant with this no theory or doctrine but something quite factual, the phenomenon of evil deeds, committed on a gigantic scale, which could not be traced to any particularity of wickedness, pathology, or ideological conviction in the doer, whose only personal distinction was perhaps an extraordinary shallowness. However monstrous the deeds were, the doer was neither monstrous nor demonic, and the only specific characteristic one could detect in his past as well as in his behavior during the trial and the preceding police examination was something entirely negative: it was not stupidity but a curious, quite authentic inability to think.[8]

The striking feature about this passage is the sharp distinction that Arendt makes between the *doer* and the *deeds*. The deeds are monstrous, but the doer (Eichmann) is *not* a monster; he is "terrifyingly normal." He was so caught up in clichés and the Nazi "rules of language" that he lacked the ability to think—to have the imagination to think in the place of other persons. It is almost as if Eichmann thought that his role in efficiently transporting persons to death camps had nothing to do with their final extermination. Arendt thought there was something sadly "comical" about Eichmann—the ruthlessly efficient "desk murderer."

Now, there are two basic questions that we can ask about Arendt's portrait of Eichmann. Is it historically accurate? Did she underestimate Eichmann's viciousness and ideological conviction? But even if we think that she did not get Eichmann "right," we can still ask: Is there something important about the concept of the banality of evil? Today, as a result of extensive historical research, we know a good deal more about Eichmann's history than Arendt knew. I believe that she tended to underestimate Eichmann's fanatical ideological commitment. Even when the Nazis knew that they were losing the war and Himmler wanted to slow the action of the death camps, Eichmann played an *active* role in sending more than 400,000 Hungarian Jews to their death in the spring and fall of 1944. I agree with the judgment of the distinguished historian of the Holocaust, Christopher Browning, when he writes: "I consider Arendt's concept of the 'banality of evil' a very important insight for understanding many of the perpetrators of the Holocaust, but not Eichmann himself. Arendt was fooled by Eichmann's strategy of self-representation in part because there were so many perpetrators of the kind he was pretending to be."[9] But I also want to quote the concluding remarks of David Cesarani, the author of the most comprehensive biography of Eichmann. Despite his many criticisms of Arendt, he comes remarkably close to Arendt's judgment:

> The *génocidaire* has become a common feature of humanity and to that extent Eichmann is typical rather than aberrant. This is not the same as saying that "we are all potential Eichmanns"; rather, that the matrices which generate the perpetrators of atrocity and genocide have multiplied. In these circumstances normal people can and do commit mass murder or engineer it."[10]

This is a statement that Arendt would surely have endorsed. But the *primary* issue is not whether "banality" is a correct description of the historical Eichmann. What is most important is that Arendt describes a *type* of person and a *type* of behavior that have become frightening and all too common in our time.

What I most admire about Arendt is her intellectual courage in taking on the toughest issues of our time. She had a strong sense that there has been a break in tradition, and the task of the thinker is to forge new concepts and categories to comprehend our times. She felt that many of the traditional ways of thinking about evil are no longer adequate for comprehending the evil that erupted with totalitarianism. We tend to demonize evildoers; they must be vicious—they are intrinsically evil. (Think of the way in which evil has been used as a polemical weapon since 9/11). But if one really wants to understand the evil of our time—or at least one of its most common and pernicious forms—then we have to understand how ordinary "normal" people can—without *thinking*—be caught up in committing or supporting monstrous evil deeds.

I believe that one of the fundamental reasons why *Eichmann in Jerusalem* stirred up so much controversy is because Arendt challenges our most entrenched (and comforting) ways of thinking about good and evil when we claim that perpetrators of evil deeds *must* be vicious sadistic monsters. In an interview that she gave after the publication of *Eichmann in Jerusalem*, she said; "As far as misunderstanding goes, the subtitle *On the Banality of Evil* really has been frequently misinterpreted. Nothing could be further from my mind than to trivialize the greatest catastrophe of our century." She goes on to say:

> As you know, there have been many attempts to trace National Socialism into the depths of Germany's and even Europe's intellectual past. I consider such attempts mistaken, and even pernicious, because they argue away the phenomenon's most conspicuous hallmark, this utter shallowness, that

something could be born in the gutter, and despite its lack of depth, can at the same time gain power over almost everyone, that is what makes the phenomenon so frightening.[11]

Susan Neiman sums up why *Eichmann in Jerusalem* is such an important contribution to understanding *one* of the faces of evil in our time—and why it is still so controversial:

> Auschwitz embodied evil that confuted two centuries of modern assumptions about intention.
>
> Those assumptions identify evil and evil intention so thoroughly that denying the latter is normally viewed as a way of denying the former. Where evil intention is absent, we may hold agents liable for the wrongs they inflict, but we view them as matters of criminal negligence. Alternatively, anyone who denies that criminal intention is present in a particular action is thought to exonerate the criminal. . . . The conviction that guilt requires malice and forethought led most readers to conclude that Arendt denied guilt because she denied malice and forethought—though she often repeated that Eichmann was guilty, and was convinced that he ought to hang. Her main point is that Eichmann's harmless intentions did not mitigate his responsibility.[12]

So what is "the banality of evil" all about? It is about something that is born in the gutter, something that has no depth, but is shallow; something that is thought-defying; something that has to do with the way in which "ordinary people" can commit evil deeds without being vicious monsters or even having evil intentions.

We still have not fully appreciated or assimilated Arendt's insights about the banality of evil. There is an enormous temptation to think about good and evil in the most simplistic and crass ways.[13] There are the good guys and bad guys, as in the old Hollywood movies about cowboys and Indians or *Star Wars*. And bad guys like Darth Vader really are "evil" to the core. They are vicious monsters who enjoy doing evil for its own sake. No one wants to deny that there are sadists and ideological fanatics. Arendt never denied this![14] But to speak about good and evil in this simplistic manner is not only inadequate for understanding evil in our contemporary world, but also it is dangerous. It is cynically used as a political weapon to obscure complex issues. This is no longer a satisfactory way to come to grips with the prevalence of *new* forms of evil that became manifest in the twentieth century and are still very much with us. We need to understand how ordinary people can be complicit with evil deeds, including genocide. And we also need to understand how political leaders and bureaucrats (who are not vicious monsters) can, by their actions, create an environment where it is all too easy to foster torture and humiliation.

One of the most disturbing remarks in *The Origins of Totalitarianism* is Arendt's claim at the end of her long study: "Totalitarian solutions may well survive the fall of totalitarian regimes in the form of strong temptations which will come up whenever it seems impossible to alleviate political, social, or economic misery in a manner worthy of man."[15] We are *not* living in a totalitarian society, but the temptation to appeal to "totalitarian solutions" is still very much with us. It should give us pause when we stop and think about how the policies of a presidential administration with its "clever" lawyers come up with Orwellian ways of redefining torture, circumventing the Geneva conventions and helping to create a climate in which the type of evil exemplified by Abu Ghraib can happen.

We still need to confront the phenomenon that Arendt identified as the banality of evil. And we still need to be alert to the ways in which evil "can overgrow and lay waste the whole world precisely because it spreads like a fungus on the surface."[16]

Facing: Book spines on the shelves of the Hannah Arendt Library at Bard College. Photo, Serena Randolph. Courtesy of the Hannah Arendt Collection, Stevenson Library, Bard College.

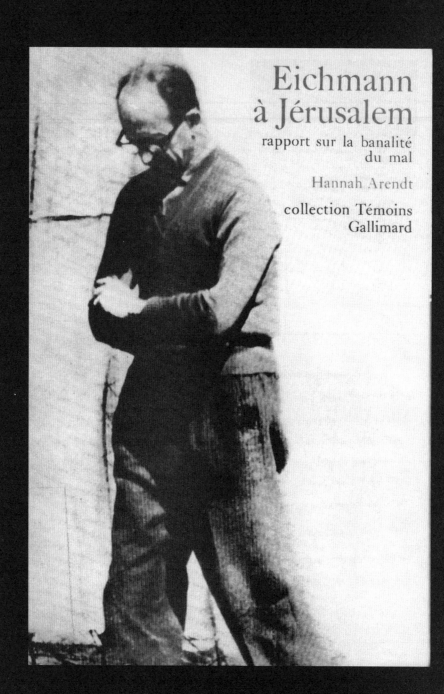

Eichmann
à Jérusalem

rapport sur la banalité
du mal

Hannah Arendt

collection Témoins
Gallimard

Banality and Cleverness

EICHMANN IN JERUSALEM REVISITED

P E T E R B A E H R

Hannah Arendt's famous argument in *Eichmann in Jerusalem* was that Eichmann was not a demon on a mission from Hell, but a crass, ludicrous, pathetic individual.[1] Faced with a media blitz that depicted him as the quintessence of perversion (how could so much evil be concentrated in one person, ran the mantralike refrain), Arendt wished to puncture such verbiage with a formula designed to show that very unremarkable people have often perpetrated the most despicable acts of modern times. Many disagree with Arendt's portrait of Eichmann, claiming that he was far more of an ideological antisemite than she realized. Others defend her, saying that, even if she were wrong specifically about Eichmann, her argument applies more generally. The point I wish to make here is rather different.

The expression "banality of evil" was destined for controversy, not least because it broke with key elements of the Judeo-Christian tradition and hence of Western civilization itself. Arendt did not want to clothe Nazis like Eichmann in the spurious grandeur of satanic greatness; yet ironically, if she had spoken of satanic *banality*, the expression, though infelicitous and strained, would at least have been historically closer to one current of that tradition. For the word Satan in early Hebrew discussion designated an obstructor; it was not a person's name, but rather a term to denote a role that a person played, or a function discharged, in God's scheme of things.[2] In the book of Job, for instance, Satan is the accuser (in Greek, *diabolos*), "one of the sons of God whose duty it is to test a person's faithfulness to God."[3] Only at a late stage of Hebrew thought, especially during the intertestamental period (c. 350 BC–AD 50), did Satan become identified with evil as such.[4] Secularized in such a way as to deprive Eichmann of God's imprimatur, such imagery could have approximated the man on trial in Jerusalem whose banality, one might say, blocked or obstructed his thought; and who became assimilated to his function as a functionary of the regime.

But Arendt spoke not about Satan, but about evil, and evil within the Judeo-Christian tradition has its roots in Persian dualism (to which the early Hebrews were exposed at the time of Exile), in which good is pitted against

Facing: Cover of Hannah Arendt's copy of the French edition of *Eichmann à Jérusalem*. Courtesy of the Hannah Arendt Collection, Stevenson Library, Bard College.

its radical antithesis. In Daniel, evil is compared to bestial forces; in Luke, it is the personification of wickedness confronting Jesus with temptation. Clearly, this is not a contest in which "banality," superficiality, and thoughtlessness have any evident place. On the contrary, evil is depicted as something radical, calculated and charged with immense metaphysical power, so that if Arendt had wanted to use the conjunction "banality of evil" persuasively, she would have needed to redefine evil itself—an unenviable task she was reluctant to attempt, but which she nonetheless falteringly did attempt when she came under attack from Gershom Scholem. In the *Origins of Totalitarianism*, Arendt had spoken about "radical evil" in a way, refracted through Kant, that was at least consistent with the tradition. Now, Scholem said, she seemed to be speaking of evil as "banal." The obvious, but still unsatisfactory, retort to this kind of objection was for Arendt to say that evil itself was not banal, but only the kind of evil personified by Eichmann—an interpretative lifejacket that Karl Jaspers threw out to her, though not before Arendt herself had responded to Scholem with the observation that evil is never radical, "that it is only extreme, and that it possesses neither depth nor any demonic dimension. It can overgrow and lay waste the whole world precisely because it spreads like a fungus on the surface. It is 'thought-defying,' as I said, because thought tries to reach some depth, to go to the roots, and the moment it concerns itself with evil, it is frustrated because there is nothing. That is its 'banality.' Only the good has depth and can be radical."[5] This vague and question-begging formulation strained credulity, and Jaspers, for one, told her so.[6]

Had Arendt not collapsed evil into banality or thoughtlessness, as she now seemed to do ("it is my opinion now that evil is never radical"), but simply confined her comments to their relationship ("the strange interdependence of thoughtlessness and evil"), she would have been on firmer ground. Her report would then have been on banality *and* evil rather than on the banality of evil. She would have been able to argue—as in fact she magnificently demonstrated—that shallowness could *under some circumstances* lead to evil. Scholem was also understandably perplexed at the shift between the notion of radical or absolute evil that Arendt had formulated in *Origins* (evil as the attempt, forged in the concentration and death camps, to make human beings superfluous, to transform, even destroy, their nature) and the new notion of evil as "thoughtlessness." Richard J. Bernstein argues, in this volume and elsewhere, that this was largely a shift of emphasis and that, if one takes Arendt's writings as a whole, including her later remarks on Eichmann in the introduction to *The Life of the Mind,* evil as rendering humans otiose and disposable is the dominant and overriding motif.[7] The point remains, however, that in the Eichmann report it is evil as banality that is highlighted. Though the phrase "banality of evil" is used only once in *Eichmann in Jerusalem*, it remained through multiple (and multilingual) editions the subtitle of the report. In addition, the emphasis on Eichmann as a crass, opportunistic, and cliché-dependent perpetrator of evil deeds is prominent throughout her discussion.[8]

We should also note that Arendt's banality argument was anticipated, at least in part, in *The Origins of Totalitarianism* itself. There she excoriated the "respectable philistines," the "job holders and good family men" who typified the "mass" man. The "characteristic personality" of this social species was "not a bohemian like Goebbels, or a sex criminal like Streicher or a crackpot like Rosenberg, or a fanatic like Hitler, or an adventurer like Göring." The mass man's epitome was Heinrich Himmler. At least it was Himmler who most shrewdly appreciated that the legions of killers he needed to organize wholesale extermination were people whose first priority was respectability and private interest. As Arendt remarked in one of the most acerbic passages of *Origins*:

> The philistine is the bourgeois isolated from his own class, the atomized individual who is produced by the breakdown of the bourgeois class itself. The mass man whom Himmler organized for the greatest crimes ever committed in history bore the features of the philistine rather than of the mob man, and was the bourgeois who in the midst of the ruins of his world worried about nothing so much as his private security, was ready to sacrifice everything—belief, honor, dignity—on the slightest provocation. Nothing proved easier to destroy than the privacy and private morality of people who thought of nothing but safeguarding their private lives.[9]

Still, between *Origins* and *Eichmann* a clear change of accent is apparent: evil as making people superfluous refers to *deeds* (of the SS), *institutions* (the death factory), and their *consequence* (extermination). Evil as thoughtlessness refers to the *barren inner world* of the *perpetrator*. This distinction emerges clearly in *Thinking*, the first volume of *The Life of the Mind*, where Arendt writes of the "manifest shallowness in the doer that made it impossible to trace the uncontestable evil of his deeds to any deeper level of roots or motives. The deeds were monstrous, but the doer—at least the very effective one now on trial—was quite ordinary, commonplace, and neither demonic nor monstrous." Arendt's hyphenated qualification ("at least the very effective one now on trial") appears to leave open the question of how other former Nazis were to be characterized. Would the banality of evil have been pertinent to, say, someone like Klaus Barbie, the Gestapo chief of Lyon, whose sadistic cruelty was proverbial and whose contempt for those he had tortured to death was evident at his own trial in 1987?[10]

The first concept of evil runs with the current of the tradition inasmuch as there is something metaphorically demonic about a project to make human beings superfluous, to try to change their nature, for in the tradition, human nature has been decided by God. (One does not have to couple this view with the contention that the killers were themselves demonic.) This explains why the simile of Hell is so often a device that Arendt employs whenever, in her early postwar work, she seeks to depict the monstrous nature of totalitarianism. But evil as "banality" remains an expression much more difficult to fathom for at least three reasons: first, because there is no integral relationship between the two concepts (that is, banal thought of itself is not evil); second, because the concept of evil seems largely redundant to explain Eichmann's inner world (banality would have done the job adequately enough); and third, because one of the richest normative terms of condemnation in our vocabulary has become obscured and diluted. At this juncture, it will be objected that I have completely missed the point, since the weight of Hannah Arendt's many arguments about totalitarianism fell on its unique character and its rupture with "the tradition." In that case, however, the concept of evil was a very blunt instrument to do the work Arendt intended, because evil is a salient part of the very tradition she believed had been superseded.[11]

Hannah Arendt's occasional descriptions of Eichmann as "normal" and "ordinary" were also unfortunate, though explicable when one understands what she meant by these terms. Arendt was fully aware that Eichmann's thoughtlessness was not normal in the sense of commonplace. Someone who shows virtually no capacity for reflection and the "dialogue of the mind" is not normal, even though such an individual may not be clinically insane. A bureaucrat who participates in mass murder is also not normal, because this is not what most bureaucrats or bureaucracies typically do, want to do, or are trained to do. An "idealist," in Eichmann's sense of a person who sacrifices everything for a conviction, is not normal, since most people are not fanatics. The *politically* significant sense in which Eichmann was normal was that, under the conditions extant in Germany during the Third Reich, he did what was expected of him; he was a conformist, a person in tune with the milieu in which he operated. To that extent, the Nazi regime had inverted our customary sense of what is normal and what is exceptional. To resist had been abnormal, while to be a compliant tool of genocide had become pedestrian.

George Orwell once criticized some of the intellectuals of his day for "silly cleverness." He was alluding to turns of phrase that are resonant but ultimately hollow or foolish. *Eichmann in Jerusalem* is a bracing "report," with a provocative argument. Arendt was a brilliant intellectual. "The banality of evil" is, however, an example of the silly cleverness that Orwell lamented.

Facing: Hannah Arendt and her husband, Heinrich Blücher, 1950s. Courtesy of the Hannah Arendt Blücher Literary Trust.

Sprache – 165 259 328 197 | Briefwechsel 220

Zionismus 44 153 189 222 314, 309

Paris 49 56 421 09 · 446

Kant 156 161

Bibliothek 153 9 . 198) 397 240 290 307 328 350
                358 374, (423 434
Palästina 208 213 . (242 (Hebr.) ´ 383
                        (248
                        (257
Folge 217 232   (455
                        (463
Welt-Familie 75, 206 221 236 238 235 241 296 !!
                170,
Zukunft 289 341 373 379 395 396 480 !!

Ernst Bloch 219 / 479 413

Deutsch 225 404 | Zitate 366

Ensslinger 252 | Hofmannsthal – 327

Depressionen 281

Buchlughs trimmler 255 258 300 302 315 380
                444
Zt. Einleitg. zum Trauerspiel 322-3

Zitate – 339 366

Kommunismus (1924) 355 382 425 ! 39 , 440 ,
                        344,
Sammler 366 381

Proust 412

Hegel 171

Baudelaire – 1915 ! – 1924 — 330

Hölderlin Hälfte – 1918 ! – 181

Trauer- Tragik 1918 ! – 182

Hofmannsthal Brief 329

Neue Beiträge – 331, 341, 457

Cii.

Quellenartikel – 419
     f. Russland

Judging the Events of Our Time

Intentions don't count in the theater. What counts is what comes out.

JEAN-PAUL SARTRE

::
J E N N I F E R   L .   C U L B E R T

I begin with a quotation from Hannah Arendt's *The Origins of Totalitarianism*: "An insight into the nature of totalitarian rule . . . might serve . . . to introduce the most essential political criterion for judging the events of our time: will it lead to totalitarian rule or will it not?"[1] I take this quotation as an invitation— an invitation to remind us that what we are called upon to do as we consider questions about the banality of evil and the threat of totalitarianism is *to judge*. To judge is not to answer questions as matters of knowledge or truth, but rather is to participate in a public quest for meaning; to determine in, for, and as a person who appears to others what the events of our time *mean*.

I hope to contribute to the discussion here by recalling one aspect of the task the editors of this volume set for us when they asked us to contemplate "Is evil banal? Is totalitarianism a threat?" Specifically, I hope to contribute by not only reminding us of *what* Arendt says about judgment but also of *how* she herself goes about judgment. To this end, in my remarks I revisit Arendt's judgment of Adolf Eichmann and his trial.[2] In my re-presentation of this judgment, I suggest that by calling attention to the theatrical quality of the Israeli House of Justice and the trial staged there, Arendt subtly underlines a claim she makes at the beginning of *Eichmann in Jerusalem*, a claim that is not often considered by critics but one that introduces an argument for which Arendt's account of the trial continues to receive much criticism.[3] The claim is that a trial resembles a play. The argument is that the trial in Jerusalem was a failure.

The opening pages of *Eichmann in Jerusalem* call attention to the theatrical nature of the courtroom where the proceedings against Adolf Eichmann, the man accused of being the architect of the final solution, take place.

"*Beth Hamishpath*"—the House of Justice: these words shouted by the court usher at the top of his voice make us jump to our feet as they announce the

Facing: Hannah Arendt's notes on the endpaper of her heavily annotated copy of Walter Benjamin's *Briefe*. Courtesy of the Hannah Arendt Collection, Stevenson Library, Bard College.

arrival of the three judges, who, bareheaded, in black robes, walk into the courtroom from a side entrance to take their seats on the highest tier of the raised platform. . . . Whoever planned this auditorium in the newly built *Beth Ha'am*, the House of the People . . . had a theater in mind, complete with orchestra and gallery, with proscenium and stage, and with side doors for the actors' entrance.[4]

After observing how the House of Justice is constructed like a theater, Arendt explicitly discusses the resemblance between trials and plays. First, she says, both trials and plays begin and end with doers. Like theater, justice for Arendt is properly concerned with action. Thus, at the center of a trial is, and can only be, the one who acts. Arendt claims that this figure is like a hero in a play. His deeds are the proper focus of the court's attention. Second, what the actor does is a matter for the spectators of the play, not the actor, to decide. From a vantage point away from the action, spectators can critically evaluate what they see. They may understand that what they see are effects, but when they seek the causes for these effects, they compromise their understanding of the meaning of the action of the play. Of course, there is no guarantee that what they understand is what the producers of the spectacle seek to represent. The fact that a trial, like a play, always contains the element of such an "irreducible risk" is a third way in which trials and plays resemble one another.[5] Indeed, both trials and plays are self-conscious productions that try to contain this risk, and the way that they may be "stage managed" to provide spectacles with prearranged results is another way in which trials and plays resemble one another.

By calling attention to the resemblance between trials and plays, Arendt reminds us that we live in an "appearing" world. In *The Life of the Mind*, Arendt describes an appearing world as a world in which "Being and appearing coincide."[6] In an appearing world, the "old metaphysical dichotomy of (true) Being and (mere) Appearance," as well as the "old prejudice of Being's supremacy over appearance," do not make sense.[7] According to Arendt, these old saws suggest that something must exist that is not appearance and that this something explains how everything appears. While Arendt does not take issue with the observation that the appearance of a particular thing arises from an invisible base, she does condemn the tradition of Western philosophy that transforms this invisible base into a cause that produces the appearance of a particular thing. This cause is then assigned a higher rank of reality than that of what it causes. Arendt says this is a logical fallacy and a colossal mistake. Try as philosophers and scientists might to uncover the higher truth underneath appearances or to interpret all appearances as a function of the life process, no one ever arrives at a region beyond appearances.[8]

Noting this, Arendt suggests: "Since we live in an appearing world, is it not much more plausible that the relevant and the meaningful in this world of ours should be located precisely on the surface?"[9] The plausibility of her suggestion invalidates our habitual standards of judgment. Arendt says that these standards are invalidated because "they are rooted in metaphysical assumptions and prejudices—according to which the essential lies beneath the surface, and the surface is 'superficial.'"[10]

It is for failing to question these metaphysical assumptions and prejudices that Arendt criticizes the court in Jerusalem. The failure is significant; as a result, the judges could not acknowledge the originality of the character of the defendant and could not see how his deeds properly related to the events of his time. In brief, the judges could not appreciate the unprecedented quality of the criminal and his actions. Consequently, those responsible for doing justice in Eichmann's case denied the appearance of something completely new in history, and in so doing, manifested an unwillingness to judge.

According to Arendt, the faculty of judgment engages human beings in a search for public meaning.[11] Like spectators at a play, judges, in the presence of others, observe what men do and strive to make sense of it. To grasp the significance of what they see, judges must not only watch but also think. The activity of thinking is concerned with what it means for something to be. In the quest for this meaning, thinking spares no certainty or received wisdom. All accepted doctrines and rules are dissolved and examined anew.

Thus, it is finally for the failure to think that Arendt criticizes the judges at Eichmann's trial. Specifically, Arendt says the judges in Jerusalem did not dare to recognize the grounds upon which Eichmann was properly brought to trial and ultimately executed. The judges were loath to do so because these grounds rest on propositions that do not conform to the conceits of "civilized" jurisprudence and the superiority of Being over appearing. However, because the judges did not have the wherewithal to challenge received wisdom, the judges did not do justice to Eichmann in Jerusalem. Traditional Western jurisprudence is based on the idea that only human actions that are informed by free will may reflect or express something in addition to or other than what is accomplished by the act itself, something calling for moral consideration.[12] The propositions upon which Eichmann's trial ultimately depended for its legitimacy are considered barbaric, Arendt says, because they assert "that a great crime offends nature, so that the very earth cries out for vengeance; that evil violates a natural harmony which only retribution can restore; that a wronged collectivity owes a duty to the moral order to punish the criminal."[13] These assertions do not attend to the will of the criminal. The only thing that matters is the violation of the appearance of a natural harmony.

Because the judges in Eichmann's trial did not dare recognize these assertions as the proper grounds of the proceedings, they failed to do justice in Jerusalem in two ways. First, when it came to understanding the criminal, as justice requires, the judges did not focus on Eichmann's actions and how his actions appeared to the world. Instead, the judges looked to Eichmann's state of mind to establish his guilt (*mens rea*), following the prosecution's lead when it asked the court to judge Eichmann not for what he did but for having an evil heart. By following the prosecution's lead and inquiring into Eichmann's internal motivations, the court failed to attend to what was new and unique about Eichmann, and ultimately condemned him on the old, familiar grounds of the intention to do wrong.

Against this claim, Arendt argues that Eichmann should have been judged not for what the judges understood to be his intentions but for what they knew to be his deeds. In other words, the judges should have come to terms with what was obvious about Eichmann at first glance; that he was neither a devil nor a clown but rather a perfectly ordinary man who, in full knowledge of what he was doing, participated in the commission of some of the most horrific atrocities of human history. According to Arendt, the trial in Jerusalem failed because the judges did not pay attention to what was in front of their eyes, but rather concerned themselves with what they assumed lay behind what they saw.

Arendt also accuses the court of failing to do justice in Jerusalem for a second reason. According to Arendt, the judges failed to apprehend the new character of Eichmann's crime. Arendt understands why it was difficult for the court in Israel to recognize its novelty—the facts of Jewish history and "current Jewish historical self-understanding" obscured the ways in which the crimes of World War II were different not only in degree of seriousness but also in essence from atrocities of the past.[14] However, according to Arendt a "crime against humanity" is not an offense committed against a group of people; it is an attack upon human diversity as such.[15] Such a crime appears as the violation of an essential fact of human life, the fact that "men, not Man, live on the earth and inhabit the world."[16] Arendt says that only in the presence of others do individual human beings exist, not merely as subjects or objects but as people. Thus, the crime with which Eichmann was charged is not a crime committed against the Jewish people per se but is rather a crime committed *on the body* of the Jewish people *against the possibility and condition of humanity* itself. By eliminating certain "races" from the surface of the earth, the policy Eichmann supported sought to destroy the plurality upon which human Being depends. By supporting such a policy, Eichmann participated in a crime against humanity.

In light of this perception of the crime with which Eichmann was accused, we can understand why Arendt honors the earth's cries for vengeance and not Eichmann's victims' calls for revenge. Arendt states that a wrongdoer is brought to justice because his act has disturbed the community as a whole, and not because "damage has been done to individuals who are entitled to reparation."[17] The grammar of this sentence makes the significance of Arendt's reference apparent. Cries for vengeance indicate (public) acts; calls for revenge indicate (private) effects. The difference between (public) acts and (private) effects is sometimes difficult to see, but Arendt insists that criminals be punished for what they *do* and not for what they will or what others invisibly suffer. In other words, Eichmann must be punished not because he wanted his actions to cause people terrible distress (a state of mind that cannot be publicly witnessed) nor because his actions actually did cause people terrible distress (an effect that also cannot be seen) but because his actions themselves did wrong.

In brief, the "barbaric" propositions that justify Eichmann's prosecution and execution, the propositions that "a great crime offends nature . . . [and] that evil violates a natural harmony," speak of the appearance of a wrong in the world. Specifically, they call attention to the *violation* of an appearance, the authentic appearance of harmony provided by the diversity of sentient beings that inhabit the world. The appearance of this harmony and its violation by the Nazis can be seen by everyone. Indeed, Arendt says the facts of Eichmann's case were never in question. Because what Eichmann did was never at issue, the judges in Eichmann's trial were called on to decide only what his actions *meant*. By contrast with Eichmann's deeds, to which the earth responds with cries for vengeance, the judges cannot observe that to which the sobs of the survivors of the Holocaust respond. The judges cannot observe the suffering these sobs struggle to express because it is an "inner" experience, one that by its nature cannot appear and be apprehended by other people, even in the mode of "it-seems-to-me." Thus, when Israeli Prime Minister David Ben-Gurion tried to use the testimony of Holocaust survivors at Eichmann's trial to teach lessons, in Arendt's eyes he succeeded only at teaching either superfluous lessons about the evil of antisemitism or misleading lessons about history that grotesquely implied that Eichmann was only an innocent executor of some mysteriously foreordained destiny.[18] According to Arendt, the prime minister's lessons went awry because the suffering to which calls for revenge correspond is a private matter, the meaning of which is not for the public to decide. Because cries for vengeance pertain to a harm done to the appearing world, they draw attention to a matter of public concern and the public can reply to the victim's demands for justice.

In sum, Arendt's view of justice in a theatrical world, a world in which Being and appearing coincide, explains Arendt's support of the long-forgotten and "barbaric" propositions that justify Eichmann's trial, conviction, and sentence. In an appearing world, cries for vengeance rather than calls for revenge call attention to a wrong that only punishment can repair. In an appearing world, punishment is not based on the quality of the wrongdoer's intentions or will nor on what others endure, but only on what the wrongdoer does, for only what a wrongdoer does is presented on the stage of life, and only what men do there too can fix the harm he does.

To conclude, then, what do I think these reflections help us see? Recall the questions before us: Is evil banal? Does totalitarianism threaten? To address these questions, I am arguing that Arendt recommends that we consider not the essence of evil but the appearance of evil. That is to say, Arendt suggests we should not be overly concerned with matters of psychology, sociology, or even history. These social-scientific approaches are not appropriate to the nature of our investigations into the events of our time. Rather, we ought to ask how evil manifests itself or appears to us. To decide this, we must emulate the judges in Jerusalem to the extent that their actions before the spectators in Jerusalem revealed their sincere desire to do justice—here, Arendt is willing to, and does, celebrate the judges. However, I also want to suggest that we ultimately model our actions on Arendt's deeds rather than those of the judges because Arendt is willing to do what the judges were not. Specifically, she is willing to judge Eichmann for what he does rather than who he is. This is particularly important when we want to appreciate what is, perhaps, before our very eyes.

Facing: Hannah Arendt in Manomet, Mass., 1950. Courtesy of the Hannah Arendt Blücher Literary Trust.

Weltbürger: 247, 340

Die Hoffnung der Tugend ... und ...
... der Dualität ... ... liegt in
... Philosophie. — (Motto?) 345

Ueberlieferung der Rothen — 1819, 26, 46

Freiheit: 41, 335; Ernst & Appell an die Freiheit.

Bezug zum Staat ... ... gegen der ... ... 91.
341

Bezug zur Politik: 92

Unsterblichkeit — 350 — ... ... der ... ...
..., die die ... ... 352.

Philosophie — ancilla vitae — 357

...
...
... ...
10te Schrift vor der Schuldigung.
303

Weltgeschichte gegen Weltbürgertum 299

Der Unwert der ... den Philosophen ...
...

Arendt's Banality of Evil Thesis and the Arab-Israeli Conflict

:: YARON EZRAHI

Following the publication of Arendt's *Eichmann in Jerusalem: A Report on the Banality of Evil*, less than two decades after the Holocaust, the early "career" of her thesis concerning the banality of evil met with intense resistance. For Jews, a belief in the banality of evil of the kind committed by Eichmann could only serve Germans in avoiding responsibility for their hideous crimes against the Jews. Arendt's thesis seemed to suggest to many Jews and non-Jews an unacceptable basis for rationalizing—it was a license for leveling Nazi crimes with other crimes of war, a license for ignoring the genocidal drive behind the extermination of most European Jews, and a license for the unique dehumanizing by efficient mechanical and technological means by which the Nazis carried out the mass executions of the Jews.

Beyond the controversy, my concern here is with the potential second "career" of the banality of evil thesis in the profoundly different context of the Arab-Israeli conflict. Considering the continual violence between the sides, the urgent problem in this context is not only how to understand evil committed in the past but how to frame it in a way congenial for the social psychology and politics of reconciliation between the antagonistic parties.

In the present situation perhaps the greatest obstacle to the politics of reconciliation is the tendency of many Israelis and Palestinians to demonize each other as essential evildoers. Such "essentialization" constitutes perhaps the greatest obstacle to getting the respective national collectives to understand each other and to move toward a more peaceful course and discourse. Currently no local leadership can form reasonable foreign and security policies in the region when its own public is grossly misinformed and profoundly ignorant about the character and drives of its adversary. Israeli and Palestinian leaders who seek compromise are seriously hampered by convoluted public opinions formed largely by a continual strife and some nine wars over sixty

Facing: Hannah Arendt's notes on the front endpaper of her heavily annotated copy of Karl Jaspers's *Rechenschaft und Ausblick*. The long paragraph on the inside cover reads: "Jaspers's attempt to make visible and communicable the ungraspable and the unconditional demands, even [unreadable] the radical relativization of any thing. This relativization is retained as the irrelevance and thanks to the itself 'unconditioned' reverence before the tradition." She then refers to p. 303. Courtesy of the Hannah Arendt Collection, Stevenson Library, Bard College.

years, as well as by a profound distrust of the will and capacity of the other side to change in the future.

Hannah Arendt's thesis provides a key to a new approach stressing the possibility that criminal acts and evil consequences have been and are now committed by individuals having a "noncriminal . . . inner life" or lacking a "diabolical or demonic profundity"; thus, the banality of evil enables us to see the religiously sanctified suicide-murderer as a spiritually empty banal individual.[1] While Arendt obviously regards massacres and the brutal killing of defenseless civilians as intrinsically evil—and while she insists that Eichmann deserved the death penalty for his deeds—the gap she sees between evil acts and their terrible consequences on the one hand and the banal inner lives of the agents of evil on the other hand opens up the way for shifting the focus to the question: how do people lacking criminal or diabolic inner life become agents of evil?

At first glance, Arendt's suggestion to replace the inner criminal intent or demonic personality of the agent of evil acts by thoughtlessness and a lack of imagination is irritating. No wonder it provoked such angry protest at the time. But one should not overlook the gravity with which Arendt treats the implications of her insistence that the banal normality of evildoers "is much more terrifying" because of the ease with which many people can become evildoers like Eichmann. In some places all it takes, she suggests, is the enactment of a dehumanizing administrative classification that can lead to what she calls "administrative massacres."[2] In other circumstances it can be the result of the readiness to enact a demonic classification of "infidels" or occupiers as guilty by sheer membership in a collective of another faith or nation. While such circumstances are enormously difficult to change in the short term, recognizing their role can lead to a more flexible historical-sociological view of criminal conduct, a view foreclosed by the essentialist attribution of evil to individuals and groups.

Critics can object that by attributing evil acts to circumstances and thoughtlessness rather than to demonic individuals or group agents, we weaken both our moral rage and our propensity to severely punish the perpetrators. It is not possible simply to overcome the drive for revenge in the face of such horrible crimes as the mass killing of children and innocent, defenseless civilians. But to the extent that we wrongly ignore the gap between the banality of evildoers and the horror of their crimes, we deprive ourselves of potent resources for changing the conditions and forms of consciousness that participate in the very production of evil.

The perspective from which the banality of evildoers can be compatible with the evil of their acts opens up a number of hopeful possibilities. If normal people can become agents of evil acts by virtue of such factors as occupation and repression imposed by their adversaries, warranted and unwarranted fear of the enemy, or educational and ideological brainwashing, then such conditions and processes can be subject to historical transformations that can induce greater future continuity between noncriminal elements of inner individual life and noncriminal normal behavior. No less important is the possibility that recognizing the banality of evildoers can—especially in the context of a national-political conflict—encourage each party to less defensively reflect upon, and be self-critical with regard to, its own crimes against the other side. This can result in a greater readiness to accept the criticism of the other side without being imprisoned and paralyzed by the charge of being essential evildoers.

The rejection of a wholesale attribution of essential criminality to whole groups has also been very congenial for Germans' ability to cope with the crimes of the Nazis and participate in a necessary process of reassessing their past jointly with their Jewish victims.[3] Again, the point about the relative (not absolute) disjunction between evildoers and evil acts is not to absolve the perpetrators of responsibility but to focus on the means to end the cycle of evil feeding on more evil across time and across generations. As Neil Smelser implies in his instructive observations on the sources and faces of terror, a pragmatic approach—so badly needed to the Israeli-Palestinian conflict—must often take a longer time perspective than a moralistic one.[4] A moralist perspective prefers that justice will be done almost immediately within the community of the living, not the dead. But effective intervention directed to prevent or reduce collective crimes requires strategies that transcend the immediate present and deal with the long-term poisonous processes that generate absolutist religious or secular forms of consciousness that breed one-dimensional deterministic conceptions of action. These are precisely the kind of processes that Hannah Arendt held can easily normalize and justify crimes against innocent civilians.

One of the most suggestive attempts to soften the dichotomies between homogenous Israeli and Palestinian perceptions of past and present had been led by the late Dan Bar-On, a professor of psychology at Ben-Gurion University. Following many years of organizing and running dialogue groups consisting of children of prominent Nazi criminals and children of Jewish Holocaust victims, Professor Bar-On turned to form mixed dialogue groups of Palestinian Arabs and Jewish Israelis. The approach in these groups was to exchange personal stories—including sharing moments of agony and terror inflicted by members of the two sides on each other—as a way to humanize each side in the eyes of the other and soften absolutist stereotypes and hostility. Eventually his efforts led him and his colleagues to produce a school textbook on the history of the region based on two largely inconsistent narratives of Israelis and Palestinians, with the intention of breaking the respective molds of homogenous consciousness based in each case on one total linear narrative.[5] Obviously, the educational process involved in composing such a textbook and making it acceptable in the two rival educational systems requires a thorough, time-consuming effort. Along the way, it is likely to be disrupted by the resistance of victims and ideologues who insist on sweeping moral condemnation, excommunication, and revenge. Hannah Arendt's thesis can be seen as a part of the intellectual and educational resources available to overcome such resistance and enhance a future-oriented pedagogy of reconciliation.

Applied in a modified form to the Israeli-Palestinian context, Arendt's banality of evil thesis can combine indeterminist impersonal sociological, cultural, and political processes underlying mutually antagonistic views of the conflict with narratives of personal tragedies. Such a pragmatic application of the banality of evil can mitigate the paralyzing demonizations of the agents of evil. This approach is also consistent with liberal democratic conceptions of the individual as at least partially educable by exposure to humanistic values and inclusive cultural forms and as having the ability to engage in reflexive self-criticism. Especially important is the process of cultivating the kind of individual consciousness that reduces the tendency of each side to justify its violence toward members of the enemy's collective as a reasonable way to punish that collective, regardless of the pain and suffering inflicted upon them as individual human beings. Both random killing of civilians by acts of terror and moral indifference to "collateral killing" of civilians by the actions of a regular army indicate an illiberal tendency to see human beings as just organs of a hostile collective organism. This, in fact, is almost a kind of political biologization of the enemy that fits the whole conflict into a Darwinian mold. Jews have a special historical reason to passionately resist such a tendency, which has emerged among some Israelis in the public discussion of the proper attitude toward cases of collateral civilian victims resulting from "target killing" of terrorists and leaders of Hamas and Hezbollah.

Contextualizing evil and distributing it more evenly between the two nations would be a contribution to diminishing future bloodshed. More specifically, I think that despite the enormous difficulties, the ability to classify a host of actions like wholesale or random killing of civilians, and particularly children, as evil without wholesale demonization of the groups from which the perpetrators came, can put Israelis and Palestinians on a path toward a more hopeful interaction. Whereas the pain and destruction inflicted by each side on the other seem from each of the two perspectives to be asymmetrical, still the ability to recognize the banality of the agents of evil on the side of the adversary increases the possibility of corrective self-reflection on one's own side. If both Israelis and Palestinians were able to attribute the acts of violence and crimes committed by each side against the other as related to particular circumstances rather than to essential character traits, they could more easily focus on manageable changes of circumstances rather than on much less feasible changes of individual or collective personality. If each side recognized its own contributions to starting or feeding more than a hundred years of violence between the two communities, it would certainly advance the goal of a future settlement. The ability to recognize that even terrorists are humans who were turned by religion, ideology, and suffering into suicide bombers or that trigger-happy Israeli soldiers are themselves victims of prejudice, brainwashing, improper education, and distorting emotional manipulations, is a first step. This step has to be reinforced by concerted efforts on each side to historicize and sociologize conditions that produce violence and reverse attempts to define the conflict in absolute metaphysical and spiritual terms.

The record of the Arab-Israeli conflict indicates that of the many measures taken by those on both sides who seek to escalate the conflict and avoid compromise, the most effective has been to define it as a war of religions. Religious faith and religious symbolism, especially when they penetrate the politics of nationalist parties, have a poor record of encouraging compromises among rival groups. This tendency is obviously also the most effective means to demonize the other groups and justify violence and sacrifice. Fanatic Jewish and Moslem religious leaders in the Middle East have proved to have great powers to spiritualize mass sacrificial murder. It is largely because of these powers to spiritualize the sacrifice of your own heroes and demonize those of the other side that the banalization of the agents of those massacres can be so important in countering murderous nationalist fundamentalism. Banalizing evil seems then more akin to a secular than a religious cast of mind. But we should not assume that it is necessarily so. There are a few Jewish and Moslem religious leaders who in recent years worked together to spiritualize peace and condemn violence.

On the domestic Israeli front, the banality of evil idea is not only valuable in de-demonizing the Arab side but also in resisting domestic "exchange demonizations" between the radical Israeli Left and the radical Right, which includes the settlers. Facile analogies between the Settlers' Youth and Hitler Youth have proved counterproductive, as have the sweeping labeling of the Left as a bunch of traitors. Such internal demonization tends to provoke overreactions that harden the Right and the Left, encouraging them toward further entrenchment in uncompromising positions. As Hannah Arendt preached but not always practiced, intellectuals and other influential figures who want to make a difference must work within the general frame of common opinions, not radically transcend them. A lot of work is still needed to expose the choices and colossal errors of judgment Israeli decision makers conceal behind the rhetoric of demonization, external threats, necessary wars, realistic pessimism, and ontological victimhood. For better or for worse, the Middle East has been the cradle of prophetic politics. The modern history of Israel in the Middle East is a combined record of the self-fulfilling prophecy of the Zionist Utopia and the negative self-fulfilling prophecies of imminent wars. I believe that were she alive now, Hannah Arendt—who was deeply concerned about the Arab-Israeli conflict—would endorse a version of the banality of evil as a part of a remedial approach to the relentless continual hostilities and violence between Israelis and Palestinians.

PART V

Judaism and Cosmopolitanism

Rahel Varnhagen

The Life of a Jewish Woman

Revised Edition

Hannah Arendt

Liberating the Pariah

POLITICS, THE JEWS, AND HANNAH ARENDT

The essay that follows is a condensed version of a piece written not long after Hannah Arendt's death in 1975. The original essay took its impetus from a request from Martin Peretz, editor of *The New Republic*, that I review Ronald H. Feldman's pioneering collection of Arendt's writings, *The Jew as Pariah: Jewish Identity and Politics in the Modern Age* (1978), which now exists in an expanded version, *The Jewish Writings*, edited by Feldman and Jerome Kohn (2007). Peretz published the review as a cover essay in *The New Republic* in 1978. I was then encouraged to expand and revise the essay for publication elsewhere, and the most complete version of the piece appeared in *Salmagundi* in 1983.[1]

The essay escaped the notice of all but a few. My disadvantage was that Jewish history and politics were never my fields. As an outsider without standing in these disciplines, there was no scholarly or political reason for my essay to be remembered. When the editors of this new volume asked me to contribute to it, I briefly considered writing something new, but in the end thought better of the idea. Since the original, full-length version of the following essay disappeared without much of a trace, I thought that reviving it in summary form, if only for archaeological purposes, might be more useful.

What qualifies me to publish another version of the essay? Insofar as there might be a positive answer to these questions, I submit the following. When I arrived at the University of Chicago as a sixteen-year-old freshman, I went to hear Arendt speak in defense of her Eichmann book. She had already come under public severe attack, even from the audience that evening. At the end of the lecture I introduced myself. She took a liking to me (even though it was difficult for me to convince her I was not a German Jew, but a descendant of Polish and Russian Jews), came to concerts I gave, and became an important figure in my undergraduate experience. She encouraged me to take courses from people whom I would otherwise never have thought of studying with, including Leo Strauss, whom she admired but with whom she disagreed. She read and helped me on my senior honors essay on Max Weber. Proof of her interest can be found in the now-published correspondence between Arendt and Karl Jaspers.

Facing: Cover of Hannah Arendt's copy of *Rahel Varnhagen*. Courtesy of the Hannah Arendt Collection, Stevenson Library, Bard College.

LEON BOTSTEIN

My relationship with Arendt derived not only from my role as a student, but also as the grandson and nephew of survivors and victims of the Holocaust. She knew that in 1939 my grandfather had refused the position of head of the Jewish Council in Lodz and fled from Poland to Russia in full recognition of the potential danger of collaborating with the Nazis. My grandfather, Maksymilian Wyszewianski, who survived and ultimately immigrated to New York in his late eighties during the early 1960s, was the first to bring my attention to Arendt's *New Yorker* articles on the Eichmann trial. I was in high school, and since his experiences in the Warsaw ghetto and labor camp were a crucial part of our contact with one another, he recommended the articles with the observation that what Arendt had written was the most honest and perceptive thing he had ever read about the Holocaust.

For those of us who were born abroad after the war but grew up in America, our parents' and grandparents' experiences during the war years were the object of intense childhood fascination. The world from which my parents emerged no longer existed. There was no hometown to visit, no gymnasium or university friends; there were only fragments represented by the random selection of survivors who gathered every Sunday in my parents' home in the Bronx. My grandfather—who studied philosophy and politics in Heidelberg, got his law degree from Kazan State University, and lived in prerevolutionary Moscow, where he married the granddaughter of the Chief Rabbi of Moscow, Leib Abramovich Kan—was articulate, learned, and kind. He helped teach me Russian, introduced me to literature, and responded unstintingly to my many questions about a world no longer visible that could be remembered only through the telling of tales.

When I, a dazed twenty-eight-year-old, was offered the Bard College presidency in 1975, Arendt played a critical, behind-the-scenes role in persuading me to take the position and in convincing the understandably skeptical Bard faculty to accept me. Because her late husband, Heinrich Blücher, had been beloved as a faculty member at Bard College, she was very kindly disposed to Bard. Indeed, she came to the campus to give me, in public, her blessing and went out of her way to indicate her confidence in me to the senior faculty in a manner that made my work here possible. I drove two of her closest faculty friends, Kate Wolff and Irma Brandeis, to her funeral in New York City.

Arendt wished to be buried in the Bard College cemetery, so in the spring of 1976 the college hosted a symposium on her work accompanied by a ceremony at which Kaddish was said. Mary McCarthy, Arendt's executor, had a long association with Bard, having taught here first in the 1940s and later in the 1980s. Her presence here further connected Arendt to Bard, particularly since Arendt had left her library to the college, where it is now maintained as a separate entity.

Beyond this residual relationship with Arendt, my qualifications on the subject are that I have remained interested in key aspects of modern Jewish history that intersect with my work in the history of music. I published a book in German in 1991 called *Judentum und Modernität* based on lectures I gave in Vienna, where during the 1989–90 academic year I shared a visiting professorship with the late J. P. Stern. That engagement with issues of Jewish history and the fate of European Jewry has deepened since the original publication of the following essay not only by my many years as president of Bard College but also by my role, since 2003, as music director of the radio orchestra of the State of Israel, the Jerusalem Symphony Orchestra. At Bard I became involved with preserving the memory and legacy of Arendt and Blücher and developing, for the first time, a Jewish presence in student life under the guidance of the Jewish studies program and faculty with expertise in Judaism and Jewish history. That faculty now includes the eminent scholar Jacob Neusner, the historian Cecile Kuznitz, and the historian and sociologist Joel Perlmann, among others. The college currently offers Hebrew and Arabic, and it continues a long tradition of teaching political theory, the faculty of which includes David Kettler and Roger Berkowitz, as well as European history, among the faculty of which is a distinguished young scholar, Gregory Moynahan, who has written extensively on Ernst Cassirer. During the period of the publication of my essay in *Salmagundi*, I was involved in a brief exchange with Martin Jay about Arendt in the pages of the *Partisan Review* in 1978. From time to time I have been drawn into documentary efforts to interview individuals who knew Arendt. I have followed the Arendt literature in amateur fashion, a habit that informs the expanded bibliography that will be found in the endnotes.[2]

Out of respect for Arendt, it is appropriate to close these introductory remarks with a few observations about the particular relevance of her views on the history of European Jews, Zionism, and Israel today. Even though there are striking continuities in the issues since her death in 1975, there have been significant changes that merit attention. For one, the American diaspora has entirely fulfilled its promise as a stable home for the remnants of European Jewry. Despite the embarrassingly small numbers allowed to enter before and immediately after 1945, the United States, by any reasonable standard, has provided a key destination place for Jews, notably in the 1950s; in 1968, when there was a large emigration from communist Poland; and between the early 1970s and the mid-1990s, when large numbers of Russian Jews came to the United States. Jews in America have become uniformly middle-class and, owing to the color of their skin, have blended easily into the majority "white" population. Even as the United States becomes less white and more diverse, antisemitism holds no promise of becoming a unifying political factor. Insofar as antisemitism exists in the United States from below in a populist form or from above, from would-be, self-styled elites, it is as a social nuisance, not a real threat or barrier. Even the high price of oil, the conflict and inherent instability in the Middle East, and the ambivalence to Judaism in the right-wing evangelical Christian embrace of Israel will not bring about a rich–poor antisemitic alliance that can form the center of new popular political movement. The (for me) embarrassing presence of an observant, once Democratic

Jewish senator and vice presidential candidate as a prominent figure in the 2008 Republican national convention is but one symptom of the integration of American Jews into both the liberal and conservative movements in American politics. Another is the existence of a stable consensus within American politics of the need for the United States to support the State of Israel. I do not believe these views to be naïve.

Furthermore, the recurring fear that Jews as a distinct entity will disappear in America through assimilation, acculturation, and intermarriage is probably exaggerated, despite demographic trends in that direction. There has been a distinct religious revival in America. But it has occurred in both Orthodox and Reform Judaism. With the general revival of religion in the late twentieth century, the United States has seen a Jewish religious renewal.

What is novel in comparison to the late 1970s is the breakdown of intra-Jewish solidarity. The essential disappearance of antisemitism has permitted the dissolution of a long-standing, pseudo-popular front among Jews. The split between Reform and Orthodox Judaism grows wider, creating the future prospect of different Jewish sects that, as in the case of Protestantism, will have distinct histories and tenuous and tense relations with one another. On the Reform side, the novelty in terms of liturgy and theology is as vital as that on the Orthodox side, where contemporary fundamentalism reveals a radical imitation of puritan American protestant habits. The historic overarching unity among Jews in European history was not the result of any uniformity or agreement among Jews, but rather the result of the sustained indiscriminate and powerful coherence of blanket antisemitism imposed on Jews. In the United States the lifting of that exogenous historical force has permitted the enormous diversity of Jewish identities to flourish unimpeded. Judaism in the United States will survive as a religion in many diverse forms, from radical fundamentalism to a fashion-driven, new age–like modernism. What will disappear are the remains of so-called secular Judaism and the notion of Jews as an ethnicity or a nation outside of Israel.

With respect to Zionism and Israel, much has changed since Arendt's death. The number of significant Jewish communities outside Israel and the United States has been reduced by immigration to both destinations. And the size of the non-American diaspora will continue to shrink. The revival of antisemitism in France and England and its persistence in countries such as Argentina and Hungary, where there still are relatively large Jewish communities, has continued to lend Zionism vitality as a political ideology outside of Israel. But within Israel it has become apparent that a distinct Israeli identity has come into being. With time, the commonality between European Jewish history, the American Jewish experience, and Israeli cultural and national identity becomes more and more tenuous.

Furthermore, within Israel there is a fundamental demographical and cultural threat to a heritage of secular Zionism, particularly that linked to socialism. Religious practice and identity have experienced an unexpected and unusual revival within Israel, even in a nominal sense among so-called secular Israelis. Arendt's concern that Israel establish itself as a secular democracy where church (so to speak) and state are separate has become for this reason all the more urgent and, unfortunately, improbable. Since the socialist legacy within Israel is in retreat, the Israel of today is far different from the country Arendt experienced during the Eichmann trial. There are new class labels and distinctions that segment rich from poor in ways reminiscent of Europe and North America. In addition, with the passage of time, Israeli culture and society are developing in a manner more coherent to the ecological and cultural environment of the Middle East. The legacy and significance of the history and tragedy of European Jewry as defining elements of modern Israel become less significant as over time Israel develops its own unique Mediterranean identity.

Perhaps the most startling consequence of this cultural development is its influence on the post-1967 record of Israel's relationship with its immediate neighbors. The occupation of key conquered territories remains in place despite the return of the Sinai, the peace with Jordan and Egypt, and the more recent evacuation from Gaza. The West Bank has been profoundly altered by a consistent policy of settlement, primarily around the city of Jerusalem. The politics behind this fact reveal the decline in influence of the heritage of Western European and American liberalism. While the patterns of occupation and settlement do not prevent a political solution that would result in two independent states, one Israeli and one Palestinian, the so-called two-state solution, once flatly rejected but now widely considered the optimal and perhaps utopian resolution of the Arab-Israeli conflict (that itself dates back to the early years of the modern Jewish settlement of Palestine), is now more and more in question.

It is highly ironic that Arendt's allegiance, along with Judah Magnes's and Martin Buber's, to the ideal of a one-state, binational political "homeland" solution is now experiencing renewed attention. In 1963 and 1975, it was dismissed as naïve at best, if not disloyal to Israel. Yet there are those both within the Israeli and Palestinian communities who believe the only hope is a so-called one-state solution that, for demographic reasons, raises the specter of Jews once again becoming a minority (and perhaps pariahs) within a single political entity. The idea of a Jewish state is therefore considered sadly by many sympathetic observers to be fatally flawed in the long term, not because of external forces but because of internal developments both within Israel and the Palestinian Authority.

My deep, lifelong admiration for Arendt has never implied agreement with all of her views. It is fair to say that her dream of a binational solution was already unrealistic in the late 1940s. In my view it remains unrealistic today, and probably undesirable. Despite close proximity and a shared history, the legacy of conflict, mutual mistrust, violence, and religious intolerance will not be easy to remove. What merits revisiting the writings of Arendt on Jewish history and Zionism is the power of her thought as a provocation to self-criticism with respect to many commonly held political beliefs. There is an inherent idealism in her writing about the possibilities of politics. I believe that the logical consequence of that idealism is the need to realize a stable two-state solution: a secular, democratic Israel with an explicit constitutional framework and a viable democratic, constitutional, secular Palestinian state that has economic potential and viable geographic boundaries. That these two states would have to work together economically and politically goes without saying. Perhaps the closest these two states can come together is in the form of a federation similar to what exists today within the European community and that has brought the historic German-French enmity to an end. The years since 1948 and 1967 have created two strong, distinct identities, one Israeli and one Palestinian, and with distinctiveness has come too much distrust to justify the idea of a single, integrated political entity. Differences, however, do not require that there be endless conflict. Therefore, for stability and peace to exist, Israel should to turn its attention, sooner rather than later, to securing its own long-term security and prosperity by enabling the creation of a coherent independent state for the Palestinians.

Here, then, is a shortened version of my original article.

Liberating the Pariah

Ludwig Wittgenstein's claim in the *Philosophical Investigations* that "the speaking of language is part of activity, or a form of life" applies precisely to Hannah Arendt's theoretical notion of political activity.[3] In Wittgenstein's enumeration of several "language games," or uses of language, one can recognize Arendt's own involvement in politics: describing, deconstructing, reporting, speculating, making up stories, and translating from one language to another. From Nietzsche and Heidegger, and through her lifelong love of poetry, Arendt grasped the philosophical centrality of language. Language was more than a mere vehicle of description, an instrument of perception, or a carrier of knowledge and thought between subject and object. Rather, speech constituted action among men, the concrete *praxis* of politics. Language—in Arendt's case, German—was also the symbol of political identity, a bridge between the discontinuous phases of her life, a continuous thread of what Heidegger called "being-in-the-world."

Speaking, as a species of political action, vindicated her view that politics is an activity larger than the wielding of power and the assertion of dominion. If politics were simply the individual and collective manipulation of varieties of violence among men or solely the art of achieving and maintaining dominion, then politics and freedom might be fundamentally conflicting notions. Yet, as

Arendt argues in *The Human Condition*—in fact in all her writing from *Rahel Varnhagen* to her unfinished work of philosophy, *The Life of the Mind*—freedom is a consequence of sustained political activity. Freedom demands political action. Politics requires speech and language as "a form of life," audible openly in shared space well beyond the private conversation.

In her focus on language, Arendt shares with writers in the semiotic and hermeneutic tradition the assumption that if politics is human, and if it centers on language and speech, then an understanding of language is central to a proper politics. Where Arendt's understanding of language significantly differs is in her implicit belief that sustained usages and meanings, in their commonsense definitions, must remain useful, be widely acknowledged, and be legitimated as a proper basis of action.

The linking of language to political action and Arendt's expectation of the probability of finding accepted, shared meanings did not presume a universal commonality of usage or language as the basis of large-scale politics. Arendt retained a consistent affection for smaller, decentralized units of political organization, rather than a utopian faith in a scheme for world government. Arendt's idealization of a public realm among small groups, each dealing with local circumstances at precise moments in history, made speaking as politics per se seemingly realistic. In contrast, speech and language functioning as politics in the public realm of a massive, centralized, modern nation-state could become banal and general; both would lose their particular and complex power. She believed that political participation by individuals in their immediate, collective historical moment through language (in the philosophic sense which Arendt used it)—although difficult in the contemporary age of electronic journalism, political formulae, and slogans—is possible in modern life. The consequence of the failure to overcome these dangers is made clear in Arendt's view of Eichmann. He was revealed by his abuse of language, his inability to think and speak without clichés. Eichmann, as an ideal type of mediocre official of the mass nation state, represented the specter of the loss of politics as speech, language, and thinking.

In view of her portrait of Eichmann, it is ironic to note that Arendt's view of language and speech as political action was formulated through and sustained by her lifelong critical confrontation with the central historical issue of her political existence: the Jewish question in modern European history. The Jewish search for freedom from powerlessness and exclusion and for the opportunity to speak and act as equal citizens in a public realm, particularly in a Diaspora, occupied Arendt in two contrasting contexts: Germany and France before 1941, and America until her death in 1975. Arendt's reading of the European Jewish secular tradition, antisemitism in the era after Emancipation, and Jewish nationalism illuminate, in part, the origins of her theory of political action. After 1948, Arendt's sense of the American political tradition and its promise, notably her interpretation of the foundations of America in the eighteenth century, became increasingly favorable and accelerated her critical distance from the Zionism of her youth. Arendt saw, in America, the authentic prospect of a political life (as she conceived politics) for Jews.

Arendt's basic theoretical claim, the separation of the social from the political, and her call for a return, in modern times, to the primacy of the political, originated in her understanding of the Jewish problem as decisively political rather than social in character. Although prewar Western and Eastern Europe contained impoverished *Ostjuden*, economic status—poverty and social class—were not, for Arendt, the key factors in the historical plight of Jewry. Social discrimination and social exclusion per se—especially as understood in the "country club" sense among privileged classes—did not, in themselves, strike her as dangerous. Obsession among certain Jews about such discrimination fueled her contempt of the self-denying Jew and the parvenus of bourgeois Jewry, who pursued assimilation, wealth, and success in order to overcome prejudice. For Arendt they focused incorrectly on what was a defensible extension of the private right of individuals to choose friends. Her view, bizarre to some, was that social inequities were the direct consequences of political freedom and compatible with the equality of citizenship.

Since social solutions to the Jewish problem—and indeed all problems of inequality—were both reprehensible and essentially ineffective, Arendt sought a solution not contingent on social identity but on politics in the autonomous sense of the "rights of men." Political justice and equality for men as citizens in the life of European nations, given permanent social differences, was perhaps a hope for Jews. Such notions had led to their legal emancipation in the late eighteenth and early nineteenth centuries. Jewish political participation in the citizenry of a commonwealth could free the Jew from being a pariah—unfree, incomplete in human terms, a stranger, and homeless—in the Western world. To support this hope, Arendt consistently referred to two periods when she believed men acted as equal political citizens, using persuasion in a socially diverse world in Aeschylus' sense: the ancient republics of Greece and Rome and the age in which Enlightenment political thought influenced political revolution.

The political vision Arendt fashioned out of her pre-1933 hope for the political future of a Jewish nation within a pluralistic Europe remained the same throughout her work: she supported a world of political federations of differing peoples and individuals. A cosmopolitan or Marxist conception of a society without different national identities failed to demand that highest human activity—speaking and acting in separate political realms. Schemes of legislated social equality and universalism, even if achievable gradually and voluntarily from below, were as deadly as sameness achieved from above by tyrannical violence, terror, and domination.

Arendt's politics, if realized—the exercise of individual speech and action in the public arena—could allow a particular Jewish character, originally developed in pariah conditions, to continue. This secular political solution to the isolation of the Jew of Europe that could permit a Jewish culture, identity, and "national" distinction to flourish in a modern Europe required a special definition of Jewish nationalism. Arendt's lifelong pride in being Jewish, in the history of the Jews and the legacy of her and others' Jewishness, sustained her image of Jewish secular culture in Europe.

What the Jew within Europe lacked before 1933 was the home, place, and public arena to exercise what equal political membership insured, the human *telos* of the *vita activa*: working and speaking freely in the public realm of a differentiated community. Nineteenth-century, race-based nationalism and separatism did not offer to Arendt a solution to ending the negative status of Jews in Europe as pariahs, as strangers. Zionism denied Jewishness as it was and denied Jews Europe as potentially a proper national home.

Nevertheless, Arendt's recognition of the need for politics, her allegiance to Jewish identity, and her experience as a young Jewess led her to Zionism less than a decade before the revisionist Zionist Vladimir Jabotinsky urged the voluntary liquidation of the European Diaspora in the late 1930s as a means of preempting the involuntary liquidation he prophesied. The creation of a separate physical homeland, a piece of territory in which Jews would not have pariah status and could speak and act in the public arena, attracted the young Arendt. Like Louis Brandeis in America, Arendt believed that a physical homeland outside of Europe could be a powerful impetus to achieving future political equality for Jews within a Diaspora. Zionism struck Arendt as the legitimate self-respecting political arena for the assertive, secular, European Jew in the darkening years of the 1920s and 1930s.

Yet because of Arendt's philosophical and theoretical views on nationalism and politics, she presumed the existence of a vital Diaspora apart from a Jewish national home even as she actively participated in Zionist organizations in the 1930s and 1940s. For Arendt, political equality in the Diaspora was a goal to be pursued along with the formation of a Jewish homeland outside of Europe in Palestine. She never contemplated immigrating to Israel, despite her lifelong emotional tie to it. Later, her American experience would vindicate her belief in the continuing vitality of a Diaspora.

Zionism, by securing a double life for Jews, would place Jews in an exemplary position that would avoid the pitfalls of the past and vindicate the human possibility that Arendt celebrated consistently: the capacity to begin anew, to give birth to new beginnings. The pariah Jewish nation would begin anew and be in the vanguard of a constructive future redefinition of nationalism and politics. The Jewish homeland in Palestine was to be a political federation with a structure that encouraged the sense of citizenship beyond race and religion. It would allow both Arabs and Jews political autonomy. It would avoid the dilemma of numerical and racial dominance. Arendt's "Enlightenment" Zionism eventually led her to advocate not a "state" but a "homeland," a term that explicitly stopped short of the idea of a Jewish state or majority control by constitutional definition.

Her break with most political Zionists in the 1940s paralleled her criticism of the confusion of social with political issues. In the prevailing conception of a Jewish state she saw an ominous triumph for social thinking, that is, race-based thinking within the political arena. Yet Arendt, as a political national-ist in her own sense, vigorously advocated during World War II a specifically Jewish army. Military service by Jews as a national group in a world struggle was an example of a proper political equality and identity for the Jews in a diverse world.

Vladimir Jabotinsky's testimony to the Palestine Royal Commission in 1937 contained the unacceptable Zionist argument that Arendt believed, by the mid-1940s, had moved from the periphery of Zionism to its very center. After conceding Arab hardships in Palestine and claiming economic benefits for the Arabs, Jabotinsky argued that being a minority in another's nation-state was not a concern: "It is not a hardship on any race, any nation possess-ing so many National States and so many more in the future."[4] Jabotinsky circumvented, in Arendt's sense, the facts of birth and particular historical distinctions among Arabs and concentrated only on Jews. Most important, from Arendt's point of view, he failed to afford the Arabs the necessary pre-conditions for freedom and political equality. Jabotinsky's program did to the Arabs what in effect had been done to the Jews. Misreading the character of the historical tragedy of the European Jews, Jabotinsky advocated a trun-cated pariah status for the Arabs. He called for Arabs to live the life the Jews had lived in Europe, as a distinct minority in a nation whose character was based on the legal legitimation of the numerical superiority of one single re-ligion and race.

Arendt's Zionist writings from the 1940s contain urgent pleas for Arab-Jewish cooperation and for new definitions of nationalism. Already in the mid-1940s, Arendt feared that chauvinism, militarism, international isolation, and the triumph of religious influences in political life (challenging the church-state separation essential to political freedom) would be consequences of the Zionism that fought for a Jewish *state*. Arendt's fears were not allayed later in 1961 when she wrote *Eichmann in Jerusalem*. In her final Zionist writings of the late 1940s, she offered a vision of a potentially harmonious, binational federa-tion in Palestine with political equality and freedom for all: a truly democratic state, appropriate for what she affectionately called "small nations."[5]

Arendt's early grasp of the long-range dangers of Jewish strife with the Arab world was prescient. She foresaw the effect of Palestinian refugees, the political isolation of the Jewish nation-state, the exclusive dependency of Israel on America, the possible tension between Israel and its liberal Ameri-can Jewish Diaspora, and the cultural pitfalls of an Israel permanently depen-dent on high military readiness.

But what can be said of her solution? The geopolitical role of Israel between the Soviet Union and the West made a small-nation solution, an "Austrian-ization" of Israel, unlikely. Well before the modern politics of oil, the utopian binational federalist rather than the nationalist internal arrangement at the close of British rule was unlikely. The gap between Arendt's political philosophy and what were generally perceived as the real options for Zionist action seemed only to grow as the Israeli state developed. The problems, however, were apparent to Arendt's critics very early.

As she saw her vision of Zionism go to defeat and oblivion, Arendt was drawn rapidly into a new, concrete focus for thinking about politics: America, her new Diaspora home, and the myth of its political origins and character. Myth in its poetic and didactic sense was the way in which Arendt used America's founding as a story and an occasion for celebrating the politics of speech and critical interpretation. Though she insisted on distinguishing fact from fiction, her historical writing reflected Heidegger's, Nietzsche's, and Walter Benjamin's challenges to the claims of historical objectivity and to the static character of historical fact. She continued to like storytelling and the didactic quality often associated with it.

For a solution to the problem of the Jewish nation, Arendt turned in the 1950s to America. An overlooked clue to the strident tone of what Arendt later conceded was the hastily written and explosive Eichmann book is the fact that she went to report on the judicial proceedings in Jerusalem on the heels of a close, affectionate reading of America's political origins and their modern consequences. In that decade she came to know America better and gained a close circle of non–Jewish American intellectual companions such as Mary McCarthy. The sharply worded criticism of Ben-Gurion and Israel in *Eichmann in Jerusalem* came from a thinker who now castigated the Jews for failing to imitate America and take advantage of the possibility of a new beginning, for not making of the Jewish state what she had come to believe was the miracle of America: a federal system of government not based on race or designed to rectify social inequalities, but established to ensure political equality among all citizens, to maintain the freedom of the public realm, social difference notwithstanding. Despite her lament over the failure of a more decentralized federal system right after the American Revolution, as envisaged by Jefferson, her admiration for American politics and its potential was strong in 1959.

In *The Human Condition*, written in America in 1958, Arendt argues that the Founding Fathers had indeed succeeded, not only where Israel failed but where the Enlightenment in Europe had failed. *The Human Condition* presupposed that the technological triumphs in space, medicine, and atomic science promised a properly nonpolitical solution to the world's basic economic and social needs, therefore decisively undermining Marxism and the domination of the social agenda in modern politics. Ironically, Arendt's recurrent praise of classical and eighteenth-century models revealed a disturbing attraction to societies built upon a system of slavery and affording only restricted access to full citizenship. Yet what *The Human Condition* argued for seemed possible in America for Jews.

In contrast to the career of the Jew in the pre-Nazi European Diaspora, the Jewish refugee's access to full citizenship, to the public world of America after 1941, was impressive. The Jewish immigrants from the years of World War II and after—Arendt's era of emigration—even if they were survivors of Auschwitz, did not arrive as a proletarian mass and did not in the main resemble the impoverished, rural, small village Jewish immigrants who came from Eastern Europe in the late nineteenth century; neither was the America they entered much like the earlier America. The refugees after 1933, however stateless, entered a Jewish community that had begun to achieve economic prosperity sufficient to eliminate the bottom stratum of a Jewish working class and the Jewish poor. American Jewry, from its late nineteenth-century immigrant origins, had become by the 1950s part of a white middle class within America.

Although social problems could not, in Arendt's terms, be properly transcended, the American Jew found that social distinctions and economic class were clearly not special problems for him. Race was the issue in America, and American Jews on that account came quickly to feel that they belonged to the majority, an event without parallel in Europe. Arendt's concept of the political as a category distinct from the social became even more plausible in a context where the standard social barriers to which Jews were accustomed did not pertain and seemed not to threaten participation by Jews in ordinary politics.

Furthermore, antisemitism appeared unlikely to become a major political or social force in America. The immigrant Jew was accepted in America as a European, much like the Irish and Italians. Nationhood, the opposite of statelessness, was bestowed on the Jew in America on Ellis Island curiously—from an Arendtian perspective—by acts of speech: naming and declaring. These were, from the point of view of Arendt's concept of politics, consequential political acts. The Jew arrived in America as a Jewish American like a German American, Irish American, or Polish American. Jews were but one of the many distinct immigrant people possessed of a European past. Jewishness became a *national* appellation in America equivalent to those more traditional European nationalities.

Masses of European Jews, Western and Eastern, came to view America as fulfilling a dream of Diaspora stability: the potential of a separate Jewish presence—secular and religious—secured by political equality and freedom. The prosperity among Jews even lessened the proverbial differences between Eastern and Western European Jews. America became the most popular option among Jews for solving the nineteenth-century Jewish question. Assimilation, conversion, poverty, and fear were not required. America outdistanced Palestine and later Israel as a Jewish national home. If Arendt had made a necessary but uneasy personal philosophical compromise by participating in Zionist activity before 1941, by 1951 her increasing sense of comfort in America made her even more doubtful about Zionism. The implicit America-Israel contrast evident in *Eichmann in Jerusalem* culminated that process.

In 1961 Arendt recognized that Ben-Gurion wanted to encourage a view of Israel as the quintessential and only legitimate future home for all Jews, especially Western Jews. Arendt's experience in Israel during the Eichmann trial heightened her awareness that the continuing evolution of Zionism on a European nationalist model threatened the balance between the Diaspora and Israel. From her vantage point in 1961, Israel challenged the viability of a permanent Jewish national life in the Diaspora. The explicit use of the Nazi crimes, not only to sustain a memory and the moral occasion for statehood in Israel but also to argue the historical logic that led to Zionism and to nationalism in Israel, cut directly against her two decades of experience in America. America vindicated the possibility of a secular political order that permitted the flourishing of a distinctly secular Jewish nation in a democratic Christian Diaspora. As a result, after 1963 the frequency with which Arendt turned her attention politically away from European and Jewish issues to American ones increased sharply.

In American democracy, Jews were then uniquely qualified by their dispersion to engage in politics in a public space in which speaking—the result of thinking—was an effective political instrument. Arendt's theory of the political was an extension, in Kantian fashion, of Jewish pariah experience into a universal norm for the future. Indeed, the influence of Kant's categorical imperative is apparent in the Arendtian proposition that speaking and thinking in the political realm are the activities that treat man as an end in himself, as the *telos* of human life. To generalize that activity universally to mankind became a political obligation. As normative to human life, the freedom of speech and thought must be secured by politics according to a Kantian model, so that language does not become an instrument of subjugation. Speech and thought, activities often exclusively private, become public and political as *ends* and means. Politics in this sense might ensure a new beginning and decrease the possibility of the transformation of radically evil ethical behavior into apparently unexceptional acts of banal routine committed by office seekers and ordinary bureaucrats, as in the Eichmann case.

The Jews, once excluded from politics and never permitted to "live as a man among men"—to be free in the full sense—could remain as they were historically (with all the characteristics of Jewishness in the secular European sense) and enter a new political realm. Neither assimilation nor strangeness would be required. The redefinition of politics in her mature thought permitted Arendt to believe she could preserve the special character of the Jew while permitting him to leave behind his pariah status and participate as an equal with other free citizens in a pluralistic society.

The difficulties of Arendt's position are many. First, Arendt consistently stressed politics as a realm for all ordinary citizens, not for an elite. Politics was the collective experience in which human values like loyalty and friendship—private virtues—flourished; yet it demanded a shared common life.

Despite this recognition of the political as common and requiring large and numerous groupings, Arendt relied on exceptional human qualities in her theory of politics and remained somewhat allergic to the actual political instincts of people. Her well-known correspondence with Gershom Scholem, in which she disclaimed any "love of a people," hints only at her ambivalence about the political as the realm of ordinary life.[6] She never overcame the conflict between her idealized notions of common citizenship, natality, and solidarity, and her idea of an uncommon individuality.

Second, Arendt's particular political thinking stood without adequate reference to the scale of the economic and demographic realities of twentieth-century politics. Arendt's favorite political models—the *polis*, the early Soviet councils, the very beginnings of revolutionary movements, the Hungarian Revolution of 1956, the small kibbutz experiments, and Jefferson's vision of permanent revolution—all involved preindustrial conditions. She never adequately came to terms with the realities of large-scale economic development, centralization of administration, bureaucracy, mass communication and transport, global demographics, and mass education.

Third and last, a crucial contradiction persisted in Arendt's critique of mainstream Zionism. In creating Israel, Jews displayed normal behavior. Once they had a home, they lost their strangeness and joined the ordinary human race as political equals. What was curious was the persisting expectations that Jews would behave more nobly than Europeans or Arabs on account of their past; that they would avoid chauvinism and militarism, perfect their democracy, and moderate the use of power itself. It was useful for Arendt to redefine politics, to make the exceptional qualities of the Jews into models and to look to the Founding Fathers and the *polis* for further support. But it was unreasonable of her to be so very disappointed in the failure of the Israelis to live up to her standards. If Jews are human, is it reasonable to expect them to form ideal political societies and behave ahistorically or exceptionally, despite a heritage derived from a history of exclusion? Or is it more appropriate to expect them to behave as others do once they enter the political realm? Arendt was aware of this dilemma and sought pragmatic answers. But the Israeli achievement of a relative political freedom continued to offend her.

Arendt's answer to this tension between the practice of politics and the redefinition of politics was her claim that the Nazi experience and the concentration camps—totalitarianism—constituted a precise moment of radical historical discontinuity. The Hitler period constituted a sharp break with the historical past and made new beginnings necessary, not only for Jews in Palestine and America but in Europe as well.

In the end, she was mostly sharply disappointed by the failure of her own people to achieve new beginnings. America, after all, possessed the political structure and the traditions that vindicated her belief—despite Vietnam and Watergate—that her concept of politics was practical and more than idle theorizing. And she stubbornly believed that Israel could have developed an American-style polity in the Middle East, given its historical preconditions.

Arendt never fully grasped the fact that in order to make a new beginning in Israel in 1948, Jews were required to shed the mantle of the "good European," to abandon their sense of a privileged spiritual superiority and to stop thinking of themselves as merely a thinking race. Jews assumed a human political role with all its potential for banal ordinariness. Though Arendt eloquently argued in her Eichmann book that Jews must be permitted—without reproach—to become entirely human, she could not help criticizing them from an ethical perspective that seemed less appropriate to the actual circumstances than she wanted it to be.

Why is the Jewish nation, perhaps unfairly, held culpable for the consequences of ordinary international political behavior and power politics more than other nations? How does one approach the fact that for the first time in modern history the Jewish nation shares in the evils of racism, cruelty, war, censorship, the irresponsible exercise of power and injustice? What is the posture of the Diaspora American Jew, persuaded by an Arendtian view of politics, toward Israel after 1967? The issue here is not the hard realities of international politics but rather the premises and character of American Jewish support and criticism of Israel—to say nothing of the rhetoric of international criticism and support. The free, political, "normal" Jew has disappointed the exceptional noble pariah except to vindicate the fact of the shared, common humanity of the Jew.

Is there any significant future for Jewish national identity as an essentially secular phenomenon in America, given the revival of religion among both Christians and Jews beginning in the last decades of the twentieth century? What if the American Jewish community opts either for complete assimilation or religious revival? What if Jews are left with a *religious* community in America and a *national* (whether combined with religion or not, as in other Middle Eastern nations) one in Israel? Perhaps Arendt was the last of a generation for which Jewish national identity could circumvent religious faith. Secular European learning and the everyday patterns of secular Jewish life, derived from the religious and social habits of the European Diaspora, created Arendt's and even Rahel Varnhagen's Jewishness. Arendt herself participated only marginally in Jewish religious life, even as a child. Is her mode of Jewish nationalism, a third option between religious sectarianism and political Zionism, still possible?

The possible disappearance of the secular Jewish national community in America would close the chapter on the legacy of a conception of Jewish national identity Arendt shared with her European contemporaries. That secular, European, post-Emancipation legacy bred Zionism and its critique; it bred the notion of a special Jewish nation held together by common experience and habits, whether dispersed or in a national home. Should this occur, the irony would be that the Arendtian conception of an autonomous realm of politics failed to achieve a goal central to Arendt herself. Only if one accepts her generous interpretation of the American political tradition and its modern potential can the plausibility of her concept of politics be vindicated. Even so, there is no assurance that a separate Jewish nation, in her sense of the word, will survive in a pluralistic America.

With the disappearance of the secular Diaspora Jew and the rise of the Israeli ethnic and religious nationalist, the Arendtian dream will have vanished. As she wrote poignantly in 1947, "In America one does not have to pretend that Judaism is nothing but a denomination and resort to all those desperate and crippling disguises that were common among the rich and educated Jews of Europe. The development of Jewish culture . . . will from now on not depend on circumstances beyond the control of the Jewish people, but upon their own will."[7] Ordinary power politics and nationalism, assimilation, and religious allegiance—processes apart from Arendt's public realm, yet acts of conscious Jewish will—may end the career of the once pariah Jewish secular nation, both in Israel and in America.

Facing: The Hannah Arendt Library at Bard College. Photo, Serena Randolph. Courtesy of the Hannah Arendt Collection, Stevenson Library, Bard College.

SONDERDRUCK AUS ERANOS-JAHRBUCH XXI

Zur Entwicklungsgeschichte der Kabbalistischen Konzeption der Schechinah

von

GERSHOM SCHOLEM

RHEIN-VERLAG ZÜRICH

1953

Hannah Arendt's Jewish Experience

THINKING, ACTING, JUDGING

:::

JEROME KOHN

The members of this panel have been asked to consider the following question: "What is the importance of Hannah Arendt's Jewish identity?" Though a response might be fashioned in categories of particularism and universalism, is there not something problematic about the question itself, even aside from Arendt's understanding of the uniqueness of every human life? What exactly does Jewish identity mean when applied to a nonreligious Jew who in much of her writing criticized the Jewish people, and who, because she dared to judge the behavior of certain Jewish leaders during the Holocaust, was cast out of Jewish communities in America, Europe, and Israel? If identity always implies some sort of sameness,[1] the sameness, for example, of a set of generic personal and behavioral characteristics by which an individual is recognized as a member of a group or collective, then it is tempting to say that her Jewish identity, without denying that it existed, holds little importance for *who* Hannah Arendt was. And this temptation becomes harder to resist if one considers the principal trains of her thought, which embrace the *human* world, *human* plurality, *human* freedom, *human* action, and the distinctive faculties of *human* minds. Arendt invites all human beings, human beings as such, to join her and think for themselves along these trains of thought, which, though they are by no means "restricted" for Jews, are not easy to see as setting forth or gathering steam from her Jewish identity.

If it is politically attached to Arendt, I find the term Jewish identity even more problematic. In a now-famous letter written to Gershom Scholem in 1963, Arendt responds to his complaint that she lacks "*Ahabath Israel*: Love of the Jewish people" by simply agreeing with him. "You are quite right," she says, and then continues, "I have never in my life 'loved' any people or collective—neither the German people, nor the French, nor the American, nor the working class or anything of that sort."[2] For Scholem "love of the Jewish people" is the inner meaning of a Jew's identity, whose sameness lies in being a part of—in *participating* in—that exclusive and excluding love. This quasi-theological, quasi-Zionistic sameness of Scholem's Jewish identity, unlike the

Facing: Inscribed title page of Arendt's copy of Gershom Scholem's *Zur Entwicklungsgeschichte der Kabbalistischen Konzeption der Schechinah.* Courtesy of the Hannah Arendt Collection, Stevenson Library, Bard College.

sameness of a set of merely outward characteristics, entails the immortality, at any cost, of "God's chosen people." The military might of the sovereign State of Israel has inflicted waste and desperation on far greater numbers of Arab men, women, and children than Arabs have inflicted on Israelis, and yet the destiny of Israel still hangs in the balance. Arendt rejects this sense of Jewish identity, as itself a rejection of the reality of the world that Jews, whether they want to or not, cohabit with people other than themselves whom they do not love.

But if we replace the word *identity* with the word *experience*, the question before us changes completely. To doubt the importance of what Arendt experienced as a Jew, the witness she bore to the unprecedented catastrophe that befell Jews in her time—as I have raised doubts first about the importance and then the existence of her Jewish identity—would be more than irresponsible. It would come closer than one could possibly wish to letting something precious and vital slip through one's fingers and disappear from sight.

That is the general point I want to make, and in what follows I will try to illustrate it. We should bear in mind that Arendt accepted having been born a Jew as a "given" of her being, a gift for which she was always grateful and never dreamed of exchanging. Distinguishing amongst: a *natural* Jewish identity that, even or especially if we are skeptical of its importance, is indisputable in Arendt's case;[3] a *religious* Jewish identity of a common creed and rites to which Arendt is not a party; and a Jewish identity of the *heart*, like Scholem's, which is alien to Arendt, may help us to appreciate the impact of her Jewish experience. A preliminary and perhaps oblique way of approaching this matter is to consider Arendt's status as a political philosopher or as a philosopher tout court.

Readers of *The Human Condition*, precisely because of its abstract generality, are hard put not to think of it as a work of political philosophy, while readers of *The Life of the Mind*, primarily because of its twofold reflective nature—it is an intertwined series of reflections on the reflexivity of mental activities—are hard put to think of it as anything other than a work of philosophy. Yet Arendt consistently denies, and nowhere more explicitly than in *The Life of the Mind*, that she is a philosopher of any stripe. For her the inherent tendency of philosophic thought, not excluding *political* philosophic thought, is to seek atemporal or absolute truths—from the nonnatural or inverted teleology of Plato's idea of the Good to Augustine's vision of the true order of the City of God within the false order of the Earthly City, and to Hegel's and Marx's demonstrations of the dialectical progression of History and historical events toward their necessary ends. Such truths transcend human affairs, even when they are conceived, as they usually are in political philosophies, as immanent in human affairs; they are at home, so to speak, in a "higher" metaphysical realm, which is all well and good as long as they are not logically or, as Arendt sometimes says, "tyranically" imposed on the essential contingency of the free realm of human action, either to determine or encompass it.

The main consideration here is that for Arendt, and no one has ever articulated this as clearly as she does, thinking and acting are fundamentally distinct activities. On the one hand, thinking discloses the self to the self, the condition of which is the thinker's *withdrawal* from the world, while on the other, acting displays the self to other selves, the condition of which is the actor's *appearance* in the world. Granted that for her the activity of thinking is not contemplative but, on the contrary, more sheerly active than acting itself, nevertheless I want to suggest that her experience of the destruction of European Jewry impelled Arendt to weigh action, whose mental spring is not thinking but the self-contradictory activity of willing, as heavier and more exigent when placed in a scale with the absolutes of philosophic thought, at least in her time.[4] More than anything else, I believe, it is the exigency of action that distinguishes Arendt's thinking from philosophy in general and political philosophy in particular. Her thinking, which she conceives as the self conversing in accord with itself, seeks a *meaningful* world, above all by finding meanings in the ever-changing appearances brought forth by human actions, rather than the truths those same appearances have been thought by philosophers to obscure. Thus, thinking as Arendt practices it need not be at odds with acting: as distinct activities, they can and usually do run parallel to each other. Indeed, it was her experience of thinking's failure to find meaning in the phenomenal world that prompted Arendt's discovery of a new "middle term," as she once said of Kant, "that links and provides a transition from theory to practice."[5] For her, if not for Kant, that "transition" leads back and forth between the activities of thinking and acting without implying their convergence. The "middle term" that Arendt discovers between the self and other selves, relating them to each other, not only precludes the search for absolutes but also heals the abyssal, anarchic freedom of the will; it "provides" the way along which new meanings enter and enrich the world through new actions.[6]

Another way to look at this is to say with Arendt that thinking, if it is to be relevant *to* experience, cannot lose contact *with* experience. I should add that the term experience here signifies the mind's imaginative encounter with *reality*, that is, with those events that affect human lives and sometimes, in extreme cases, destroy parts of the human world. A part of that world was deliberately destroyed in her lifetime, and Arendt remembers and laments the diminishment of both the world and its experience, the loss itself perhaps even more than what was lost: "It is not merely that a people or a nation or a given number of individuals perishes, but rather that a portion of our common word is destroyed, an aspect of the world that has revealed itself to us until now but can never reveal itself again."[7] If the thinker's withdrawal is both the condition *and* the phenomenological description of understanding the past, of endowing it with meaning, the activity of thinking cannot but be strained when the experience of what has passed is intentionally obliterated, as it was in totalitarian societies, first by systematic lies and then by means of violence.

That the activity of thinking originates in experience is crucial for Arendt. Even before Plato unequivocally said so, that initiatory experience was of wonder, an admiring wonder, directed not at what our senses perceive, but at the invisible harmony of the whole, sometimes called the beauty of the cosmos, which the most apparent of appearances may hint at, but only the mind's eye can bring into focus, make still, and behold.[8] Admiring wonder is a response to what is *not* called forth by men, but to what calls forth from men hymns and odes of praise in the case of poets, and reasoned accounts, of which Aristotle's four causes or reasons why are a prime example, in the case of philosophers. Two and a half millennia after Plato, however, the existential experience of European Jews living in the twentieth century was more likely to have been of horror, not the least aspect of which was the blinding of their minds' eyes to their own reality. Jews were denied the solitude of withdrawal, obstructed from exercising their imaginations in the inner dialogue of thought, constrained from living in accord with themselves, deprived of their humanity, and thereby rendered unfit to live among men (*inter homines esse*). Vast numbers of Jews were brutally *prevented*—and this was planned and organized by men—from understanding why they suffered, from recognizing, *re-cognizing*, their familiar world in the factitious world into which they were uprooted and hurled not by fate but by force. What issues from the experience of horror is non-meaning, a sense of nothingness, a revulsion, or, in Sartre's word, *nausea* at the opaque omnipresence of sheer existence, of nothing but existence. Is not that in every conceivable sense the opposite of philosophic wonder?

Today our shame at what humans are capable of doing to their fellow humans, a distant cousin of horror, has become so prevalent that at times thinking, even when not obstructed, seems to be going out of style all by itself. Now the question becomes whether there is still enough wonder left in us to rouse a thinking that in its withdrawal remains circumscribed by the experience of shame. I believe this question, which has seldom been asked explicitly, informs much of the contemporary interest in Arendt's thought, and perhaps even more in a way of thinking that reflects its own unusual, perhaps unique, originating experience. That experience, whose seed was planted in Arendt's youth, is of a *relation* between "the speechless wonder of gratitude" for "what is as it is" and "the speechless horror at what man may do and what the world may become."[9] At first sight so bewildering, this relation is essential for understanding Arendt: what rises between wonder and horror and connects them is the possibility of the new, that is, of action. What matters most in the present context is that the imaginative experience of a new beginning is called forth in response to the conjunction of wonder with horror, not from one and then the other.

In this sense Arendt's thought can be seen as an *approchement* to a world from which the freedom that lies in men's ability to act is ultimately ineradicable. More than anything else, I believe, that is why her way of thinking has become exemplary for those who cannot ignore their need to feel at home in a world into which they never asked to be born. For, and here Arendt acknowledges an affinity with Hegel,[10] an active thinking that refuses to acquiesce in the reality of what it itself cannot change issues in a self-understanding—indeed, a self-illumination—that almost always reconciles the thinker even to an inimical world. That is a lot more than the ancient "consolations of philosophy," but it is not yet the discovery of the "middle term" that links thought to action.

Hannah Arendt was a thinker who acted only rarely, when she "couldn't help it,"[11] as, for instance, when she escaped from Germany by the skin of her teeth in 1933. A few months after the burning of the Reichstag in February of that year, Arendt was enlisted by her friend Kurt Blumenfeld, the head of the Zionist organization in Berlin, to collect antisemitic statements whose sources were not Nazi propaganda but "professional clubs" and "professional journals." The collection was intended to show Jews and others outside of Germany, who for the most part were unaware of it, the extent to which antisemitism permeated ordinary, respectable German society, that is, the same society that did next to nothing to resist Hitler's rise to power. Why did Arendt do this, considering that she "was not a Zionist" and "politically . . . had nothing to do with Zionism"? Moreover, she already believed that conditions for Jews "would just get worse and worse." Well, in her own words, "I did not intend to run around Germany as a second-class citizen," and this "very intelligent idea" of Blumenfeld's "gave me the feeling that something could be done after all." It was a lost cause, of course, and for her efforts in its behalf Arendt was arrested. But "the official who arrested" her turned out, against all odds, to be "a charming fellow," and she "made friends" with him. When he said, "I got you in here [and] I shall get you out again," she "relied" on his "open, decent face" rather than on the lawyer dispatched by the Zionist organization to aid her. That lawyer "was himself afraid," in an admittedly frightening situation, and she sent him packing at the official's urging: "Don't get a lawyer! . . . Jews don't have any money now. . . . Save your money!" The official was good to his word; he did get her out of jail, and Arendt forthwith crossed the German border "illegally"—her "name had not been cleared" from the police register—*gratified* that she was no longer "innocent," no longer "a bystander," but someone who had made a decision and "done something."[12] In short, she had acted—with courage, with luck, and with the indispensable support of a most unlikely friend.

I do not want to belabor this perhaps minor incident. Arendt spoke of it in public only once, and then with embarrassment, saying it was "of no consequence."[13] Nevertheless, anyone familiar with her fully developed understanding of action cannot but recognize some of its elements in this recounting of what transpired not simply because Arendt *was* a Jew—that was yet to come—but also because she *acted* for the sake of Jews. These elements include the determination to do something that *can* be done, which Arendt later elaborates as the actuality of freedom experienced only in action; the inability of thought to determine the outcome of any specific action in advance, which later becomes the ever-present element of risk, of chance, and contingency in all action; and the trust placed in someone other than oneself, that is, the fact that no one can act alone, which Arendt will come to see as the joy, and in a sense the miracle, of acting together, of acting in concert with one's fellow men to change the world.

But let me return to antisemitism, surely one of Arendt's great topics. While still in Germany, and later as a stateless exile in France from 1933 to 1941, in her late twenties and early thirties, Arendt sought to understand how antisemitism had grown in Germany, of all places, where the emancipation of Jews had been associated with the struggle for human freedom since the Enlightenment. In the eighteenth century, Gotthold Lessing and his friend Moses Mendelssohn, and after them J. G. Herder, who was critical of the Enlightenment ideal of an ahistorical, universal humanity, strove to liberate Jews from the *mentalité* of the ghetto. The liberation of Jews became "official" with the Emancipation Edict of 1812, that is, in the wake of the French Revolution and the Declaration of the Rights of Man, followed by Bonaparte's victories in 1806–7 and the French occupation of Prussia. Arendt's main point is that not Lessing, Mendelssohn, nor Herder, nor the Edict of 1812, which in any case was never passed into law, succeeded in emancipating Jews. True, the *social* assimilation of Jews was now more viable than before, but Jews took no part in anything like a *public* realm where they could raise their voices and take responsibility for the future of German Jewry. The assimilation of Jews into German society[14] and their lack of responsible political action are the kernels that grew into Arendt's well-known and controversial distinction between social and political life,[15] and they mark the beginning of her career as a conscious pariah among her own people.

After 1812 and before 1823 Arendt discerns a historical moment when the absolutist Prussian monarchy, the power of the state, lacked the support of both the aristocratic and bourgeois classes. The Junkers wanted the ancient privileges attached to their hereditary properties, which had been attenuated by the monarchy, reinstated, and the bourgeoisie wanted a constitution that would legally establish and secure its financial and economic interests. The monarchy resisted the demands of both of these classes as diminutions of its own power, but it is more consequential for our purposes that the mutual opposition of the aristocrats and the bourgeoisie to the monarchy by no means united them. On the contrary, the conservative aristocrats mounted a blistering attack on the bourgeoisie's "cosmopolitanism," its predilection for international trade, and its accumulation of wealth as subversive of the German "spirit." Worst of all, the aristocrats declared the bourgeoisie to be a disintegrative and destructive force within the German nation. At the same time, the peasant class, which felt itself exploited by the premiums exacted on loans negotiated by ingenious bourgeois capitalists, that is, for reasons not wholly dissimilar to those of the Junkers, also despised the bourgeoisie. To salvage its own position in German society, the bourgeoisie shifted the attack of the aristocrats and the enmity of the peasants to the Jews, which is to say that the most liberal class in Germany did all it could to revive the feudal hatred of Jews as usurers, laying every charge against itself on Jewish doorsteps. For Arendt this marks a turning point in the history of German Jews.

When the monarchy, above all class distinctions but dependent on popular support, accommodated to a degree the demands of both the aristocracy and the bourgeoisie and offered a degree of protection to the peasantry, the reinvigorated prejudice against Jews played a major role in restoring and rebalancing the class structure of German society. A political crisis was averted when every class and also the monarchy readily agreed that Jews, now looked upon as a caste within the various strata of society, were "the 'real' usurers"— which, of course, was not true, and had not been true since the Middle Ages. In 1823 the Law for the Estates of the Provinces "for the first time . . . linked the right to elect and be elected [to public office] to a person's being 'in communion with a Christian church,'" which was "an open revocation of the Edict of 1812."[16] So much for the Enlightenment's "inalienable" rights of man. To top it off, the civil rights of German Jews, which finally were enacted into law in 1869, did not alleviate but instead exacerbated society's prejudice against them. For it was then that the danger of the civil equality of a "foreign" people living within the German national state, which had been hinted at by the aristocracy in regard to the bourgeoisie, was deemed real. The breadth and depth of the social prejudice against Jews, as we have seen, prompted Arendt to act in 1933, the result of which was the abrogation of her civil rights, statelessness, and exile. Soon after 1933, Hitler found, in promulgating his antisemitic ideology, that the outdated hatred of Jews as usurers, and even more so as politically dangerous intruders,[17] was the easiest thing to export to countries with strong Catholic and/or nationalist identities, such as Poland, where far greater numbers of Jews resided than in Germany. From this constellation in modern German Jewish history, in part experienced through her capacious imagination and in part in her person, Arendt learned a lesson she never forgot, namely, that the assimilation and the emancipation of a people in a land that is not their own exist in *inverse* proportion. Social assimilation comes at the price of forfeiting political emancipation, and political emancipation at the price of jeopardizing social assimilation.[18] Upon arriving in New York in 1941, Arendt was pleased to find that the sheer diversity of the people, their customs, and habits left nothing "American" to assimilate to, at least for herself. Her stand *for* emancipation and *against* assimilation aligned her, for a while, with Zionism as the only authentic Jewish political movement.

During the Second World War, Arendt called for an international Jewish army, not just a Jewish brigade within the British army (though she appreciated that as well). Her call to Jews all over the world was not to immortalize the Jewish people by sacrificing their own and others' lives, but to act for the *freedom* of their people by combating their oppressors. A Jewish army fighting the Nazis under a Jewish flag would be an unequivocal sign to the world that Jews *are* a free people. At this same time Arendt distinguished between a people and a polity, and it is in accord with this distinction that a few years later she spoke of a "right to have rights."[19] A "right to have rights" cannot be a civil or human right in the usual sense, since it is a right that trumps the experience of European Jews whose civil and human rights were systematically nullified by the Nazis in camps (or "laboratories," as Arendt called them) designed for that purpose. Again it is a question of action, in this instance the fundamental action of founding a polity, whose laws and institutions for the first time would enable Jews to make binding treaties, military alliances, and trade agreements with other polities. The *political* right of Jews to enjoy civil and human rights would no longer be in question, since it would be manifest to, and recognized by, other states and nations throughout the world.

There is not time now to go into this matter in the detail it deserves, but it should be noted that Arendt broke with Zionism over the nature of this new polity. She contended not for a Jewish nation-state based on the model of European nation-states, which is what Zionists wanted and eventually got, but for a Jewish homeland or *Heimat* within a federated Palestinian state. Arabs and Jews are neighbors in the small land of Palestine, but can live as neighbors only in a secular state whose political structure is revolutionary and opposed, from beginning to end, to the equally revolutionary structure of "the so-called totalitarian state," both of which are simultaneously present in Arendt's mind in the late 1940s.[20] In a federated Palestinian state, two distinct peoples would have "a common government . . . rest[ing] on Jewish-Arab community councils." Power and authority would flow upward from this "lowest and most promising level of proximity and neighborliness," and not downward from above. In Arendt's words, which now appear prescient, "Local self-government and mixed Jewish-Arab municipal and rural councils, on a small scale and as numerous as possible, are the only realistic political measures that can eventually lead to the political emancipation of Palestine." The state envisioned by Arendt might then become a "natural stepping stone for a . . . greater federated structure in the Near East and the Mediterranean area" whose power potential would be immense—an autonomous political entity, to be sure, but one that eschews *national* sovereignty.[21]

This, too, turned out to be a lost cause, but when Israelis, Arabs, and others in or outside the Middle East dismiss the idea of a federated Palestinian state as unrealistic, they implicitly accuse Arendt of lacking political judgment—which is ironic since she is the first political thinker to thematize political judgment. She lacks judgment in the eyes of those who regard the possibilities of action from the point of view of their own or their people's self-interest. But for Arendt the hallmark of judgment is the disinterestedness, or impartiality, that allows the judge, through his imagination, to see with his own eyes from standpoints that are not his own and may differ from his people's. In other words, though she is a Jew, Arendt's political identity is not Jewish but that of an active world spectator, a *Weltbetrachter*,[22] and the sole yet crucial "sameness" in that identity resides in the community of spectators who also exercise their imaginations in judging. Human judgment is far removed from Hegel's notion that History is the final judge in human affairs (*Die Weltgeschichte ist das Weltgericht*), for, unlike History, the activity of judging does not go on behind the backs of actors but is the other side of action. In fact, judgment is operative in actors insofar as their actions reveal the *principles*— which the Greeks thought of as *aretai* or excellences—that inspire them. In the last analysis, the spontaneity of actors *is* their judgment that, along with the principles of their actions, they themselves as actors are fit to appear in the world, regardless of the perils that always await them, and regardless, too, of their success or failure.

Apart from seeing from the points of view of others, many others, as many as possible, political judgment is feckless, no more than an opinion among opinions. Arendt understands political judgment as *refined* opinion, in analogy, one could say, to the way oil must be refined before it can propel a vehicle. No polity, no people, no party has a premium on judgment. When the distinguished Palestinian writer Sari Nusseibeh, in his political memoir *Once Upon a Country*, called for a binational secular state, as had Arendt many years before, Arabs derided him as an "Arab who wants to be a Jew," and Jews as "the most dangerous Arab alive." To Hannah Arendt, who was a Jew, and to Sari Nusseibeh, who is an Arab, the core of the Arab-Israeli conflict is the inability—or refusal—of both Jews and Arabs to see themselves from the other's point of view.

Though Arendt wrote about Jews and Jewish affairs during four decades, from the 1930s to the 1960s, I have been trying to shed some light on the ways in which her political thought in general is anchored in her experience as a Jew. In this sense, her Jewish experience is literally the foundation of her thought: it supports her thinking even when she is not thinking about Jews or what pertains only to Jews. To put it in a way suggested earlier, Arendt's most abstract concepts and ideas grow from an experiential ground, and they thrive, as great trees thrive, because they remain rooted in that ground. On the other hand, the power of her political thought can be fully grasped if and only if her ideas strike chords and resonate in the experiences of others, however different they may be from hers. Her most original, profound, and yet elusive concept of human plurality, the uniqueness and hence dignity potential in every human life, and the host of ideas surrounding it, developed out of her experience of political antisemitism. By calling upon Diaspora Jews, that is, Jews who for centuries had lived dispersed in different nations and cultures, to show *who* they are by joining together to combat their common oppressor, Arendt first disclosed plurality as the condition of action, and action itself as the experience of freedom, the latter being the origin and raison d'être of politics as she understands it.[23] As the condition of action, since no one acts alone, plurality is likewise the condition of human solidarity, for only when the plain fact that "not a single man but Men inhabit the earth"[24] is fully registered can the fundamental meaning of political life, which is to share the earth with others, be fully recognized. Today's instantaneous communications make it theoretically more feasible than ever before to encounter others as neighbors in one world regardless of where they live. This political encountering of others as separate *and* related, distinct *and* equal may be in the throes of being born right now. But if it is not to be stillborn, the plurality and dignity of human lives will have to be experienced by men and women all over the world, and their experience obviously cannot and need not be the same as Arendt's.

We have seen how Arendt's urge to think and find meaning in the world, rather than truth beyond the world, was instigated by her need to understand the rise of antisemitism in Germany. In Arendt's native land, where distrust of Jews had become a widespread social prejudice over the previous hundred years, Hitler transformed that prejudice into a "valid" political ideology, that is, an ideology approved as the *truth* of Nature by world-alienated masses, in Germany and elsewhere.[25] The consequences of that transformation were unprecedented, precipitating from the denial of the right of Jews to appear in public to, in the ensuing darkness, the insignificance of their right to live. Although Arendt was never in a Nazi concentration or extermination camp, in 1940 the government of France, not yet Vichy but the Third Republic, could legally—because Germany had stripped her of citizenship in 1933—intern her as an "enemy alien." The irony that at the time France and Germany were on the brink of war, and that she had fled Germany to seek asylum in France, is striking. It may be idle to speculate on the role her internment by the French played when, a decade later, Arendt *imagines* the terror of the Nazi camps, the "radical evil" of rendering the lives of Jews, simply because they were Jews, along with the lives of everyone else touched by that terror, "superfluous," that is, interchangeable and expendable, in the attempt to "accelerate" Nature's plan to evolve a superior or master "Aryan" race. The power of Arendt's imagination, which is fully manifest in her writing, enables readers of *The Origins of Totalitarianism*, most of whom today lack experience of or relatable to a totalitarian society, to experience vicariously an evil that cannot be "understood" or "explained" by any known "evil motives," such as "self-interest, greed, covetousness, resentment, lust for power, [or] cowardice."[26] For the first time in human history, according to Arendt, the hitherto disguised *root* of evil appeared in the world unmasked.

Arendt's idea of one supreme human right, the "right to have rights," hangs upon the experience of having lost one's accustomed place, rights, and legal standing as a citizen. Thus it might be thought to originate in human superfluousness, except, as she sees it, the worthlessness of an individual life eludes experience: to be superfluous is to be deprived of "the reality of experience," of "*common* sense," of "contact with [one's] fellow men." In every respect the polar opposite of human plurality, the meaning of human superfluousness can be thought today probably only through the experience of what Arendt calls "loneliness." Even more than being forced out of a particular, familiar community, the experience of loneliness is of "not . . . belong[ing] to the world at all."[27] The one supreme right is therefore the "right to the human condition itself," which "can and can only be guaranteed by the comity of nations." Thus, while negating superfluousness, the idea of a "right to have rights" is embedded in the freedom experienced by a plurality of human beings joined in action to generate new or regenerate exhausted political entities. This highest of rights transcends "the rights of a citizen [by] being the right of man to citizenship,"[28] which is to say that its realization would afford, as no formal contract can afford, men and women qua citizens the experience of *political* equality, the only sense, after all, in which plural and unique beings can be conceived as equal. It should be noted that political equality does not entail the sameness of equals in the sense of a national, religious, or ethnic identity, of social uniformity, let alone the sameness of superfluous human lives, the latter being nothing but a logical deduction of totalitarian ideologies. What Arendt means by political equality demands far more from citizens than entering a voting booth alone once or twice every few years to cast ballots for candidates of their choice. The experience of political equality is of one's own and one's peers' responsibility for their nation's actions, and of their ability to join together and act into their nation's future. This experience is most likely to be realized in a revolutionary council state, such as Arendt strove to see established by Jews and Arabs in Palestine. By showing its rarity, her book *On Revolution* appeals less to scholars and students of revolution and more to those who, though they may be citizens of a state, and though that state may be a modern constitutional democracy, have nevertheless experienced political inequality, perhaps the foremost harbinger of loneliness.[29]

What we have not yet seen, and in conclusion will turn to, is how the "right to have rights" *corresponds* to the specific meaning Arendt gives, in *Eichmann in Jerusalem: A Report on the Banality of Evil*, to the new concept of a "crime against humanity," and to her judgment of that crime.[30] In 1961 Adolf Eichmann stood trial in Jerusalem, and Arendt attended his trial because she wanted to see in the flesh a man responsible for the deaths of literally millions of Jews, men, women, and children who had committed no crime and posed no threat to the German Reich. Her experience in the Jerusalem courtroom may have been her culminating experience as a Jew; it was certainly the catalyst of her discovery of the power of judgment, which is indeed the culmination of her political thought. The case of Eichmann is complex, and one way of approaching it is to note how frequently we hear clerics and other moralists bemoan the increasing number of people who seem proud of their liberation from moral and religious prohibitions, of their dismissal of, or impassivity toward, the commands of conscience. Those words do not fit well with Arendt's experience of Eichmann, and certainly they do not capture what she means when she speaks of "the banality of evil." But they may account for the striking recurrence of that phrase in our everyday language, as well as in the media, to characterize a certain type of crimes, such as the killing of a passerby for his watch or wallet. In such a crime we have difficulty relating the motive of the criminal, say to buy something, to taking a human life. And if the purchase turns out to be crack cocaine, and the criminal a drug addict who has lost control over what he does, we are still likely to call his crime "unthinkable"—primarily, I suspect, because we cannot imagine ourselves committing it. In such a case we do not say, "There, but for the grace of God, go I." Despite its unthinkability, however, his crime *is* thought of as an instance of "the banality of evil," not to excuse it, but somehow to reconcile ourselves to a society in which this sort of criminal behavior—less rare, perhaps, than it used to be—is believed to emanate from the lack of a moral disposition. "The banality of evil" has also been used, and for much the same reason, to characterize the unfortunate U.S. policy of "aggressive interrogation"—in plain language the torture of prisoners, who may be no more than suspects, in the "war against terror." The motive of men to torture other men is never moral: it can be the pragmatic motive of *discovery*, or the highly questionable one of *evidence*, or, more important in this context, the "unthinkable" one of willfully degrading and humiliating a fellow human being. In disparate acts, which recently have included the random shooting of students in a lecture hall of an Illinois university, the dumping by Florida police officials of a quadriplegic from his wheelchair, and the abandonment of infants by their mothers, it is the antimoral *motivation* of the transgressors that we seek to comprehend in what has now become a catchword, "the banality of evil."

Arendt's experience as a Jew facing Eichmann is very different. She sees in him a particular perpetrator of a political crime that has far greater consequences for the world than immoral or amoral acts ever have. "In the center of moral considerations of human conduct," she writes, "stands the self; in the center of political considerations of conduct stands the world."[31] In this partially Kantian view, moral transgressions, regardless of who else is harmed, always shatter the integrity of the transgressor. The political crime against humanity, on the other hand, corresponds to the "right to have rights," insofar as the former denies what the latter promises, a chance for men and women to actualize their potential freedom, which becomes manifest in the world whenever they speak and act together as equal citizens of polities. When Arendt saw Eichmann in the dock, he struck her as an ordinary man, neither especially intelligent nor especially stupid, even though what he did was not in the least ordinary. He was not a psychopath; he murdered no one with his hands; but by *identifying* himself with what he called "the household use" of Kant's categorical imperative,[32] and with the cooperation of Jewish leaders, he organized the mass transport of Jews across Europe to extermination camps where, in unfathomable loneliness, they were metamorphosed into living corpses before being destroyed. Because Arendt chooses not to overlook the role that Jewish leaders played in the destruction of their people, she was accused of absolving Eichmann and blaming his victims. That is a pure distortion of what she says, which has nothing to do with the absence and everything to do with the *uselessness* of traditional moral standards throughout "respectable European society—not just in Germany but almost all European countries, not only among the persecutors but also among the victims."[33] Because she now calls the evil that arose with this uselessness, which she observes specifically in the person of Eichmann, not radical but "banal," Jews on three continents ostracized Arendt. This may recall her exile from Germany thirty years before, and it is probably the most political consequence to date of her concept of "the banality of evil."

To Arendt, the banality of Eichmann's crime against humanity ensues from his inability to think, which she apprehends in the extraordinary triteness of the clichés that flowed from his mouth regardless of what he talked about. This was his "distinction," the distinction of a "buffoon," the only sense, perhaps, in which he was not entirely ordinary, and Arendt goes on to say that the independence of the activity of thinking, absent in Eichmann, can condition those who enjoy it against evildoing.[34] Yet, under the law, no one is condemned for not thinking, for what does not go on in his mental life, but for what he does and why he does it. This is the crux of the matter. Arendt agrees with the judgment of the court that Eichmann should be hanged, but not because, as the court held, he had "base motives." What she sees in Eichmann is that he had not an unknowable evil motive (as she implied in speaking of radical evil) but *no motive whatsoever*. He did his "duty" as a "law-abiding citizen" of Nazi Germany,[35] and therefore anticipated rising within the ranks of the Gestapo, but contrary to what has sometimes been alleged, his motivation cannot be attributed to "careerism." To advance his career did not *move* him to erase Jews from the face of the earth, any more than he would have murdered a superior to take his place in the bureaucracy where they both held jobs. He was not in any perceptible sense morally corrupt, and above all he was not an antisemite; he harbored no "ill feelings" against the Jews he dispatched to their deaths.[36] The conclusion of Arendt's judgment addressed to Eichmann reads:

> Let us assume, for the sake of argument, that it was nothing more than misfortune that made you a willing instrument in the organization of mass murder; there still remains the fact that you have carried out, and therefore actively supported, a policy of mass murder. For politics is not like the nursery; in politics obedience and support are the same. And just as you supported and carried out a policy of not wanting to share the earth with the Jewish people and the people of a number of other nations—as though you and your

superiors had any right to determine who should and who should not inhabit the world—we find that no one, that is, no member of the human race, can be expected to want to share the earth with you. This is the reason, and the only reason, you must hang.[37]

In other words, the crime against humanity is against the human status of plurality, "against the very nature of mankind," *the* political crime for which Eichmann was indicted, as Arendt sees it, not just by the people of Israel but also by all the peoples of the world. His crime against human plurality was "perpetrated upon the body of the Jewish people . . . only the choice of victims, not the nature of the crime, could be derived from the long history of Jew-hatred and antisemitism," and that choice was not Eichmann's.[38] To judge his crime requires no proof of the perpetrator's intention or motive to do wrong, nor of his guilty conscience, for in doing his "duty," in being *duty-bound*, Eichmann was extremely conscientious. Arendt knows that what she says flies in the face of the age-old moral principles that inform the law, but that is her main point: moral standards of human conduct, which originate in the accord of the two-in-one in the activity of thinking,[39] did not apply in judging the crime of the particular man who appeared before her in the Jerusalem courtroom. That the judges in the trial did not view Eichmann as Arendt did, and that neither do most of us, is due to the undoubted difficulty of distinguishing the activity of judging from that of thinking. By sending to their deaths masses of people he did not even dislike, Eichmann's crime against humanity included, since he was no demon, his own humanity. It was his inability to think what he was doing, both in the war and during his trial, which defies thought and releases, at least in Arendt, the power to comprehend and judge what thinking cannot endow with meaning—the terrifying banality of the evil done to the world by this one thoughtless man.[40]

Arendt does not seek reconciliation to a world in which such evil once appeared and for that reason is "more likely" to reappear "than its initial emergence could ever have been," and on a far greater scale.[41] The reconciliation she seeks is to a world that strives to prevent its recurrence, that is, to a world in which its previous unprecedented occurrence is kept unprecedented. That is not something thinking can do, since that activity, as Arendt understands and practices it, does not affect what happens in the world, even if it affects what thinking individuals refuse to do when they appear in the world. Arendt's point, I believe, is not simply to encourage thinking but to revivify it, since thoughtless evil, which unlike radical evil has no root for thinking to latch on to and thus no experience for thinking to remain bound to, tends to render thinking men and women themselves superfluous. What else could she have meant when in 1964, writing about "The Destruction of the Six Million," she says that a "reappraisal of our mental habits" is not only now required but also so "agonizing" that it threatens to make our humanity "*irrelevant*"?[42]

Eichmann was unable to think what he had done, and Arendt, who excels at thinking, cannot think it either. The only meaning of such evil is paradoxical: its "banality" stymies the faculty of thinking that alone can give it meaning. Arendt suggests that, because it has no root, banal evil is "extreme" and "can overgrow and lay waste the whole world."[43] She also suggests that, because it is "word-and-thought defying,"[44] it is *essentially* evil. But that does not mean it is "nothing," or "insubstantial," or a "lack of being" as the great tradition of philosophic thought, in which the unity of thinking and being is presupposed, has maintained.[45] From a psychological perspective, her judgment that Eichmann "must hang" comports with her love of the diversity of human life and her abhorrence of its destruction. Yet her invocation of the death penalty is not to punish Eichmann—there is no punishment commensurate with his crime—but to indicate that a human world can neither forgive nor contain a man who never hesitated to fill boxcars with human beings and ship them to death camps, much as cattle are shipped to slaughterhouses, a man, that is, who in sheer indifference to his own humanity never elected "to share the earth" with others. Because she sees in Eichmann a man "who should never have been born," Arendt repeats the judgment of Jesus Christ: "It were better for him that a millstone were hanged about his neck, and he cast into the sea" (Luke 17:2).[46] It were better *for him*.

The power of judgment is the link between thinking and acting that Arendt long sought and here discovers, as probably only she could discover it. Her judgment cleaves the *meaningless* meaning of a world-destructive crime from what henceforth the world can afford to let appear in it. It is her *decisive* judgment that never again can a human being "be expected to want to share the earth with" such a man as Eichmann. Arendt's judgment is an arrow shot into the past, which, its target struck, revivifies her thinking. She will not "think the unthinkable" (which is always a contradiction), but she will reveal an abundance of meanings in phenomena and events that have passed, are passing, or are anticipated. *Thinking*, the first part of *The Life of the Mind*, abounds with new meanings, and the reader who discovers the world of which they are the meanings will find for himself that thinking sets limits to what he is willing to do. That is the negative correlate of the power of judgment to halt the indeterminable oscillation of the will in men of action, the will's inability to decide to act, not in necessity, to which it is not subject, but as Buridan's ass is said to have starved to death while standing unfettered between two equally tempting bales of hay. It is no wonder, considering all that it relieved her of, that Arendt wrote *Eichmann in Jerusalem* in a "state of euphoria."[47] The ability to judge, however, is an *autonomous* faculty of the human mind, and by no means a readily applicable "middle term."

Arendt's judgment of Eichmann as the motiveless perpetrator of a crime that could destroy the world is clearly for the sake of the world, and she writes *Eichmann in Jerusalem* to tell the story of a man whose life exemplifies the extremity of such thoughtless, unthinkable evil. But to experience the import of her judgment requires an "enlarged mentality," as Kant called it, to make present to the mind what is not present to the senses—not a sense datum but a complex political image of the concrete reality of human freedom, distinctness, and equality as *undermined* by Eichmann's deeds against that reality. Arendt's judgment of Eichmann, whose emblematic significance is his disappearance from the world, claims agreement, since by itself it cannot prevent the recurrence of his crime, a restriction on the scope of judgment that is all too evident and of which she is fully aware. To claim agreement, after her book's entirely unexpected reception, is, I believe, the principal reason she undertook to explain and justify the concept of "the banality of evil" in the remarkable series of essays that precede *The Life of the Mind*.[48] In these writings she seeks not the passive consent of her readers but instead to draw them into the silent dialogue of her thinking, to induce them to think with her as far as she can guide them. Only then, at the boundaries of thought, may they actively assent to the validity of her judgment of a man who, without thinking what he was doing, did all he could to obliterate human plurality from the face of the earth, and with it every trace of dignity from human lives. In the eventuation of that assent, Eichmann's execution, unlike his life, becomes thinkable, indeed most meaningful, provided only that the mind's eye sees in the gallows—under which Eichmann stood "elated"—the threshold to a renewed and lightened world, which each one of us, Jew and non-Jew alike, *can* elect to cross.

Facing: Shy Abady, *Smoke*, 2004, mixed media on paper, on wood.

W·H·AUDEN

CITY WITHOUT
WALLS
and Other Poems

To Hannah
with love
from
Wystan

RANDOM HOUSE   NEW YORK

The Pariah as Rebel

HANNAH ARENDT'S JEWISH WRITINGS

RON H. FELDMAN

Hannah Arendt was born in 1906 in Germany and died in 1975 in New York. Between those bookends, her life played out during what she termed the "dark times" of the twentieth century. She was a political and cultural critic, publishing many essays and books, and she is now considered among the elite of the German Jewish culture that produced so many great literary, scientific, and artistic figures. Arendt's reputation as one of her generation's most gifted political thinkers rests on two major books, *The Origins of Totalitarianism* and *The Human Condition*, both published in the 1950s, and a slew of other essay collections.

Still, Arendt is probably best remembered as the author of *Eichmann in Jerusalem*, first published as a series in the *New Yorker* in 1963 and then as a book in 1964. Its now-famous subtitle was *A Report on the Banality of Evil*, a line that has been much quoted and much misunderstood. The appearance of this book about the trial of Adolf Eichmann, one of the leading Nazi organizers of what is now called the Holocaust, created a heated controversy in the Jewish community. At that time she was viciously attacked, especially for her assertion that Jewish leaders throughout Europe had "cooperated in one way or another, for one reason or another, with the Nazis,"[1] during the Holocaust. Many people were under the impression that the "banality" in the subtitle of the book demeaned the suffering of the Jews during the Holocaust, and her accusations against Jewish leaders meant that, "We are asked, it appears, to confess that the Jews, too, had their 'share' in these acts of genocide,"[2] as put by her onetime friend, the great Jewish historian Gershom Scholem. Arendt clarified her position by saying that the tragedy of the Jewish leaders was that they "were *not* traitors or Gestapo agents and *still* they became the tools of the Nazis."[3] Nevertheless, she was accused of being a self-hating Jew and largely read-out of the Jewish community.

As will be clear in what follows, I have a much more positive evaluation of Arendt's Jewish politics. I will not dwell on the Eichmann controversy, but given that my focus is on Arendt's Jewish writings, it is prudent at least to

Facing: Inscribed title page of Hannah Arendt's copy of W. H. Auden's *City Without Walls*. The inscription reads: "To Hannah with love from Wystan." Courtesy of the Hannah Arendt Collection, Stevenson Library, Bard College.

acknowledge this famous episode. Indeed, in retrospect, it is worth pointing out a double irony that has come to pass. Israeli Prime Minister David Ben-Gurion's political purpose in having Eichmann captured in Argentina, brought to Jerusalem and put on trial was to teach the world about the Holocaust, antisemitism, and the justification for a Jewish state. While Arendt concluded that Eichmann was guilty and should be hanged, she was critical of the "show trial" aspect of the proceedings, where many witnesses to the Holocaust took the stand even if their relevance to Eichmann's personal role was indirect. Arendt believed that a trial should turn on the guilt of the accused. The double irony is this: for Ben-Gurion it is ironic that Arendt's report is still read and is the main way the Eichmann trial is remembered today; yet, for Arendt it is equally ironic because, despite her criticism of the trial, she has become Ben-Gurion's long-term publicist for the main message of the trial, which was to show the world the horrors of the Holocaust.

I want to begin my exploration of Arendt's political positions and analyses by focusing on what "Jewishness" meant to her. As she writes in her famous response to Gershom Scholem, "I have always regarded my Jewishness as one of the indisputable factual data of my life, and I have never had the wish to change or disclaim facts of this kind."[4] That is, her Jewishness is a given; we might say that Arendt is an "essentialist" when it comes to being Jewish. This is the underpinning of her biting criticism, written long before the Eichmann controversy, of those Jews who sought to escape their Jewishness (especially through celebrity and fame), whom she called the "parvenus." To use a concept she would explore in *The Human Condition*, Jewishness is part of her "natality" and, because of the place and time in which she lived, this fortuitous and uncontrollable circumstance of her birth determined the basic parameters of her fate.

Yet, before the late 1920s, "Jewishness" was not the most important thing in her background or life; like most German Jews, she was culturally more German than Jewish, more secular than religious. Her education was in the classics: she learned Greek but not Hebrew. While she was interested in theology, as demonstrated in her dissertation on Saint Augustine, this was *Christian* theology analyzed from a secular philosophical perspective. And while the *Jewish Writings* includes a 1935 essay lauding Martin Buber as the "true leader" of German Jewish youth because he was able to "rediscover the living roots of . . . [Judaism's] past to build an even greater future,"[5] this is notable because it is a rare instance of documented interest in Jewish philosophy. In general, we cannot call Arendt a "Jewish philosopher or theologian" in the sense of Martin Buber, Franz Rosenzweig, Herman Cohen, or even Gershom Scholem, to name a few German Jewish luminaries; she did not engage with the Jewish textual tradition.

Rather, Arendt's Jewishness is adamantly secular and political. As for so many German Jews, its significance was thrust upon her by the rise of Nazism, but her response was not preordained or typical. As she says in a 1964 interview with Günter Gaus, "my personal problem was political. Purely political! I wanted to do practical work—exclusively and only Jewish work."[6] In the German Jewish milieu of that period, simply the commitment to Jewish politics is significant, because this commitment to the Jews as a *people* is already an action and argument in opposition to Jewish assimilationists, whether secular—those seeking to pass as non-Jews because their Jewish background was simply irrelevant (or so they thought)—or religious, who claimed they were loyal "Germans of the Mosaic persuasion." Nazi antisemitism had foreclosed these options for being accepted as part of the German nation, which meant that Jewishness had become a personal problem for every German Jew. Arendt deliberately chose to affirm loyalty to the Jewish people, and she became a political person by way of Zionist activity.

After escaping Germany in 1933, she worked in France for Youth Aliyah, assisting young Jews leaving Germany for British Mandate–era Palestine. This job gave her a chance to see the Yishuv (as the pre-state Jewish-Zionist community in Palestine was called) in person when she escorted a group that traveled from France. After escaping to America in 1941 she wrote essays and, after the war, worked for Jewish Cultural Reconstruction and Schocken Books.

Although Arendt was quite critical of aspects of Theodor Herzl's Zionist philosophy, her personal transformation into a Zionist in the face of antisemitism bears many similarities to that of political Zionism's founder. For both Arendt and Herzl, their German cultural education was more significant than their Jewish education, and they had little interest in what we might call "Judaism," that is, Jewish religion or philosophy. After becoming politicized, Arendt, also like Herzl, did not display any newfound personal interest in specifically Jewish religion, philosophy, or literature, but was focused on political and historical issues. Therefore, while we might not want to describe Arendt as a Jewish philosopher, we could legitimately describe some of her writing as that of a Jewish political theorist, like Herzl and other Zionists (and anti-Zionists, for that matter).

In another important passage from her interview with Gaus, Arendt says, "I arrived at the conclusion which I always, at the time, expressed to myself in one sentence, a sentence which clarified it to me 'When one is attacked as a Jew, one must defend oneself *as a Jew.*' Not as a German, not as a world-citizen, not as an upholder of the Rights of Man."[7] This passage helps us make sense of what many readers find surprising, the lack of any overtly feminine or feminist positions in her writing, despite another "fact" of Arendt's natality, namely that she was a woman.[8] In my mind, the key reason for the lack of explicit feminist analysis in her writings is that *Arendt was politicized as a Jew*, not as a woman.[9] To invert Y. L. Gordon's famous emancipation motto, "Be a man on the street and a Jew at home," one might even say that Arendt was "a Jew on the street and a woman at home," in correspondence to the distinction between public and private realms that she develops into a key feature of her political theory.[10] It seems that Arendt assumed that she was the intellectual equal of men, and her status as a woman simply did not matter when it came to issues of either philosophy or politics.

Arendt celebrated her path, the type of person she was, in her essay "The Jew as Pariah: A Hidden Tradition." As distinct from Isaac Deutscher's famous analysis of "non-Jewish Jews"[11] who played an important part in European life, Arendt's focus was on Jews who simultaneously affirmed their Jewishness and Europeanness, whom she calls the "pariahs," those "who were great enough to transcend the bounds of nationality and to weave the strands of their Jewish genius into the general texture of European life . . . those bold spirits who tried to make of the emancipation of the Jews that which it really should have been—an admission of Jews *as Jews* to the ranks of humanity."[12] By affirming their Jewish particularity and their Europeanness, they became marginal to both European and Jewish communities. This, of course, was Arendt's fate. She was committed to, yet critical of, both inheritances and her intellectual corpus as a whole is colored by the struggle of being accepted as a Jew in the modern world.

On the Jewish side, as a secular person she had lost the religious Judaism of her ancestors and sought refuge in the concept of a Jewish people. In particular, she finds a model for the politicized "Conscious Pariah" in Bernard Lazare, a contemporary of Herzl's who briefly joined Herzl's Zionist movement but then quit because of political differences. As Arendt writes, for Lazare "the territorial question was secondary—a mere outcome of the primary demand that 'the Jews should be emancipated as a people and in the form of a nation.' What he sought was not an escape from antisemitism but a mobilization of the people against its foes." What Lazare learned, according to Arendt, is that when the Pariah enters politics, he or she becomes a rebel.

While Arendt became known as a rebel in the wake of the 1963 publication of *Eichmann in Jerusalem*, the origins of her role as critic, pundit, and gadfly can be traced back to the 1930s. For example, *The Jewish Writings* includes a previously unpublished seventy-five-page essay entitled "Antisemitism," which was drafted in the late 1930s, about the same time she was completing her biography of Rahel Varnhagen, an early-eighteenth-century German Jewish socialite. This was probably intended to be part of a future book, and some of the materials were refined and included in the first part of *The Origins of Totalitarianism*, which is also entitled "Antisemitism." Nevertheless, the focus is different, and we find here an extensive critique of both assimilation and Zionism as not answering the real needs of the Jewish people.

Arendt writes, "Whereas nationalist historiography is based on the uncritical assumption of a distance on principle between Jews and their host nation, assimilationist historians opt for an equally uncritical assumption of a 100 percent correspondence between Jews and their entire host nation."[13] The problem with both is that they "arise out of a shared Jewish fear of admitting that there are and always have been divergent interests between Jews and segments of the people among whom they live."[14] Both views strip "the relationship between Jews and their host nation of its historicity."[15] The Zionists simply turn the assimilationists' views "upside down. Where the former imagined they had become *like* the German people, the latter respond: No, as antisemitism proves, we are totally *foreign*." For Arendt, this ahistorical theory "appears to conform perfectly to the National Socialists who crystallize their worldview of a *volksgemeinschaft* [ethnic community] in antisemitism." It is from this point of critique that Arendt begins a long investigation into the emancipation, its failures, and the historical position of Jews in Europe as linked to the state as such, part of which eventually found its way into *The Origins of Totalitarianism*.

One of the Zionist policies Arendt disagreed with, for example, was what was called "The Transfer Agreement," which allowed the transfer during the 1930s of some Jewish people and property from Nazi Germany to Palestine in the form of German-manufactured merchandise. While anti-Zionists point to this agreement as "proof" that Zionists collaborated with the Nazis, Arendt is critical from a Jewish perspective, arguing that "it seemed unwise for a Jewish political agency to do business with an antisemitic government."[16] This, she claimed, was a confusion of the proper "distinction between friend and foe."[17] Here she felt the Zionist Organization prioritized the building up of the Jewish homeland in Palestine over the interests of the Jewish people to oppose its enemies.

From 1941 to 1945, Arendt wrote columns in German for the New York–based *Aufbau*; these have been translated and published in *The Jewish Writings*. One of her main themes was advocating for the creation of an independent Jewish army to fight the Nazis. For example, in November 1941 Arendt writes that the Jewish people should "join the battle against Hitler as Jews, in Jewish battle formations under a Jewish flag."[18] She continues this theme until the end of the war, criticizing the Jewish and Zionist establishment, including plutocrats, philanthropists, and rabbinic "leaders" for not advocating this position more strongly to the Allies and rallying the Jewish people to action.[19] Arendt saw the issue as a practical one: close to a third of world Jewry was on the verge of annihilation, and a Jewish army could "at least *attempt* to replace the rules of extermination and the rules of flight with the rules of battle."[20] In the long term, without an army the Jews would not have a place at the peace table; fighting the war *as Jews* was a way to legitimate the Jewish demands for freedom, including the right to a homeland in Palestine.

Related to this enthusiasm for military action, Arendt celebrated the phenomenon of the Warsaw Ghetto fighters, the Jewish partisans, Jews in the Soviet army, and the Palestinian Jewish Brigade of the British army as "aspects of the same great struggle—the Jewish people's struggle for freedom."[21] It is significant, she claims, because it represents a fundamentally new political attitude among Jews: "Gone probably forever, is that chief concern of the Jewish people for centuries: survival at any price. Instead, we find something essentially new among Jews, the desire for dignity at any price."[22] On this point

Arendt shares the position of many Zionists, who were strongly critical of the "the diaspora Jew" and hoped to create a "new Jew" who would be unafraid to stand up for themselves physically and politically, thereby becoming the basis for remaking the Jewish people as a secular, political, territorial Jewish nation. Arendt saw the fighters as the vanguard of this phenomenon.[23] Yet she also cautioned that this desire for dignity rather than survival can result in a dangerous "readiness for suicide"[24] that later came to be called "the Masada complex." Moreover, Arendt strongly rejected one group that also advocated the formation of a Jewish army, the right-wing Zionist Revisionists, a party she heartily rejected as "terrorist" and "Fascist."[25]

As the war progressed, Arendt became increasingly distraught at the lack of action among Jews in the face of news concerning the concentration camps and mass murder of Jews. Indeed, reading Arendt's *Aufbau* articles reveals how much it was possible to know about these events during the war if one was paying attention, despite the claims of many people after the war to not have known what was happening.

From 1945 to 1948 Arendt was also a critic of the Zionist movement's policy advocating the establishment of a Jewish state. Instead, she stood with a small minority (including Martin Buber and Judah Magnes) that advocated a binational state as part of an internationally negotiated and agreed settlement in Palestine. Like Buber and Magnes, her reasons were not in principle anti-Zionist: she believed that in the post–World War II period the nation-state system was passé and would be replaced either by federations of peoples (perhaps on the model of the United States, USSR, or British Commonwealth) or by empires. Arendt made an important distinction between a Jewish *homeland* and a Jewish nation-state. "Palestine can be saved as the national homeland of Jews only if . . . it is integrated into a federation."[26] She feared that the demand for a Jewish State would result in failure: in the worst case, it would lead to military defeat, which if it occurred so soon after the Holocaust might be the beginning of the "self-dissolution of the Jewish people."[27] At best, a Jewish state that could not establish peace with its neighbors would ruin the positive achievements of Zionism in Palestine, eventually leading to a chauvinism that "could use the religious concept of the chosen people and allow its meaning to degenerate into hopeless vulgarity."[28]

Arendt's worst fears about the demise of the state of Israel and the decline of its political culture proved wrong. Nevertheless, she was prescient concerning the prominent role that the military and nationalist thought would take in Israeli politics, the difficulty of resolving the Arab-Israeli conflict when both sides refuse to give up on their nationalistic perspectives and claims, and how Israel would become dependent on the financial and political support of diaspora Jewry, especially in the United States—clearly not a situation of independence and true sovereignty. One might say that, to use Arendt's terminology, the pariah people gave birth to a pariah state.

Overall, what we see in Arendt's writings of the 1930s and 1940s is her engagement in "Jewish politics." Her attempt was to find a different way through the positions of the assimilationists and the state-oriented Zionists. Her focus, instead, was on what she called the "Jewish people," which was a concept that encompassed but went beyond political Zionism's practical focus on building up the homeland in Palestine. The homeland was important as a center for Jewish cultural pride and renewal, but it was not a political answer to the immediate threat that Nazism posed to European Jewry. For Arendt, the "lifeboat" solution of a Jewish state was insufficient because of the urgency and magnitude of the Holocaust. In taking on this view, she was speaking from the perspective of a conscious Pariah, a rebel à la Bernard Lazare. Arendt was concerned with the fate of the masses of Jews in Europe under the Nazis, which she felt needed to be the main front.

Arendt wanted to have the Jews recognized as a European nation, and in 1940 she wrote that Jews should have representation in "a European parliament" because the Jews were an integral part of the peoples of Europe.[29] "For the first time, Jewish history is not separate but tied up with that of all other nations. The comity of European peoples went to pieces when, and because, it allowed its weakest member to be excluded and persecuted."[30] This view, which insistently integrates the Jews and Europe, is reflected in Arendt's formulation of the concept of a "crime against humanity" in *Eichmann in Jerusalem*:

> It was when the Nazi regime declared that the German people not only were unwilling to have any Jews in Germany but wished to make the entire Jewish people disappear from the face of the earth that the new crime, the crime against humanity—in the sense of a crime 'against the human status,' or against the very nature of mankind—appeared. . . . The supreme crime . . . was a crime against humanity, perpetrated upon the body of the Jewish people, and . . . only the choice of victims, not the nature of the crime, could be derived from the long history of Jew-hatred and antisemitism.[31]

Arendt was already thinking beyond the nation-state system when she advocated a federation as a solution to the Arab-Israeli conflict. She felt that while the Jews had the right to live as a community in their "homeland," she identified herself as a "non-nationalist" who believed that a federation of Middle Eastern peoples was the best way to assure the Yishuv's safety and vitality.[32] She was in favor of a Jewish homeland, and despite her opposition to statehood continued to be concerned with the welfare and fate of Israel, even as she was critical of certain aspects and policies. While Buber and Magnes clearly counted themselves as "Zionists," I would categorize Arendt as a "non-Zionist,"[33] not an "anti-Zionist." Despite her opposition to statehood, she was not anti-Zionist in the fashion of the assimilationist or religious Jews, for whom Zionism's assertion of Jewish nationalism was anathema, or of non-Jews who rejected the Jews' right to build a national home in Palestine, such as the Arabs.

Arendt's attitude was that of a loyal critic, and criticism is not self-hatred. As she puts it in her letter to Scholem, "there can be no patriotism without permanent opposition."[34] Jewish politics, like all politics, is based on answering the fundamental question: What is best for our community—or, in this specific case: What is good for the Jews? In my view, Arendt is "loyal" because she counts herself as part of the community effected by the answers to this question—a "critic" because she is often disapproves of the powers that be and the policies they are practicing, which she sees as *bad for the Jews*. Whether or not one agrees with her positions, this is the perspective of a Jew, not that of a world-citizen or an upholder of the Rights of Man.

The issue at stake here is one that continues to be a challenge: the parameters of loyal criticism within the Jewish community. This is an issue in both the diaspora and Israel, but it plays out differently in each venue.

The organized "leadership" of the American Jewish community was (and continues to be) mostly a self-selected, voluntary group of wealthy philanthropists that is largely governed in the traditional diaspora fashion going back to the Court Jews, which Hannah Arendt critiqued as a plutocracy that "embraces prominence, philanthropy, and political representation."[35] As Arendt puts it in an *Aufbau* article, "the misfortune of the Jewish people . . . has been that the parvenu has been more important than the pariah; that Rothschild was more representative than Heine. . . . Donning the mask of the philanthropist, the parvenu poisoned all Jews, forcing his ideals upon them."[36]

One aspect of this plutocratic system is that the range of self-criticism is limited: the American Jewish community continues the diasporic tradition of being nervous about fitting in and getting along with the gentiles. Jewish identity and politics in the postwar era has focused on two topics: remembering the Holocaust and supporting Israel. This is best understood as a Jewish civil religion, a paradigm of destruction and redemption that focuses and displaces Jewish identity away from contemporary America toward places that are distant in time and place.[37] Far outweighing the importance of traditional Jewish religious practices, during the second half of the twentieth century this became the focus of public Jewish identity, defining contemporary Jews to both themselves and the gentiles. Hannah Arendt, of course, engaged both these issues at length, but her critical perspectives on both topics—an internal critique from a Jewish point of view—was like touching a high-voltage third rail, engendering reactions she did not anticipate.

The question of "loyal opposition" is also alive in Israel. Of course, it is worth noting that there is a qualitative difference between Jewish politics in the diaspora and Israel, for unlike the philanthropic politics of the diaspora, in Israel there is a very vigorous democratic political life, where the parliament is based on proportional representation, the government is always a coalition of many parties, and where views of every sort are part of daily debate. Yet, Arendt was neglected in Israel—one might even say boycotted—until the 1990s. Since then there has been a rediscovery of Arendt among younger scholars and intellectuals, and she has begun to take on an iconic stature as a *Jewish* political thinker who went beyond traditional Zionism. In 1997 an International conference on Hannah Arendt was held in Israel, organized by Steven Aschheim, and in 2003 a conference of Israeli scholars took place, organized by Idith Zertal and Moshe Zuckermann. Both conferences produced collections of essays, the first in English and the second in Hebrew.[38] Arendt's works are beginning to be translated into Hebrew—starting with *Eichmann in Jerusalem* in 2000. More than this, her image is entering into the realm of art and literature. In November 2006 there was an exhibit in Jerusalem of a series of portraits of Arendt by the Israeli artist Shy Abady, an exhibit that appeared in Germany the prior year.[39] [Abady's portrait of Arendt, "Dark Times," appears as the frontispiece to this volume.—Eds.] In 2006 a work of fiction, *The Visitation of Hannah Arendt*, by Michal Ben-Naftali appeared in Hebrew, describing hypothetical conversations between Arendt and the author.[40] Part of this interest in Arendt is fueled by the development since the mid-1990s of "post-Zionism," and some look to Arendt as a precursor.[41] Regardless of the label, Arendt's thought and image are being used as models for how to engage in Jewish politics while going beyond the timeworn domestic Israeli civil religion of Zionism that sees the Jews as eternal victims.

Whether one agrees with Arendt's particular positions on Jewish political issues, I contend that her stance is of lasting significance: she assumes the existence of a Jewish people and a Jewish polity that is sufficiently strong, proud and secure that all Jews have an inherent right to engage in vigorous political debate. While I have never agreed with all of Arendt's views, I find her Jewish writings to be a continuing model for engaged Jewish political speech.

Nevertheless, I want to make it clear that even if a "Jewish" Hannah Arendt can be reclaimed, this does not mean we should categorize or ghettoize her work as a whole as a "Jewish" political theory. Her experience as a Jew in the twentieth century, as someone who worked for Jewish organizations and wrote about Jewish political concerns in the 1930s and 1940s, is an important basis and background for her later work. Ultimately we need to see her as one of those "pariahs" who, as Arendt wrote, "were great enough to transcend the bounds of nationality and to weave the strands of their Jewish genius into the general texture of European life."

In this sense, the Jews were an example for Arendt, perhaps the first victims, but not only the first victims. Indeed, Arendt rejects the politics of victimization, which has become so popular today, where each interest group seeks to portray itself as wronged and thereby, somehow, absolved of responsibility for the world as a whole and its place therein. Arendt's critiques of Jewish emancipation, of Zionism, and of Jewish leadership rest on the premise that all people, even those who are oppressed and persecuted, nevertheless bear *some* responsibility for the world. Through their responses to their situation, even the victims play a role in co-creating and maintaining a human world of freedom that is shared by all people, a possibility that exists anew at every moment.

The Dolphin

FOR HANNAH,

GIVEN NOT JUST SIGNED,

WITH ALL LOVE

FROM

[signature]

NOW YEAH NOVEMBER 1973

Hannah Arendt's Jewish Identity

The topic of Hannah Arendt's Jewish identity can be approached from many directions. In this essay, I am going to consider Arendt in the context of the vision of world history articulated by her teacher and mentor Karl Jaspers, in which her people, the Jews of Palestine, were considered as one of the "Axial Age" peoples.

In the later years of the Second World War, when Arendt was writing *The Origins of Totalitarianism*, Jaspers was writing *The Origin and Goal of History*. His book, published in 1949, came into her hands as she was finishing hers. They both knew that they shared the project of thinking about what kind of history was needed for facing the events of the war and the Holocaust and for considering how the world might be after the war. They agreed that the needed history should not be national or for a national purpose, but for humankind.

When he was writing *The Origin and Goal of History*, Jaspers was not the first to observe that in the period of approximately 900–800 BC to 400–300 BC, five great peoples had reached pinnacles in their development, generating civilizations that were exemplary ever after among their descendants. But Jaspers was the first historian to grasp the significance for his own time of the fact that, independently—or relatively independently—of each other, in China, India, Persia, Greece, and Palestine, these five peoples had stepped out of their domination by mythical, tribal ways of thinking and supported something new: the emergence of philosophers or sages or prophets who were open to the wider world—who were cosmopolitan—and who reflected on how their people should organize themselves politically. The Taoists and Confucians in China, the Vedantic sages in India, the Zoroastrians in Persia, and the Jewish prophets in Palestine were teaching and preaching while a line of philosophers, scientists, poets, and political leaders in Greece created a legacy in which political freedom was more central than in any of the other traditions.

The legacies of each of these peoples were quite distinct, Jaspers argued,

:: ELISABETH YOUNG-BRUEHL

Facing: Inscribed title page of Hannah Arendt's copy of Robert Lowell's *The Dolphin*. The inscription reads: "For Hannah, Given not just signed, With all love from Cal, New York, November 1973." Courtesy of the Hannah Arendt Collection, Stevenson Library, Bard College.

but they had in common their attention to the world as it was before them and as it might be—they did not invoke mythic golden ages in the past or submit to simple determinisms or concepts of fate. It was this common thread that Jaspers thought could be taken up from the Axial Age people by modern people who found themselves living at a historical juncture, in a world made one by a worldwide war and by technological developments that had united all peoples, for better or for worse.

In the world after the war, Jaspers wrote, modern people could have an experience of opening to the world and thinking in a cosmopolitan way about the future of the human species: They could be self-conscious about their shared humanity, or they could suffer further the ill effects of their own prejudices and technological progress, which had made the worldwide war possible. He posed a great Either/Or. And over the next decade he elaborated on his view, especially by writing the articles that he drew together in *The Atom Bomb and the Future of Mankind*, first published in Germany in 1961.

Jaspers and Arendt had lost direct contact with each other when she fled Germany in 1933, but when they were able to renew their relationship by correspondence and then by Arendt's visits to the Jaspers's postwar home in Basel, Switzerland, the two (later joined by Arendt's husband, Heinrich Blücher) had many conversations about what the cosmopolitan thinking of the Axial Age descendants might be like. She spoke about this publicly when she delivered two addresses about Jaspers himself—"Karl Jaspers: Citizen of the World?" and "Karl Jaspers: A Laudatio," both published in *Men in Dark Times*—but her ideas were present throughout their correspondence (now published) and, *inter linea*, in her books, especially *The Human Condition*. They are also present in all of her writings on "the Jewish question," which Jerome Kohn and Ron Feldman have now so helpfully collected in the volume called *The Jewish Writings*, published in her centenary year, 2006. There, as in the antisemitism section of *The Origins of Totalitarianism*, the cosmopolitan tradition that was established for the Jews by their Axial Age prophets is continually invoked as an antidote to tribalist Jewish thinking, parochial and governed by mythic notions about the Jews as a chosen people, an exceptional people, transcendently oriented rather than in and of this world and its interrelated peoples.

It is Arendt's Jewish identity—not just the identity she asserted in defending herself as a Jew when attacked as one, but more deeply her connection to the Axial Age prophetic tradition—that made her the cosmopolitan she was, while Jaspers's cosmopolitanism was more learned than inherited and reinforced by group experience. He learned from Kant (*History with a Cosmopolitan Intent*) and the Germans indebted to Kant, right on up through Jaspers's older contemporary Max Weber, a world historian who counted among his friends the Sinologist Richard Wilhelm and the Indologist Heinrich Zimmer.

Neither Arendt nor Jaspers ever made a survey of the ingredients of cosmopolitan thinking that they shared and appreciated in each other, but I would like to do so here—in a very rudimentary fashion—as a tribute to them both, and to the common ground of the North German Protestant teacher and his Prussian Jewish student.

Key to cosmopolitan thinking is the capacity for and exercise of "enlarged mentality" (in Kant's phrase). Arendt often invoked this capacity for thinking your way into the viewpoint, the position, the experience, of other people, past and present (perhaps future, too). You ask yourself how the world would look and feel to different people (without thinking that you could have their experience or be them). In a sense, this capacity—a capacity requiring imagination—is the capacity to appreciate the plurality of people, the fact that no person's experience is the same as any other's. But this appreciation comes from making the effort of enlarging your own experience by imagining others'—to the point of potentially embracing all.

The second ingredient of cosmopolitan thinking is what Jaspers called "a sense of history." To both of them, this meant primarily a sense for the unpredictability of human affairs. Arendt emphasized throughout her writings the events and eras she considered to be "unprecedented" (and thus not predictable on the basis of what has been). No person, no group, has a privileged view of history or a vantage point that is advantaged. Only a world historical sense—one embracing all times, all peoples, all precedents—can ultimately judge an event or an era unprecedented. Judging an event or an era unprecedented is a necessary step in judging what is needed after a break in history or in tradition, when old ways of thinking and acting will not do for new realities.

The third ingredient of cosmopolitan thinking is what might be called a sense of the *human* condition—or the human conditions as they change over time, not fixed once and for all. How, Arendt asked, are the basic elements of human life affected by change, affected through historical differences? Humans exist on earth, for example, but they have learned to leave their earthly condition for space travel; they are living beings, but they have learned to manipulate the genetic ingredients of life, so now their life condition is to a degree manufacturable. But each condition—she named six: earth, life, world, natality, mortality, plurality—although susceptible to change, is *human*, common to all mankind, so only cosmopolitan thinking can compass it. Jaspers, for his part, spoke of "boundary situations" common to all people.

And fourth, I think this cosmopolitan thinking that Arendt and Jaspers were considering in the immediate postwar period depended upon an appreciation of what I, as a psychoanalyst, would call unconscious desires and motivations. The word "unconscious" was not part of Arendt's vocabulary, and both she and Jaspers were decidedly hostile to psychoanalysis (he wrote his critique into his *General Psychopathology*). Nonetheless, I think that the psychoanalytic terms point to something they both understood deeply: that people are shaped by their particular historical experiences—Arendt by her experience as a Jew—but that they are also moved, usually unconsciously, by needs and experiences and conditions shared by all human beings (understandings first articulated or made conscious in the Axial Age cultures). Arendt, for example, was as aware of the human need to act politically as any thinker of her generation, and Jaspers (so their postwar correspondence shows) knew this well. Particular historical experiences make people look and behave and sound more different than they are, as an aphorism by Kant's contemporary Georg Christoph Lichtenberg that Hannah Arendt once quoted to me conveys: "People do not think about the events of life as differently as they speak about them."

Facing: Portrait of Hannah Arendt by Fred Stein, taken for the jacket of Arendt's book *Men in Dark Times* (1968). Copyright Fredstein.com.

HANNAH ARENDT

vies politiques

TEL gallimard

Jewish to the Core

SUZANNE VROMEN

Hannah Arendt was born Jewish and undoubtedly remained Jewish until she died. This fact must be stressed, because as recently as 2001 she was accused by the intellectual historian Richard Wolin of being a "non-Jewish Jew," an expression he adopted from the Marxist biographer Isaac Deutscher for intellectuals for whom Jewish parentage was nothing more than a biographical accident.[1] Contrary to Wolin, the lifelong continuity and importance of her Jewish identity must be emphasized despite the doubts, fierce criticisms, and uproar against her in the wake of the publication of her book *Eichmann in Jerusalem.*

What did Arendt's Jewish identity mean to her and how did it evolve over time? First of all, her experience as a Jew was the foundation of all her thinking, and her Jewishness was inseparable from her work as a whole. In fact, her essentialist position as laid out in her 1963 letter to the scholar Gershom Scholem, in which she stated that being Jewish was an indisputable fact of her existence, precluded the possibility of assimilation.[2] Hers was a political Jewishness, a commitment to a people, not to Judaism as a religion. Politicized by the rise of Nazism, Arendt chose to become a pariah, adopting the model of Bernard Lazare, a French Jewish journalist and Dreyfusard, who actively confronted antisemitism and demanded that Jews should be emancipated as a people. For Lazare, when the pariah enters the political realm, he is a rebel fighting both external and internal enemies, and Arendt's stance was to become a rebel within the Jewish world.[3]

Second, Arendt was different from other Jewish thinkers prominent in the twentieth century, such as Franz Rosenzweig, Gershom Scholem, and Leo Strauss. While these scholars had an ahistorical appreciation of what it meant to be a Jew, Arendt undertook, through different stages, a historically rooted critique of the Enlightenment and of beliefs in Jewish assimilation.

In order to understand Arendt's relationship to her Jewish identity, it is helpful to distinguish four separate phases in her life. The first extends from her childhood to the late 1920s. The second ranges from the late 1920s to the

Facing: Hannah Arendt's copy of the French edition of *Vies Politiques.* This is a French translation of *Men in Dark Times,* with the addition of Arendt's essay "Martin Heidegger at 80." Courtesy of the Hannah Arendt Collection, Stevenson Library, Bard College.

end of the Second World War. The third is the Cold War experience in America during which she wrote *The Origins of Totalitarianism*. The fourth is the Eichmann period and its aftermath.

In the first phase, she never questioned the stability of her German Jewish identity, and, I might add, she acknowledged little interest in politics. Late in the 1920s, as she was facing increasing explosions of political antisemitism all around her, she recognized the need for political participation. Moreover, with the end of her relationship with Heidegger, she realized the fragility of her position as an exotic Jewish woman and examined it indirectly by writing the biography of Rahel Varnhagen. Let me emphasize that *Rahel Varnhagen*, Arendt's first book, was undoubtedly a parallel to her life. She keenly understood Varnhagen and at the same time was critical of her. This project was Arendt's first analysis of the negative Jewish experience of assimilation and antisemitism. Varnhagen, a highly educated Jewish woman at the turn of the nineteenth century, organized a prominent salon in Berlin where writers, artists, and aristocrats, Jews and Gentiles, exchanged ideas and socialized in an intimate environment, temporarily realizing the utopian aspiration of the Enlightenment and of emancipation. This enlightened and tolerant world was, however, eminently fragile, and it crumbled when the rights granted to Jews were rescinded after Napoleon's defeat. The salon was Rahel's social reality, the space where she was socially recognized. When it disappeared, Varnhagen the social climber discarded her Jewishness by assimilating through baptism, love affairs, and marriage. She followed the trajectory of a parvenu, trying to enter circles closed to Jews, becoming an "exception." Eventually, at the end of her life, she rejected self-hatred and assimilation, exclaiming on her deathbed that she would not have wanted to miss the fact that she had been born a Jew. Simply stated, she came back to her roots. In contrast, Arendt never left her roots; this is the very significant difference between her and Rahel.

The manuscript has a long history. It was nearly finished when she left Germany in 1933. In France, encouraged by both Heinrich Blücher and Walter Benjamin, Arendt added two final chapters. Finally, after the war, in 1952 she sent the manuscript to Karl Jaspers. He responded with one of the longest letters of their correspondence, still convinced of the possibility of post-Enlightenment German-Jewish coexistence.[4] He pointed out the autobiographical nature of the work and then accused her of seeing Rahel only in the context of the Jewish question and not as a total human being. He objected to the negative way she presented the Enlightenment, and he scathingly reproached her for her loveless view of Rahel and her belief in the impossibility of assimilation.

Arendt did not yield to his vehement criticisms. She answered him that the reality of social assimilation did not allow Jews to really live fully.[5] The manuscript, with corrections and updated preface, was finally published in 1957.

In that second phase, she never tried to recast a Jewish culture in the German context. When she left Germany in 1933, she ultimately chose the route of Zionism. Until her internment in the camp of Gurs in 1940 as an enemy alien, she worked in Paris for Youth Aliyah, taking a group of children to Palestine in 1935, and then for the Jewish Agency. In 1941, she arrived in the United States, where she became a steady contributor to the German Jewish immigrant newspaper *Aufbau*.

During World War II, Arendt called for an international Jewish army. Such an army would satisfy the desire of dignity and legitimate claims for freedom, including a home in Palestine. I think that this was probably not a new idea for Arendt; Heinrich Blücher, the German Communist she fell in love with in Paris and married, presented it to her in 1936. Relatively early in their relationship, Blücher sent Arendt a long letter on what he called the Jewish war. He called for a Jewish combat unit against fascism in Spain and, caught in his rhetoric, even for Jewish freedom legions around the world.[6] At the time, Arendt did not accept his idea that Jews had to bring armed salvation to the world, but it may have inspired her to write in 1941 her second *Aufbau* article, in which she argued that the Jewish people needed an army for reasons of identity as well as defense.[7]

Having arrived in the United States as a homeless and stateless refugee, Arendt keenly enjoyed the privilege of citizenship. One can discern, however, in the Arendt-Blücher correspondence repeated instances of angst, or reactions to political events with caution or desire to flee. For example, in May 1952 Blücher warned her to stay clear of Berlin lest she fell into a Russian trap.[8] Arendt replied that if it were not safe she would not go to Berlin, even though she could expect to be flown out because she had an American passport and an official invitation.[9] Her passport was one year old! More dramatically, after Malenkov resigned in 1955, Blücher anticipated trouble and suggested Bard College as a meeting place in case of emergency.[10]

During the war and in the late 1940s, Arendt grew increasingly critical of various Jewish leaders and mainstream Zionism. She opposed the search for a political solution to antisemitism through the establishment of a state, for it was predicated on a flight from the Gentile world. She advocated local self-government based on joint Jewish-Arab municipal and rural councils. She envisioned a federation of Mediterranean peoples, and above all she wished power to rise from the bottom, not to be imposed from the top down. Arendt doubted that a Jewish state would be tenable. If the war for Jewish independence failed, it might lead to the dissolution of the Jewish people, and this was her greatest fear. Prescient about the problem what to do with the Arab populations, she sided with Judah Magnes and his vision for a binational state. Perhaps what needs to be noted within the framework of this session is how deeply involved she was in Zionist politics and how much they mattered to her, then and for the rest of her life. After the creation of the state of Israel, she remained greatly concerned with the pariah status thrust on Israel in international politics and hoped for some better situation.

In the third phase of her life, after the end of the Second World War, her writings were framed by her desire to explain the failure of culture and civilization. Arendt's reflections on the meaning of freedom, on the human condition, on revolutions, and on democracy had their source in her experiences as a Jew. Yet, in the dialogue between Jaspers and Arendt after the end of the war, a certain cosmopolitan thinking developed in their writings and was shared in their correspondence. In fact, Arendt's ideas reflect a constant tension between cosmopolitan thinking and a more tribal defensive one. In this context cosmopolitan thinking meant openness to the multiplicity of experiences in the world, a feel for the new in history, a sense of the basic human condition and an appreciation for desires and motivations reflected in historically specific aspirations of people. Here it is not possible to discuss in detail the tension between the universal and the particular found in Hannah Arendt. Let me just mention that a recent article on Arendt argues that she used a concept of cosmopolitanism that does not conceive of the relation of universal and particular as an either—or, it is both. The author, Natan Sznaider, concludes that "the idea of an intimate connection between morality and identity is Arendt's answer to what it means to maintain a tension between the universal and the particular."[11]

This tension between the universal and the particular is perhaps best illustrated by examining some of the reactions to *Eichmann in Jerusalem* and Arendt's virtual excommunication from Jewish communities. The public misunderstood her, for Eichmann could be judged, even though the evil he committed could not be thought. It led Arendt to a long reflection on the difference between thinking and judging. The Jewish community castigated her, but the book was in fact an important contribution because it transformed research and discussion in the Holocaust. Let me elaborate this last point. From her very first writings Arendt rejected a lachrymose conception of Jewish history in which Jews were described as victims and martyrs. Early on, she stressed the need for understanding one's historical situation. This emphasis shaped her indictment of the Jewish leadership in her book on Eichmann, an indictment based on Nazi archival data. The reactions to her book spurred serious research in Jewish sources, which uncovered complex situations at different stages of the extermination process and diversity of responses, yielding a nuanced understanding of choiceless choices. Most importantly, the book opened the way to correcting the formerly unacknowledged bias in Holocaust research toward heroic martyrology and denial of any human corruptibility.

Arendt believed that what was important about Jewish pariahs was the combination of their Jewishness and Europeanness. She came to America as a German Jewish exile. She made her reputation as a European intellectual, an exceptionally brilliant woman, and a bearer of "high culture." German remained her language, and she always pointedly said that she remained a German Jew to the end. For literary executors she chose a German and an American, Lotte Kohler and Mary McCarthy. It is in an amusing way that she introduced Mary McCarthy to her childhood friend, Kurt Blumenfeld, then living in Israel: "McCarthy is a very good friend of Irish descent, has a Jewish grandmother . . . is enormously intelligent and is very American."[12]

On a final note, an examination of Arendt's identity clearly illustrates that to be Jewish is not a univocal concept. This is the reason why one can object to Gershom Scholem when he reacted to the Eichmann book by accusing Arendt of failing to be a daughter of the Jewish people. For Scholem there was just one way of being Jewish: you supported Palestine, you supported what Jews did in Palestine forever. Arendt exemplified that one can be Jewish in many ways. Because she put so much emphasis on speech as action, she enjoyed being able to have a public forum in the United States where she could be openly Jewish and not have to justify herself either as a parvenu or as a pariah. She stopped being a pariah when she came to America. She certainly was never a parvenu here or elsewhere. A complex personality, she was Jewish to her core, but determined to be so in her very own way.

PART VI

Thinking in Dark Times

USA

Drucksache

FREIBURG 'BREISGAU
17.12.52. 13.
b

(17b) FREIBURG
17.12.52

Frau Dr Hannah Arendt

130 Morningside Drive

New - York 27

Abs.
Heidegger
Freiburg : Br.
Zähringen
Deutschland.

Thinking Big in Dark Times

:: DRUCILLA CORNELL

In dark times we need to resist the temptation to miniaturize the human spirit, to paraphrase Amartya Sen's telling phrase.[1] We have to think big, even if we often feel overwhelmed and powerless before a world that acts from thoughtless myths and the reputed commands of ruthless gods. Indeed, we need to risk affirmative, moral, and ethical speech, knowing all the while that great ethical and moral ideals have indeed been soiled and profaned and debased, to echo a poem of Auden's that Arendt so loved.[2]

At the heart of Arendt's work is her conviction that the European tradition of moral thought has crumbled, not because of the failure of human beings to live up to their standards, or even because of philosophical inadequacy. Rather, the tradition of human dignity has succumbed to the brutal reality of the twentieth century, a reality that has undone the tradition by confronting us with acts and behavior that simply fall outside or beyond the reach of these measures or ideals. To quote Arendt:

> Antisemitism (not merely the hatred of Jews), imperialism (not merely conquest), totalitarianism (not merely dictatorship)—one after the other, one more brutally than the other, have demonstrated that human dignity needs a new guarantee which can be found only in a new political principle, in a new law on earth, whose validity this time must comprehend the whole of humanity while its power must remain strictly limited, rooted in and controlled by newly defined territorial entities.[3]

Before the horror show of the twentieth century, Arendt argues that "morality has become shabby and meaningless, and no effort to rebuild it will effectively revitalize the great moral and ethical ideas."[4] To the degree that ideals remain in the discourse of revolution, they are distorted into ideologies that threaten to prop up totalitarianism.

To judge and question Arendt's conclusions about the fate of ethical and moral ideas, we need, of course, to read the decline of Europe and European traditions somewhat differently from how she does. After all, Franz Fanon,

Facing: Envelope from Martin Heidegger to Hannah Arendt, dated December 17, 1952. Courtesy of the Hannah Arendt Collection, Stevenson Library, Bard College.

who reminded us that the reconstruction of the great ideals of humanism could truly begin only with the demise of colonialism, remained committed to the possibility of a new humanity through the very struggle for liberation. As he so aptly put it:

> We must leave our dreams and abandon our old beliefs and friendships from the time before life began. Let us waste no time in sterile litanies and nauseating mimicry. Leave this Europe where they are never done talking of Man, yet murder men everywhere they find them, at the corner of every one of their own streets, in all the corners of the globe. For centuries they have stifled almost the whole of humanity in the name of a so-called spiritual experience. Look at them today swaying between atomic and spiritual disintegration.[5]

While Arendt saw this demise and the crisis of ideals it manifested, she did not—indeed thought she could not—offer new ideals in their place.

In the spirit of questioning Arendt's judgment of modern European ideals, I want to offer two examples of the role of moral and ethical ideals from the new South Africa. The first is the connection between the moral ideal of dignity, as it has been established as the *Grundnorm* of the entire South African Constitution,[6] and then deployed to justify the horizontal application of the Constitution.[7] Horizontal application, in short shift, means the legally radical claim that all social actions are open to constitutional review.[8] For example, the question whether or not discriminatory social gatherings violate any person's dignity is, in South Africa, a constitutional issue. I will say more about this.

The second example is the South African Constitution's commitment of the current South African Constitutional Court to the ideal of humanity as this both demands and promotes a notion of cosmopolitan right.[9] Furthermore, the African National Congress (ANC) has strived to develop an ethical and not simply an instrumental foreign policy.[10] Arendt often argues that foreign policy should not be a political matter. In the new dispensation of South Africa, foreign policy is not just political, but also an explicitly ethical matter.

The South African Constitution was politically enacted in its current form only after a bitter battle that led to the complete breakdown of the negotiations in 1992. The political lines were in part drawn around the issue of the horizontal application of the Constitution. Horizontal constitutional jurisdiction is unique to South Africa, and it was gained in South Africa only after the ANC and Pan African Congress (PAC) withdrew from the constitutional negotiations under the slogan, "No privatization of Apartheid." In 1993 the impasse was overcome, and the National Party conceded to the demand for a horizontal application.[11]

In the United States, we have vertical application of the Constitution. Our Bill of Rights protects individuals from state action that violates their fundamental freedom protected therein. In the social plane, individuals confront each other primarily as private legal actors. The Constitution, in other words, only in certain circumstances such as in discrimination law, reaches into the social interaction of civil society. In Germany, there is indirect application of the spirit of the German Constitution. The significance of this indirect application of the Constitution in Germany is that constitutional principles can inform particular disputes in the private law. The spirit of dignity is to pervade the entire constitutional schema of post–World War II Germany. Direct horizontal application of the South African Constitution takes a major step beyond even the German Constitution's commitment to dignity as the constitutional sprit that must be brought to bear in all legal disputes. To repeat, horizontal application means in principle that every single action between human beings in civil society can potentially raise a constitutional issue.

In South Africa, direct horizontal application means in principle that every single action between human beings in civil society can come up for constitutional review.[12] Since the Constitution enshrines the ethical principle of dignity in South African legal life, every person is legally required to treat others, in all their interactions, with dignity. Thus all actions between individuals, even those actions that might occur in private homes or in civil society more generally are potentially governed by the Constitution and are therefore subject to constitutional review. The South African Constitution, then, runs directly against Arendt's insistence that we need a private realm of difference and that any kind of state imposed equality leads to some form of tyranny. This fear of legally imposed equality and legal interference in the sphere of civil society of the private can be seen in Arendt's essay "Reflections on Little Rock."[13] Famously, Arendt disagreed with the U.S. Supreme Court decision to enforce integration legally:

> The moment social discrimination is legally enforced, it becomes persecution, and of this crime many Southern states have been guilty. The moment social discrimination is legally abolished, the freedom of society is violated, and the danger is that thoughtless handling of the civil rights issue by the Federal government will result in such a violation. The government can legitimately take no steps against social discrimination because government can act only in the name of equality—a principle which does not obtain in the social sphere.[14]

Indeed, to underscore her fear of legally imposed equality in social and private life, Arendt further states, "What equality is to the body politic, its innermost principle—discrimination is to society."[15] Of course, Arendt is not alone here. Indeed her fear of state regulation of civil society may well be the core idea of neoliberalism; state regulation of social life is treated either with suspicion or disdain.

Although I strongly disagree with her argument against state regulation of racial discrimination, Arendt is also seeking to demonstrate her own rich evocation of the power of judging in this essay. She wrote this essay after viewing a photograph of a young black woman hounded on all sides by whites, protected only by a white friend of her father's. Arendt is clearly deeply affected by the photo. As she writes,

> The point of departure of my reflections was a picture in the newspapers showing a Negro girl on her way home from a newly integrated school: she was persecuted by a mob of white children, protected by a white friend of her father, and her face bore eloquent witness to the obvious fact that she was not precisely happy. The picture showed the situation in a nutshell because those who appeared in it were directly affected by the Federal Court order. My first question was what would I do if I were a Negro mother. The answer under no circumstances would I expose my child to conditions which made it appear as though it wanted to push to its way into a group where it was not wanted.[16]

Arendt also tries to imagine herself as a white mother:

> My second question was: what would I do if I were a white mother in the South. I would try to prevent my child's being dragged into a political battle in the school yard. In addition, I would feel that my consent was necessary for any such drastic changes no matter what my opinion of them happened to be. I would agree that the government has a stake in the education of my child insofar as this child is supposed to grow up into a citizen, but I would deny that the government has any right to tell me in whose company my child received its instructions. The rights of parents to decide such matters for their children until they are grown-ups are challenged by dictatorships.[17]

Interestingly, in this experiment to imagine the two mothers, there are no fathers. The essay, however, is written through the effort to envision, through different perspectives, to imagine before her own eyes, and of course before our eyes, as she asks us to see with her the dilemmas of legally enforced integration. In other words, she is trying to use the photo and our response to it as an example of reflective judgment, and of an enlarged mentality that will allow all of us to agree and to see that for *us* legalized integration is wrong.[18]

As I have suggested, part of Arendt's concern is that legal government of the social and the private is integral to what she calls totalitarianism. Arendt, however, has unavailable to her the South African constitutional understanding of dignity as that which both demands horizontality, and yet at the same time, resists legislation or, worse yet, edicts, which would run afoul of the person's dignity and freedom. Whether or not this restoration of dignity, as both the moral ideal and the *Grundnorm* of the Constitution, can resist turning into a mechanical screech is, of course, itself a huge question, but it is one that the South African Constitutional Court has been fearless in attempting to answer.

Indeed the South African Constitution can arguably provide us with a new principle of humanity to which Arendt calls us, even if she does so through a reinterpretation of the moral and legal significance of dignity. It is dignity as it actually functions in the state's regulation of social life in the name of equality that is also used to stand against totalitarianism and the violation of individual freedom.[19]

Let us now turn to my second example of how the new South Africa and the South African Constitution specifically seek to develop a new principle of humanity as the basis of understanding the relationship between international law and the ideal of dignity as the *Grundnorm* of the South African Constitution.[20] The Constitutional Court combined the works of Immanuel Kant and Hans Kelsen.

For Kelsen, in his pathbreaking work on international law,[21] if we are to consider it to be a valid legal order, including one that can protect human rights, international law must be established as a higher normative system that determines the national legal order's three spheres of validity. These are the territorial, the geographical; the temporal, the period of the legal existence; and indirectly, through the medium of national legal order, and through international norms, all the rights of personality.[22] There are two points that Kelsen emphasizes in this work. The first is that a state must concede to the international law the right to regulate its territorial, temporal, and personal spheres if it is to be a legal system that can be reconciled with an international legal order.

Kelsen's second point is that municipal law and international law must constitute an inseparable whole. He is a strong defender of the monist version of the relationship between international law and municipal law. He advocates a world system premised on the *civitas maxima* and the ideal of perpetual peace—a world community that would be faithful to the ideal of dignity of all persons, and all national sovereignty would thus be subjected to those principles. The only legitimate war would be a war against those parties who had violated international law, and that would be decided by an international court. All unilateral forms of aggression, thus, are forbidden.

The purpose of Kelsen's work is to develop a universal system of law with specialized judicial organs, one whose function is to ascertain the initial breach of international norms and execute appraisals of offending states—always done by the international body. Kelsen argues against state sovereignty as traditionally understood as having legal mastery in its own territory. He argues, more importantly, that the submission of national sovereignty is absolutely necessary to establish an international law and the minimum norms of personality that we now take as at the core of human rights. In his work on international law, Kelsen dares to think big. He is arguing against the idea that laws arise within national state boundaries, and that the only civil rights are state-enforced civil rights. A Kelsonian approach to international law would argue that we have to rethink the very basis of law and sovereignty in order to institutionalize human rights. Kelsen, as it is well known, was a positivist, and we are very far from having a system of international law in place, although there have been significant developments in the Kelsonian direction.

Without a positive system of international law, the *Grundnorm* that Kelsen attributes to the world legal system needs to be adopted on a national level. That adoption is, in a profound sense, what the South African Constitution accomplishes. Section 39(1) (c) of the South African Constitution articulates that in interpreting the Bill of Rights, the Court must consider international law.[23] So, in a sense, the Constitution pays fidelity to the governing power of these laws rooted as they are in the principle of humanity, even before the establishment of the world system that Kelsen has advocated.

Former Constitutional Court judge Justice Laurie Ackermann—one of the leaders of the dignity jurisprudence movement in South Africa—argues that the South African Constitution as it aspires to the great Kantian ideal of the Kingdom of Ends is seeking to bring in to existence a law more worthy of the idea of the principle of humanity.[24] But Justice Ackermann has also rigorously developed the significance of §39(1)(c) and the importance of the international and foreign law as these point us to an ultimate international system of law rooted in the ideal of humanity. In all of his decisions, where it was apposite to do so, he carefully reviewed international law as it paves the way for the Kelsonian ideal.

In South Africa, human rights themselves are grounded either in the moral ideal of dignity, for those like Justice Ackermann who are rooted in the tradition of German idealism, or in uBuntu, for those like Justice Yvonne Mokgoro who are rooted in the South African tradition. Both ideals appeal to the principle of humanity as the basis of legality of the South African Bill of Rights.[25] In a rightfully famous case, Justice Mokgoro said that in South Africa you are a human being before you are a citizen.[26] She powerfully argued that in the new South Africa, all human beings should promote uBuntu. Justice Mokgoro defined uBuntu in the *Makwanyane* decision as follows:[27]

> Generally, *ubuntu* translates as *humaneness*. In its most fundamental sense, it translates as *personhood* and *morality*. Metaphorically, it expresses itself in *umuntu ngumuntu ngabantu*, describing the significance of group solidarity on survival issues so central to the survival of communities. While it envelops the key values of group solidarity, compassion, respect, human dignity, conformity to basic norms and collective unity, in its fundamental sense it denotes humanity and morality. Its spirit emphasises respect for human dignity, marking a shift from confrontation to conciliation. In South Africa *ubuntu* has become a notion with particular resonance in the building of a democracy. It is part of our "rainbow" heritage, though it might have operated and still operates differently in diverse community settings. In the Western cultural heritage, respect and the value for life, manifested in the all-embracing concepts of *humanity* and *menswaardigheid* are also highly priced.

Justice Mokgoro could have decided the case narrowly. The case concerned Mozambican refugees, and the central issue was whether or not certain benefits should be extended to those refugees. A possibility for a narrower decision would have been that these benefits should be extended to Mozambican refugees because of the harm done under apartheid to the territory of Mozambique. However, Justice Mokgoro did not decide on that basis. Instead, she eloquently argued that the Mozambican refugees had become part of the South African community and should therefore be treated with due respect. But she also appealed to the principle of humanity explicit in uBuntu. With Justice Mokgoro, we have another example of someone who dares to think big, who thinks through a new principle of humanity rooted in uBuntu.

To conclude: In his article, "The Legal Nature of the South African Constitution"[28] before he stepped down from the bench, Justice Ackermann argued that the South African Constitution is grounded in the moral ideals of dignity and uBuntu, and that it can never be final—these are moral ideals that can never be fully realized in any positive legal system. Of course, the legal system must aspire to these regulative ideals according to Justice Ackermann, and indeed, section 1 of the South African Constitution institutionalizes them as the basis of the new South Africa. If the regulative ideal of the new South Africa is nothing less than the Kingdom of Ends or uBuntu, then it is up to every South African to hear the appeal of moral ideals and struggle to live up to them. This task is certainly one that demands that we resist the miniaturization of the human spirit.

Martin Heidegger

Zeit und Sein

En hommage à Jean Beaufret

Für

Hannah

Martin

F.J.

12. Jzl. 1968

PLON

Crimes of Action, Crimes of Thought

ARENDT ON RECONCILIATION, FORGIVENESS, AND JUDGMENT

:: SHAI LAVI

In the winter of 1932–1933, correspondence between Martin Heidegger and Hannah Arendt was abruptly terminated. It requires little imagination or speculation to understand the cause of the long and lasting silence between the two. More disquieting for some, above all for Arendt herself, was the revival of this relationship, beginning in February 1950. For Arendt, Heidegger posed a problem bigger than the romantic drama depicted by some of her biographers, and a moral dilemma that went far beyond the failings of one individual. Arendt's confrontation with Heidegger involved more weighty concerns, and it is these that led her to contemplate the phenomenon of reconciliation, forgiveness, and judgment.

Three months after their unsettling reunion, in a letter dated May 16, 1950, Heidegger writes to his former student: "Oh you! Most trusted one. . . . *You are right about reconciliation and revenge*. I have been thinking about that a great deal. In all this thinking, *you* are so near."[1] Heidegger recalls "a walk in the valley," presumably referring to a conversation he had with Arendt during her earlier visit to Freiburg in March. Though the content of the conversation between the two remains unknown, some hints regarding Arendt's thinking on these matters can be gathered from her recently published *Denktagebuch*.

Reconciliation and revenge were central themes in Arendt's writing after the war and became decisive in her relationship with Heidegger. Together with blame and guilt, wrong and evil, and forgiveness and resignation, reconciliation and revenge became word-thoughts through which Arendt contemplated two very different and novel human failings that the war had revealed. The first failing, to which Arendt responds, concerns the crimes performed under the Third Reich, crimes that led to the systematic extermination of millions of people with the active participation and tacit cooperation of entire political regimes; the second, more theoretical but no less definitive, was the failure of the *vita contemplativa*. Putting personal matters aside, Arendt read Heidegger's moral failure during the Nazi regime not as the wrong of an individual human being but of philosophical thinking as such. Both these crimes,

Facing: Inscribed cover of Hannah Arendt's copy of an offprint of Martin Heidegger's *Zeit und Sein*. The inscription reads: "For Hannah. Martin." Courtesy of the Hannah Arendt Collection, Stevenson Library, Bard College.

of human action and of human thinking, demanded Arendt's attention not merely because of their novelty and gravity, but also because they put into question the ability, long taken for granted, of the legal system and of philosophical thinking to correct their failings from within.

One can identify three moments in the writings of Hannah Arendt where she contemplates the proper response to human failings. In each case, she strives to come to terms with both the crimes of human action and the failures of human thought. The first appears in her *Denktagebuch* notes from June 1950. To anyone familiar with her later discussion of forgiveness and its central role in her book on *The Human Condition*, this earlier discussion of similar themes may come as a surprise. In these notes, Arendt rejects not only revenge but also forgiveness as a proper response to crime. Both fail to ground a political community, which to her can be founded only on the basis of human equality.

Revenge, Arendt argues in line with a long tradition of political thought, cannot be the basis of a political community because it is grounded in natural rather than political equality. When the avenger claims that his act of revenge revisits upon the wrongdoer the same (equal) act that he himself has done, the notion of equality he relies on is the natural equality of the experience of pain. Such equality is based on an experience that human beings share with the animal kingdom, and therefore cannot serve to ground a uniquely human polity.

Arendt's rejection of forgiveness is more nuanced. She objects to the prevailing notion that forgiveness is rooted in human equality, specifically in the notion that all human beings share, by virtue of their humanity, the capacity to do wrong and consequently the power to forgive. Rather, she contends, "The gesture of forgiveness destroys the equality and with it the fundamental human relationship so radically that after such an act no relationship is possible any longer."[2] Forgiveness becomes possible only under the principle of qualitative difference, as in the power of God to forgive humankind or of parents to forgive their children. Though Christian forgiveness seems to be based on human equality, this is not a worldly equality, but rather an otherworldly equality grounded in the abstract determination that all individuals share in a common original sin. In political terms, forgiveness must be ruled out because it is founded on negative solidarity, on the abstract equation of what the perpetrator actually did with what the victim might have done.

Arendt's rejection of the abstract notion of universal guilt is not merely a rejection of the political viability of forgiveness, but also a rejection of a dominant aspect of philosophical thinking. Here and in many of her later writings, she contrasts the concreteness of political action with the abstractness of philosophical thinking. It is in this way that she wishes to overcome the failings of philosophical thinking.

In place of both forgiveness and revenge, Arendt offers reconciliation as the proper response to wrongful deeds. She illustrates the phenomenon of reconciliation with the potent image of wrongfulness not as an inner stain on the soul, but as a burden one carries on one's shoulders. Reconciliation entails a willingness on the part of the wronged to carry the burden together with the wrongdoer. This notion of reconciliation has little to do with Christian forgiveness, for there is no possible way to undo past crimes, but only the possibility of a mutual recognition that a wrong has been committed, and that if nevertheless the wrongdoer and the wronged can continue walking together, it is only to the extent that both continue to carry the wrong. From a political point of view, reconciliation creates worldly solidarity. For the wrongdoer, the burden is a result of her own doing, and for the person coming to terms with the wrong, it becomes a gift of destiny that one accepts.[3] To become reconciled with a wrong thus does not unburden the wrongdoer. Instead of attempting to undo the past, reconciliation encourages acceptance of the past as given.

In this sense, reconciliation has its source in, but is not identical with, the fundamental attunement of "gratitude for what is given."[4] Famously, Arendt discusses fundamental gratitude when she identifies as a Jew and writes: "There is such a thing as a basic gratitude for everything that is as it is; for what has been given and not made."[5] As the fundamental attunement of gratitude, reconciliation accepts the past as that which has passed and is no longer within the ambit of human control. However, reconciliation also differs from the fundamental attunement of gratitude, because it harbors an element of renewal and spontaneity. Unlike fundamental gratitude, which responds to that which is always already given, reconciliation is an active gesture of acceptance that must be regenerated anew each time. Its spontaneity lies in its chosen acceptance of the past.

On the basis of her explication of reconciliation, Arendt formulates one of several notions of radical evil later to follow. Radical evil, in these earlier writings, is that which one cannot accept and become reconciled with. It is that of which one cannot say, "this too could have happened." Radical evil is that which never should have happened.[6]

Arendt next makes a substantive attempt to respond to human failings of thought and action in the third part of *The Human Condition*. Here, she develops her more familiar account of forgiveness—as opposed to reconciliation and revenge—as a necessary foundation of human action. "Without being forgiven," she writes, and thus without being "released from the consequences of what we have done, our capacity to act would, as it were, be confined to one single deed from which we could never recover."[7] Since nothing in the doing of a wrong necessitates forgiveness, forgiveness becomes for Arendt a paradigm of action, a spontaneous rebirth of a future, unbound to the past. As in her earlier notes, Arendt rejects revenge. Revenge appears as the precise opposite of forgiveness. It is merely an automatic reaction to the past wrong, and as such it is bound to the wrong in a way that leaves the avenger trapped in the past.

The Arendt of *The Human Condition*, however, does not merely abandon reconciliation and revive the notion of forgiveness. Instead, she fundamentally alters her understanding of the human relation to the world and of human temporality, and this leads to a change in her critique of philosophical thinking. Whereas in her earlier account of reconciliation, human beings were receivers of the gift of destiny, now, in her more familiar analysis of forgiveness, man assumes the position of shaper of his own destiny. Philosophy, perhaps most clearly Heidegger's philosophy, which Arendt identified with the passive acceptance of destiny, is contrasted with the political act of taking responsibility for the future.

Following her new account of forgiveness, Arendt also offers a new understanding of radical evil. Radical evil no longer signifies that which one cannot accept, but rather that which one cannot forgive. Radical evil marks, in other words, the limits of man's power, and it is precisely when the human will confronts its own impotence that it is compelled to eradicate radical evil. Arendt writes, "All we know is that we can neither punish nor forgive such offenses and that they therefore transcend the realm of human affairs and the potentialities of human power. . . . Here, where the deed itself dispossesses us of all power, we can indeed only repeat with Jesus: 'It were better for him that a millstone were hanged about his neck, and he cast into the sea.'"[8]

Arendt's thinking on the questions concerning reconciliation, forgiveness, and revenge as responses to human evil does not end with *The Human Condition*. There is a third moment in Arendt's writings where she offers yet another response to the same set of questions. Admittedly, this third moment is much harder to pinpoint. It is not located in one place; presenting an even greater challenge, it does not discuss the questions of forgiveness, revenge, and radical evil under their explicit names.

Her final attempt to reflect on the problem is famously captured in Arendt's turn away from the notion of radical evil to the banality of evil. The new form of evil that Arendt identifies is thoughtlessness. Thoughtlessness is not a revolt against reason and should not be confused with irrationality. To the contrary, it is the ability to act rationally without thinking. Eichmann becomes an extreme example of such a possibility, unable to rise above the logic of bureaucracy and the clichés of utter conformity.

In this reconceptualization of evil as thoughtless, Arendt asks: If crime is thoughtless, what is the proper response to it? Arendt confronts this question in the conclusion of her *Report on the Banality of Evil*. Though adamant in her support of Eichmann's execution, the justifications she gives for the punishment are less clear. To judge solely by her argument in the book itself, it seems that she may be contemplating these matters in the spirit of revenge. In a familiar passage, she openly admits,

We refuse, and consider as barbaric, the propositions that "a great crime offends nature, so that the very earth cries out for vengeance; that evil violates a natural harmony which only retribution can restore; that a wronged collectivity owes a duty to the moral order to punish the criminal." And yet I think it is undeniable that it was precisely on the ground of these long-forgotten propositions that Eichmann was brought to justice to begin with, and that they are, in fact, the supreme justification for the death penalty.[9]

But if it is indeed revenge that Arendt has in mind here, it is of a very different nature than the phenomenon discussed in her earlier writings. Revenge is no longer a claim based on natural equality, but is now synonymous with justice as retributive punishment. Arendt's allusion to revenge in the Eichmann trial should be read in light of her discussion of violence during the 1960s. Revenge, which had been condemned in her writings from the 1950s as merely reactive, acquires a new significance in her writings on violence in the 1960s. In her famous analysis of Melville's *Billy Budd*, Arendt presents the young sailor's violent act in response to absolute evil not as vengeful, but rather as pure good.[10] Similarly, in her writings on violence, in a book by that title, Arendt argues that violence and rage are at times the only appropriate response to injustice.[11] Admittedly, in both her analysis of *Billy Budd* and her more general account of violence, she refuses to attribute political status to such spontaneous acts of violence, continuing to insist on their nonpolitical nature. Still, it is only to the violent character of these acts to which she objects, while embracing the notion of the spontaneity of judgment that inheres in acts of violence.

Arendt again ascribes a political significance to judgment as a spontaneous unmediated response to evil when she discusses the riddle of the exceptional individuals who refused to cooperate with the Nazi regime. In her lectures from the 1960s, collected in *Responsibility and Judgment*, she writes that it was not on the basis of systematic thinking, contemplation, and reasoning that some exceptional individuals found within themselves the power to resist becoming part of the totalitarian regime.[12] What stood between decent human beings and the regime's atrocities can only be characterized as the capacity for unmediated thinking that is judgment. Once someone began to consider matters, to weigh the advantages and disadvantages of cooperating with the new regime, all was already lost. In an insight, which is no doubt still relevant today, Arendt explains that one can always justify one's actions; it is always possible to convince oneself that it is better to collaborate with a totalitarian regime and partake in daily routines of human rights violations than leave this in the hands of someone with lower moral standards. Reason alone, she argues, could never provide the ground for moral strength in the face of immoral demands. The only real ground for resistance was an internal conviction that ruled out cooperation from the outset.

Judgment for Arendt is the ability to act not according to rules, but in an unmediated response to the singularity of the case at hand. In the final analysis, the banality of evil lies precisely in the incapacity to judge, namely, to discern the singularity of the case at hand. It is precisely the capability of judgment that is absent in thoughtless evil, and it is only through an act of judgment that this wrong can be corrected.

Like reconciliation and forgiveness, judgment emerges spontaneously, but its spontaneity is very different from that of both its predecessors. Whereas reconciliation was grounded primarily in passive acceptance, and forgiveness in active doing, judgment opens a third possibility of interrelation between humankind and world. Whereas reconciliation consisted of an acceptance of the past and forgiveness of an overcoming of the past for the sake of the future, judgment seems to be less concerned with the problem of time. It emerges with respect to the present, to the case at hand that requires discerning judgment, as if the future and past were reunited in the present.

The turn to judgment is yet another way in which Arendt wishes to confront the failings of both human action and philosophical thinking. Here Arendt identifies the latter not simply with abstract thinking but, more precisely, with the construction of coherent systems of thought. The seemingly impenetrable fortress of systematic logic has proved to be ever so fragile when faced with the pressing call to pass judgment in a singular and nonreplicable historical situation. It is interesting to note that, precisely on this point, Arendt comes closer than ever to the critique that Heidegger himself had launched against philosophical thinking, and that her solution, the turn to judgment, bears a close resemblance to Heidegger's understanding of proper philosophical thinking.

To conclude, Arendt's writings on judgment are not merely her third and final attempt to deal with the crimes of thought and action to which she continuously returned in the years after the war. It would seem that her study of judgment led Arendt to question her earlier presuppositions on the nature of evil deeds and misleading thoughts. In her notebooks as well as *The Human Condition*, Arendt assumed that an unbridgeable abyss separates radical evil from ordinary human action and that, similarly, political action and philosophical speculation are irreconcilable. As her thinking matured, Arendt seems to have become aware of the difficulty of expelling even the worst forms of evil from the realm of human action and even the best forms of philosophy from the life of the mind. Her inquiry into judgment should not be read as an attempt to come to terms with, become reconciled with, or forgive the atrocities of human action and the failings of philosophical thinking. In the final analysis, judgment did not provide Arendt with a solution to the questions that troubled her so badly: how to distinguish good from evil or demarcate philosophical thinking from political thought. For her, judgment emerged as at best a deeper way of reformulating precisely these challenges.

Facing: Books from the Hannah Arendt Library at Bard College. Photo, Serena Randolph. Courtesy of the Hannah Arendt Collection, Stevenson Library, Bard College.

... IN DIE METAPHYSIK

Vorträge und Aufsätze   Teil I

Vorträge und Aufsätze   Teil II

Vorträge und Aufsätze   Teil III

EXISTENCE AND BEING

Martin Heidegger

Für

Hannah

Martin

22. *April* 1971

Martin Heidegger :

Pensivement

Solitude and the Activity of Thinking

R O G E R   B E R K O W I T Z

"The true predicaments of our time," Hannah Arendt wrote, "will assume their authentic form only when totalitarianism has become a thing of the past."[1] The totalitarianisms in Germany and the Soviet Union were only symptoms of these true predicaments, of what Arendt early on calls the mass society characterized by "organized loneliness."[2] Later, covering the trial of Adolf Eichmann, she would come to see that the bond between totalitarianism and loneliness is the phenomenon of thoughtlessness.

I have long been struck by Arendt's suggestion that totalitarianism depends on thoughtlessness and that thoughtlessness is itself rooted in the experience of loneliness. Loneliness, she writes, is the "common ground for terror, the essence of totalitarian government."[3] As the "experience of being abandoned by everything and everybody," loneliness deprives one of a common sense and a common world; cut off from the experience of taking another seriously, of hearing the voice of conscience, and of listening in other ways, lonely men are uniquely susceptible to the delusional fellowship promised by ideological and totalitarian fantasies. Thrust back on his own insecurity, the lonely man is prone to embrace a coherent and stable world offered by ideological extremism.

Observing Adolf Eichmann during his trial in 1961, Arendt was confirmed in her earlier speculations regarding the connection between loneliness and totalitarianism. Eichmann, she argued, was a joiner; he craved, more than anything else, "being a member of something or other"; he feared, above all, to live alone, without orders and directives, cut off from an organization or group that would give his life direction and meaning.[4] Fearing the loneliness that permeates the bourgeois world defined by private interests, Eichmann, Arendt writes, sought out a movement that gave his life sense. He was an "idealist" in the sense that he "*lived* for his idea" whatever the idea was, because that idea gave significance to his insignificant life.[5] In thrall to the movement and its ideas, Eichmann was prepared to sacrifice everything and do anything that was asked of him. Thus does loneliness open the door to thoughtlessness. Barricaded behind an impenetrable fortress of clichés, Eichmann traded his

Facing: Inscribed cover of Hannah Arendt's copy of an offprint of the French edition of Martin Heidegger's *Pensivement.* The inscription reads: "For Hannah. Martin. 22. April 1971." Courtesy of the Hannah Arendt Collection, Stevenson Library, Bard College.

human power to think for the power of membership in a mass movement. It is this refusal to think—his "inability to *think*"—that frustrates all communication with others and defines Eichmann's loneliness even amidst his immersion in a movement.[6] And it was this "absence of thinking—which is so ordinary an experience in our everyday life, where we have hardly the time, let alone the inclination, to *stop* and think"—that Arendt came to see as the dangerous wellspring of evil in modern times.[7]

Thoughtlessness, like the loneliness that nourishes it, is hardly new. As we all know, the activity of thinking is rare. Yet, what makes thoughtlessness especially dangerous today is the fact—Arendt insists we recognize it as a fact—that we are the first people in history for whom the authority of tradition—like the authority of custom, religion, and truth—has evaporated. Malicious men have always and will always exist; yet, ordinary albeit thoughtless men could, in earlier times, be restrained from evil by the force of habit, the authority of tradition, and even the commands of religion. Arendt recognized that throughout most of modern history, traditions are absorbed into a common sense that contributes to the building of a shared and public world, the worlds of law and politics. She also saw that the retreat of traditional standards leads common sense and politics to atrophy as well. Since traditions are what root us in a common world, the decay of tradition is the factual basis of our political crisis. Shorn from tradition and left rootless, modern individuals are lonely. Thrust back on themselves, men and women yearn, Arendt suggests, for nothing so much as a home.

The "isolated human being" amidst the breakdown of tradition and the uprooting of friendships, loses his place in the world, and "seeks his place only from his belonging to a movement."[8] The last hundred years are witness to what men are capable of in the service of a movement. And today, the current struggle between jihad and democratic capitalism has extended further the proof of mankind's potential for depravity. Time was that blowing oneself up in public, torturing enemy soldiers, and disappearing people without a trial—and doing so in accordance with legal procedures or religious sanction—was the very mark of an uncivilized people. Today, suicide bombings and legalized procedures of torture burst the bounds of common sense. To take seriously our modern predicament is to recognize that once burst, it is not clear whether the public bonds of tradition and common sense can be put together again.

How do we begin to try? Do we try? Arendt's political project asks the question, and it remains for her a question of how and if politics can, or even should, found an ethical world. Can we who live without traditions nevertheless make a human world in which we live and act together?

In the face of this question, Arendt teaches the supreme importance of thinking. Arendt's question—the question that drives so much of her work from *The Origins of Totalitarianism* through *The Life of the Mind*—is whether, in the absence of tradition, thinking can halt the temptation of human evil. "Could the activity of thinking as such," she asks, "be among the conditions that make men abstain from evil-doing or even actually "condition" them against it?"[9] Thinking—the habit of erecting obstacles to oversimplifications, compromises, and conventions—is an important part of Arendt's answer to Lenin's famous question: What is to be done?

To reflect on the political importance of the activity of thinking suggests that the space of politics may not be limited to its traditional abode within the public realm. Indeed, I want to suggest that Arendt's defense of political action requires attention not only to the public but to the private as well. What has been overlooked amidst all the attention to Arendt's defense of the public realm of politics over and against the rise of the social is her equally strong insistence upon a vibrant and secure private realm where active thinking is possible, secured from the unthinking habits, common opinions, and constraints of the social.

Of course, the public realm is important to Arendt's conception of political action. She writes, "Action needs for its full appearance the shining brightness we once called glory, and which is possible only in the public realm."[10] With some justification, therefore, Arendt scholars have focused their critical gaze on political action and sought to "discover a set of criteria that will isolate genuinely political action from its various simulacra."[11] There is a widespread view critiqued by a number of the essays in this volume that Arendt seeks an idea of politics that is purified of all practical, social, and private activities.

What is often ignored by the single-minded focus on the boundary of Arendtian politics is her equally emphatic call for the protection of a private realm as a sphere of dignity; the "sacredness of privacy," she writes, "was like the sacredness of the hidden, namely, of birth and death, the beginning and end of the mortals who, like all living creatures, grow out of and return to the darkness of an underworld."[12] Similarly, Arendt repeatedly returns to a quotation from Cato, "Never is he more active than when he does nothing, never is he less alone than when he is by himself."[13] The solitary thinker is, for Arendt, deeply enmeshed in the public web of action and politics.

The private, Arendt insists, is not necessarily the realm of loneliness that is opposed to politics and action. Nor is the private an economic realm concerned with the pursuit of individual interests. Instead, the private can be a space of solitude that is the necessary prerequisite for the activity of thinking. Indeed, it is solitude that nurtures and fosters thoughtfulness and thus prepares individuals for the possibility of political action. What Arendt teaches is that in dark and lonely times we must not seek only the company of others in public; just as importantly, we must be vigilant in protecting the sanctuaries of solitude from which the activity of thinking is born. To combat the loneliness of the modern world, Arendt suggests, requires solitude, which she sees as the cradle of thinking.

It is important to remember that the thinking that happens in solitude is different in kind from the public rationality of political thought. To think is not the same as to reason. Indeed, in the project of building a world, Arendt warns us against the seductions of reason. Arendt forces us to confront the fact that it is rational for a democratic government charged with protecting its citizens to do so, as the slogan goes, by any means necessary. It is rational for guerrilla fighters to promote their cause through terror. Indeed, the normalization of terror and torture shows how ordinary men can reason themselves into justifying what ought to be unthinkable. Thus, reason, Arendt writes, "fits man into the iron band of terror."[14] Reason, Arendt warns, reasons, it does not think.

Against reasoning that fits men with the dead weight of answers, Arendt insists that thinking proper be understood as a kind of action. "When everybody is swept away unthinkingly by what everybody else does and believes in, those who think are drawn out of hiding because their refusal to join in is conspicuous and thereby becomes a kind of action."[15] Thinking separates individuals from the mass and inoculates the thinker from the contagion of conformity. Thus, the activity of thinking is the last barrier to the lonely and conformist uniformity of the blood-dimmed tide.

To orient herself in the activity of thinking and its foundation in solitude, Arendt rightly looks not to theories but to models. This makes sense. Given the way Arendt thinks, a rigid conceptual analysis risks distorting her point. She is a brilliant associative thinker who often begins with an image or idea or event and allows her thought trains to proceed from there and radiate outward. So perhaps the best way to pursue what Arendt means by the fertile relationship between solitude and thinking is to inquire more deeply of the examples she gives.

Two thinkers—Socrates and the German philosopher Karl Jaspers— appear and reappear as Arendt's examples that shed light on the power of thinking in dark times. What unites Jaspers and Socrates in Arendt's imagination is their shared ability to replace the thoughtlessness of loneliness with the thoughtfulness of solitude.

Loneliness, Arendt writes, is the loss of the experience of being with others that can strike one even when and especially when one is with others and lost in and among them. In contrast to loneliness, solitude demands that one actually is alone; and yet, in the being alone of solitude, "I am 'by myself,' together with my self."[16] It is in solitude, Arendt sees, that we are least alone. Amid the plurality that attains in solitude, there is the possibility for the activity of thinking that interrupts totalitarianism and fosters political action.

I want, briefly, to sketch Arendt's extraordinary accounts of these two models of solitary thinking in dark times.

When she writes about Karl Jaspers in her book *Men in Dark Times*, Arendt is struck by his internal exile where he stood entirely separate, independent, and alone. Although he remained in Germany and did not join the armed or peaceful resistance, Jaspers was politically relevant because he appeared in public as a living refutation of the Nazi regime. While some might condemn him for staying in the country, Arendt argues that Jaspers's dignified and silent resistance spoke volumes, and she suggests that his dignified presence in the world was itself at the very heart of political action.

Jaspers, Arendt writes, is possessed of "*humanitas*," by which she means "something that was the very height of humanness because it was valid without being objective."[17] *Humanitas* is not objective. It is not rational, at least not in the sense of something that can be demonstrated or deduced. Neither is *humanitas* subjective, a property of an isolated individual. Instead, *humanitas* is a "personal element beyond the control of the subject"—that which defines a man as who he is and never leaves him.[18] The magnificence of Jaspers's *humanitas*, Arendt writes, is that in the darkness of total domination, he stood firm as a beacon to the ultimate triumph of humanity over barbarity.

This striking personal element of Jaspers's *humanitas* is, for Arendt, a public act—a beacon—but one rooted in the solitude of his thinking. What Jaspers manifested to all whom he encountered was "a confidence that needed no confirmation, an assurance that in times in which everything could happen one thing could not happen. What Jaspers represented then, when he was entirely alone, was not Germany but what was left of *humanitas* in Germany."[19] Alone, Jaspers was anything but lonely. If loneliness is marked by an inability to think, Jaspers's solitude is a being at home in a "region of reason and freedom," in a "space forever illuminated anew by a speaking and listening thoughtfulness."[20] In dark times in which public affairs and politics tend to shatter rather than inspire thoughtfulness, solitude is a refuge that harbors the proper realm of thinking. And not simply thinking. The solitary act of thinking is, for Arendt, inevitably an activity of politics.

Arendt is struck, too, by the solitude of Socrates—the one pure example she admits of the thinking man. In the *Life of the Mind* and in her essay "Socrates," she emphasizes Socrates' discovery that solitude is "the necessary condition for the good functioning of the polis."[21] Socrates' solitude is marked by what Arendt names the dialogue of the "two-in-one," the fact that when he is alone he is not alone but "by himself." Socrates is actually with his other self. This other self—figured as Socrates' *daimon*—is that divine voice to whom Socrates goes home; he is that "very obnoxious fellow who always cross-examines him."[22] The *daimon* is what interrupts the individual's sovereign and unitary self. The importance of thinking, and hence of solitude, is that thinking interrupts the oneness, certainty, and confidence that allows ideology to overwhelm thought. The Socratic thinker is a gadfly who stings citizens and also himself and thus arouses them from the satin sleep of conformity to the activity of thinking.

In asking herself where the activity of thinking originates, Arendt answers that thinking is born from the experience of "absolute solitude."[23] It is only in solitude that the murderer can encounter himself, as when Richard III encounters himself in Shakespeare's play:[24]

What do I fear? Myself? There's none else by:
Richard loves Richard: that is, I am I.
Is there a murderer here? No. Yes, I am:
Then fly: what! From myself? Great reason why:
Lest I revenge. What! myself upon myself?

For Arendt, it is in solitude that Richard comes face to face with his con-science, his other self—the one who, gadfly-like, stings us into thinking. Only someone who has the experience of "talking with himself" is someone who understands the danger that he might contradict himself—he may, for exam-ple, commit a murder and then have to live with himself, a murderer, for the rest of his life—only such a thinker can develop a conscience. This is why Ar-endt writes that "living together with others begins with living together with oneself."[25]

Arendt also addresses the intimate connection between solitude and think-ing in her speech celebrating Heidegger's eightieth birthday. It is there that she recalls the "rumor" that originally brought her to Heidegger's lecture hall. It was the rumor that Heidegger was teaching thinking; namely, that against the scholarship of universities, Heidegger broke with the tradition, those "dark times" in which philosophy had become an academic exercise. It is against philosophy that Arendt, building upon Heidegger, describes her own passion for thinking as necessarily "something solitary."[26] In all spoken dialogue there remains something unspeakable; there is, in truth, always that which "cannot be fully made to ring through language," something, she in-sists, that "does not communicate itself either to others or even to the person involved." While Arendt forever remains suspicious of a thinking that has its place fully outside the world, she nevertheless wants to "honor thinkers"[27]—especially those thinkers such as Socrates and Jaspers whose thought bursts the bounds of solitude in which it originates.

For both Jaspers and Socrates, the thinking that emerges from solitude is as loud and as active as glorious speech could ever be; thinking, she insists, can be of even greater consequence than traditional political activism. In Jaspers's silence in the face of Nazism and Socrates' humble refusal to escape his ulti-mate sentence by the Athenians are manifest activities of thinking that shine brightly in dark times. And it is in dark times, when everybody is swept away unthinkingly, that those who think come to act in their refusal to join in.

It is Arendt's profound belief in the power and need for thinking in soli-tude that drives her controversial and widely loathed essay "Reflections on Little Rock." Arendt provocatively argues against governmentally mandated integration of the public schools. Her position has been heavily and at times rightly critiqued; Arendt herself, in a letter to Ralph Ellison, withdrew her claim that forced desegregation sacrificed black children in a struggle their parents were unwilling to fight themselves. And yet few commentators have fully grappled with Arendt's warning, never withdrawn, that in mandating how parents educate their children we risk eviscerating the realm of the private that is the necessary foundation of solitude, the activity of thinking and even of politics. Whatever one thinks of Arendt's conclusion—and it is difficult to endorse her willingness to allow segregated public schools—the provocation of her arguments demands attention.

In the Little Rock essay, Arendt distinguishes three realms of life: the public, the social, and the private. While the public, or political, realm is governed by equality and the social realm by inequality, the private realm is the realm of exclusivity and uniqueness. The "rule of uniqueness" that Arendt attributes to the private sphere will always conflict both with the political demand for equality and the social demand for discrimination against certain kinds of people and behavior. While the private can coexist with the political, it, like the political, is particularly endangered by the rise of the social. As Arendt writes, "The rules of uniqueness and exclusiveness are, and always will be, in conflict with the standards of society precisely because social discrimination violates the principle [of uniqueness], and lacks validity for the conduct, of private life."[28] And given the increasing power of the social world of conformity, "not many people are left who know the rules of and live a private life."[29] The great threat today is that the drive to remedy the inequalities characteristic of the social realm will overwhelm not only the political realm, in which only political equality is at issue, but also the private realm, where the drive for political and material equality threatens the sacred dignity of unique individuals. And it is this very private realm, the realm of uniqueness, where one can retreat from both equality and sameness to the experience of solitude.

Arendt insists that we recall the importance of solitude for politics as well as for thinking. For, if it is the activity of thinking that might originate a politics that would ward off evil, Arendt reminds us that thinking originates in the experience of solitude. Solitude, she writes, is what makes possible the two-in-one of thinking; it is solitude, therefore, that is "the necessary condition for the good functioning of the polis, a better guarantee than rules of behavior enforced by laws and fear of punishment."[30] To preserve the realm of solitude, and thus the activity of thinking upon which politics depends, Arendt emphasizes the essential value of privacy. The protection of the private sphere includes the right to marry someone of any race, a right she defends as integral to the dignity and uniqueness of the private sphere, and also the right to raise one's children as one will. These rights must, she writes, remain the private business of every person.[31] We must, she argues, safeguard the right of every person to be unique and different within the four walls of his or her home.

The private right to uniqueness resonates, Arendt writes, nowhere more than in a parent's rearing of children. There is no greater right of privacy, a right of living as one thinks right, than the right to raise one's child as one sees fit. "To force parents to send their children to an integrated school against their will means to deprive them of rights which clearly belong to them in all free societies—the private right over their children and the social right to free association."[32] What offends Arendt in the Little Rock case is not the ideal of desegregation, but the danger that well-intentioned governmental attacks on social discrimination will erode the walls of privacy that nourish the possibility of thinking and of acting—and thus of uniqueness and plurality. Since the space for solitary thought depends on the protection of a vibrant private realm, the protection of privacy is a necessary first step in the cultivation of thoughtful political action.

To think in private is not easy. Nor is it easy today to defend and protect the right to privacy in the name of thinking. For it is surely the case that the call for and the protection of privacy can all too easily be turned away from a foundation for the activity of thinking and toward a defense of thoughtless individualism and hateful racism. All too often, advocates of privacy yearn for the lonely and bourgeois pursuit of interests—from accumulating wealth to cooking and even to philosophizing. There is a difference between an individualist and a thinker. And yet the need for thinkers militates for the protection of individuals.

Thinking is a difficult business. It requires a separation from the world, a passion for truth, and a willingness to let go of the affairs of the world. In the name of and out of care for the world, thinking requires a distance from the world.

To stand apart from the public does not mean to stand alone. Arendt distinguishes solitude, the conversation one has with oneself, from loneliness, the experience of the absence of being with others. To hole up in the lonely refuge of one's psyche is to lose one's humanity, which can appear only in public.

While the experience of thinking might begin in solitude, it can only be brought to fruition when one "ventures into the public realm."[33] What Jaspers and Socrates combine is the ability to live doubly, both in solitude and in public. When such persons appear as beacons of dignity, they inspire us. There is, Arendt writes, something fascinating about someone's being inviolable, untemptable, unswayable. Something fascinating, and also deeply political.

There may be no thinker in the canon of political thinking more similarly attuned to the political relevance Arendt attributes to the dignity of the solitary thinker than Ralph Waldo Emerson. Emersonian self-reliance is possessed by those who follow the inflexible string that colloquially is called one's backbone. Trust thyself, Emerson counsels, and hear that iron string that every hearts vibrates to. As Emerson writes, "He only who is able to stand alone is qualified for society."[34] Emerson's imperative, to take up the divine idea allotted to each one of us, resonates with Arendt's Socratic imperative, to be true to yourself.

Are Emerson and Arendt fooling themselves? Are we truly to believe that thinking in solitude can be the animating source of politics?

The answer depends on our understanding of politics. If politics is about policies, if it is what happens in legislatures and courts and in administrative agencies, if it is about the distribution of power in society, then dignity seems quite foreign to politics. Similarly, if politics is about the rational organization of a state, personal dignity fits uneasily with the pursuit of political ends. Clearly, politics is about policies, and it is about the rational pursuit of ends.

And yet, there is also another idea of politics, one that has its beginning in Plato's claim that the politician is an educator. For Plato as for Thoreau, the political actor is one who awakens himself and others to the claim that the just and the good make upon us. As Arendt understands it, politics in this sense is the unification of a multitude. As the activity of unifying, politics is based on the activity of revealing, of showing to a people the common ground of their unity.

If Arendt's politics depends on the actions of those who can and do stand apart, her elitism is that of neither an oligarchic nor a hereditary elite; it is, rather, an elitism of those who have had the experience of freedom, whether in public or in private. The free are a self-selected elite who, knowing both the joy and the precariousness of freedom, seek to "protect the island of freedom they have come to inhabit against the surrounding sea of necessity."[35] In her attunement to the phenomenon of freedom, Arendt discovers islands of freedom in revolutionary action and inner exile. What unites both public and private activities of freedom is their separation from the predictable, statistical, ordinary, and normalizing demands of our modern world. Against the social scientific demand that the world be lawful, understandable, and thus improvable, Arendt holds out the possibility of action. What elitism seeks is neither rule nor power, but spaces of freedom. Some of those spaces are public and political. One such space, however, is the private life of solitude.

PART VII

Sites of Memory

WALTER BENJAMIN

zum Gedächtnis

Institut für Sozialforschung 1942

Exile Readings

HANNAH ARENDT'S LIBRARY

:: REINHARD LAUBE

On May 1, 1972, the photographer Jill Krementz took a picture of Hannah Arendt in her library.[1] As Lotte Kohler remembers it, this library was set up partly in the dining room of Arendt's Riverside Drive apartment and partly in the study of her husband, Heinrich Blücher, who had died in 1970. After Hannah Arendt's death in December 1975, Lotte Kohler and Mary McCarthy were faced, as executors of her will, with the task of liquidating the New York apartment and with it the library that was located there. While Arendt had already entered into agreements during her lifetime with the Library of Congress and the German Literary Archive in Marbach concerning the unpublished and handwritten portions of her literary effects, such agreements did not as a rule cover books.[2] So Lotte Kohler thought she had to find a solution for this extensive working library. She first offered the volumes to the New School, which would have taken them but could not install the collection as an entity. The question was how best to handle the library. In fact, Arendt and Blücher had already entered into an agreement with Bard College in 1963 to donate their joint libraries to the college after their deaths.[3] Although Kohler did not know of this circumstance, she nevertheless, in the summer of 1976, approached the president of Bard College, where Heinrich Blücher had taught as a philosophy professor for many years. Leon Botstein had been a former favorite student of Arendt's, and she had even forwarded his research questions in 1966 on the discussion of Max Weber's *Science as Vocation* to Karl Jaspers.[4] Botstein accepted the libraries, and so the books were brought to the place where both Hannah Arendt and Heinrich Blücher are buried, and where they had in fact wanted them to be. Individual books out of the collection, however, came into the hands of friends and students. Through Lotte Kohler, in this way, dedication copies of writings by Martin Heidegger also went to the German Literary Archive in Marbach; she also supplemented the holdings in the Hannah Arendt Collection of Bard College with books and offprints with Heidegger's handwritten inscriptions.[5]

Facing: Hannah Arendt's hectographed typescript of Walter Benjamin's last work, "On the Concept of History," which was posthumously edited by Max Horkheimer and Theodor W. Adorno after Benjamin committed suicide while trying to escape France in 1940. The title page reads, "Walter Benjamin, In Memoriam." Courtesy of the Hannah Arendt Collection, Stevenson Library, Bard College.

The library of the philosopher and political thinker, Hannah Arendt (1906–1975) is a part of her literary effects that must first be described in its extent and historically conditioned makeup. Beyond that, the question arises of the apt way of tracking her use of these materials and her reading, as well as the references in the catalogue, peculiar to this collection and its individual volumes. Of central importance, finally, is how a nonarbitrary examination can yield conclusions about the processes of textual genesis and Hannah Arendt's readings under the circumstances of her emigration.

The Collection

Lotte Kohler cannot remember a catalogue system in the library in the New York apartment except for a distinction between *philosophy* and *literature*. The collection that arrived at Bard in 1976 and that was installed as a unit contains more than 4,000 volumes, periodicals, offprints, brochures, and incidentals (*Akzidenten*). Some 3,100 of these titles have been catalogued so far and installed all together in a single room, ordered according to the classifications of the Library of Congress. This means that the original order of the library is not retained, although in the uncatalogued portion it is possible to gain an impression of how things had been put together: for example, yards of shelving devoted to French literature purchased in Paris, the literature of and about Walter Benjamin together with a hectographed version of his essay "On the Concept of History," and yards more devoted to various individuals and themes. In general, the distinction between literature and philosophy noted by Lotte Kohler gets to the heart of a library that consists of several collections, which can in turn be reconstructed on the basis of ownership registers and annotations in the volumes.

One part of the library originates in the possessions of Hannah Arendt's first husband, Günther Stern, and his father. So, for example, Matthias Baumgartner inscribed his 1911 study of St. Augustine to his Breslau colleague, William Stern. His son, Günther, after his doctoral examination in Freiburg in 1924, made a note in a copy of Edmund Husserl's *Ideen-Schrift*: "Gift of Husserl on my departure from Freiburg." Husserl's *Logical Investigations* is marked with an ownership stamp, numerous annotations, and a sketch drawing of Socrates. In the first edition of Max Weber's *Science as Vocation*, as in the works of Georg Simmel, the handwriting of Günther Stern (Anders) can be identified. It may be that Max Weber's posthumous work on *The Rational and Sociological Foundations of Music* (Munich 1924) points toward Stern's Frankfurt habilitation project in philosophy of music, as the contemporary editions of Brecht may do with regard to Stern's employment, through Brecht's good offices, at the *Börsen-Courier*, where "Stern" turned into "Anders." Arendt and Stern not only worked together on such topics as Rilke's *Duineser Elegien*, but each also wrote a review of Karl Mannheim's *Ideologie und Utopie* (Bonn 1929), which appeared, respectively, in the periodicals *Die Gesellschaft* and *Archiv für Sozialwissenschaft und Sozialpolitik*. The collection contains an underlined and annotated unbound review copy of the book. In addition, Hannah Arendt received an offprint of Mannheim's celebrated talk at the Zürich Sociological Congress on "Competition as a Cultural Phenomenon," *Die Bedeutung der Konkurrenz im Gebiet des Geistigen*, inscribed "with heartiest regards."[6] Other partial contents of the collection are books that had belonged to Martha Beewald, Hannah Arendt's remarried mother. Her ownership stamp can be found in Karl Jaspers's *Spiritual Situation of Our Times* (*Zur geistigen Situation der Zeit*, Berlin/Leipzig 1932), as well as in Rilke editions. Heinrich Blücher used the library together with his wife, and his annotations reveal such focal points of his interests as Nietzsche and editions of military history. There is thus an edition of Carl von Clausewitz's *On War* (Dresden 1901), a work for which there is evidence that it was read by his wife as well.[7]

What is remarkable is that Hannah Arendt was able to rescue books out of earlier places of residence and phases of life to New York. In Königsberg in 1924, Felix Perles made his student a present of an edition of Joseph H. Hertz's *Jewish Thoughts and Thoughts on Judaism* (*Jüdische Gedanken und Gedanken über Judentum*, Leipzig 1924) that he had supplied with an introduction; and this contains the handwritten dedication, "To his dear student, Hannah Arendt, in friendly remembrance." We also have the book that Martin Heidegger announced to Hannah Arendt in his letter of February 1925: "The demonic has struck me. . . . As *symbol* of my gratitude accept this small book. It is at the same time an emblem of this semester."[8] With the help of the collection it is now actually possible to solve the mystery of which gift book was involved. Plato's *Symposium*, edited in 1913 by Eugen Diederichs, contains the ownership stamp "Arendt," as well as the dedication, "Marburger W[inter] S[emester] 1924/5. M." Plato's *Symposium* is a symbol indeed. More important, however, is that from the securing of volumes from her working library in various places until they could reach New York, we can infer a deliberate safeguarding of the collection. In Paris, books were deposited with friends such as Anne Weil-Mendelssohn; and she had already given a copy of her Rahel Varnhagen Manuscript to Käthe Fürst for safekeeping in 1933, not to be recovered until 1945.[9]

The countless dedicatory volumes and offprints in the Arendt library clearly indicate the network within which she moved. This included old and new teachers, colleagues, and friends—among them Walter Benjamin, Rudolf Bultmann, Martin Heidegger, Karl Mannheim, Karl Jaspers, Hans Jonas, Gershom Scholem, Dolf Sternberger, Paul Tillich, and Benno von Wiese, as well as Wystan Hugh Auden, Hermann Broch, and Uwe Johnson and artists such as Lewin Alcopley. Clues for the reconstruction of these networks as reflected in the library are provided by her address book, through which she assured contact with the discussion partners and friends whose productions can be met with on her bookshelves.[10] The handwritten dedications both establish and document personal and intellectual contacts, and they offer exceptional evidence that calls for a more detailed reading.[11] Who are the people who sent their publications to Hannah Arendt, when, and which of them supplied the books with what sorts of dedications, dedicatory poems or other texts in dedication? Benno von Wiese, for example, supplies his dissertation on Friedrich Schlegel, *A Contribution to the History of Romantic Conversations* (*Ein Beitrag zur Geschichte der romantischen Konversationen*, Berlin 1927) with a small text on his understanding of a "philosophical question"; and Paul Tillich uses poetic language to dedicate an edition of Rainer Maria Rilke's *Book of Images* on Christmas 1942, and in another gift—*The Socialist Decision* (*Die sozialistische Entscheidung*) of 1948—he calls up a "community of spirit." Worth special notice are also the offprints of Gershom Scholem, with which he recommends a "bit" of Jewish theology, as well as the numerous dedications by Martin Heidegger, who sent monographs and offprints to New York.[12] Heidegger also presented Hannah Arendt with his new publications during her visits to Freiburg. That emerges clearly, above all, from two dedications dated on February 7, 1950, the day of their first reunion after the Second World War. *Der Feldweg* (Frankfurt, 1949), like *Holzwege*, contains a handwritten dedication marking the occasion of their reunion in Freiburg. Arendt gives thanks for the latter in a letter of February 9, and, somewhat later, writes to Heinrich Blücher about her reading in it: "I looked into the *Holzwege* of Heidegger: a considerable work. I'll bring it home. Much of it is remarkable and much of it is unbelievably wrong and crazy."[13]

Arendt's library, as a unifying collection derived from different sources and as a network of relations, establishes—through selection, safekeeping and mode of appropriation—a prestructured thought-and-reflection space that opens up, with the volumes it preserves, a range of possibilities for reading and reflection that can be scrutinized retrospectively as a collection with a clear profile. A striking example is Kant. When Hannah Arendt was asked in a television interview with Günter Gaus in 1964, which later became famous, about the reasons for her selection of philosophy as her subject, she answered: "Well, yes, I had read Kant. You may well ask why I read Kant. Somehow the question came down to a choice between studying philosophy and jumping off a bridge."[14] Reading philosophy is thus about more than understanding and rational reconstruction. It is, quite emphatically, also self-preservation ("*conservatio sui*"). And it is a fact that the *Kantgesellschaft* listed among its newly registered members for the year 1921 the name of the fifteen-year-old "Hannah Arendt from Königsberg."[15] A number of Kant editions can be found in her library, including a much-read and profusely marked-up Meiner edition of the *Critique of Pure Reason* of 1926.[16] Additional pillars of memory constructed by this collection are philosophers from Plato to Heidegger and Jaspers, writers from Heinrich Heine to Franz Kafka. "From poets we expect truth" is the title of a book that reveals the importance of literature for Hannah Arendt and the literary network within which she lived.[17] But also jurists—among them Ernst Rudolf Huber, Theodor Maunz, and Carl Schmitt, who serve as reminders of the juristic legitimation of exclusion from legality—form substantial components of the collection and the memory that is represented by it.

For the profile of the collection as a whole, it is decisive, for one thing, that on the basis of the various partial collections, it is possible to identify sites of memory that indicate both a working collection and a traditional philosopher's reference library. That applies in the case of Arendt above all to the Kant editions, or in the instance of the books transmitted from Stern, to the Simmel volumes, including first editions such as the *Problems of Philosophy* (*Hauptprobleme der Philosophie*, Leipzig 1910) or collections of articles such as *The War and Decisions of the Spirit: Speeches and Articles* (*Der Krieg und die geistigen Entscheidungen: Reden und Aufsätze*, Munich 1917). Even if the reading of Kant, the reception of Heidegger, or the controversies with Schmitt served not only the investigation of these authors and their works, but also—like the readings of Heine, Kafka, and Broch—her self-description, supporting the search for and registration of sites of memory, the library was above all a working bibliography and thus not a bibliophilic or encyclopedic collection in the tradition of scholarly libraries. Hannah Arendt's involvement in the securing of books of Jewish origins in the framework of Jewish Cultural Reconstruction doubtless sensitized her to the importance of collections of printed bearers of memory.[18]

In her library, the various partial collections and the outstanding dedicated volumes indicate the importance of provenances and a differentiated web of relations. The books of this collection convey, in Benjamin's words, "pictures" and "remembrances" of the places of acquisition, earlier standpoints, and previous possession.[19] Above all, nevertheless, it is Hannah Arendt's projects and work themes that can be recovered from the assemblage of the literature.

The collection thereby reflects it own history as well as a conception of science as work (*Wissenschaft als Arbeit*) that had definitively displaced the idea of the universe of knowledge (*Kosmos des Wissens*) in the course of the nineteenth century. While the profiles of scholarly library collections were traditionally encyclopedic in design, new demands were made of libraries of the nineteenth and twentieth centuries as a result of the upheavals of modernity as well as a new concept of science as research (*Wissenschaft als Forschung*).[20] The collections must now increasingly accommodate the research process and the completion of projects.[21] That applies as well to researchers' book collections that take on the character of working libraries. Hannah Arendt's collection gives no sign of either bibliophilic or encyclopedic interests. Filling the bookshelves are rather literature and works appropriate to Hannah Arendt's grand projects. This applies no less to her contributions on Franz

Kafka, Walter Benjamin, and Hermann Broch as to her book projects, among which the extensive literatures for *The Origins of Totalitarianism* and *Eichmann in Jerusalem* deserve special mention. Her extensive correspondence—now partly in print—also permits conclusions about her formative readings. Early in the gestation of her magnum opus, for example, she writes about the utilization of useful libraries and reports to Heinrich Blücher, "I am reading Tocqueville and Shakespeare and I mess around with human rights in despair [*murkse . . . verzweifelt*]. I cannot and cannot get the history straight."[22]

It was a part of Hannah Arendt's reading to insert a handwritten index on the endpaper in back of the books she had worked through. Page numbers are noted next to central concepts, turns of phrase, and names; and important matters are emphasized with single and multiple underlinings, and occasionally comments. In addition, there are inserts in the form of notepaper on texts of the most varied origins. Thus there was a postcard from Walter Benjamin to Hannah Arendt dated 1937 located in Hans Prinzhorn's *Body—Soul—Unity: A Core Problem of the New Psychology* (*Leib–Seele–Einheit. Ein Kernproblem der neuen Psychologie*, Potsdam 1927),[23] or the typescript of a poem by Friedrich Gundolf enclosed in his *Shakespeare: His Essence and Work* (*Shakespeare. Sein Wesen und Werk*, Berlin 1928).

Before we can enter more deeply, by way of examples, into the course of her readings in, exile and therefore before the significance of the traces of those readings can be demonstrated, we must first address ourselves to the question of how uncovering the meaning of collections in general, as well as information specific to individual examples, are prerequisites to answering the question about the profile of collections and the significance of readings.

Opening up the Collection

All research into provenance interested in the profile of a collection, as well as its composition of particular volumes bearing ownership and dedication marks or traces of reading or use, presupposes an uncovering of provenances. The present-day Weimar librarian Jürgen Weber has called attention to the need for such documenting of information about the origins and use of individual volumes and collections, and he has cited it as an example of librarianship problems in the restitution of National Socialist booty.[24] In case of faulty collection management, such holdings can simply be no longer found. The precondition for the kind of successful research into provenance that works with copy- and collection-specific evidence is thus a methodical expansion of collection practices, which pays attention—in addition to the bibliographic identification of an edition, noting author, title, place and year of publication, as well as a contents-centered substantive elucidation employing keywords and systematization—to the individual materiality and contexts of a collection. In the recent Weimar model of a cooperative provenance register, the demands of a clarification specific to individual examples are met by means of "Recommendations for the notation of provenance" and a "Thesaurus of provenance concepts," building on the American thesaurus, *Provenance Evidence*.[25]

The description and investigation of the Hannah Arendt Library have to do with precisely these problems of provenance notation, in order to make possible research into provenance in this collection, which has been until now opened up only in the sense of being kept together as a unit, with a catalogue that is as yet incomplete. In 2006, on the occasion of the one-hundredth birthday of the philosopher, the library of Bard College was able to provide a centralized Web-based access to the collection together with an Arendt portal that bundles access to offerings associated with it, such as digital pages and information about additional sources. What is decisive, however, is that all the itemized data relating to the catalogued volumes have been marked, "Arendt, Hannah – Personal library" and thereby coded as a collection and subject to computer search in this context. In addition, there are references to dedications, marginalia, and ephemera inserted in the volumes, such as postcards, notes, and manuscripts. They are searchable online, even if a comprehensive search by means of a thesaurus of provenance concepts is not available and the current selection of provenances does not as yet offer a unified picture of the collection. As search keywords for dedications, marginalia, and enclosures in the individual books in the collection, such expressions as "Arendt marginalia," "Arendt ephemera," and "Arendt dedications" are available, although these are as yet limited to a provisional state of the collection's catalogue. In the domain of "Image Gallery," access is provided to digitalizations of revealing individual pieces of the collection, while under the heading of "Digital Project" there is documentation of current and completed work utilizing the holdings of the Arendt Library.

In this way, the collection is made visible as a site of memory, which gives insight, through intelligible indicators of provenance, into the meaning of readings—of readings that leave a residue in marginalia, of handwritten entries that permit conclusions about the appropriation and thereby the interpretation of what was read, as well as about processes of textual generation. Marginalia, notes, journals, and manuscripts document forms of productive appropriation and processing, which are absorbed in publications or remain invisible in published work. Attention to the working library opens a new range of possibilities for contextualizing and interpreting the published works, which becomes visible in its intertextuality. It becomes possible to observe as well what was worked through but left latent in the publications.

The Readings

Barbara Hahn has called attention to an impressive example of processes of appropriation while reading. She tells the story of a volume in the Arendt library, which the philosopher received as a present from a casual travel companion in the course of a trip through Germany on assignment for Jewish Cultural Reconstruction. At issue is Ernst Jünger's war diaries, *Emanations* (*Strahlungen*, Tübingen 1949), supplied with a dedication in February 1950 and intensively worked through. The reading is put to use in "The Aftermath of Nazi Rule: Report from Germany" (1950). Ernst Jünger's *The Forest Path* (*Der Waldgang*, Frankfurt, 1950) similarly shows tracks of work, as well as numerous comments, although these did not find entry in any of her publications.[26] As further examples of pregnant readings, I want to drawn on two pillars of the site of memory that is the Hannah Arendt Library—two authors, who were, with the glosses she applied, formative for the reader Hannah Arendt: Carl Schmitt and Martin Heidegger.

In her 1948 essay on existential philosophy, Hannah Arendt called Heidegger the last Romantic and likened his "total irresponsibility" to that of Friedrich Schlegel and Adam Müller.[27] This designation remains incomprehensible without the Weimar debate about "political romanticism" in which Carl Schmitt had launched a general assault against modern forms of the [bourgeois] civic public sphere (*bürgerliche Öffentlichkeit*). The interpretation of romanticism became a schematic framework for social interpretation and an intellectual weapon in the political conflicts of the time.[28] Among Hannah Arendt's early contributions may be listed her essay on the Adam Müller Renaissance, which appeared in the *Kölnischer Zeitung*.[29] The appropriate selection of Müller texts is to be found in her library, duly annotated: *Vom Geiste der Gemeinschaft, Elemente der Staatskunst, Theorie des Geldes* (Leipzig 1931). Although Arendt seizes upon the interpretive figure of "political Romantic" with Schmitt, she then turns it against him, as well as against Heidegger. In *Elemente und Ursprünge totaler Herrschaft* (*The Origins of Totalitarianism*, Frankfurt, 1955) she describes Schmitt's *Political Romanticism* as "the best work on this subject, to which we will also revert more frequently in what is to come," and she reiterates her attacks on Adam Müller and Friedrich Schlegel, "who are symptomatic to the present day of the intellectual lack of seriousness [*Verspieltheit*] . . . in which just about any opinion can temporarily find a home. No reality, no event, no political idea can escape them because all these are nothing but occasions for their actual Romantic games."[30] Arendt also considered Schmitt's observations about the "specifically German variety of the pretentious bourgeois (*Spießer*)," the cultivated philistine, to be an "outstanding formulation," so excellent, in fact, that she applied it in a letter in defense of Jaspers against Curtius's critique during the Goethe Year: "Have you seen Curtius's attack on Jaspers?" Arendt wrote to Dolf Sternberger. "Hitler really achieved nothing; he could not even free the German people from these idiotic cultivated philistines."[31]

In commenting on Schmitt's strategies of justification after 1945, Arendt invoked precisely the qualities with which Schmitt had earlier characterized the representatives of "political Romanticism." In the margin of Schmitt's *Ex Captivitate Salus* (Cologne 1950), Arendt notes its "total mendacity": to Schmitt's reference to the "possibility of a total exclusion from legality [*Entrechtung*]," Arendt remarks in the margin of the now ostensibly "excluded jurist": "Earlier this never worried him (at all)!" Schmitt's comparison of his situation with "the condition of hunted game," Arendt dismisses with the remark, "he evidently never belonged to the hunters himself." His conception of a *"kat-echon"*—from the Greek word meaning "to restrain"—in his article on Tocqueville, which praises the capacity for insight of the defeated, she comments upon with the observation, "Without any kat-echon at all, T[ocqueville] would have been clear that aggressive war remains aggressive war and mass murder remains mass murder." Schmitt's description of a relationship of recognition in which I recognize someone as an enemy if he is in a position to call me into question, Arendt summarizes as follows in a marginal note: "Whoever calls me into question is my enemy."[32]

Arendt's library offers a collection of thoroughly worked-over Schmitt editions, which also includes *Der Nomos der Erde im Völkerrecht des Jus Publicum Europaeum* (*Nomos of the Earth in the International Law of European Public Law*), an example of a title that appeared in 1950, like *Ex Captivitate Salus*, similarly marked by a toxic scrutiny of Schmitt's argumentative strategies. Anyone who takes up Hannah Arendt's copy and opens it to the rear endpaper receives a summary of her reading and thereby at the same time insights into her manner of working. Here are the conclusions from the reading in the form of theses, with corresponding page numbers: so, for example, "retaining soil from 'blood and soil'"; "the inability to understand the contract that rests on promise is typical. The only German who understood this was Nietzsche"; "Not even listed in the index"; "Schmitt the only student of Hobbes"; and "Schmitt actually the jurist of the geopoliticians."[33]

Her exile's perspectives on German postwar attempts at self-description are especially manifest in the marginalia to the main text, as with the following pregnant formulation from Arendt's pen: "The world spirit moves dialectically—Human beings do nothing, and above all the Germans, nothing at all! Belgian neutrality . . . the U-Boat campaign, Hitler—*simply never happened*."[34] "The question of war guilt fundamentally falsified!"—this is the tenor of Arendt's commentary at another place; and she notes, with regard to Schmitt's account of the Munich Pact of September 1938, "Fantastical! England sacrificed [Czechoslovakia] and that! is how it came to war!"[35] At another place, she interprets Schmitt's treatment of the League of Nations: "In short the League of Nations is responsible for the Second World War because it could not prevent it."[36] "International law," as Arendt reads Schmitt, "relates [always only] to Europe. The question of justice or injustice [*Recht oder Unrecht*] is altogether excluded. E.g., the mass murder of stateless individuals is legally possible."[37] Beyond that, Schmitt's style as a "pose of danger " is remarked,[38] and his anti-Americanism, always unmistakably highlighted: "As if Europe had gone to ruin because of America!"[39] Schmitt's reading of Kant is characterized as "really . . . the epitome of malicious distortion," or, elsewhere, he is subjected to an ironic mock sympathy: "Poor Schmitt: The Nazis said Blood and Soil—he understood soil and the Nazis meant *blood*."[40] Abruptly condensed and acid interpretations of what is read characterize the annotations, as well as indications throughout of Schmitt's latent obscuring of factual evidence, responsibilities, and the absent tradition of contractual thinking: "Thus I may murder, as long as I am on a trip," "Unjust is only what is prohibited," and the contract "cannot even be found" in the index of the book.[41]

An additional way of working through her readings can be found in Arendt's intellectual journals (*Denktagebücher*), where Schmitt's *Nomos of the Earth* is mentioned, as well as Heidegger's interpretation of the allegory of the cave, another emotional reading that has as its object, as was true of political romanticism, a central interpretative schema. The allegory of the cave in the seventh book of *The Republic* was similarly a key text in Weimar debates, and this did much to shape Arendt's reflections on the polis, its historic and contemporary reality, and the cultivating role of philosophy.[42] Martin Heidegger, for his part, repeatedly drew on the allegory of the cave during the 1920s as a way of introducing the study of philosophy and his conceptions of "truth." It was none other than Günther Stern (Anders) who recalled in 1946 the special importance of this Platonic dialogue for Heidegger.[43] Arendt's use of the cave as starting point can be read not only in her reviews and contributions to political philosophy, but also in her personal copy of Heidegger's *Platons Lehre von der Wahrheit* (Plato's Doctrine of Truth).[44] The significance that Arendt assigns to Plato's original text and Heidegger's glosses also become evident from the numerous annotations and references to the Greek key concepts in her copy of the English translation by Francis MacDonald Cornford.[45] Underlinings and comments refer to a debate about Plato, one which was carried out as a debate about the "polis" of modernity and thereby about (bourgeois) civil society. It manifests itself as well in the conflict about sociology of knowledge, the concept of *Bildung* (cultivation) and the function of the sciences. It is not decisive that Arendt praises Heidegger's "grand interpretation of the cave analogy,"[46] and at the same time bemoans his lack of a political philosophy; what is decisive is the presence of an interpretative figure in which the cave remains the site of modern society that needs to be transcended by the truth claims of philosophy.[47]

In conclusion, then, I want to call attention to a discovery in the Arendt library that humorously brings into focus the traditions that can be traced in the collection as well as the ways they are called into question in the course of reading—that is, precisely the presence of contradictory perspectives. At issue is a previously unknown typescript of a poem by Friedrich Gundolf about "The History of Philosophy." In untranslatable jingles, the last verse goes something like this:

Everyone saws off [*sägt*] the absolute
whereupon the previous question rested
by means of new questions, and turns
into means what had been thought of as an end.
Each "That" turns into "If," every "What" turns into "How'"
The progress of Philosophy.[48]

TRANSLATED BY DAVID KETTLER

so, daß sie das, wovon sie ausgeschlossen ist, ebensowenig kund hat
wie das, was ihr zugeteilt ist. Dieser eigentümliche Ausschluß be-
stimmt die spezifische Einzigkeit der dy. aloges und dessen, wovon
sie mächtig ist. Dieser Ausschluß gibt wiederum den Hinweis auf die
Wesenszugehörigkeit der steräsis zur Kraft, auf die wir früher schon
hingewiesen haven. Das ist der entscheidende Gehalt dieses Kap.: daß
darin die wesenhafte Nichtigkeit, und das will sagen: die innere Endlichkeit, jeder Kraft als solcher aufleuchtet. Endlichkeit, das heißt
nicht, daß die einfach irgendwann erlahmt - sondern die wesenhafte
Endlichkeit der dy. liegt in der von ihr mit Schranken selbst gefor-
derten Zwiespältigkeit, der Notwendigkeit des Sich-Entscheidens nach
der einen oder der anderen Seite. Wo Kraft und Macht herrscht, da ist
notwendig Endlichkeit -und daher ist Gott nicht mächtig, und die All-
macht ein Begriff, der, wie alle seine Genossen, sich in Dunst auf-
löst, wenn man ihn zu denken versucht. Aber auch, wenn Gott mächtig
ist, dann ist er endlich, um jedenfalls etwas anderes als der gemeine
Begriff, der Gott zum Allerweltswesen herabwürdigt.
Die Interpretation des 2.Kap. führte uns wiete weg von dem anfänglich
sich bietenden Bild, wonach es sich lediglich um eine Einteilung der
dy. in redegeführte und redelose zu handeln schien. Jetzt muß klar
geworden sein: es handelt sich um die Aufhellung des Wesens der dy.
kata kinäsin überhaupt, in dem Sin, daß die ganze Betrachtung in
eine urapfüngliche Dimension zurückverlegt wird, damit die Gesamtun-
tersuchuneg und Beantwortung der Frage sich zusammenschließt: Was ist
die dy. kata kinäsin?
Aus dieser gesammelten Durchdringung des Wesens der dy. werden wir
durch den Beginn und den Verlauf des 3.Kap. herausgerissen. Wir sto-
ßen damit auf das erste froße Hindernis, das sichnach diesem verlok-
kenden Anfang der ganzen Untersuchung dem Verfolg einer einheitlichen
Aufbaus der ganzen Abhandlung in den Weg legt. Die Entscheidung über
die Zugehörigkeit oder Nicht-Zugehörigkeit gewisser Stücke hängt ab
von dem je erreichten Grad des sachlichen Verständnisses. Das gilt
nun gerade für das folgende Kap., das man bisher viel zu leicht gen-
nommen hat und nehmen mußte, weil Metaph. Th längst schon mit Hilfe
der abgegriffenen Schulbegriffe für dy. und en.: potentia und achus
gemein gemacht wirden, und unser Sinn für die darin behandelte Frage
längst stumpf gewordenist.

Metaph. Th 3
Es sei zunächst kurz an sen Hauptaufriß der ganzen Abhandlung erinnert.
Es gilt, die beiden Phänomene dy. und en. kata kinäsin nachihrer ge-
wissen Bedeutung zuerst zu erörtern und dann überzugehen zu der Be-

Remembering Hannah
AN INTERVIEW WITH JACK BLUM

:: ROGER BERKOWITZ

On the final day of the conference Thinking in Dark Times, celebrating Hannah Arendt's one-hundredth birthday, a group of attendees gathered by Hannah Arendt's gravesite to hear Arendt's friend Jack Blum offer some remembrances of her. Blum's stories, some humorous, others poignant, offered a glimpse of Arendt's life in a way that her published writings do not. Blum, a student of Heinrich Blücher, Arendt's husband, also offered insights into Arendt and Blücher's loving and intellectually rich relationship. The stories struck those who gathered in a light rain as meaningful and worth preserving for a wider audience. Toward that end I arranged to record Blum's reflections with the aim of publishing them in this volume. The interview, excerpted here, took place at Blum's house near Washington, D.C., during the summer of 2007.

RB: How did you meet Hannah Arendt?

JB: I was a student of Heinrich Blücher's at Bard [class of 1962]. I knew of Hannah, but I had never really met her. At the point when I left Bard and came down to Columbia Law School, I would regularly go to visit Heinrich at the Morningside Drive apartment. And visiting Heinrich, of course, Hannah would be there. I first got to know her serving tea and cookies while I would be sitting there talking to Heinrich. He had his students. She had her students. We were nodding acquaintances, but we didn't really get to know each other terribly well.

The point where I began to get to know her very well was when I was the one picked to deliver the eulogy at Heinrich's funeral on behalf of his students—a

Facing: Page 88 of Hannah Arendt's personal typographic copy of Martin Heidegger's 1931 lecture course on Book Theta of Aristotle's Metaphysics. Arendt must have carried this manuscript with her through Paris and to New York. It was found in a brown file envelope that bears the title "Interpretationen aus der antiken Philosophie. Aristotle—Metaphysik—Buch Θ." The file envelope is dated summer semester, 1931. The manuscript is underlined throughout. Here Arendt emphasizes a passage that reads: "The inner finitude lights up every force as such. Finitude, that does not mean it at some point simply wanes—rather the essential finitude . . . lies in the self-demanded division, the necessity of a self-decision for one or the other side. Where force and power reign, there is necessarily finitude—and thus is God not powerful, and the omnipotent, a concept that, as all of its comrades, dissolves itself in mist when one seeks to think it." Courtesy of the Hannah Arendt Collection, Stevenson Library, Bard College.

copy of that eulogy, by the way, is in the Bard Library as part of the collection of papers I gave to the library. She was very much taken by the eulogy, and she sent me a handwritten letter saying, "You understood Heinrich so well, I really want to get to know you better." So the next time I was up in New York I went to see her. By then I had graduated from law school and was working in Washington for the U.S. Senate. So the next time I was up in New York I called, and we had dinner together, and we would do that with some regularity over the next couple of years, whenever I was in New York, or from time to time she would be in Washington and she would call me or there was an event in Washington that we would both participate in. It was in the course of all that that I got to know many of her circle of friends and many of Heinrich's old friends whom I hadn't known while Heinrich was alive. So that is how I got to know her.

RB: You said you met her first serving cookies. Could you tell us about her and Heinrich as a couple?

JB: First of all, I don't think she ever took umbrage at the idea that it that was beneath her dignity to serve cookies and tea. That was not the kind of person she was. It was a perfectly appropriate thing and wasn't an issue. She was just very hospitable and warm, and if I hadn't known that she was a well-known writer and thinker, I would have thought, well, he is married to this very nice lady who does a nice job of serving cookies and tea.

You need to understand, she loved that guy so intensely, I cannot even begin to describe it. I remember going with her, it was sometime after he died, she invited me to come with her to a performance of Bach's *St. Matthew's Passion* in a church, and she saw that as a tribute to Heinrich, and the emotion was just immense. I think that in many ways he was her reality check, her anchor, and her inspiration. He would talk about certain kinds of issues that she then spun into her essays that she wrote for the *New Yorker*. He would talk about it and she would spin it into an essay, which he could never do.

I did have occasion before he died to see the two of them together interacting. They thought almost as one person. You could hear him start a sentence and her finish it. She'd start a sentence and he'd finish it. And you could also see the degree to which his ideas permeated her work. Now the very difficult proposition here is that he never really wrote anything. The only thing we have are the transcribed tapes [now in the Bard library]. Everything else he did was oral. A lot of that dynamic and the degree to which he influenced her is something you'll never see, because none of it is down on paper anywhere.

RB: Where do you see his influence on her the most?

JB: What I see is his intense ability to deal with the world as it is, and look at it and to think critically about it. This is a guy whose entire life was non-academic, was totally tied to figuring out how to survive and how to deal with some of the most god-awful experiences of the twentieth century, and they were god-awful experiences. He lived through the trenches in World War I. He was born in 1899. His father, I gather, was either dead or had left before he was born. His mother was dirt poor. He struggled every inch of the way. He then winds up in the German army in World War I. He comes out into a time when there's no work, when people are in complete turmoil. And he is looking at fascism trying to take over Germany, and I am talking about early. And he then begins to figure out what do I do and whom I ally myself with to stop this thing that I see coming. He thought at the time that the only open possibility was the Spartacists. He wound up as a street orator for Rosa Luxemburg. He was one of the most successful and compelling speakers they had—this from the accounts of Lotte Kohler and others who knew him well. And he did all of that under an assumed name. And then after the war he was living in the middle of terrible economic chaos and thinking how to survive. At one time he was involved in writing and directing musicals in musical theater. What he was trying to do all this while was desperately trying to figure out what is it that I have lived through here that permitted this unbelievable horror to take place that I wasn't able to do a damned thing about. I think that both of them spent a lot of time coming to grips with what happened. First the World War I experience, followed by this complete disintegration of German society into Nazism. They both struggled to comprehend the complete failure of any kind of political ideas that anyone had to be useful, to stop what was happening. And then also, watching friends and colleagues wind up in the middle of it and not capable of understanding and seeing what they were in the middle of.

RB: These are two people who were both at certain points in the 1930s were politically active in brave and dangerous ways, and then became epitomes of teachers and thinkers in the United States. Did Hannah Arendt remain political?

JB: Hannah was very much involved in the anti-McCarthy movement. She was one of the founders of the National Committee for an Effective Congress. The National Committee for an Effective Congress was founded by a former student of Heinrich's at Bard. That guy had worked in Washington for Maurice Rosenblatt. Quite accidentally, I got to know Rosenblatt in a totally different context. In fact, I wound up as in effect his trustee and guardian and executor of his will. But the National Committee for an Effective Congress was what mobilized the fight against McCarthy. She was one of the people willing to take that on; she took that risk. She understood the importance of doing that and the threat that McCarthyism posed in ways that an awful lot of people at the time did not—those who just said, "Oh, I just don't want to be a participant"—because she could see echoes of what had happened in Germany in what was going on with McCarthy. She was very much involved in that. And I was with her on what had to have been the twentieth anniversary of McCarthy's censure. There was a reception at the home of Laughlin Phillips—the family that established the Phillips Gallery in Washington. He had been one of the people and Dean Sayer, and a lot of the original collection of people along with the founders of NCEC were at the reception. I remember being with her at that reception. For her that was a very important thing to have been involved in. But beyond that, I don't think she got involved in things political. That was really the point; she did her political things, but she was much more focused on the academics.

RB: Did she ever express discomfort with teaching as opposed to acting?

JB: No I don't think they were ever at all uncomfortable with the idea of teaching. I think Heinrich viewed teaching as doing. I think Heinrich viewed giving people philosophical insights as assisting the creative process. His view of it was that philosophy as practiced, as opposed to taught, is the queen of all creative activity. And that if you give people the ability to think philosophically, you will inspire every other kind of positive creative activity, whether it is politics, music, or art, in any field, sciences, if people are taught to ask the right kinds of questions about what they are doing and what they are looking at, it will enormously enhance the work product and bring it to a kind of transcendent level that it wouldn't have otherwise.

Hannah told one story about Heinrich, saying he couldn't do anything. He couldn't make a pot of coffee. He'd get all the measurements wrong and the coffee was terrible. This guy couldn't do things. But could he think? Absolutely.

Now, in Hannah's case it was a little bit different. Here is a woman who in her thirties had behaved heroically, bringing people from behind German lines and rescuing them at great personal risk. But one occasion that comes to my mind along these lines was when she called me one day and said, "You have to come to New York."

I said, "What's going on?"

She said, "Well, they're turning our apartment building into a condominium and the tenants are all fighting and I need your help."

So I come up to New York and she said, "The problem is all the tenants are fighting over how to pay a lawyer to represent the tenants. All the tenants are arguing over whether the amount each apartment should be assessed to pay the lawyer should be based on the number of bedrooms, the number of square feet, the number of windows—she said they are all crazy because the differences are minuscule and the end result if they don't agree to hire a lawyer is going to be a catastrophe. So I need you to go to the meeting and speak for me."

So I am mystified at all this. But I go to the meeting, and I say I am speaking on behalf of Mrs. Blücher, that is how she wished to be known there, and we feel that everyone has to agree to hire a lawyer and it doesn't matter how we figure out how to pay. In the end, they come to an agreement. And then we go back to her apartment and I say, "Hannah, I don't understand this. Here you are a foremost political scientist, a political thinker, and you are asking me to make this simple-minded presentation to get these people to stop fighting with each other. Couldn't you have done it?"

And she said, "You have to understand there is an enormous difference between knowing what should be done and actually doing it. And this is something that I can't do." And she said, "even faculty meetings where there is dissension, I feel very uncomfortable and I hate them. And I don't want to be part of that kind of political process."

RB: What was Hannah Arendt's relationship with New York intellectuals?

JB: Hannah and Heinrich had for many years a famous New Year's Eve party. It was the intellectual event of the season. Then there came a moment when Norman Podhoretz published a book called *Making It*. And it was about how he, Norman Podhoretz, had made it in the New York intellectual world because by god he had been invited to the famous New Year's Eve party. Well, she read the book, and my then wife and I were in New York visiting her. And she said, "This is the first truly pornographic book I've ever read." She said, "I am announcing the party is cancelled." And she turned to us and said, "I'd like you to help me organize a smaller party for real friends."

RB: Do you read much of what is written about Hannah Arendt? And what do you think of it?

JB: There are times when I read it and I get mad and I stop reading it because I get mad because it is not doing me or anybody else any good to continue. And I don't know what to say about it other than that sometimes I am surprised. And the thing I am most surprised by is how people try to parse every nuance of what she did in some academic theoretical way when, if there is one thing to take away from both Hannah and Heinrich, it is that what you should be doing is thinking critically about what is happening to you now, not why they said this or did that. They produced their work struggling with what happened to them. And you should be thinking about what they did not in terms of how to take that and mold it into something else, but in terms of how to take that and use it as a model for how you struggle with the mess you're in right now.

RB: Which of Arendt's books most influenced you?

JB: I confess that I am not very good at reading academic philosophy, and I struggled at times, particularly as a student, because this isn't easy reading. It is only after hearing her talk and getting to know her that suddenly the stuff I read that was so hard lights up in a different way.

So for example, I think one of the most important books that she wrote is

The Human Condition. Why is it important? Because what she does is make I think the most important point all of us have to deal with, which is that none of us start on this planet with a perfectly clean slate, saying, "and here's how we can remake the world and we can go out and do that." And in fact, we are in a particular setting, in a particular time, we're given our parents, we're born in a particular language and place. All of this has a real role in shaping where we are and what we're doing. And, most importantly, we have to work on our own experience and accept what we are given and figure out where to go from there, rather than to say, "Wouldn't it have been wonderful if I had been given this, that, and the other thing?"

The other book that has intrigued me is the book that she didn't finish, but Mary McCarthy did, *The Life of the Mind.* And there the idea—and this is a real set of problems that bothered Heinrich to no end as well—is thinking very carefully about thinking. The question as she framed it and as she and Heinrich discussed it is: When you are thinking, to whom are you talking? And when you're debating an issue in your own mind, with whom are you debating? And what happens when you're actually talking to someone else? How does that suddenly unify and where does the composite that you're giving to somebody else come from? These are very difficult questions to play around with.

RB: Are there any other memorable stories about Hannah Arendt you'd like to share?

JB: I had one memorable evening sitting with her and [W. H.] Auden, and she introduced me to Auden as the man who taught her English and who was very helpful in editing her work, which I thought was astonishing. Who would've known? And then I heard the tale of how she and Mary McCarthy cleaned Auden's apartment. What happened was that they knew that he was living in absolute filth with his lover in this apartment on the Lower East Side, and they couldn't bear it, and so the two of them went down there with buckets and mops and literally got down on the floor and cleaned the apartment.

RB: That is quite a story! There is a book by Jacques Taminiaux called *The Thracian Maid and the Professional Thinker,* referring to Arendt and Martin Heidegger respectively. I wonder what he would make of Arendt scrubbing Auden's floor.

JB: It is part of who Hannah was.

RB: Thank you so much for such an insightful talk.

JB: Thank you.

Facing: The gravestones of Heinrich Blücher and Hannah Arendt Blücher, Bard College Cemetery. Photos, Serena Randolph. Courtesy of the Hannah Arendt Collection, Stevenson Library, Bard College.

HANNAH ARENDT BLUCHER
BORN HANOVER GERMANY
OCT. 14, 1906
DIED N.Y. N.Y.
DEC. 4, 1975

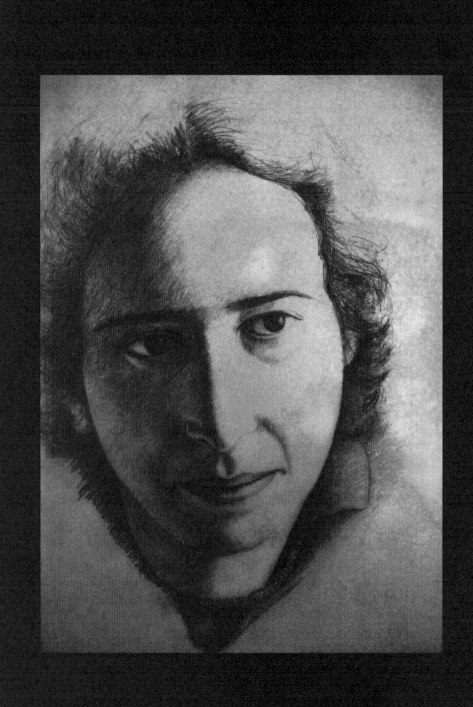

My Hannah Arendt Project

:: SHY ABADY

During my German-language studies at the Goethe Institute in Tel Aviv in 2003, I came across Hannah Arendt's *Eichmann in Jerusalem*, the only one of her books that had been translated into Hebrew at the time. There it was, standing behind a window in the institute's foyer. On its jacket, Adolf Eichmann wore a white shirt, looking like the most typical and ordinary person in the world. Soon the book was in my hand; the reading experience was thrilling. Sharp, direct, cynical—and yet sensitive and convincing—the book offered a wide perspective on a new form of evil. Hannah Arendt entered the life of my mind.

A short time later, during a flight back to Tel Aviv from a visit in Berlin, I had a chat with the woman sitting beside me. I soon found out that she was an art curator working on a big project planned for Tel Aviv's ninety-fifth anniversary. Her vision was to cover the front wall of the Tel Aviv municipality building with 240 portraits made by more than two hundred Israeli artists. The portraits would depict people whom the city decided to honor by naming streets after them. Each portrait would then be enlarged to the size of three by four square meters, large enough to cover together the entire building. I thought it would be good to participate in such an exhibition, and I already had an idea in mind, but I said nothing to the curator. Instead, I set an appointment with her in my studio to discuss my participation in the exhibit.

In preparation for the meeting, I started sketching Hannah's image, hoping I could convince the curator to include a portrait of Arendt in the exhibit. But the meeting was disappointing. She responded to my proposal with a definite no. "No street in Tel Aviv [or for that matter, in Israel] is named after Arendt," she said. The forty-year boycott was more successful than I had imagined. It was hard to forgive the woman who portrayed one of the main perpetrators of the final solution as a simple-minded bureaucrat rather than as the architect of the Nazi extermination machine. In addition, Arendt had not been afraid to touch the open wounds of the cooperation between the Nazi regime and the Jewish councils during the Holocaust, and she did not hide her criticism of the way the Eichmann trial was designed to serve Zionist ideology. The fact that this sober and harsh account came from a Jewish woman that was per-

Facing: Shy Abady, *Dark Times*, 2004, mixed media on paper.

sonally affected by the events—she fled Germany in 1933 and was for several years active in Zionist organizations—made her book even more unbearable for many Jewish-Israeli readers. And her close relation before and after the war with her teacher, the great German philosopher Martin Heidegger, who became known as a Nazi supporter, made things even more complicated for her in the eyes of many Jewish readers. No one in Israel, except for a small segment of the academy, wished to commemorate Arendt's name, legacy, or writings. It even took nearly forty years to translate *Eichmann in Jerusalem: A Report on the Banality of Evil* into Hebrew.

But the curator's refusal came too late. I was already captivated by the intriguing and elusive face and image of Hannah Arendt—as well as by her life story.

The artistic process always poses its challenges, but it is especially demanding when it concerns the presentation of a specific figure. How does one translate a life story into artistic form without making the work overly illustrative? How can the subjective impression that the image has on the artist be communicated to an audience for which this image already has its own significance? How can I express my thoughts and words in silent colors? In the past, I had confronted similar questions working on the portraits of the legendary Polish-Russian dancer and choreographer Vaslav Nijinsky. His talent, sensuality, and tragic life—Nijinsky spent his last thirty years in a mental institute—captivated me, and led me to dedicate two exhibitions to his image, movement, and body. I continue to face similar challenges in my present work, a tribute to the life and work of an Israeli-Romanian poet and writer, Radu Klapper.

With Arendt these questions were as challenging as ever. From the outset, I was fascinated not only by her writings, ideas, and sharp observations on the tragic events of the twentieth century, but also by her face—the face of a handsome young woman. Experience and world events transformed her inner and outer appearance, etching her life story on her face. Her life story was that of an intellectual Jewish woman who experienced the European turmoil of the twentieth century and tried to understand the sources of human evil and violence.

The series started by tracing her portrait from a very young woman to her old age. The source materials included unfamiliar photos of Arendt at different stages of her life. On the unpresumptuous and intimate medium of paper, I started to give my interpretations to these photos. With a sketch pencil I tried to catch the elusive expressions of her face and penetrating gaze. The curator of the exhibition at the Jewish museum in Frankfurt, Erik Riedel, called this technique *sfumato* (literally, Italian for smoky), a technique of very gentle passes between the shades developed by Leonardo da Vinci. After my drawings were complete, I added glazes of oil colors and lacquer and then attached the glazed drawings to wooden panels. At a certain moment in my work, I realized that portraits on their own would not be enough to capture

Arendt's world. I decided to add another layer of complexity to the series and began drawing conceptual images and symbols representing Arendt's life and writings.

I also introduced a new technique—the use of an electric pen. In a way, I was prompted by my work as an art teacher. From time to time, I explain to my students that they should experiment with new techniques, and one of the examples I gave them was the electric pen, a tool that burns the wood's surface, creating dark marks on it. The heat, the smoke, and the destruction that turns into reconstruction seemed to me appropriate to Arendt and the series. For one of the works, I decided to draw an ancient cascade, borrowed from the Gauloise cigarette package, as a symbol of Arendt's connection to ancient European history as well as her being a heavy smoker. Other electric-pen drawings included a cigarette butt, a sabra plant in a flowerpot, and two portraits of Arendt.

Tali Tamir, an Israeli curator who wrote one of the texts in the exhibition catalogue, described the further development of the series: "As a painter, Shy Abady approaches the portrait of Arendt using several techniques and styles, understanding that no style can fully epitomize her personality. While he does not aim to perpetuate her one official portrait, he seeks, or rather attempts, to hunt out the multitude of her faces and her elusive and suggestive complexity."

After the series was completed, I suggested it to the Jewish Museum of Frankfurt. They had certain hesitations and were somewhat baffled by the possibility that an Israeli artist would present in a central Jewish museum in Germany a "pro-Arendt" exhibition. The long time that had passed did not fully quell the anger and resentment that the Jewish-Israeli world had toward Arendt. Eventually they decided to go forward with the project.

A very short time after the successful meeting I had at the Frankfurt Jewish museum, I visited Todtnauberg, a small town in the Black Forest near Freiburg, where Heidegger's famous hut is located. There he hosted many visitors before and after the war, and among them was Hannah Arendt. Under the strong impression from the pastoral landscape and its contrast to the tumultuous events concerning Heidegger, his relationship with Arendt, and the war, I created the last work in the series. It is a triptych in which Heidegger, Arendt, and a fox appear in the foreground of the hut, inspired by Arendt's ironic essay "Heidegger the Fox."

The exhibition was first presented at the Jewish Museum of Frankfurt and was greeted favorably by the public and the media. The exhibit opened at a momentous time, during the commemoration of the thirtieth anniversary of Arendt's death. After Frankfurt, the exhibition traveled to the Heinrich Böll Gallery in Bremen and later on to the Hannah Arendt Center in Oldenburg.

Finally, in October 2006, the exhibition arrived in Jerusalem. Forty-five years after Arendt's historical visit to the city during the Eichmann trial, a small circle closed. Arendt's one-hundredth birthday was celebrated across the world, and on the heavy walls of the historical building of the "Jerusalem artist's house," her paintings were hung side by side, along with a small number of excerpts from her work. Having the exhibition in Jerusalem was very significant for me. I saw the importance in presenting her image to an Israeli audience. Two panels discussing Arendt, art, politics, memory, and rejection took place in the gallery with a wide range of participants, including an actress who played the role of Arendt, reading her incisive letter responding to Gershom Scholem, who accused her of betraying her own people.

I was glad for my small contribution to the discussion of Arendt's legacy. I was also encouraged by the power of art to open new venues into the life and work of Hannah Arendt and to stimulate a public discussion on the relevance of her views to contemporary Israeli politics.

Finally, allow me to return to the portrait exhibition on the Tel Aviv municipal building. After the curator refused my Arendt proposal, I was asked to draw Betzalel, the first biblical artist. Since no one, of course, knows what Betzalel looks like, and given the fact that I was already in the middle of my Arendt "obsession," I decided to use the facial details of young Hannah Arendt as the base of the Betzalel portrait. And so it came to pass, that from the big municipal building watching over the streets of Tel Aviv, alongside 239 portraits of other important figures, was the denied image of Hannah Arendt.

Notes

Introduction: Thinking in Dark Times ∗ Roger Berkowitz

Thomas Keenan, Jenny Lyn Bader, and Wyatt Mason read and offered generous and helpful comments on earlier versions of this essay.

1. Bertold Brecht, "To Those Who Follow in Our Wake (An die Nachgeborenen)," trans. Scott Horton, *Harper's*, January 2008.

2. Hannah Arendt, *Men in Dark Times* (San Diego: Harcourt Brace Jovanovich, 1983), viii.

3. Ibid., ix.

4. Al Gore, *The Assault on Reason* (New York: Penguin Press, 2007), 2, 26.

5. Nazism taught Habermas that when we abandon universal values, there is a grave danger that the horrors of the twentieth century will reappear. "We have to stand by our traditions," he writes. Jürgen Habermas, "On the Public Use of History." See generally the excellent account of Habermas's work by Tracy B. Strong and Frank Andreas Sposito, "Habermas' Significant Other," in *The Defense of Modernity: The Cambridge Companion to Habermas*, ed. Stephen K. White (New York: Cambridge University Press, 1995).

6. Hannah Arendt, *The Origins of Totalitarianism* (New York: Harvest Books, 1973).

7. Ibid., 475.

8. Ibid., viii; Hannah Arendt, *The Human Condition* (Chicago: University of Chicago Press, 1958), 5; Hannah Arendt, *The Life of the Mind* (New York: Harvest, 1981), I, 5.

9. *Gorgias* 482bc, cited in "Some Questions of Moral Philosophy," in *Responsibility and Judgment*, ed. Jerome Kohn (New York: Schocken Books, 2005), 90.

10. Eyal Weizman, "665/The Lesser Evil," on the *Research Architecture Roundtable*," http://roundtable.kein.org/node/802 (accessed May 15, 2009).

11. Hannah Arendt, "Personal Responsibility Under Dictatorship," in Kohn, *Responsibility and Judgment*, 19.

12. See Shai Joshua Lavi's excellent book *The Modern Art of Dying* (Princeton: Princeton University Press, 2005).

13. Arendt, "Personal Responsibility Under Dictatorship," 19. See also Arendt, *The Human Condition*, 42–43.

14. Arendt, "Personal Responsibility Under Dictatorship," 48.

15. Ibid., 21.

16. Arendt, "Some Questions of Moral Philosophy," 78.

17. Arendt, *The Life of the Mind*, I, 192.

Reflections on Antisemitism ∗ Christopher Hitchens

1. Hannah Arendt, *Origins of Totalitarianism*, preface to the 3rd ed. (New York: Harcourt Brace Jovanovich, 1973) xxiv–xxv.

2. Hannah Arendt, *Between Past and Future* (Penguin Books, 1968), 4.

3. Ibid., 5.

4. Elisabeth Young-Bruehl, *For Love of the World* (New Haven: Yale University Press, 1982), 399.

5. Victor Sebestyen, *Twelve Days* (New York: Pantheon, 2006).

6. Ibid.

7. Christopher Hitchens, "Suez," *Grand Street*, Winter 1986. See also Keith Kyle, *Suez: Brit-*

ain's End of Empire in the Middle East (New York: Palgrave, 2003).

8. Kyle, Suez.

9. Young-Bruehl, For Love of the World, 391.

10. Ibid, 10.

11. Rebecca West, Black Lamb and Grey Falcon (New York: Penguin Books, 1995), 961.

A Discriminating Politics * Uday Mehta

1. Amartya K. Sen, Freedom as Development (New York: Oxford University Press, 1999).

2. Hannah Arendt, "On Humanity in Dark Times: Thoughts About Lessing," in Men in Dark Times, trans. Clara and Richard Winston (San Diego: Harcourt, 1983), 331. The later part of this essay is the shared product of many conversations with Professor Faisal Devji.

3. Hannah Arendt, The Promise of Politics (New York: Schocken Books, 2005), 105–106.

4. He makes this point in several entries of Hind Swaraj (Cambridge: Cambridge University Press, 1997), ed. Anthony J. Parel.

5. Arendt, The Promise of Politics, 100.

6. M. K. Gandhi, "The Khilafat," in M. K. Gandhi, The Collected Works of Mahatma Gandhi (New Delhi: Publications Division, Ministry of Information and Broadcasting. Government of India, 1965), Vol. 17, March 23, 1921, 177–178.

7. M. K. Gandhi, "The Meaning of the Khilafat," September 18, 1921, 190.

8. M. K. Gandhi, "Khilafat: Further Questions Answered," June 2, 1920, 170.

9. M. K. Gandhi, "The Question of Questions," March 10, 1920, 145–147.

10. M. K. Gandhi, "Khilafat and the Cow Question," December 10, 1919, 141.

11. The corrosion of everyday relations though the mediation by a third party is a recurring and deep strain in Gandhi's thought. As early as 1909 his analysis of the empire and its effects pointed to this feature of power. "The fact is that we have become enslaved, and, therefore quarrel and like to have our quarrels decided by a third party," he wrote, and similarly, "But, when we do quarrel, we certainly do not want to engage counsel and to resort to English or any law courts. Two men fight; both have their heads broken, or

one only. How shall a third party distribute justice amongst them?" Hind Swaraj, 54 and 57.

12. Arendt, The Promise of Politics, 99.

Hannah Arendt's Political Engagements * Seyla Benhabib

1. See Jonathan Schell's introduction to the new edition of On Revolution (New York: Penguin Books, 2006), xi.

2. See Samantha Power's introduction to The Origins of Totalitarianism, new edition (New York: Schocken Books, 2004); and Michael Massing, "Trial and Error," New York Times, October 17, 2004.

3. Martin Jay first voiced this view of Arendt's "political existentialism." See Martin Jay and Leon Botstein, "Hannah Arendt: Opposing Views," Partisan Review 45, no. 3 (1978). I have considered in more detail the matter of Hannah Arendt's "existentialism" and "decisionism" in my contribution to the Festschrift for Martin Jay, entitled "From The Dialectic of Enlightenment to The Origins of Totalitarianism and the Genocide Convention: Adorno and Horkheimer in the Company of Arendt and Lemkin," in The Modernist Imagination: Essays in Intellectual History and Cultural Critique. For Martin Jay on His 65th Birthday, ed. Warren Breckman, Peter E. Gordon, A. Dirk Moses, Samul Moyn, and Elliot Neuman (New York: Berghahn Books, 2009), 299–330. Richard Wolin repeats the claim of Arendt's "decisionism" in Heidegger's Children: Hannah Arendt, Karl Loewith, Hans Jonas, and Herbert Marcuse (Princeton: Princeton University Press, 2001), 67. Dana Villa, although more sympathetic to Arendt than either Jay or Wolin, also defends a version of Arendt's "political existentialism" in Arendt and Heidegger: The Fate of the Political (Princeton: Princeton University Press, 1996), 53–55. George Kateb early on voiced a certain anxiety about "Arendt's existentialism," of her view of politics as being devoid of ordinary moral and normative constraints, in Hannah Arendt: Politics, Conscience, Evil (London: Rowman and Allanheld, 1984). That there are such passages in Arendt's works is

beyond doubt, just as there are many others pointing us toward what I have called her "reluctant modernism"; see Seyla Benhabib, *The Reluctant Modernism of Hannah Arendt* (Thousand Oaks, Calif.: Sage, 2004); however, I am asking how considerations of Arendt's own political agency should further complicate her view of the political.

4. See Max Weber, "Politics as a Vocation," in *From Max Weber: Essays in Sociology*, trans. and ed. by H. H. Gerth and C. Wright Mills (New York: Oxford University Press, 1958), 77–129, 115.

5. For accounts of this period, see Elisabeth Young-Bruehl, *Hannah Arendt: For Love of the World* (New Haven: Yale University Press, 1982), 42, and Hannah Arendt and Kurt Blumenfeld, *Die Korrespondenz. "In Keinem Besitz Verwurzelt,"* ed. Ingeborg Nordmann and Iris Piling (Berlin: Rotbuch Verlag, 1995).

6. See Hannah Arendt, *Eichmann in Jerusalem: A Report on the Banality of Evil*, rev. ed. (New York: Penguin Books, 1994), 230; the recently published Arendt-Benjamin correspondence also provides good insight into the lives and psychology of the German Jewish exiles in this period. See *Arendt und Benjamin. Texte, Briefe, Dokumente*, ed. Detlev Schoettker and Erdmut Wizisla (Frankfurt: Suhrkamp, 2006). See also Seyla Benhabib, "Arendt's *Eichmann in Jerusalem*," in Dana Villa, ed., *The Cambridge Companion to Hannah Arendt* (Cambridge: Cambridge University Press, 2000), 65–85.

7. For an account of Sperber and Koestler's friendship, the German and German-Jewish left communities in their Paris exile, and Sperber's reaction to *Darkness at Noon*, see David Cesarani, *Arthur Koestler: The Homeless Mind* (New York: Free Press, 1998).

8. Hannah Arendt, *The Origins of Totalitarianism* (New York: Harcourt Brace Jovanovich, 1979), 292.

9. For a discussion of this period, see Young-Bruehl, *For Love of the World*, 173–180; Benhabib, *The Reluctant Modernism*, 35–60; Jeffrey Isaac, *Arendt, Camus and Modern Rebellion* (New Haven: Yale University Press, 1992), 206–216.

10. For the early edition, see Hannah Arendt, *The Jew as Pariah: Jewish Identity and Politics in the Modern Age*, ed. Ron Feldman (New York: Grove Press, 1978); Jerome Kohn and Ron Feldman, eds., *Hannah Arendt: The Jewish Writings* (New York: Schocken Books, 2007).

11. For an excellent account of this movement, see Raluca Eddon, "Israel, 'A Light Unto the Nations'? Hannah Arendt, Gershom Scholem, and the Founding of the Jewish State" (PhD dissertation, Yale University, 2004).

12. This idea is voiced several times in Arendt's "Zionism Reconsidered," *Jewish Writings*, 163. Steven Aschheim also discusses Arendt's preference for "federative solutions" in the context of the Middle East and refers to a suggestion, floated by Abba Eban in 1948, that a federation consisting of Israel, Turkey, and Christian Lebanon be entertained. See S. Aschheim, "Hannah Arendt's Trials," *Times Literary Supplement*, September 28, 2007.

13. For more detailed analyses of Arendt's critique of the nation-state, see Benhabib, *The Reluctant Modernism*, 43–47.

14. See Young-Bruehl, *For Love of the World*, 232–233.

15. See Hannah Arendt, *On Revolution* (New York: Viking, 1963); Hannah Arendt, *Crises of the Republic* (New York: Harcourt, Brace and Jovanovich, 1969), which includes the essays "Lying in Politics," "Civil Disobedience," "On Violence," and "Thoughts on Politics and Revolution."

16. Hannah Arendt, "Reflections on Little Rock," *Dissent* 6, no. 1 (1959): 50. Reprinted in Hannah Arendt, *Responsibility and Judgment*, ed. Jerome Kohn (New York: Schocken Books, 2003). See also my discussion in *The Reluctant Modernism*, 146ff.

17. Ralph Ellison, *Who Speaks for the Negro?* (New York: Random House, 1963), 343–344.

18. See her remarks on the black students' occupation of campuses in *Crises of the Republic*, 120ff., and in particular 121 n. 32, where she cites Bayard Rustin's critique of the students.

19. Reprinted in *Responsibility and Judgment*, 257–277.

20. See Giorgio Agamben, *Homo Sacer: Sovereign Power and Bare Life*, trans. Daniel Heller-Roazen (Stanford: Stanford University Press, 1998), 126ff. See also Giorgio Agamben and Kevin Attell, *State of Exception* (Chicago: University of Chicago Press, 2005). In his article "Arendt's Insights Echo Around a Troubled World," Edward Rothstein writes, "Hannah Arendt was a philosopher of the exceptional," conflating the exceptional with the unprecedented and the new. E. Rothstein, "Arendt's Insights Echo Around a Troubled World," *New York Times*, October 9, 2006.

21. Carl Schmitt, *Political Theology: Four Chapters on the Concept of Sovereignty*, trans. George Schwab (Chicago: University of Chicago Press, 1985), 5. See also *The Concept of the Political*, trans. George Schwab (Chicago: University of Chicago Press, 2007), 45ff.

22. For further discussion, see Benhabib, *The Reluctant Modernism of Hannah Arendt*, 185–193.

23. Wolin, *Heidegger's Children*, Chapter 3.

24. Jeremy Waldron, "Arendt on the Foundations of Equality," in *Politics in Dark Times: Encounters with Hannah Arendt*, ed. Seyla Benhabib (New York: Cambridge University Press, forthcoming).

25. In American politics as well, since the 2006 conference for which this essay was originally written, a new social movement around President Barack Obama's candidacy emerged, which during his campaign excited a new generation to concern itself once more with the *res publica*, the "public thing," in the Arendtian sense.

What Does It Mean to Think About Politics? ∗ Mark Antaki

1. Hannah Arendt, *The Life of the Mind, Volume I: Thinking* (New York: Harcourt Brace Jovanovich, 1978), 176. See also Hannah Arendt, "Thinking and Moral Considerations," in *Responsibility and Judgment* (New York: Schocken Books, 2003), 163.

2. The first part of this essay, on the negative involved in thinking, draws on Mark Antaki, "The Critical Modernism of Hannah Arendt," *Theoretical Inquiries in Law* 8 (2007): 251.

3. Arendt, *Life of the Mind*, I:176.

4. Hannah Arendt, *Eichmann in Jerusalem: A Report on the Banality of Evil* (New York: Viking Press, 1964).

5. Arendt, "Thinking and Moral Considerations," 178.

6. Ibid., 184.

7. Ibid.,185. Arendt explains that, for Socrates, thinking required friendship.

8. In the text, "otherness" is meant more broadly and refers also to the "uniqueness" Arendt associates with human plurality. See Hannah Arendt, *The Human Condition* (Chicago: University of Chicago Press, 1958), 176, where she explains that "human distinctness is not the same as otherness— the curious quality of *alteritas* possessed by everything that is."

9. Arendt, "Thinking and Moral Considerations," 177; see also *Life of the Mind*, I:176. On nihilism, see also Martin Heidegger, "Nietzsche's Word: 'God is Dead,'" in *Off the Beaten Track* (Cambridge: Cambridge University Press, 2002).

10. Arendt, "Thinking and Moral Considerations," 176.

11. Ibid., 188.

12. Ibid.

13. Ibid.

14. Ibid., 189.

15. Note the title and aim of Reinhart Koselleck, *Critique and Crisis: Enlightenment and the Pathogenesis of Modern Society* (Cambridge, Mass.: MIT Press, 1988).

16. Hannah Arendt, *Men in Dark Times* (New York: Harcourt Brace, 1968), 76.

17. George Orwell, "Politics and the English Language," in *Orwell's Nineteen Eighty-Four: Text, Sources, Criticism*, ed. Irving Howe (New York: Harcourt Brace Jovanovich, 1982).

18. Hannah Arendt, *On Revolution* (New York: Viking Press, 1963), 49–52. Arendt describes how the events of the French Revolution— and not those of the American Revolution— became the script for future revolutions.

19. Hannah Arendt, *Between Past and Future: Eight Exercises in Political Thought* (New York: Penguin, 1968), 13.

20. See generally the essays in *Between Past and Future*.

21. See Martin Heidegger, *Parmenides* (Bloom-

ington: Indiana University Press, 1992), 89ff.

22. Arendt, *The Human Condition*, 7.

23. Hannah Arendt, *The Promise of Politics* (New York: Schocken Books, 2005), 93.

24. Max Weber, "The Profession and Vocation of Politics," in *Weber: Political Writings*, ed. P. Lassman (Cambridge: Cambridge University Press, 1994), 310–311.

25. Carl Schmitt, *The Concept of the Political* (New Brunswick, N.J.: Rutgers University Press, 1976), 26.

26. Julien Freund, *L'Essence du politique* (Paris: Sirey, 1965), 94.

27. Ibid.

28. Arendt, *The Promise of Politics*, 117.

29. Ibid.

30. Hannah Arendt, "Thoughts on Politics and Revolution," in *Crises of the Republic* (New York: Harcourt Brace Jovanovich, 1972), 229–233.

31. Arendt, *The Human Condition*, 200.

32. Ibid., 73.

33. See, for example, Hannah Pitkin, "Justice: On Relating Private and Public," *Political Theory* 9 (1981): 327–352.

34. Arendt, *The Promise of Politics*, 117.

35. Arendt, *On Revolution*, 79.

36. See Hannah Arendt, *Lectures on Kant's Political Philosophy* (Chicago: University of Chicago Press, 1982).

37. See Immanuel Kant, *Groundwork of the Metaphysics of Morals* (New York: Harper Torchbooks, 1964).

A Lying World Order: Political Deception and the Threat of Totalitarianism * Peg Birmingham

1. Hannah Arendt, "The Seeds of a Fascist International," in *Essays in Understanding*, ed. Jerome Kohn (New York: Harcourt Brace, 1994), 145.

2. Hannah Arendt, *Origins of Totalitarianism* (New York: Harcourt Brace, 1951), 8–9.

3. Arendt, "The Seeds of a Fascist International," 146–147.

4. Ibid.

5. Hannah Arendt, "Truth and Politics," in *Between Past and Future* (New York: Penguin, 1977), 238.

6. Ibid.

7. Ibid., 229.

8. Frank Rich, *The Greatest Story Ever Sold* (New York: Penguin Press, 2006), 3.

9. Hannah Arendt, "On the Nature of Totalitarianism," in *Essays in Understanding*, 354.

Lying and History * Cathy Caruth

1. Hannah Arendt, *The Human Condition* (Chicago: University of Chicago Press, 1998), 177–178.

2. Ibid., 207.

3. Ibid., 8–9.

4. Hannah Arendt, "Truth and Politics," in *Between Past and Future* (New York: Penguin Books, 1954), 236.

5. Freud's extended analysis of this phenomenon is to be found in *Beyond the Pleasure Principle*, in *The Standard Edition of the Complete Psychological Works of Sigmund Freud*, ed. James Strachey (London: Hogarth, 1963–74), vol. 18.

6. Arendt, "Truth and Politics," 239. For an excellent analysis of deception in Arendt, see Peg Birmingham, "A Lying World Order: Deception and the Rhetoric of Terror," *The Good Society* 16, no. 2 (2007): 32–37.

7. Ibid.

8. Ibid., 249.

9. Ibid., 250–251.

10. For an analysis of the performative dimension of the lie and its relation to historicity in Arendt (and others), see Jacques Derrida, "History of the Lie: Prolegomena," in *Without Alibi*, ed. Peggy Kamuf (Stanford University Press, 2002), 28–70.

11. Arendt, "Truth and Politics," 252.

12. Hannah Arendt, *The Origins of Totalitarianism* (New York: Harcourt Brace, 1976), 262.

13. Ibid., 252–253.

14. Hannah Arendt, "Lying in Politics," in *Crises of the Republic* (New York: Harcourt Brace, 1972), 4.

15. Ibid., 3–4.

16. Ibid., 7.

17. Ibid., 8–9.

18. Ibid., 9–10.

19. Ibid., 11.

20. Ibid., 14.

21. Ibid.

22. Ibid., 15.

23. Ibid., 17.

24. Ibid., 17–18.

25. Ibid., 28.

26. Ibid., 29.

27. Ibid., 39, 36.

28. Ibid., 35.

29. Ibid., 42.

30. Ibid., 37.

31. It should be noted that Arendt is in part responding, in her essay, to Daniel Ellsberg's own analysis of the Pentagon Papers in his essay "The Quagmire Myth and the Stalemate Machine," which had been published earlier; its final version appears in his *Papers on the War* (New York: Simon & Schuster, 1972). In this essay, Ellsberg describes a "stalemate machine" at the heart of the war process that oscillates between deception and self-deception on the part of the government; Arendt argues, on the contrary, that "the deceivers started with self-deception." Arendt, "Lying in Politics," 35.

32. Arendt, "Lying in Politics," 39.

33. Ibid., 40.

34. Ibid., 43.

35. Ibid., 39.

36. There is interesting work on the atomic bomb and its effects in relation to the images it produced as well as the kind of technology invented in order to make images of it. One interesting book on the former topic is Akira Mizuta Lippit's *Atomic Light (Shadow Optics)* (Minneapolis: University of Minnesota Press, 2005).

37. Arendt, *The Origins of Totalitarianism*, 478.

38. Arendt, "Lying in Politics," 13.

39. Arendt, *The Origins of Totalitarianism*, 267.

40. On half-erasure in a literary context, see Paul de Man, "Shelley Disfigured," *The Rhetoric of Romanticism* (New York: Columbia University Press, 1984).

41. Ellsberg, *Papers on the War*, 36.

42. Arendt, "Lying in Politics," 245.

43. It is interesting that Neil Sheehan, a reporter who published the Pentagon Papers articles in the *New York Times* and then later published a book compilation of them, said that reading them the first time "was like an explosion going off in our mind" ("Remembering the Viet Nam War: Conversation with Neil Sheehan," interviewer Harry Kreisler, University of California at Berkeley, Institute of International Studies, available online at http://globetrotter.berkeley.edu/conversations/Sheehan/sheehan-con0.html).

44. Daniel Ellsberg, "Secrecy Oaths: A License to Lie?" *Harvard International Review* 2004.

45. Ellsberg, *Papers on the War*, 80.

The Experience of Action * Patchen Markell

My thanks go to Kirstie McClure, Dan Slater, Verity Smith, and especially Jason Frank for conversations and advice.

1. Plato, *Statesman* 305d, 305e, trans. Christopher J. Rowe (Indianapolis: Hackett, 1999).

2. On these issues, see also the chapter "Revolution and Reiteration: Hannah Arendt's Critique of Constituent Power," in Jason Frank, *Constituent Moments: Enacting the People in Post-Revolutionary America* (Durham, N.C.: Duke University Press, 2009).

3. Hannah Arendt, *On Revolution* (New York: Penguin Books, 1977).

4. Elisabeth Young-Bruehl, *Hannah Arendt: For Love of the World* (New Haven: Yale University Press, 1982), 402, 404.

5. Bernard Bailyn, ed., *The Pamphlets of the American Revolution, 1750–1776*, vol. 1, *1750–1763* (Cambridge, Mass.: Harvard University Press, 1965); the introduction to which became Bernard Bailyn, *The Ideological Origins of the American Revolution* (Cambridge, Mass.: Harvard University Press, 1967); Gordon Wood, *The Creation of the American Republic, 1776–1787* (Chapel Hill: University of North Carolina Press, 1969); J. G. A. Pocock, *The Machiavellian Moment* (Princeton: Princeton University Press, 1975).

6. See, for example, John Higham, "The Cult of the 'American Consensus': Homogenizing Our History," *Commentary* 27, no. 2 (February 1959): 93–100.

7. Louis Hartz, *The Liberal Tradition in America: An Interpretation of American Political Thought Since the Revolution* (New York: Harcourt, Brace and World, 1955); Daniel J. Boorstin, *The Genius of American Politics* (Chicago: University of Chicago Press, 1953) and *The Americans: The Colonial Experience* (New York: Random House, 1958); Clinton Rossiter, *Seedtime of the Republic: The Ori-*

*gins of the American Tradition of Political Lib-
erty* (New York: Harcourt, Brace and World,
1953).

8. Boorstin, *Genius*, 68; see also Rossiter, *The
First American Revolution: The American Colo-
nies on the Eve of Independence* (New York:
Harcourt, Brace and World, 1956), 6.

9. Higham, "Cult of the 'American Consensus,'" 94.

10. Boorstin, *Genius*, 3. Boorstin's explicit list
of tyrannies includes "naziism, fascism,
and communism," but his pointed characterization of the effort to export an American "philosophy" abroad as "un-American"
(1) suggests the salience of McCarthyism as
well. Early in 1953, Boorstin—who had been
a Communist Party member briefly in the
late 1930s—had appeared before the House
Un-American Activities Committee, where
he proved a cooperative though not exactly
enthusiastic witness, naming names, prof-
fering his anticommunist credentials, and
affirming the unfitness of active Communist Party members for University employment, though stopping short of an endorsement of HUAC's activities.

11. Arendt, *On Revolution*, 68, 99, 154, 239.
Compare Rossiter, *First American Revolution*, 57.

12. Arendt, *On Revolution*, 99, 154, 239; Vernon
Louis Parrington, *The Colonial Mind, 1620–
1800*, vol. 1 of *Main Currents in American
Thought* (New York: Harcourt, Brace and
Company, 1927), 267–278; Charles A. Beard
and Mary R. Beard, *The Rise of American
Civilization*, vol. 1, *The Agricultural Era* (New
York: Macmillan, 1927), 297–335. Arendt
never suggests that constitution making
is *inherently* counterrevolutionary. Indeed,
without naming Beard or Parrington, she
explicitly *rejects* the claim that American
constitution making "either defeated the
revolution or prevented its full development," on the grounds that such a claim
involves a conceptual error, a failure to distinguish "liberation" from "freedom" and so
to see revolutionary freedom and constitution making as at least potentially comple-
mentary (*On Revolution*, 142). It is Arendt's
indifference to the economic dimensions of
the American Revolution and founding that
marks her real distance from such historians as Parrington and Beard.

13. Arendt, *On Revolution*, 18–35.

14. Boorstin, *The Americans: The National Expe-
rience* (New York: Random House, 1965); *The
Americans: The Democratic Experience* (New
York: Random House, 1973).

15. Boorstin, *Genius*, 36, 95.

16. Boorstin, *Colonial Experience*, 82, 84.

17. Ibid., 235.

18. Arendt, *On Revolution*, 34.

19. Ibid., 120; see also 165–169.

20. Boorstin, *Genius*, 54ff, 8. On the history of
appeals to the epistemic authority of experience in Europe and America, see Martin
Jay, *Songs of Experience: Modern American
and European Variations on a Universal Theme*
(Berkeley: University of California Press,
2005).

21. In Arendt's own German translation of *On
Revolution* (*Über die Revolution* [Munich:
Piper, 1965]), "experience" is consistently
rendered with *Erfahrung*, with its suggestion of a movement or journey, rather than
Erlebnis, which, as Jay has observed, has
acquired a stronger connotation of immediacy (Jay, *Songs of Experience* 11 and passim).

22. This is one reason that such compelling
critiques of the category of "experience"
as Joan Scott's seem to me not to cut very
deeply against Arendt's invocations of
"experience": for Arendt, the point of the
invocation of experience is not to provide
"uncontestable evidence" for an identity-
claim, which was the use of the concept
against which Scott's critique was directed.
(See Joan W. Scott, "The Evidence of Experience," *Critical Inquiry* 17 [Summer 1991]:
777.) More generally, we might say, Arendt's
use of "experience" is distinctive because
she manages both to insist on the importance of the first-personal perspective *and*
to deny that actors themselves have privileged access to the meaning of their own
experiences.

23. Arendt, *On Revolution*, 44.

24. Ibid., 41, 44.

25. Ibid., 37, 44 (emphasis added).

26. See, for example, Hannah Arendt, *The
Human Condition* (Chicago: University of
Chicago Press, 1958), 230–233.

27. Arendt, *On Revolution*, 33. For a discussion of the experience of pleasure in action as a motivating force in a contemporary social movement, see Elisabeth Jean Wood, "The Emotional Benefits of Insurgency in El Salvador," in Jeff Goodwin, James M. Jasper, and Francesca Polletta, eds., *Passionate Politics: Emotions and Social Movements* (Chicago: University of Chicago Press, 2001) 267–281. Thanks to Dan Slater for directing me to this essay.

28. This obscurity becomes especially clear in the last chapter of *On Revolution* and especially in Arendt's sympathetic but critical account of Jefferson's oscillation between the celebration of anticonstitutional rebellion and the celebration of constitution making (233–235). See also 33, 52, 154–155.

29. Ibid., 220.

30. Arendt, *The Human Condition*, 182–183.

31. This reading resists the usual view of Arendt—not without ground, but in my view incomplete—as, in Jay's words, "championing a kind of *politique pour la politique* reminiscent of *l'art pour l'art*," which "ignores the instrumental purpose of action." Jay, *Songs of Experience*, 176–177.

32. Arendt, *On Revolution*, 221.

33. An earlier expression of the thought in this paragraph appears at the end of my "The Rule of the People," 13.

34. Arendt, *On Revolution*, 223 (emphasis added).

35. Ibid., 233.

36. The passage is from an essay Arendt delivered to the American Political Science Association in 1960, early in her work on *On Revolution*, which was later incorporated in part into the book: Arendt, "Action and the 'Pursuit of Happiness,'" in Alois Dempf, Hannah Arendt, and Friedrich Engel-Janosi, eds., *Politische Ordnung und Menschliche Existenz: Festbage für Eric Voegelin zum 60. Geburtstag* (Berlin: C. H. Beck, 1962), 9. See also Arendt, *On Revolution*, 155, 218–220.

37. Arendt, *On Revolution*, 235 (emphasis added).

38. Ibid., 57.

39. Arendt, "Action and the 'Pursuit of Happiness,'" 9; see also *On Revolution*, 129.

40. One might think here of Stanley Cavell's meditations on the nature of theatricality in the latter part of his Vietnam-era essay "The Avoidance of Love: A Reading of *King Lear*," in *Must We Mean What We Say? A Book of Essays* (New York: Cambridge University Press, 1976).

41. See Arendt, *On Revolution*, 248ff.

42. This is the function of thinking Arendt would later emphasize in "Thinking and Moral Considerations," now collected in Hannah Arendt, *Responsibility and Judgment*, ed. Jerome Kohn (New York: Schocken Books, 2003).

43. Arendt, *The Human Condition*, 168–171.

44. Arendt, *On Revolution*, 220.

45. Arendt, "Action and the 'Pursuit of Happiness,'" 2.

Dissent in Dark Times: Hannah Arendt on Civil Disobedience and Constitutional Patriotism * Verity Smith

1. See especially Jürgen Habermas, "Constitutional Democracy: A Paradoxical Union of Contradictory Principles," *Political Theory* 29, no. 6 (December 2001): 766–781.

2. Frank Michelman, *Brennan and Democracy* (Princeton: Princeton University Press, 1999), 4.

3. This in spite of several important essays that focus explicitly on Arendt's constitutionalism, including George Kateb, "Death and Politics: Hannah Arendt's Reflections on the American Constitution," *Social Research* 54, no. 3 (1987): 605–616; Robert Burns, "Hannah Arendt's Constitutional Thought," in *Amor Mundi: Explorations in the Faith and Thought of Hannah Arendt*, ed. James W. Bernauer (Dordrecht: Martinus Nijhoff Publishers, 1987), 212–216; Jeremy Waldron, "Arendt's Constitutional Politics" in *The Cambridge Companion to Hannah Arendt*, ed. Dana Villa (Cambridge: Cambridge University Press, 2001), 201–219.

4. See, for example Dana Villa, *Politics, Philosophy, Terror: Essays on the Thought of Hannah Arendt* (Princeton: Princeton University Press, 1999), 203, 258.

5. For the former, see Bernard Yack, *The Problems of a Political Animal: Community, Conflict, and Justice in Aristotelian Political Thought* (Berkeley: University of California Press, 1993). For deliberative democratic

readings, see especially Jürgen Habermas, "Hannah Arendt: On the Concept of Power," in *Philosophical-Political Profiles* (Cambridge, Mass.: MIT Press, 1976), 171–188; Seyla Benhabib, *The Reluctant Modernism of Hannah Arendt* (Thousand Oaks, Calif.: Sage, 1996). And for agonistic interpretations, see Sheldon Wolin, "Hannah Arendt: Democracy and the Political," *Hannah Arendt: Critical Essays*, ed. Lewis P. Hinchman and Sandra K. Hinchman (Albany: SUNY Press, 1994), 289–306; and Bonnie Honig, "Declarations of Independence: Arendt and Derrida on the Problem of Founding a Republic," *American Political Science Review* 85 (1991): 97–113.

6. Hannah Arendt, "Civil Disobedience," in *Crises of the Republic* (New York: Harcourt Brace Jovanovich, 1972), 79.

7. Ibid., 83–84.

8. Jürgen Habermas, *The Structural Transformation of the Public Sphere* (Cambridge, Mass.: MIT Press, 1989).

9. See, for example, Frank Michelman, "Law's Republic," *Yale Law Journal* 97, no. 8 (1988): 1493–1537.

10. The secondary literature contains many brief or passing references to Arendt's use of Montesquieu, but few that systematically examine his profound influence on her thought. A rare exception is Anne Amiel, "Hannah Arendt lectrice de Montesquieu," *Revue Montesquieu* 2 (1998), which focuses on Arendt's debts to Montesquieu's typology of forms of government in *Origins of Totalitarianism* and in some of her unpublished work. The most extended treatment to date remains Margaret Canovan's seminal account of Arendt's debts to classical republicanism in *Hannah Arendt: A Reinterpretation of Her Political Thought* (Cambridge: Cambridge University Press, 1992), which profoundly revises her own earlier (1974) interpretation of Arendt in light of Arendt's unpublished writings.

11. Arendt's unpublished notes, lectures, drafts, and correspondence are archived at the Hannah Arendt Papers at the Library of Congress. The relative neglect of Montesquieu's influence in what is otherwise a voluminous secondary literature may be because the first waves of Arendt schol-arship came out without reference to this material.

12. Indeed, the copy of *The Spirit of the Laws* housed in the Arendt Collection at Bard College is replete with underlining or marks next to almost every instance in which the word "principles" is used, particularly when paired with "energetic" or "animating." At the top of the first page of Book III ("Of the Principles of the Three Kinds of Government"), she has written "Principles even stronger than *laws*." (See the Arendt Collection, Bard College. Bard Library Call #: Arendt JC 179.M74 1949.)

13. Some of this material is developed in "Karl Marx and the Tradition of Western Political Thought," lectures, Christian Gauss Seminar in Criticism, Princeton University, first and second drafts, 1953. Container 75, Hannah Arendt Papers, Manuscript Division, Library of Congress.

14. See Montesquieu, *The Spirit of the Laws* (III.1) I usually follow the translation of Anne Cohler, Basia Miller, and Harold Stone (New York: Cambridge University Press, 1989) but sometimes return to the version in *Oeuvres completes de Montesquieu*, ed. Roger Callois (Paris: Pleiade, 1949–1951) to modify their translation.

15. *Description of Proposal*, Rockefeller Correspondence, 1959. Container 25, Hannah Arendt Papers, Manuscript Division, Library of Congress.

16. Many of the more extended meditations on Montesquieu are in lecture notes and other unpublished manuscripts. But see also "Understanding and Politics" and "On the Nature of Totalitarianism (an Essay in Understanding)" in *Essays in Understanding*, ed. Jerome Kohn (New York: Harcourt Brace, 1994); and "Montesquieu's Revision of the Tradition," in *The Promise of Politics*, ed. Jerome Kohn (New York: Schocken Books, 2005).

17. Hannah Arendt, "On the Nature of Totalitarianism: An Essay in Understanding," in *Essays in Understanding: 1930–1954*, ed. Jerome Kohn (New York: Harcourt Brace, 1994), 329.

18. Ibid., 330.

19. See Hannah Arendt, *On Revolution* (New York: Viking Press, 1963), 189, 197.

20. Tzvetan Todorov, *On Human Diversity: Nationalism, Racism, and Exoticism in French Thought*, trans. Catherine Porter (Cambridge, Mass.: Harvard University Press, 1993).

21. See *Spirit of the Laws*, III.10, IV.2, XXI.20, XXII.12.

22. In his seminal *Montesquieu et le problème de la Constitution francaise au XVIII seicle* (1927), Ely Carcassone stresses that this politics of contestation and disobedience comprises a fundamental part of the constitutional order itself.

23. *Spirit of the Laws* (emphasis in original), II.2.

24. Hannah Arendt, "What Is Freedom?" in *Between Past and Future: Eight Exercises in Political Thought* (New York: Penguin Books, 1977), 153.

25. *On Revolution*, 234.

26. Arendt, "Civil Disobedience," 94.

27. Ibid., 85.

28. Ibid., 88.

29. Ibid., 94–101.

30. Ibid., 92.

31. Ibid., 76.

32. Ibid., 96.

33. Ibid., 102.

Promising and Civil Disobedience: Arendt's Political Modernism *

J. M. Bernstein

1. Sheldon Wolin, "Hannah Arendt: Democracy and the Political," *Salmagundi* 60 (1983): 18. Bracketed comments are my interpolations.

2. My thought is that this conception of civil disobedience is the political analogue of the notion of fugitive experience and fugitive ethics I developed in my *Adorno: Disenchantment and Ethics* (New York: Cambridge University Press, 2001), Chapter 9.

3. Friedrich Nietzsche, *On the Genealogy of Morality*, Trans. Maudemarie Clark and Alan J. Swenson (Indianapolis: Hackett, 1998), 35.

4. For an account of artistic modernism that forms the background to these remarks, see my *Against Voluptuous Bodies: Late Modernism and the Meaning of Painting* (Stanford, Calif.: Stanford University Press, 2006).

5. Hannah Arendt, *On Revolution* (New York: Penguin, 1963), 145.

6. Ibid., 146

7. Hannah Arendt, *The Human Condition* (Chicago: University of Chicago Press, 1958), 237.

8. Ibid., 246. For an elaboration of Arendt's notion of forgiveness in the context of Hegel's, see my "Evil and Forgiveness: Hegel's Poetics of Actions," in *Beyond Representation*, ed. Richard Eldridge (New York: Cambridge University Press, 1995), 34–65.

9. Arendt, *The Human Condition*, 237.

10. Nietzsche, *On the Genealogy of Morals*, Second Treatise.

11. Stanley Cavell, *A Pitch of Philosophy: Autobiographical Exercises* (Cambridge, Mass.: Harvard University Press, 1994), 104.

12. Stanley Cavell, *Philosophical Passages: Wittgenstein, Emerson, Austin, Derrida* (Malden, Mass.: Blackwell, 1994), 65.

13. Jürgen Habermas, "Hannah Arendt's Communications Concept of Power," *Social Research* 44, no. 1 (1977): 3–25.

14. Arendt, *On Revolution*, 174.

15. Hannah Arendt, *Crises of the Republic* (New York: Harcourt Brace Jovanovich, 1972), 150.

16. Arendt, *On Revolution*, 175.

17. Ibid., 212–213.

18. Immanuel Kant, *Critique of Judgment*, trans. Werner S. Pluhar (Indianapolis: Hackett, 1987), 308.

19. Ibid., 283.

20. Arendt, *On Revolution*, 202.

21. Arendt, *Crises of the Republic*, 88.

22. Ibid., 76.

23. Ibid., 56.

24. Jacques Ranciere, *Disagreement: Politics and Philosophy*, trans. Julie Rose (Minneapolis: University of Minnesota Press, 1999), 89.

Is Evil Banal? A Misleading Question * Richard Bernstein

1. See Margaret Canovan's discussion of Arendt's "thought-trains" in her introduction to *Hannah Arendt: A Reinterpretation of Her Political Thought* (New York: Cambridge University Press, 1994).

2. The passage appears in the "Concluding Remarks" of the first edition of *The Origins of Totalitarianism* (New York: Harcourt Brace, 1951), 433.

3. Hannah Arendt, *The Origins of Totalitari-*

anism, 3rd ed. (New York: Harcourt Brace Jovanovich, 1968), 438.

4. Hannah Arendt, *The Jewish Writings*, ed. J. Kohn and R. H. Feldman (New York: Schocken Books, 2007), 471.

5. For a detailed analysis of the meaning of radical evil and its compatibility with the banality of evil, see my discussion in *Hannah Arendt and the Jewish Question* (Cambridge, Mass.: MIT Press, 1996).

6. Hannah Arendt, *Eichmann in Jerusalem* (New York: Viking Press, 1965), 252.

7. Ibid., 287.

8. Hannah Arendt, "Thinking and Moral Considerations: A Lecture," *Social Research* 38, no. 3 (Fall 1971): 417.

9. Christopher Browning, *Collected Memories: Holocaust History and Postwar Testimony* (Madison: University of Wisconsin Press, 2003), 3–4.

10. David Cesarani, *Eichmann: His Life, Crimes and Legacy* (London: Heinemann, 2003).

11. Arendt, *The Jewish Writings*, 487.

12. Susan Neiman, *Evil in Modern Thought* (Princeton: Princeton University Press, 2004), 271–272.

13. See my critique of the recent abuse of evil in *The Abuse of Evil: The Corruption of Politics and Religion Since 9/11* (London: Polity, 2006).

14. In *The Origins of Totalitarianism* (453–454), Arendt distinguishes the "blind bestiality of the SA" from "cold and systematic destruction of human bodies" by the SS.

15. Arendt, *Origins of Totalitarianism*, 459.

16. Arendt, *The Jewish Writings*, 71.

Banality and Cleverness: Eichmann in Jerusalem Revisited * Peter Baehr

1. Hannah Arendt, *Eichmann in Jerusalem: A Report on the Banality of Evil* (New York: Penguin, 1965).

2. Num. 22.32; also 1 Sam. 29:4, 1 Kings 5:4, Job 1–2.

3. I am not recommending the phrase "satanic banality" but saying only that *if Arendt felt compelled* to use concepts of religious origin to describe Eichmann, this would have made a little more sense than the banality of evil.

4. Donald Taylor, "'Theological Thoughts About Evil," in *The Anthropology of Evil*,

ed. David Parkin (Oxford: Basil Blackwell, 1985), 34. See also the entries under Evil and Satan, by Samuel A. Meier and Hector Ignacio Avalos respectively, in Bruce M. Metzger and Michael D. Coogan, eds., *The Oxford Companion to the Bible* (New York: Oxford University Press, 1993), 208–209, 678–679.

5. I have been quoting from "'Eichmann in Jerusalem": An Exchange of Letters Between Gershom Scholem and Hannah Arendt,'" in *The Jew as Pariah: Jewish Identity and Politics in the Modern Age*, ed. Ron Feldman (New York: Grove Press, 1978), 240–251.

6. Hannah Arendt-Karl Jaspers, *Correspondence, 1926–1969*, ed. Lotte Kohler and Hans Saner (New York: Harcourt Brace, 1992), 542. Letter of Jaspers to Arendt, December 13, 1963.

7. Richard J. Bernstein, *Hannah Arendt and the Jewish Question* (Cambridge, Mass.: MIT Press, 1996), 137–153.

8. See Arendt, *Eichmann in Jerusalem*, 36–55, 62, 78, 82, 86, 126, 135, and passim.

9. Hannah Arendt, *The Origins of Totalitarianism* (New York: Harcourt Brace Jovanovich, 1968), 338.

10. Hannah Arendt, *The Life of the Mind Volume I: Thinking* (New York: Harcourt Brace, 1978), 5.

11. After I made this comment, Richard Bernstein gently tasked me for persistently using the term "the tradition." He correctly noted that Western civilization is made up of many traditions. I agree with him. However, "the tradition" is Arendt's expression, not my own.

Judging the Events of Our Time * Jennifer L. Culbert

1. Hannah Arendt, *The Origins of Totalitarianism* (New York: Schocken, 2004), 27.

2. Hannah Arendt, *Eichmann in Jerusalem: A Report on the Banality of Evil* (New York: Penguin, 1964).

3. An exception to this general rule is Leora Y. Bilsky, "When Actor and Spectator Meet in the Courtroom: Reflections on Hannah Arendt's Concept of Judgment," *History & Memory* 8, no. 2 (Fall/Winter 1996): 137–173.

4. Arendt, *Eichmann in Jerusalem*, 3–4.

5. Ibid., 266.

6. Hannah Arendt, *The Life of the Mind* (New York: Harcourt Brace Jovanovich, 1978), 30.

7. Ibid., 27.

8. Ibid., 26.

9. Ibid., 27.

10. Ibid., 30.

11. Ibid.

12. See Sir William Blackstone, *Commentaries on the Laws of England*, vol. 2, ed. William Carey Jones (London: Claitor's, 1976).

13. Arendt, *Eichmann in Jerusalem*, 277 (citing Yosal Rogat).

14. Ibid., 267.

15. Ibid., 268.

16. Hannah Arendt, *The Human Condition* (Chicago: University of Chicago Press, 1958), 7.

17. Arendt, *Eichmann in Jerusalem*, 261.

18. Ibid., 19.

Arendt's Banality of Evil Thesis and the Arab-Israeli Conflict * Yaron Ezrahi

1. Hannah Arendt, *Eichmann in Jerusalem: A Report on the Banality of Evil* (New York: Viking Press, 1964), 278, 288.

2. Ibid., 288.

3. The Nazi biologization of the Jews as essentially evil boomeranged following the war, when some German relatives of Nazi murderers internalized so deeply the warning against any contact with Jewish blood as to refuse having children lest they give birth to monsters like their Nazi relations.

4. Neil J. Smelser, *The Faces of Terrorism: Social and Psychological Dimensions* (Princeton: Princeton University Press, 2007).

5. Dan Bar-On, *Tell Your Story: Creating Dialogue Between Jews and Germans, Palestinians and Israelis* (Beer-Sheva: Ben Gurion University, 2006) (in Hebrew).

   For more on this challenge to master narratives, see Nita Schechet, *Disenthralling Ourselves; Rhetoric of Revenge and Reconciliation in Contemporary Israel* (Madison, N.J.: Fairleigh Dickinson University Press, 2009), 21–22. On Arendt's related concepts of collective responsibility and agonistic reconciliation, see 94–131; see also Hannah Arendt, "Collective Responsibility," in *Amor Mundi*, ed. James W. Bernauer (Dordrecht: Martinus Nijhoff, 1987), 43–50.

Liberating the Pariah: Politics, the Jews, and Hannah Arendt *
Leon Botstein

1. See "Liberating the Pariah: Politics, the Jews, and Hannah Arendt," *Salmagundi* 60 (Spring–Summer 1983), 73–106.

2. Since the publication of a longer version of this piece in 1983, there has been an enormous amount of literature on Arendt and Jewish issues. The following is an incomplete but representative array of writings on the subject: Dagmar Barnouw, *Visible Spaces: Hannah Arendt and the German-Jewish Experience* (Baltimore: Johns Hopkins University Press, 1990); Seyla Benhabib, "The Pariah and Her Shadow: Hannah Arendt's Biography of Rahel Varnhagen," *Political Theory* 23, no. 1 (1995): 5–24; Richard J. Bernstein, *Hannah Arendt and the Jewish Question* (Cambridge, Mass.: MIT Press, 1996); Morris Kaplan, "Refiguring the Jewish Question," in *Feminist Interpretations of Hannah Arendt*, ed. Bonnie Honig (University Park: Pennsylvania State University Press, 1995); Norma Claire Moruzzi, *Speaking Through the Mask: Hannah Arendt and the Politics of Social Identity* (Ithaca: Cornell University Press, 2003); Gabriel Piterberg, "Zion's Rebel Daughter: Hannah Arendt on Palestine and Jewish Politics," *New Left Review* 48 (November–December 2007): 39–57; Amnon Raz-Krakotzkin, "Binationalism and Jewish Identity: Hannah Arendt and the Question of Palestine," in *Hannah Arendt in Jerusalem*, ed. Steven Aschheim (Berkeley: University of California Press, 2001), 165–180; Jennifer Ring, *The Political Consequences of Thinking: Gender and Judaism in the Work of Hannah Arendt* (Albany: SUNY Press, 1997); David Suchoff, "Gershom Scholem, Hannah Arendt, and the Scandal of Jewish Particularity," *The Germanic Review* 72, no. 1 (Winter 1997): 57–76; Natan Sznaider, "Hannah Arendt's Jewish Cosmopolitanism," *European Journal of Social Theory* 10, no. 1 (2007): 112–122; Suzanne Vromen, "Hannah Arendt's Jewish Identity: Neither Parvenu Nor Pariah," *European Journal of Political Theory* 3, no. 2 (2004): 177–190; Richard Wolin, "The Ambivalences of German–Jewish Identity: Hannah Arendt

in Jerusalem," *History and Memory* 8, no. 2 (Fall 1996): 9–35; and Moshe Zimmermann, "Hannah Arendt, the Early 'Post-Zionist,'" in Aschheim, *Hannah Arendt in Jerusalem*, 181–193.

3. Ludwig Wittgenstein, *Philosophical Investigations* (New York: Macmillan, 1953), 11.

4. Vladimir Jabotinsky, "Evidence Submitted Before the Palestine Royal Commission," in Arthur Hertzburg, *The Zionist Idea: A Historical Analysis and Reader* (New York: Harper & Row, 1959), 562–563.

5. See Hannah Arendt, *The Jewish Writings*, ed. Jerome Kohn and Ron H. Feldman (New York: Schocken Books, 2007), 343–345, 372–373.

6. See F. A. Krummacher, *Die Kontroverse: Hannah Arendt, Eichmann und dei Juden* (Munich: Nymphenburger Verlagshandlung, 1964), 207–222, 245–251.

7. Arendt, *The Jewish Writings*, 302.

Hannah Arendt's Jewish Experience: Thinking, Acting, Judging *

Jerome Kohn

1. From the Latin root *idem*, meaning "same."

2. Hannah Arendt, *The Jewish Writings*, ed. Jerome Kohn and Ron H. Feldman (New York: Schocken Books, 2007), 466–467.

3. Some may object to the word "natural," preferring perhaps "cultural," but not Arendt. She says explicitly that being a Jew for her "is *physei* and not *nomô*" (ibid., 466).

4. Yet not only in her time: "What Hamlet said is always true: 'The time is out of joint; O cursèd spite / That ever I was born to set it right!'" Hannah Arendt, *The Promise of Politics*, ed. Jerome Kohn (New York: Schocken Books, 2005), 203.

5. Hannah Arendt, *Lectures on Kant's Political Philosophy*, ed. Ronald Beiner (Chicago: University of Chicago Press, 1982), 36.

6. This is the overall project of her last, uncompleted, and underappreciated masterwork, *The Life of the Mind*, in which her thought is unmistakably *political*, but from an entirely new perspective.

7. Arendt, *The Promise of Politics*, 175.

8. For this and what follows on the experience of wonder, see Hannah Arendt, *The Life of the Mind*, Vol. I, *Thinking* (New York: Harcourt Brace Jovanovich, 1978), 141–151.

9. Hannah Arendt, *Essays in Understanding 1930–1954*, ed. Jerome Kohn (New York: Schocken Books, 2005), 445. In *Thinking*, Arendt speaks of "the intimate connection that binds the thought of Being and the thought of nothingness together" (149).

10. See Arendt's remarks about Hegel in *Hannah Arendt: The Recovery of the Public World*, ed. M. A. Hill (New York: St. Martin's Press, 1979), 303.

11. Ibid., 304.

12. Arendt, *Essays in Understanding*, 5–6.

13. Ibid. The occasion was a 1964 televised interview with Günther Gass, who was adept at getting Arendt to tell a number of stories that otherwise she kept for her inner circle or "tribe," as she called it.

14. The assimilation of Jews in Germany is a tremendously complex matter that cannot be gone into here. It is treated in detail by Arendt in *Rahel Varnhagen: The Life of a Jewish Woman* and in the first part of *The Origins of Totalitarianism*, "Antisemitism."

15. Hannah Arendt, *The Human Condition* (Chicago: University of Chicago Press, 1958), 22–37.

16. Arendt, *The Jewish Writings*, 111, 121 n. 24.

17. The Nazi propaganda machine used *The Protocols of the Elders of Zion*, a forged document purporting to reveal Jews as the secret dominators of the world, to support Hitler's ideology.

18. Though this is not the place, it would be interesting to test Arendt's theorem in the case of African Americans, which, in part because of institutional slavery, differs from that of Jews. The history of African Americans begins when they were brought to this country as chattel, while the history of European Jews ends when the Nazis turned them into chattel. Still, there is nothing that rightly can be called a *social* prejudice against African Americans before Lincoln's Emancipation Proclamation freed them from a condition in which they had no social status at all, not even that of a caste. That was in the South, and in the abolitionist North, where slavery was renounced, the gradual acceptance of African Americans changed into a cruel form of social discrimination only after the same proclamation.

19. Hannah Arendt, *The Origins of Totalitarian-ism*, 4th ed. (New York: Harcourt Brace, 1968), 296–302.

20. For the structure of "the so-called totalita-rian state," see ibid., 389–459.

21. Arendt, *The Jewish Writings*, 400–401. Later, in *The Human Condition* and *On Violence*, Arendt analyzes power and sovereignty as antithetical concepts.

22. A world spectator is sharply to be distin-guished from a world citizen. Arendt, after Kant, views a world government as the greatest tyranny imaginable (*Lectures on Kant's Political Philosophy*, 44).

23. See Hannah Arendt, *Between Past and Future* (New York: Viking Press, 1968), 146.

24. Hannah Arendt, *The Origins of Totalitaria-nism*, 1st ed. (New York: Harcourt Brace, 1951), 439, and repeated in all of Arendt's major works.

25. Ideological "truth" is the dark underbelly or perversion of the philosophic truth discussed here. For Arendt's account of the spread of world alienation and the emer-gence of mass men, see *The Human Condi-tion*, 245–325.

26. Arendt, *The Origins of Totalitarianism*, 4th ed., 459. In this respect, radical evil is not coextensive with genocide, which in fact (if not in name) is as old as human history. Even the Turks' genocide of Christian Armenians, often evoked as analogous to the Holocaust, had the transparent "politi-cal" motive of shoring up the disintegrating Moslem Ottoman Empire.

27. Ibid., 474–475.

28. Arendt, *The Origins of Totalitarianism*, 1st edition, 437, 439.

29. Today Barack Obama's appeal is to such citi-zens of the United States of America.

30. "Crimes against humanity" were first announced in the trials of high-ranking Nazi officials at Nuremberg, in which, in Arendt's opinion, they were never suffici-ently distinguished from "war crimes" and "crimes against peace."

31. Hannah Arendt, *Responsibility and Judg-ment*, ed. Jerome Kohn (New York: Schocken Books, 2003), 153.

32. Hannah Arendt, *Eichmann in Jerusalem: A Report on the Banality of Evil* (New York: Viking Press, 1963), 136.

33. Ibid., 116–126; the quoted words are on 125–126.

34. Arendt, *Thinking*, 3–5.

35. The brilliant, devastating center of *Eich-mann in Jerusalem* is Chapter VIII, "Duties of a Law-Abiding Citizen."

36. Arendt, *Eichmann in Jerusalem*, 30. For a ful-ler account of Eichmann's "incorruptibility" than can be offered here see Jerome Kohn, "Arendt's Concept and Description of Tota-litarianism," *Social Research* 69, no. 2 (Sum-mer 2002): 621–656.

37. Arendt, *Eichmann in Jerusalem*, 279.

38. Ibid., 253–272 (the quotations are on 268 and 269). Nevertheless Arendt, unlike her friend and mentor Karl Jaspers, believed the trial of Eichmann was rightly held in Israel, under Israeli law, absent "an inter-national criminal court" and "an inter-national penal code."

39. Arendt, *Responsibility and Judgment*, 185–189.

40. This limiting case, in which the impotence of thinking liberates the faculty of judg-ment, has no bearing on the lack of politi-cal judgment in such a thinker as Martin Heidegger.

41. *Eichmann in Jerusalem*, 273.

42. Arendt, *The Jewish Writings*, 493 (emphasis in the original).

43. Ibid., 471.

44. Arendt, *Eichmann in Jerusalem*, 252.

45. Kant, who destroyed that equation and first introduced the notion of "radical evil," is an exception. For the "nonbeing" of evil, see Jerome Kohn, "Evil and Plurality," in *Han-nah Arendt: Twenty Years Later*, ed. Larry May and Jerome Kohn (Cambridge, Mass.: MIT Press, 1996), 147–178.

46. Arendt, *Responsibility and Judgment*, 125.

47. *Between Friends: The Correspondence of Han-nah Arendt and Mary McCarthy, 1949–1975*, ed. Carol Brightman (New York: Harcourt Brace, 1995), 168.

48. These essays, which include "Some Ques-tions of Moral Philosophy," are collected in *Responsibility and Judgment*, 17–189.

The Pariah as Rebel: Hannah Arendt's Jewish Writings ✳ Ron H. Feldman

1. Hannah Arendt, *Eichmann in Jerusalem* (New York: Harcourt Brace, 1964), 125.

2. Gershom Scholem, *On Jews and Judaism in Crisis* (New York: Schocken Books, 1976), 304.

3. Hannah Arendt, *The Jewish Writings*, ed. Jerome Kohn and Ron H. Feldman (New York: Schocken Books, 2007), 497.

4. Ibid., 466.

5. Ibid., 33.

6. "'What Remains? The Language Remains': A Conversation with Günter Gaus," in *Essays in Understanding, 1930–1954*, ed. Jerome Kohn (San Diego: Harcourt Brace, 1994), 12.

7. Ibid., 11–12. This position, by the way, was reflected in a 1941 *Aufbau* article in which she wrote, "One truth that is unfamiliar to the Jewish people, though they are beginning to learn it, is that *you can only defend yourself as the person you are attacked as*. A person attacked as a Jew cannot defend himself as an Englishman or Frenchman." Arendt, *The Jewish Writings*, 137.

8. Of course, Arendt does discuss Jewish women, both as ghetto fighters (for example, the *Aufbau* article, "A Lesson in Six Shots," *The Jewish Writings*, 217–219) and in her historical research on German socialites (see "Original Assimilation," *The Jewish Writings*, 22–28, and *Rahel Varnhagen: The Life of a Jewish Woman* [New York: Harcourt Brace Jovanovich, 1974]).

9. There is a lively discussion in the secondary literature concerning Arendt's feminism. See for example, Bonnie Honig, ed., *Feminist Interpretations of Hannah Arendt* (University Park: Pennsylvania State University Press, 1995).

10. This idea of Arendt as a woman at home was also conveyed at the end of the conference where this paper was initially presented. During a visit to the gravesites of Hannah Arendt and Heinrich Blücher at Bard College, Jack Blum (Bard '62), who was a student of Blücher's, told stories of his friendship with them. Blum related that when he visited Blücher at their home in New York City, Arendt acted the role of the German *hausfrau*, serving food and drink. It was only later, as he got to know the couple, that Arendt's own intellectual stature became clear. [This story is retold in the interview published in this volume,

"Remembering Hannah: An Interview with Jack Blum."—Eds.]

11. Isaac Deutscher, *The Non-Jewish Jew and Other Essays*, ed. Tamara Deutscher (New York: Oxford University Press, 1968).

12. Arendt, *The Jewish Writings*, 275.

13. Ibid., 50.

14. Ibid., 51.

15. Ibid., 50.

16. Ibid., 415.

17. Ibid., 415.

18. Ibid., 137.

19. Ibid., 162, 165.

20. Ibid., 160.

21. Ibid., 214.

22. Ibid., 386.

23. Ibid., 200.

24. Ibid., 387.

25. Ibid., 417. See, for example, the *Aufbau* article "Philistine Dynamite" (*The Jewish Writings*, 208–211) from June 1944 and her December 1948 letter to the *New York Times* (*The Jewish Writings*, 417–419) criticizing Menachem Begin, who would become prime minister in 1977, shortly after Arendt's death.

26. Ibid., 195.

27. Ibid., 395.

28. Ibid., 450.

29. Ibid., 131. It should be noted that Arendt is very Eurocentric and displays little knowledge of non-European Jewry.

30. Ibid., 274.

31. Arendt, *Eichmann in Jerusalem*, 268–269.

32. See, for example, "Peace or Armistice in the Near East?" in *The Jewish Writings*, 423–450, especially 446–450.

33. See, for example, her use of the term in "To Save the Jewish Homeland," in *The Jewish Writings*, 394.

34. Ibid., 467.

35. Ibid., 71.

36. Ibid., 141.

37. The origins of my views and formulations of this subject can be found in Jacob Neusner's book *Stranger at Home: "The Holocaust," Zionism, and American Judaism* (Chicago: University of Chicago Press, 1981).

38. Steven Aschheim, ed., *Hannah Arendt in Jerusalem* (Berkeley: University of California Press, 2001); Idit Zertal and Moshe Zuckerman, eds., *Hannah Arendt: A*

Half-Century of Polemics (Hebrew) (Tel Aviv: Hakibbutz Hameuchad, 2004).

39. Shy Abady, *The Hannah Arendt Project* (art exhibit, Frankfurt, 2005).

40. Michal Ben-Naftali, *The Visitation of Hannah Arendt* (Hebrew) (Tel Aviv: Hakibbutz Hameuchad, 2006).

41. See, for example, Moshe Zimmermann, "Hannah Arendt, the Early 'Post-Zionist,'" in Aschheim, *Hannah Arendt in Jerusalem*, 181–193.

Jewish to the Core * Suzanne Vromen

1. Richard Wolin, *Heidegger's Children: Hannah Arendt, Karl Löwith, Hans Jonas, Herbert Marcuse* (Princeton: Princeton University Press, 2001).

2. See the complete text of her letter in *The Jewish Writings*, ed. Jerome Kohn and Ron H. Feldman (New York: Schocken Books, 2007), 465–471.

3. For further clarification of the term "pariah" and its opposite, "parvenu," as used by Arendt, see my article "Hannah Arendt's Jewish Identity: Neither Parvenu nor Pariah," *European Journal of Political Theory* 3, no. 2 (2004): 177–190.

4. Hannah Arendt and Karl Jaspers, *Correspondence, 1926–1969*, ed. Lotte Kohler and Hans Saner (New York: Harcourt Brace Jovanovich, 1985), Letter 134, August 23, 1952, 192.

5. Ibid., letter 135, September 7, 1952, 200–201. This is not the only time that Arendt was accused of being loveless. Many years later, Gershom Scholem accused her of lacking any love for the Jewish people in her book on Eichmann.

6. *Within Four Walls: the Correspondence Between Hannah Arendt and Heinrich Blücher, 1936-1968*, ed. Lotte Kohler (San Diego: Harcourt, 2001), August 21, 1936, 14–18.

7. Arendt, *The Jewish Writings*, 136–139.

8. *Within Four Walls*, 172.

9. Ibid., 179.

10. Ibid., 227

11. Natan Sznaider, "Hannah Arendt's Jewish Cosmopolitanism Between the Universal and the Particular," *European Journal of Social Theory* 10, no. 1 (2007): 112–122.

12. Hannah Arendt and Kurt Blumenfeld . . . *in keinem Besitz verwurzelt':Die Korrespon-*

denz, ed. Ingeborg Nordmann and Iris Pilling (Munich: Piper, 1995), letter 74, May 19, 1957, 191. My translation.

Thinking Big in Dark Times *
Drucilla Cornell

1. Amartya Sen, *Identity & Violence: The Illusion of Destiny* (New York: Penguin Books, 2006).

2. W. H. Auden, "We Too Had Known Golden Hours," *Collected Shorter Poems, 1927–57* (New York: Random House, 1967), 318.

3. Hannah Arendt, *The Origins of Totalitarianism* (New York: Harcourt, Brace, 1951), 9.

4. As cited in Jerome Kohn, "Thinking/Acting," *Social Research* 57 (1990): 117.

5. Frantz Fanon, *The Wretched of the Earth* (New York: Grove Press, 1963), 311.

6. Section 10 of the Constitution of the Republic of South Africa states, "Everyone has inherent dignity and the right to have their dignity respected and protected."

7. Section 1 of the Constitution of the Republic of South Africa.

8. For an excellent discussion on the radical significance of horizontality, see, generally, Johan van der Walt, *Sacrifice and Law: Towards a Post-Apartheid Theory of Law* (Johannesburg: Wits University Press, 2005).

9. In the *Khosa* case, Justice Mokgoro argued that in South Africa you are a human being before you are a citizen, in extending certain welfare benefits to Mozambican refugees. See generally, *Khosa and Others v Minister of Social Development and Others; Mahlaule and Others v Minister of Social Development and Others* 2004 (6) SA 505 (CC).

10. For an interesting discussion of the complexity of this attempt to develop an ethical foreign policy, see Patrick Bond *Talk Left Walk Right* (Scottsville, South Africa: University of KwaZulu Natal Press, 2006).

11. For a discussion on the debate over horizontality, see Richard Spitz and Matthew Chaskalson *The Politics of Transition: a hidden history of South Africa's negotiated settlement* (Johannesburg: Wits University Press, 2000), 268–279.

12. Van der Walt, *Sacrifice and Law*, 39.

13. Hannah Arendt, "Reflections on Little Rock," in *Responsibility and Judgement* (New York: Schocken Books, 2003), 193.

14. Ibid., 209.

15. Ibid., 205.

16. Ibid., 193.

17. Ibid., 195.

18. See, generally, Hannah Arendt *Lectures on Kant's Political Philosophy,* ed. R. Beiner (Chicago: University of Chicago Press, 1982).

19. See Justice Ackermann's discussion of the relationship between freedom and dignity in *Ferreira v Levin NO and Others; Vryenhoek and Others v Powell NO and Others (No 2)* 1996 (4) BCLR 441 (CC).

20. Section 39(1)(b) of the South African Constitution states, "When interpreting the Bill of Rights, a court, tribunal or forum must consider international law."

21. Hans Kelsen, *Principles of International Law* (New York: Rinehart, 1952).

22. Ibid.

23. Ibid.

24. L. W. H. Ackermann, "The Legal Nature of the South African Constitutional Revolution" (2004) *New Zealand Law Review*, 650.

25. See, generally, *Khosa and Others v Minister of Social Development and Others; Mahlaule and Others v Minister of Social Development and Others*, note 10.

26. Ibid.

27. *S v Makwanyane and Another* 1995 (6) BCLR 665 (CC), paragraph 308.

28. Ackermann, "Legal Nature," 633.

Crimes of Action, Crimes of Thought: Arendt on Reconciliation, Forgiveness, and Judgment * Shai Lavi

1. Hannah Arendt and Martin Heidegger, *Letters, 1925–1975*, ed. Ursula Lutz (San Diego: Harcourt, 2004), letter from May 16, 1950.

2. Hannah Arendt, *Denktagebuch 1950–1973* (Munich: Piper, 2002) 1:3.

3. Ibid., 6.

4. The term Arendt uses is "Dankbarkeit für das Gegebene," ibid., 4.

5. This letter can be found in *The Jew as Pariah,* ed. Ron H. Feldman (New York: Grove Press, 1978), 246.

6. Ibid., 7.

7. Hannah Arendt, *The Human Condition* (Chicago: University of Chicago Press, 1958), 237.

8. Ibid., 241.

9. Hannah Arendt, *Eichmann in Jerusalem: A Report on the Banality of Evil* (New York: Penguin, 1994), 247.

10. Hannah Arendt, *On Revolution* (New York: Viking Press, 1963), 78–83.

11. Hannah Arendt, *On Violence* (New York: Harcourt, 1969), 63.

12. Hannah Arendt, *Responsibility and Judgment* (New York: Schocken Books, 2003), 49–146, and especially 77–79.

Solitude and the Activity of Thinking *
Roger Berkowitz

I would like to thank Jenny Lyn Bader and Jennifer Culbert, who read and commented on earlier drafts of this essay.

1. Hannah Arendt, *Origins of Totalitarianism* (New York: Harcourt Brace Jovanovich, 1973), 460.

2. Ibid., 478.

3. Ibid., 475.

4. Hannah Arendt, *Eichmann in Jerusalem* (New York: Penguin Books, 1977), 32.

5. Ibid., 42.

6. Ibid., 49.

7. Hannah Arendt, *Life of the Mind* (San Diego: Harcourt Brace Jovanovich, 1978), 4.

8. Arendt, *Origins of Totalitarianism*, 324.

9. Arendt, *Life of the Mind*, 5.

10. Hannah Arendt, *The Human Condition* (Chicago: University of Chicago Press, 1958), 180.

11. Dana Villa, *Arendt and Heidegger* (Princeton: Princeton University Press, 1996), 20. See also Hannah Fenichel Pitkin, "Justice: On Relating Public and Private, *Political Theory* 9 (1981): 327–352.

12. Arendt, *The Human Condition*, 62.

13. Arendt, *Origins of Totalitarianism*, 476; Arendt, *The Human Condition*, 325.

14. Arendt, *Origins of Totalitarianism*, 475.

15. Arendt, *Life of the Mind*, 192.

16. Arendt, *Origins of Totalitarianism*, 476.

17. Hannah Arendt, *Men in Dark Times* (San Diego: Harcourt Brace Jovanovich, 1983), 73.

18. Ibid., 73.

19. Ibid., 76.

20. Ibid., 76, 79.

21. Hannah Arendt, "Socrates," *The Promise of Politics* (New York: Schocken, 2005), 24.

22. Arendt, *Life of the Mind*, 188.

23. Arendt, "Socrates," 20–21.

24. Arendt cites Richard's war with his conscience in *The Life of the Mind*, 189.

25. Arendt, "Socrates," 21.

26. Hannah Arendt, "Heidegger at 80," in *Arendt-Heidegger Letters* (San Diego: Harcourt, 2004), 155 (citing Hegel's letter to Zillman from 1807).

27. Ibid., 161.

28. Hannah Arendt, "Reflections on Little Rock," *Dissent*, January–February 1959, 53.

29. Ibid.

30. Arendt, "Socrates," 24.

31. Arendt, "Reflections on Little Rock," 53, 55.

32. Ibid., 55.

33. Arendt, *Men in Dark Times*, 73–74.

34. Ralph Waldo Emerson, *The Fugitive Slave Law* (New York: Modern Library, 2000).

35. Hannah Arendt, *On Revolution* (New York: Penguin, 1991), 276.

Exile Readings: Hannah Arendt's Library ∗ Reinhard Laube

For a critical reading of and suggestions for the following article, I am indebted to Ursula Ludz and Carsten Dutt. I owe grateful thanks above all to the Director of Libraries at Bard College, Jeffrey Katz, who supported my work in the Arendt Library in more ways than I can list. Special thanks to David Kettler—and not only for translating this article.

1. See the print in Jill Krementz, *The Jewish Writer* (New York: Henry Holt, 1998).

2. For the contracts with Marbach and Washington executed during Arendt's lifetime, see Bernhard Zeller, *Marbacher Memorablien II. Aus der Museums- und Archivarbeit 1973–1985* (Marbach: Deutsches Literatur Archiv, 2000), 234ff. Marbach was to receive all the materials connected to the Heidegger archives that were deposited there. Additional materials and supplements to the partial collection are indicated in the online catalog *Kallias*, http://dla-marbach.de/opac .kallias/index.html. The digitalized Hannah Arendt collection in Washington can be consulted on the website of the Library of Congress: http://memory.loc.gov/ammem /arendthtml/arendthome.html.

3. This donation was made in two letters; the first, from Blücher and Arendt to Dr. Reamer Kline, President of Bard College, dated January 30, 1963, and the second, from Dr. Kline to the Blüchers, dated February 11, 1963. These letters can be viewed in the Hannah Arendt Papers collection at the Library of Congress in a folder entitled *Blücher, Heinrich—Correspondence—Bard College, Annandale-on-Hudson, NY—1952–1969*. They were recently rediscovered by Alexander R. Bazelow while doing research in the Library of Congress. These letters, however, are only accessible on site.

4. Hannah Arendt: Letter to Karl Jaspers, November 3, 1966, in Hannah Arendt and Karl Jaspers, *Briefwechsel 1926–1969*, ed. Lotte Kohler and Hans Saner (Munich: Piper, 1985), 694.

5. This account of the history of the Arendt library is based on information from Lotte Kohler secured by Ursula Ludz in the course of preparing a research project in October 2005. I thank Ms. Ludz for making her interview notes available to me.

6. See David Kettler, "Arendt on Mannheim," which also describes Arendt's marginalia and relates them to Arendt's review (www .bard.edu/arendtcollection/kettler.htm). See also in that location Peter Baehr, "Sociology and the Mistrust of Thought: Hannah Arendt's Encounter with Karl Mannheim and the Sociology of Knowledge" (http://bard.edu/arendtcolection/ pdfs /SocioMistrust.pdf).

7. Elisabeth Young-Bruehl, *Hannah Arendt: Leben, Werk und Zeit* (Frankfurt: Fischer, 2004), 230.

8. Martin Heidegger: Letter to Hannah Arendt, February 27, 1925, in *Hannah Arendt / Martin Heidegger. Briefe 1925 bis 1975 und andere Zeugnisse aus den Nachlässen*, ed. Ursula Ludz (Frankfurt: Fischer, 1998), 14.

9. Information kindly supplied by Ursula Ludz. See Hannah Arendt, Letter to Heinrich Blücher of August 1945, in *Hannah Arendt / Heinrich Blücher. Briefe 1936–1969*, ed. Lotte Kohler (Munich: Piper, 1996), 139.

10. Hannah Arendt, *Das private Adressbuch 1951–1975*, ed. Christine Fischer-Defoy (Leipzig: Koehler & Amelang, 2007).

11. See Reinhard Tgahrt and Helmut Mojem, eds., *Vom Schreiben 6 Aus der Hand oder was mit den Büchern geschieht, Marbacher Magazin* 88/89 (Marbach: Deutsche Schillergesellschaft, 1999); Volker Kaukoreit, Marcel Atze, and Michael Hansel, eds., *"Aus meiner Hand dies Buch..." Zum Phänomen der Widmung, Sichtungen. Archiv, Bibliothek, Literaturwissenschaft* 8/9 (Vienna: Turia and Kant, 2005–6).

12. See the offprint of Gershom Scholem, "Tradition und Kommentar als religiöse Kategorien im Judentum," *Eranos-Jahrbuch* 31 (1962). A reproduction can be found in the image gallery of the Hannah Arendt Collection (Bard College), www.bard.edu /arendtcollection/imagegallery.htm.

13. Hannah Arendt, Letter to Heinrich Blücher, February 19, 1950, in Hannah Arendt and Heinrich Blücher, *Briefe 1936–1969*, 218. The dedicatory volumes are today a part of the collection of the GLA Marbach, together with a photo of Martin Heidegger, which he also dedicated to Hannah "on the sixth of February, 1950." A reproduction can be found in Hannah Arendt / Martin Heidegger, *Briefe 1925 bis 1975 und andere Zeugnisse aus den Nachlässen* (Frankfurt: Klostermann, 1998), figure 9.

14. Hannah Arendt, interview with Günther Gaus (October 1964) in *Ich will verstehen. Selbstauskünfte zu Leben and Werk. Mit einer vollständigen Bibliographie*, ed. Ursula Ludz (Munich: Piper, 1996), 53.

15. *Kant-Gesellschaft, Neuangemeldete Mitglieder für 1921. Ergänzungsliste 2: Juni–Dezember 1921.* Entry: Hannah Arendt, Königsberg i. Pr. In *Kant-Studien* 26 (1921): 157.

16. According to information received from Hans Saner (Basel), Karl Jaspers later gave her parts of his *Akademie* edition.

17. See Barbara Hahn and Marie Luise Knott, eds., *Von den Dichtern erwarten wir Wahrheit* (Berlin: Matthes & Seitz, 2007); see also Wolfgang Heuer and Irmela von der Lühe, eds., *Dichterisch denken. Hannah Arendt und die Künste* (Göttingen: Wallstein Verlag, 2007); Wolfgang Heuer and Thomas Wild, eds., *Hannah Arendt. Text+Kritik. Zeitschrift für Literatur* 166/167 (2005).

18. See Elisabeth Gallas, "Gedächtnisspuren. Restitution jüdischer Kulturgüter nach 1945 und ihre Wirkungsgeschichte am Beispiel des Offenbach Archival Depot," Simon Dubnow Institute for Jewish History and Culture at the University of Leipzig, *Bulletin* VIII (2006): 74–85; Young-Bruehl, *Hannah Arendt*, 268ff.

19. See Walter Benjamin, "Ich packe meine Bibliothek aus. Eine Rede über das Sammeln," in *Gesammelte Schriften*, ed. by Tilman Rexroth (Frankfurt: Humblot, 1972) 4:396.

20. Wolfgang Harms, "Gelehrtenbibliothek," in *Lexikon des gesamten Buchwesens* (Stuttgart: Hiersemann, 1991), 122.

21. See Bernhard Fabian, *Buch, Bibliothek und geisteswissenschaftliche Forschung* (Göttingen: Vandenhoeck + Ruprecht, 1983), 23–55; Fabian, *Der Gelehrte als Leser. Über Bücher und Bibliotheken* (Hildesheim: Olms George, 1998), 3–32; Uwe Jochum, *Kleine Bibliotheksgeschichte* (Stuttgart: Hiersemann, 1999), 130ff.

22. Hannah Arendt, Letter of July 8, 1946, to Heinrich Bücher, in Hannah Arendt and Heinrich Blücher, *Briefe 1936–1969*, 141.

23. The postcard is edited in *Arendt and Benjamin. Texte, Briefe, Dokumente*, ed. Detlev Schöttker and Edmund Wizila (Frankfurt: Piper, 2006) 129. Compare also the digitalization on the pages of the Bard College Library.

24. See, most recently, Jürgen Weber, "NS-Raubgut und hidden collections—Herausforderungen für ein neues Sammlungsmanagement," in *NS Raubgut in Bibliotheken. Suche. Ergebnisse. Perspektiven, Zeitschrift für Bbliothekswesen und Bibliographie*. Special Issue 94, 177–186 (in press).

25. Jürgen Weber, "'The copy in hand': Voraussetzungen und Ziele exemplarspezifische Erschließung," *Bibliotheksdienst* 36 (2002): H, 5, 614–624; Weber, "Kooperative Provenienzerschließung," *Zeitschrift für Bibliothekswesen und Bibliographie* 51, no. 4 (2004): 239–245; "Empfehlungen zur Provinienzerschließung der Arbeitsgemeinschaft Alte Drucke (AAD)" beim Gemeinsamen Bibliotheksverbund. GBV (2003) http://aad.gbv.de/empfehlung /aad provinienz.pdf; T-PRO, *Thesaurus der Provinienzbegriffe*, www.klassik-stiftung.de /einrichtungen/herzogin-anna-amalia-bibliothek/projekte/provenienzportal

//informationsmittel/t-pro.html; *Provenance Evidence—Thesaurus for Use in Rare Book and Special Collections Cataloguing*, (Chicago: American Library Association of College and Research Libraries, 1988).

26. Barbara Hahn, '*Lesen: Ernst Jünger*' in *Hannah Arendt—von den Dichtern erwarten wir Wahrheit* (Berlin: Ausstellung Literaturhaus Berlin, 2006), 54–56. See also the reference to Jünger's *Strahlungen* in "Hannah Arendt im Gespräch with Joachim Fest. Eine Rundfunksendung aus dem Jahre 1964," www.hannaharendt.de/download/fest_interview.pdf .

27. Hannah Arendt, *Sechs Essays* (Heidelberg: Duncker & Humblot, 1948), 66.

28. Hans-Christof Kraus, "Die Jenaer Frühromantik und ihre Kritik der Moderne," ZRGG 47, no. 3 (1995): 205–230; Günter Meuter, "Bataille statt Debatte. Zu Karl Schmitts 'Metaphysic' des Politischen und des Liberalen," *Aus Politik und Zeitgeschichte* 51/96 (December 1996): 23–33; Reinhard Blomert, *Intellektuelle im Aufbruch. Karl Mannheim, Alfred Weber, Norbert Elias und die Heidelberger Sozialwissenschaften der Zwischenkriegszeit* (Munich: Piper, 1999) 150ff.; Reinhard Laube, *Karl Mannheim und die Krise des Historismus. Historismus als wissenssoziologischer Perspektivismus* (Göttingen: Vandenhoeck + Ruprecht, 2004) 444ff.

29. Hannah Arendt, "Adam Müller Renaissance," *Kölnische Zeitung*, September 13 and 17, 1932.

30. Hannah Arendt, *Elemente und Usprünge totaler Herrschaft. Antisemitismus, Imperialismus, Totalitarismus* (1955) (Munich: Piper, 2003), 369.

31. Hannah Arendt, Letter to Dolf Sternberger of May 29, 1949, *Nachlaß Dolf Sternberger*.

32. Carl Schmitt, *Ex Captivitate Salus* (Cologne: Duncker & Humblot, 1950). Hannah Arendt's marginalia are located on pages 32, 60, 77, 81, and 89. The interpretive schema of the defeated's capacity for insight has been taken up, among others, by Reinhart Koselleck in the context of his historical anthropology; Koselleck, *Erfahrungswandel und Methodenwechsel. Eine historisch-anthropologische Skizze* (Frankfurt: Kloster-

mann, 1988), and again in Koselleck, *Zeitschichten. Studien zur Historik* (Frankfurt: Klostermann, 2000), 27–77.

33. Carl Schmitt, *Der Nomos der Erde im Völkerrecht des Jus Publicum Europaeum* (Cologne: Duncker & Humblot, 1950).

34. Ibid., 272.

35. Ibid., 221.

36. Ibid., 219.

37. Ibid., 183.

38. Ibid., 285.

39. Ibid., 232.

40. Ibid., 141 and 211.

41. Ibid., 67, 249, and 308.

42. Hannah Arendt, *Denktagebuch 1950–1973* (Brochure IX, X and XIX, July and September 1952 and September 1953), ed. Ursula Ludz and Ingeborg Nordmann (Munich: Piper, 2002), 217f, 243, and 455.

43. See Reinhard Laube, "Platon und die Sophisten," in *Nationalsozialismus in den Kulturwissenschaften*, ed. Hartmut Lehmann and Otto Gerhard Oexle (Göttingen: Vandenhoeck + Ruprecht, 2004), 2:148f.

44. Martin Heidegger, *Platons Lehre von der Wahrheit* (Frankfurt: Klostermann, 1997).

45. *The Republic of Plato*, translated with introduction and notes by Francis MacDonald Cornford (New York: Oxford University Press, 1956).

46. Hannah Arendt, "Was ist Autorität?" (1956), reprinted in Arendt, *Zwischen Vergangenheit und Zukunft. Übungen im politischen Denken 1*, ed. Ursula Ludz (Munich: Piper, 1994), 180 n. 19.

47. For the implication of Hannah Arendt's political philosophy, see the contributions in *Hannah Arendt: Hidden Tradition—Untimely Actuality, Deutsche Zeitschrift für Philosophie*, special issue (2006); Alphons Söllner, *Zwischen Europa und Amerika—Hannah Arendt's Wanderung durch die politische Ideengeschichte* (in press).

48. Friedrich Gundolf, *Geschichte der Philosophie*. Typescript. The text reads: "Jedweder sägt das Absolute / Worauf der vorige Frage rhte / Mit neuer Frage ab und macht ? Zum Mittel was als Zweck gedacht. / Jed Dass wird Ob, jed Was wird Wie: / Der Fortschritt der Philosophie.

Contributors

Shy Abady, artist

Mark Antaki, Professor of Law, McGill University

Peter Baehr, Professor and Head of the Department of Politics and Sociology, Lingnan University, Hong Kong

Seyla Benhabib, Eugene Meyer Professor of Political Science, Yale University

Roger Berkowitz, Academic Director, The Hannah Arendt Center for Ethical and Political Thinking, Bard College; Assistant Professor of Political Studies and Human Rights, Bard College

J. M. Bernstein, Distinguished Professor and Chair, Department of Philosophy, The New School University

Richard J. Bernstein, Vera List Professor of Philosophy, The New School University

Peg Birmingham, Chair and Professor of Philosophy, DePaul University

Jack Blum, Chairman of Tax Justice Network, USA

Leon Botstein, President, Bard College

Cathy Caruth, Winship Distinguished Research Professor of Comparative Literature and English, Emory University

Drucilla Cornell, National Research Foundation Chair in Customary Law, Indigenous Values and the Dignity Jurisprudence, University of Cape Town Law School; Professor of Political Science, Women's Studies, and Comparative Literature, Rutgers University

Jennifer L. Culbert, Professor of Political Science, The Johns Hopkins University

Yaron Ezrahi, Gersten Family Professor of Political Science, Hebrew University of Jerusalem

Ron H. Feldman, Department of Theology and Religion, University of San Francisco

Christopher Hitchens, author and journalist

George Kateb, Professor Emeritus, Political Science, Princeton University

Jeffrey Katz, Dean of Information Services and Director of Libraries, Bard College; Executive Director, The Hannah Arendt Center for Ethical and Political Thinking, Bard College

Thomas Keenan, Director of the Human Rights Project and Associate Professor of Comparative Literature, Bard College

Jerome Kohn, Director of The Hannah Arendt Center, The New School University

Reinhard Laube, Scientific Researcher, University of Bielefeld

Shai Lavi, Senior Lecturer and Director, The Taubenschlag Institute of Criminal Law at the Tel Aviv University Faculty of Law

Patchen Markell, Professor of Political Science, University of Chicago

Uday Mehta, Clarence Francis Professor in the Social Sciences, Amherst College

Verity Smith, Department of Social Studies, Harvard University

Suzanne Vromen, Professor Emeritus of Sociology, Bard College

Elisabeth Young-Bruehl, Center for Psychoanalytic Training and Research, Columbia University

Index